BUILDING LARGE KNOWLEDGE-BASED SYSTEMS
Representation and Inference in the Cyc Project

OTHER WORKS BY DOUGLAS LENAT

Building Expert Systems, with Frederick Hayes-Roth & Donald A. Waterman, Addison-Wesley, Reading, Massachusetts, 1983.

Knowledge-Based Systems in Artificial Intelligence, with Randall Davis, McGraw-Hill, New York, 1982.

Knowledge Representation, Addison-Wesley, Reading, Massachusetts, 1988.

The Ontological Engineer's Handbook, 2nd edition, with distinguished colleagues, Addison-Wesley, Reading, Massachusetts, 1997 (forthcoming).

BUILDING LARGE KNOWLEDGE-BASED SYSTEMS

Representation and Inference in the Cyc Project

DOUGLAS B. LENAT
R. V. GUHA

Addison-Wesley Publishing Company, Inc.
Reading, Massachusetts • Menlo Park, California • New York
Don Mills, Ontario • Wokingham, England • Amsterdam • Bonn
Sydney • Singapore • Tokyo • Madrid • San Juan

Many of the designations used by manufacturers and sellers to distinguish their products are claimed as trademarks. Where those designations appear in this book and Addison-Wesley was aware of a trademark claim, the designations have been printed in initial capital letters (e.g., Knowledge Craft) or all capital letters (e.g., KEE).

Library of Congress Cataloging-in-Publication Data

Lenat, Douglas B.
    Building large knowledge-based systems:
representation & inference in the CYC project /
Douglas B. Lenat, R.V. Guha.
        p.   cm.
    Bibliography: p.
    Includes index.
    ISBN 0-201-51752-3
    1. Artificial intelligence.   2. Expert systems
(Computer science)   3. System design.   I. Guha, R. V.
II. Title.   III. Title: CYC project.
Q335.L45   1989
006.3 — dc20   89-15091
                                                                CIP

Cover design by Hannus Design Associates
Text design by Joyce C. Weston
Sponsoring Editor: Ted Buswick
Production Coordinator: Sandra Hutchinson
Set in 10-point Palatino by Compset, Inc., Beverly, MA

ABCDEFGHIJ-HA-89
First printing, December 1989

CONTENTS

4. Representation: What and Why?   149

5. A Glimpse of Cyc's Global Ontology   171

ACKNOWLEDGMENTS

We would like to thank all the members of the Cyc project, past and present, who have contributed their ideas, code, and units. Mary Shepherd has been of special and invaluable help throughout the life of the Cyc project, serving in different roles as the project matured. We also thank Mark Derthick, who wrote the epistemological-heuristic level translator; David "Gumby" Wallace and John "Bop" Huffman who wrote much of the very low-level CycL code; and Karen Pittman, Nick Siegel, and the other users of the system, without whose efforts (and bug reports) CycL and Cyc would not be the language and KB they are today.

We also would like to offer special appreciation to several individuals outside our research group: to Stuart Russell for helping thrash out "Stuff"; to Mike Huhns and Larry Stephens for starting to clean up "slot space"; to Marvin Minsky, for helping to work out some of the Structure/Function details; to Bruce Porter and his students, who endured earlier versions of Cyc and provided valuable feedback to us during that period; to Mike Travers, for coding the MUE editor; and to John McCarthy, for posing really annoying (and useful) questions early on in Cyc's evolution. We also thank the participants of our January, 1989, Cyc Workshop, at Stanford; their critiques of our ideas have helped lead us to many of the significant improvements we've made in the past year.

Many of the ideas woven into Cyc's interface are based on the Knoesphere article [Lenat et al, 1983], Hypertext, Smalltalk, Balance of Power, and other pioneering HI work, which in turn owes a debt to Alan Kay, Ted Nelson, Chris Crawford, Nick Negroponte, and many other HI pioneers.

We have received a great amount of help from our colleagues and friends at MCC, including early crucial support from Bob Inman, Joe Scullion, and Woody Bledsoe. Judy Bowman, our secretary, has helped the project—and the production of this book—run relatively smoothly.

Our intra-MCC collaborators, including Elaine Rich, Jim Barnett, and numerous Human Interface researchers, continue to help expand and test the system. Our extra-MCC collaborators, such as John Mc-Dermott and David Marques's group at DEC, have done likewise, and we wish to acknowledge their help as well. This is also the place where one would typically say "Support for this project was provided by Darpa grant #xyz"; but in Cyc's case, 100% of our support has been provided by far-sighted American companies: Bellcore, CDC, DEC, Harris, Kodak, NCR, and, in earlier years, also by Honeywell and Sperry.

Finally, we would also like to thank the 1990–94 AI community for their terrific cooperation and collaboration in growing and testing Cyc. So get busy!

PREFACE

In this book, we would like to present a surprisingly compact, powerful, elegant set of reasoning methods that form a set of first principles that explain creativity, humor, and common-sense reasoning — a sort of "Maxwell's Equations" of Thought. Yes, we'd like very much to present them, but, sadly, we don't believe they exist. We don't believe that there's any shortcut to being intelligent; the "secret" is to have lots of knowledge. *Knowledge* doesn't have to be just dry almanac-like facts, of course; much of what we need to know to get by in the real world is dynamic: problem-solving methods and rules of thumb.

The majority of work in knowledge representation has been concerned with the technicalities of relating predicate calculus to other formalisms, and with the details of various schemes for default reasoning. There has been almost an aversion to addressing the problems that arise in actually representing large bodies of knowledge with content. The typical AI researcher seems to consider that task to be "just applications work." But there are deep, important issues that must be addressed if we are to ever have a large intelligent knowledge-based program: What ontological categories would make up an adequate set for carving up the universe? How are they related? What are the important things most humans today know about solid objects? And so on. In short, we must bite the bullet.

And that's just what we have been doing at Microelectronics and Computer Technology Corporation (MCC) for the past five years. So, instead of a thin article on Maxwell's Equations of Thought, you are holding a thick book that talks about the past and current state of Cyc: the massive knowledge-base project on which we've been working.

MCC was to be America's answer to ICOT. In 1983, under the direction of Admiral Bobby Inman, a consortium was formed with a score of members such as DEC, CDC, Bellcore, Kodak, NCR, and Harris. Its charter was to carry out large, high-risk, high-payoff, decade-sized projects. When, in mid-1984, Lenat and Shepherd were ready to begin implementing the Knoesphere vision [Lenat et al., 1983], MCC was the natural place at which to launch that project.

At the heart of that vision, and at the heart of the ensuing Cyc project, is the reliance upon a huge knowledge base, one that spans most of what humans call common sense. These are the millions of facts and heuristics that *define* what we routinely assume "our listener" already knows about the world, be they a professor, a waitress, a six-year-old child, or even a lawyer.

The book begins by explaining the need for such a machine-understood embodiment of consensus reality. Later chapters cover the various difficult choices we are facing in developing this knowledge base, and what solutions and work-arounds we are adopting. Some of these choices include finding adequate solutions to various representation "thorns": how to handle time, space, substances, belief, awareness, causality, intentions, emotions, and so on. Other tough choices include deciding which categories to carve the world up into, and which relationships are important enough to define explicitly. For instance, we'd like to say that fire engines are red. Should we define

RedObject (the set of all red objects) or
red-p? (a predicate that tests whether an object is red or not) or
color (a function that relates an object to its color)

To summarize the book's contents in more detail, Chapter 1 presents the Cyc "philosophy" or paradigm. Chapter 2 presents a global overview of Cyc, including its representation language, the ontology of its knowledge base, and the environment in which it functions (browsing and editing tools, multi-person knowledge server, etc.).

Chapter 3 goes into much more detail on the representation language, including the structure and function of Cyc's metalevel agenda mechanism; this chapter should be considered optional, especially on first reading through this book. It also covers the "dynamics" of reasoning in Cyc: how and why Cyc draws on two dozen different built-in inference mechanisms, of varying levels of specificity (and concommitant efficiency). Some of these may be familiar (inverse slots, inheritance, constraint-checking, demons, if/then rules), some less so (inContextVersions, classification, genlSlots, refinements), and some are rather exotic "plausible inference" mechanisms (determinations, constraint resolution, plausibly closing worlds, following metaphorically sensible links).

Chapter 4 presents heuristics for ontological engineering, the principles upon which Cyc's ontology is based. Chapter 5 then provides a glimpse into that global ontology of knowledge.

Chapter 6 explains how we "solve" (i.e., adequately handle) the various tough representation thorns (substances, time, space, structures, composite mental/physical objects, beliefs, uncertainty, etc.) In addition, it discusses the handling of intelligent agents, organizations, voluntary action, multiple models, etc.

In chapter 7, we survey the mistakes that new knowledge enterers most often commit. Chapter 8, which is the concluding chapter, includes a brief status report on the project, and a statement of our goals and timetable for the coming five years.

We've phrased much of this preface in the present tense — "are facing," "are adopting" — because this book is a snapshot of research in progress. We're in our fifth year of a ten-year project, and perhaps one of the biggest surprises is that we're still on schedule. The amount of knowledge we'll need to represent is ten times larger than we thought at first; but we have developed tools that enable us to enter knowledge ten times as quickly as expected.

Most of our time has been spent on developing tools and finding adequate "thorn-clippers," and as a result our language and interface tools and top-level ontology are much further developed than the very detailed levels of the knowledge base.

Treat this as fair warning! If you want to see the full corpus of "What Every Intelligent Machine Ought To Know," you should wait for our 1994 book, not this one. But if you're interested in a sneak preview, and in hearing about the problems we faced to get to our present stage, then read on.

1. The Cyc Philosophy

1.1. Thin Ice

In July of 1962, some Lincoln Labs scientists, urged on by Marvin Minsky, decide to play a rather interesting practical joke on the Computing Center. They write a Begging Program, a program whose job control card (remember batch?) says to give it two minutes of CPU time. All the program does is wait 90 seconds, then print a message on the operator's teletype, "I am almost finished; I need 60 more seconds, please." Then it waits 45 seconds and prints "Almost done; one more minute, please." And so on. After twenty minutes, the operator kills the job. Totally deadpan, the programmer complains when he gets the printout showing he was charged for twenty minutes:

Programmer: The JCL card says 2 minute time limit!

Operator: Yeah, but the program kept asking for more time.

Programmer: So what? It always does that!

In early 1971, a patient talks to the ELIZA psychiatric counseling program.

Patient: *My dog's mother died last week.*

Eliza: Tell me more about your mother.

The patient is impressed with the subtlety and perception of the program at digging into his subconscious. Of course, what the program did was to simply ignore most of the words because it did not understand them. It really just understood him to say "*My . . . mother . . .*", and it printed out its standard response for that case.

In July of 1976, a medical diagnosis program is told about a follow-up visit by a patient on whose case it had worked the previous

1

week. The program asks for the patient's blood pressure and temperature again. It then asks for the patient's birthdate and gender this
week.

In February of 1980, a skin disease diagnosis program is told about a
"patient" that is a 1969 Chevrolet.

Program: Are there spots on the body?

User: *Yes.*

Program: What color spots?

User: *Reddish-brown.*

Program: Are there more spots on the trunk than elsewhere?

User: *No.*

Program: The patient has measles.

In June of 1983, a machine learning program is given hundreds of
concept definitions, from half a dozen different fields, and begins to
look for interesting new discoveries. It finds a few, but, in each case,
begins to thrash after a while. It's almost as if there were some quantity of discovery-energy stored up in the program; this energy is
quickly used up, after which the program seems to wind down.

In October of 1987, an expert system authorizes a car loan to someone who stated, on his application, that he'd worked at the same job
for twenty years. A good risk? Perhaps, but the individual also stated
he was 18 years old.

In March of 1989, a natural language researcher is worrying about
how to get her program to figure out correctly which kind of "pen" is
meant in these two sentences:

The pig is in the pen.
The ink is in the pen.

She realizes that, for the examples her system is supposed to handle, she can just distinguish the two cases on the basis of containing
solid versus liquid objects. This is only a fair-weather solution, however (that is, after it rains there may be puddles in the pen, and ink
clots in the other kind of pen).

In January of 1993, a minor earthquake shatters a glass-lined drum
of virulent material at Oak Ridge National Labs (ORNL). The program

that guides spill-handling procedures there asks numerous questions and recommends dumping a particular chemical on the spill. It asks for the name of the spilled material, so the user assumes it knows what the stuff is. Unfortunately, the program was written in the 1980's, before there were any biologically active materials stored at ORNL. The program does use the compound's name, of course, in some way: it appears here and there on its printed report the next morning.

In June of 1995, at 4:20 a.m., a warning bell sounds at a nuclear power plant just outside Paris. A tired technician, about to go off-shift, is confronted with a program's recommendation to close valve #802 immediately. People often go along with a fallacious argument, nodding continuously, if the argument has some plausible justification for each step. The technician does just this, as he reads the accompanying paragraph-sized justification that is displayed with the program's recommendation. He then goes off to close the valve.

Some of the preceding examples are true; some are apocryphal. The point is that computer programs are being given ever more responsibility, ever more complex tasks, and ever more sophistication. But their *apparent* intelligence and sophistication still vastly exceed the true depth of their understanding and the breadth of their capabilities. They are especially susceptible to failure when confronted with novel or unexpected situations. They are, if not complete idiot-savants, at least extremely *brittle*.

1.2. Overcoming Brittleness

Why aren't human beings brittle in the way computer programs are? How do we cope with novelty? Largely by finding some related case and propagating the differences to this new one. That is, we do one of the following:

- Match some similar situation and adjust it slightly (= remember)

- Match some apparently far-flung situation (= analogize)

- Fall back on general knowledge (= use common sense)

- Try to learn more about this new situation (= recur)

That fourth case is perhaps a special case of the third. In any event, it is a *recursion*, in which our "problem" changes from "X" to "learn more about X," and any of the above four methods can now be tried on that new problem. (Yes, any of these four methods! You can spend time solving X, or learning more about X, or learning more about how to better learn about problems like X, or . . . .)

The first three cases above (and hence, ultimately, the fourth) depend on having a large base of both general and specific knowledge to consult. As Marvin Minsky said in his afterword to Vinge's *True Names*, "the more we know, the more we can learn." Unfortunately, the flip side of that is: "If you don't know much to begin with, you can't learn very much very quickly." That flip side comes into play every time we build and run a program that doesn't know too much to begin with, especially for tasks like semantic disambiguation of sentences, or open-ended learning by analogy.

Expert systems finesse this need for knowledge; they restrict their tasks so much that they can perform relatively narrow symbol manipulations that nevertheless are *interpreted* meaningfully (and, we admit, usefully) by human users. But having just a thin veneer of competence and understanding is the cause of their brittleness; it's why they can make mistakes that no human being ever could, often without even knowing that they're out of their range of competence. It's also why they can't readily communicate and cooperate with one another.

So the mattress in the road to AI is lack of knowledge, and the anti-mattress is knowledge. But how much does a program need to know to begin with? The annoying, inelegant, but apparently true answer is: a non-trivial fraction of *consensus reality* — the millions of things that we all know and that we assume everyone else knows. If I liken the stock market to a roller-coaster, and you don't know what I mean, I might liken it to a seesaw, or to a stormy sea. If you still don't know what I mean, I probably won't want to deal with you any more.

The necessary knowledge includes not just static facts, but also heuristics and other problem-solving methods. Moreover, selecting a base of knowledge for AI purposes involves making some hard choices about which categories, individuals, relations, representations, etc., to include. The Cyc group at MCC is attempting to build a single intelligent agent whose knowledge base contains these tens of millions of entries. We believe such a system will be a useful, perhaps necessary, platform on which to undertake the next generation of work in expert systems, natural language understanding, and machine learning.

Earlier, we said that brittleness can be overcome largely by drawing on specialized knowledge, by falling back on increasingly general knowledge, or by analogizing to specific but superficially disparate knowledge. The first case is pretty clear — it's the basis for expert systems, for example. Let's look at an example of each of the other two cases — general knowledge and analogy — to see more precisely how and why we think they should work in Cyc.

1.3. Falling Back on General Knowledge

Here's a typical expert system (ES) rule, from the task of deciding whether a credit card company should authorize a purchase or not:

> IF the purchase-price is greater than the remaining-balance
>   and you query "Are there unusual circumstances this month?"
>   and the purchaser responds "Yes"
> THEN authorize the purchase

Brittleness arises because the program doesn't really understand the meaning of the various terms, such as *unusual circumstances, purchase-price, remaining-balance, authorize, purchase,* or even *Yes* and *query.*

So in an expert system, much of the meaning of the terms is in the eye of the beholder. This is a sort of "free lunch" when it works; it gives the illusion of depth of understanding. A human being, and likewise an expert system, can push those terms around without thinking deeply about them most of the time. But then one is confronted with something a little bit nonstandard, and there the divergence between the expert and the expert system becomes apparent. The human expert can easily think of many reasons why the above rule might have led to an incorrect conclusion.

For instance, let's just focus on the term *query* in the above rule. Figure 1-1 is a fragment of the tree of knowledge above Asking&Answering (the name for the process of one person querying another and getting a response back from them). Please don't study the diagram in detail at this time, and please don't study the constraint syntax or predicates; just notice that there are some links from Asking&Answering up to more general concepts, and that there are some constraints listed on those general concepts.

We can derive failure modes for Asking&Answering by negating the various constraints that are listed there at that node, and at each ancestor of Asking&Answering. Even in this trivial example, we find a dozen plausible ways that the rule might give the wrong answer, such as:

- The question was so wordy that the listener forgot the first part by the time the last part was spoken.

- The communications link went down during the querying or replying action.

- The listener could not clearly make out the words they were being asked.

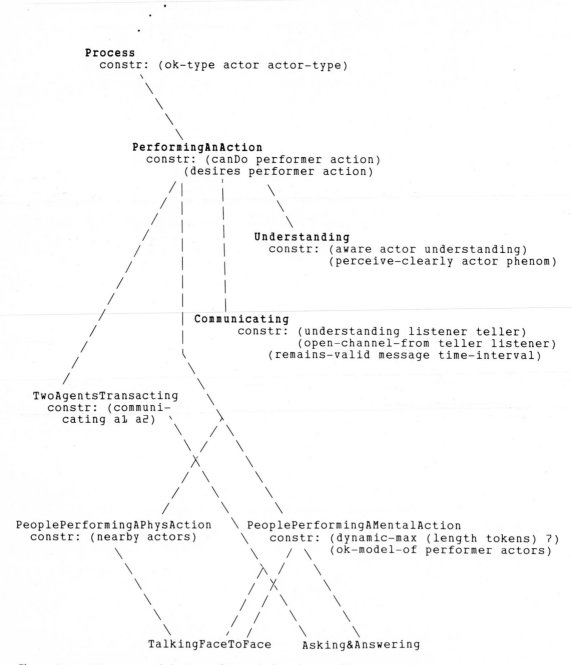

Figure 1–1: A Fragment of the Tree of Knowledge above Asking&Answering

- The listener misunderstood some terms (e.g., *unusual circumstances*) in the question.

- The listener was not aware of being asked a question.

- The questioner was asking the wrong person.

- The listener did not want to tell the questioner the truth.

- The listener was unable physically to utter a response.

Notice that the same bits of knowledge that can help find ways a credit card expert system rule might fail can also find ways in which the following medical diagnosis rule might fail;

> IF the intake-interview is in progress, and the-doctor asks
>   the-patient "Do you suffer from x" and the-patient responds
>   "Yes"
> THEN assert x as a patient-symptom

There the failure modes include the same sorts of things listed above for the credit card rule, plus the possibility that the questioner isn't really a doctor after all; or even the possibility that there is no second person at all (maybe the first person's problem is that he is hallucinating); or that the patient's symptom changed (either went away or began manifesting itself) right after the now-incorrect answer was given; etc.

It is often difficult to make a convincing case for having a consensus reality knowledge base (KB), because whenever one cites a particular piece of common sense that would be needed in a situation, it's easy to dismiss it and say "well, we would have put that into our expert system as just one more (premise on a) rule." For instance, in diagnosing a sick twenty-year-old coal miner, the program is told that he has been working in coal mines for 22 years (the typist accidentally hit two 2s instead of just one). Common sense tells us to question the idea of someone working in a coal mine since age -2. Yes, if this sort of error had been foreseen, the expert system could of course question it also. The argument is, however, that we could keep coming up with instance after instance where some additional piece of common sense knowledge would be needed in order to avoid falling into an inhumanly silly mistake.

For example, here are a few more. How about a diagnosis program that is told about a pregnant woman whose age is 103 and weight is 40; obviously someone switched those two pieces of data. Or how about a grandmother whose age is entered as 9. Or twins whose ages are different. Those examples just touch on a few *age*-related mistakes that common sense could catch, and *age* in turn is just one of the thousands of attributes that Cyc already knows about. (A rough estimate puts the number of such attributes at 15,000 by 1994.)

Most of the time, as we operate in the real world, we draw on compiled experiences — on very abstract, simplified "black-box" models. When we drive to work in the morning, we can't and don't rethink the route we take, the running condition of the car's engine, etc. But if some unexpected problem develops — the route is suddenly bumper to bumper, or the car begins stalling out — we're able to open up the black box and reason at the next more detailed level, and the next, and so on, until we get to the right level at which the problem can be handled. So we're definitely not arguing for first-principle reasoning all the time; for cognitive economy, intelligent programs and people must "compile away" the general knowledge and assumptions to produce efficient, special-case rules and procedures. The danger comes in programs' not having that basic knowledge available as a back-up. Such is the source of brittleness.

1.4. Analogizing to Far-flung Knowledge

The previous subsection illustrated how to cope with novelty by falling back on increasingly general knowledge. What of falling back on analogy? You may think that analogy is just an isolated curiosity, or a literary device that has dramatic power but no real heuristic power. See for yourself. Here is a partial analogy between treating a disease and waging a war:

```
Treating a Bacterial Infection    Fighting a War
enemyType: Disease                enemyType: MilitaryForce
enemyLocal: Bacteria              enemyLocal: EnemyTroops
protagonistType: Physician        protagonistType: Soldier
enemyProcess: Infecting           enemyProcess: Invading
protagProcess: ClinTreating       protagProcess: MilRepulsing
usefulPreprocess: Diagnosing      usefulPreprocess: J2ing
usefulTactics: Vaccination        usefulTactics: MilContainment
locale: BodyPart                  locale: GeographicRegion
emotionalCharge: Low              emotionalCharge: High
```

Often, analogy *is* used as little more than a dramatic device. For example, one news reporter might make use of the difference in emotionalCharge to dramatize the plight of a dying child, by describing "his brave battle, his war against the infection that has invaded his body . . ." Conversely, a government news agency might use that difference to downplay the horror of a firefight, by describing it in clinical terms like *sterilization action*.

Although this usage is common, it is (as regards Cyc) the least interesting and powerful use of analogy. Analogy has two other uses: to suggest brand new concepts and to help at fleshing out their details. Let's look at how the above analogy may be used in these two ways.

Notice that some of the concepts on one side are analogues of those on the other side. But Vaccination and MilContainment aren't analogues. In fact, they each have no analogue (yet) on the other side. Such asymmetry is bound to happen, and this is an opportunity: let the analogy guide the search for new, useful concepts on each side.

For instance, maybe we should define a medical analogue of *military containment*, and a military analogue of *vaccination*. The former might be *medical containment* — for example, the use of a tourniquet on a venomous snakebite, or the use of quarantine on a virulent plague. The military analogue of vaccination might be *fortifying* or *propagandizing*. To take the analogy even more seriously, the military vaccination might entail letting a small group of enemy soldiers overrun some territory before our friendly forces secure it, as a way of driving home to the local populace just how bad the enemy is.

The example above illustrated the utility of analogy as a *guide for defining* new concepts. Analogy can also help *flesh out* the new concepts. For instance, what precisely is *medical containment* containing? What does it locally contain? How should one do it? To answer those questions, go to the *military containment* concept, look up the answers there, and map them back using the existing analogy:

```
MilContainment
   usefulTacticIn: Fighting-a-war
   containedType: MilitaryForce
   containedLocal: EnemyTroops
   attributeLimited: Mobility
   howTo: Bound&Isolate
   counterTactic: (Threaten containedArea)
   containedArea: GeographicRegion
```

That suggests that medical containment, in the case of treating a bacterial infection, is containing a disease, and, more locally, bacteria. It might be done by surrounding and isolating the infected part of the body.

We could carry through a similar procedure to guess at the values of various slots on the military analogue of *vaccination*.

The example above, leading to military vaccination and to medical containment, illustrates that analogy can be useful in suggesting new concepts and in fleshing them out. That shows that analogy does have quite significant potential heuristic power. Moreover, as Lakoff and Johnson argue quite convincingly in *Metaphors We Live By*, analogy is far more pervasive than one might at first imagine, appearing in almost every sentence we utter.

Our sentences and our thoughts are riddled with analogies (such as "riddled with"), which in turn are built on analogies, and so on, like the skins of an onion. At the core of the onion is a small tangle of very primitive somatic metaphors such as forward, backward, up, down, hungry, tired, pain, push, see, breathe, sleep, and eat.

It's easy to imagine how this massive dependence upon analogy and metaphor might have come about: We understand (and communicate) "which," not "what"; that is, we perceive (or transmit) something that's already well known plus a small set of changes. Learning and understanding and speaking occur at, and can modify, only the fringe of what we already know. So even if we began as neonates with largely non-analogical knowledge, as we live our lives new skins of the onion are continually added on.

1.4.1. Why Analogy Works Frequently. The previous subsection argued that analogy is frequently useful and discussed specifically *how* it might be useful. But *why* is it frequently useful? The answer to that lies in the nature of the world we happen to inhabit and the state of our understanding (and perhaps our capacity to understand). Three aspects of our world, and ourselves, make analogy frequently useful to us as human beings:

1. The moderate amount of novelty with which we're confronted

2. The moderate number of distinct causes in the world

3. The mediocre ontology and "knowledge metric" we have

NOVELTY. If the world were very volatile and chaotic and wildly unpredictable, analogizing would avail us little; it would almost always fail. If it were totally staid and static and unchanging, we'd have little need for analogy; memory would suffice.

CAUSALITY. Analogies that have no common root cause are superficial and weak and, more often than not, no good for more than literary divertissement. If there were a zillion disparate causes in the world, analogy would usually be superficial and powerless in this fashion. On the other hand, if there were no variety of causal mechanisms in the world (for example, only one emotion, only one method of physical propulsion, only one kind of chemical reaction, etc.), there wouldn't be much power in classifying which of those causes were behind something. (In fact, there wouldn't be much point in having those terms, either.)

KNOWLEDGE METRIC. If we had a terribly wrong view of the world, analogy would lead us even further into error (for example, thinking that the cosmic objects and meteorological phenomena are sentient, one might try to bribe them with offerings.) If we had a terrific grasp of the world, we'd always *know* precisely what knowledge was relevant to our present dilemma, and exactly how it should be applied. We wouldn't need analogical leaps into the possibly relevant. In many situations, we have ṣome knowledge as to what aspects may be relevant to the decision-making problem, but we don't know how to "compute" the correct decision from those aspects. Analogy is useful because it allows us to find other situations to borrow from, situations in which we know some clearly (in)correct decision.

In other words, analogy is a useful heuristic method to employ because we and the world happen to fall near the midpoint of those three axes. (It is largely a matter of individual preference and belief whether one considers this coincidence to be an accident, or part of a conscious Design, or nothing more than a reflection of the current limits of human cognitive abilities.) A skewing along any one of these axes would reduce the power of analogizing.

1.4.2. How To Analogize.

Okay, so reasoning by analogy can be great, is frequently used, and is perhaps even indispensable. Now, how do we get a program to do it? Uemov [1970] drily notes:

> When analogy is successful it is called 'deep,' 'strict,' 'scientific' and so on. When it fails, it is called 'superficial,' 'loose,' 'unscientific' and so on. Naturally, there is a question as to how these two types of analogy can be distinguished before the practical realization takes place.

The simplest model for analogy is that of structurally mapping slots of one frame to slots of another frame. This must be generalized to include mapping between one network of frames and another network of frames; it must also include knowledge-guided reformulation to reveal commonalities between imperfectly matching entries, and likewise between imperfectly matching slots.

EXAMPLE 1. Consider the statement "Fred is ursine." Presumably that means to map TypicalBear (and the cluster of units associated with TypicalBear) to Fred (and the cluster of frames associated with Fred).

We might want to map the TypicalBear's qualitative size (Large, compared to the typical TypicalWoodlandCreature) to Fred's qualitative size (Large, compared to the TypicalHumanMale.) That was easy, because both the slot (qualitativeSize) and the value (Large) were the same. Frequently, though, either the two slots or the values are different. For example, we might map the Bear's clawLength and clawSharpness to various attributes of Fred's fingernails, which would be a cross-slot mapping. We might map some absolute numeric values (such as 800 pounds) to different numbers, and so on.

How can a program automatically find these, and other good mappings? That is, how does it notice to even try to do this, and how does it manage to carry it out?

To answer these important questions, let's ask: why might a person make that analogy and utter the statement "Fred is ursine"? If you think about it for a minute (as we did), the surprising answer is that this is not a powerful analogy after all, it's just a nice, powerful, and compact way of communicating (in parallel) a few facts that just happen to be true.

There is no causal connection here, just coincidence. All the speaker was doing was (a) compacting his message, and (b) injecting a little humor and hyberbole and variety into his speech. So it's not hard to imagine that a program could notice that a good match exists between Fred and TypicalBear, and that TypicalBear is well known to the typical listener, and, if the current problem is to describe Fred to that listener, then the program could decide to refer to Fred as ursine in order to communicate a lot about Fred all at once.

A large fraction of human use of "analogy and metaphor" is not analogy or metaphor at all, then, but rather falls into this category of merely compacting a message by finding superficially similar "analogues." Let's turn to an example of a "real" analogy.

EXAMPLE 2.   "Mowgli is wolflike." This sure seems similar to example 1, at least on the surface. What's different about it? Here, in contrast to example 1, there is a *causal connection* underlying the analogy, because Mowgli (the character from Rudyard Kipling's *Jungle Book*) was raised by wolves. One's upbringing is a strong determiner of one's attitudes toward food, shelter, possessions, ethics, life, death, music, physical conditioning, and so on. If we ask you whether Fred (from example 1) likes to catch fish, or what method he uses to catch them, or whether he cooks them before he eats them, etc., it's unlikely that the answers from TypicalBear will prove to be reliable guesses. But if I ask you whether Mowgli likes to catch fish, or what method he uses to catch them, or whether he cooks them before he eats them, etc., then you would expect to be able to guess the answers by looking at TypicalWolf. To answer Uemov's skepticism, we remark that there's not too much bias in this example, because we (the authors) don't know much about Mowgli or about wolves. We have no idea whether wolves eat fish, or how they catch them, etc. But we'd be surprised to learn that there's any episode in *The Jungle Book* that shows ways in which Mowgli and the wolves differ on diet, hunting methods, table manners, or other upbringing-dependent attributes.

There are several routes by which a program might first suspect this analogy:

1. By noticing that Mowgli was raisedBy Wolves, and that raisedBy strongly *determines* many other important properties. (Following Russell [1988], we say that "Properties x and y *determine* z" to mean that most objects sharing the same value for their x and y properties will likely have the same z values as one another. For example, age and neighborhood *determine* languageSpoken. Two individuals of the same age, who reside in the same neighborhood, are likely to speak the same language.)

2. By noticing that there are some unusual (uncommon) similarities between various attributes of Wolf-003 (some particular wolf) and Mowgli — such as their tableManners, howlingFrequency, goals, dreads, and gait; and then either
   a. Trying to "explain" these by finding some deeper, independent attribute(s) that determined them, and/or
   b. Trying to extend the analogy to other (not necessarily "deep") attributes to probe its boundary, simply because extending it is a cost-effective way of getting more information into the KB.

3. By some external clue, hint, or reference. "External" means "explicitly provided" by a human user, the surrounding text in the novel, or some very far-flung source.

4. By random search for analogies. This is a special case of all three of the preceding methods, and is probably too inefficient to make it worth trying to automate, at least on conventional serial computers. Perhaps the human brain does some of this random searching "in the background," unconsciously, and with a high factor of parallelism. If so, and if it is indeed a relatively rich source of useful analogies, then some specialized piece of parallel hardware might be warranted.

5. By noticing that "our problem, X, is very reminiscent of problem Y, which we've already worked on and know a lot about; and analogies of type Z helped us a lot with Y, so maybe analogies similar to Z will help with X." This may be viewed as a variant of method 2b above, where X and Y are noticed as similar and then the usefulAnalogies slot of Y is mapped back to X.

In order to get these various schemes to work (excepting number 3, *deus ex machina*), the system must have access to a large knowledge base, a rich space in which to prospect for matches. Most of the five schemes also require deep understanding of the knowledge in the KB, to permit obscure or imperfect (but still promising) matches to be made, to sort out the superficial from the significant matches, to posit and judge the plausibility of a common causal explanation for the similarities, and to decide along which other axes (slots) to search for further similarities that would extend the analogy.

We've glossed over some hard issues — perhaps *the* hard issues — in successful analogical reasoning, namely how *exactly* to pick a promising analogy, how to develop it, to which as-yet unmatched slots the match should be (attempted to be) extended (for example, usefulTactics), and to which slots it should not be extended (for example, inventor). Other critical issues are how to tell if the phenomenon going on is really "exploiting a hitherto unrecognized common generalization," how to tell if the analogy is superficial and not worth extending any more, when to rely on it, and so on.

Our basic approach to answering all these questions is "divide and conquer." That is, we posit that *analogy* is a vague English word covering a multitude of types of inference. The types of analogical reasoning can be usefully arranged in a space whose dimensions include things such as the nature of the boundary (where the analogy breaks down), the nature of the analogues (for example, the hardness of each analogue's field), the nature of the attributes being matched, the purpose of the analogizer, and so on. Each cell in that n-dimensional matrix represents a type of analogical reasoning, and each of those types deserves to be teased out separately and studied. A bundle of heuristics can then be assembled for each cell, though of course many of the heuristics would apply to whole sections of the matrix.

We hope to tame analogy through this two-pronged attack:

1. Breaking down the phenomenon into its various subtypes and then handling each one

2. Having a realistically large pool of (millions of) objects, substances, events, sets, ideas, relationships, etc., to which to analogize.

As we remarked a few paragraphs back, successful analogizing depends on the second prong above, so most of our efforts to date on Cyc have focused on building up that large KB, not on working out the details of the various kinds of analogical reasoning.

1.5. The Representation Trap

The careful reader may have noted a possible hole in our discussion of the brittleness of current expert systems: First, we criticized them for merely containing opaque tokens and pushing them around. Yet our example of "having more general, flexible knowledge" was nothing more than having more (and more general) tokens and pushing *them* around!

Yes, all we're doing is pushing tokens around, but that's all that cognition is. What makes our tokens "better" is that they aren't tied to solving some particular problem. Naturally, all programs are built on some primitives (predicates, frames, slots, rules, functions, scripts). But if you choose task-specific primitives, you'll win in the short run (building a program for that narrow domain) but lose in the long run (you'll find yourself painted into a corner when you try to scale the program up.)

Given a specific task, the necessary knowledge can be represented in a number of ways; in particular, it is often possible to cheat by using long predicate names. For example, we might use the predicate WellTrained (or the attribute wellTrained) to indicate that some creature was well trained. *We* know that WellTrained horses have been well trained, and that WellTrained implies Trained. But both facts would have to be told explicitly to the system; it doesn't speak English. So we could have named that predicate P00089, or Untrained, and its understanding would have been no different (for example, its behavior when facing a problem involving horse training would have been no different).

Here is a typical example of how to solve a problem dishonestly, in this case that of deciding whether something can live in a desert. Consider a program that contains the following four if/then rules:

(IF (LivesNearWater x) THEN (NOT (LivesInDesert x)))
(IF (LaysEggsInWater x) THEN (LivesNearWater x))
(IF (Amphibian x) THEN (LaysEggsInWater x))
(IF (Frog x) THEN (Amphibian x))

Now suppose we assert: (Frog Fred). We could use the above rules to conclude that Fred does not live in the desert. Note that the knowledge isn't adequate to let the system conclude such things as:

Fred sometimes gets wet.
Fred lays eggs.
Fred is alive.
Fred doesn't live in the Sahara.

Fred doesn't live on the surface of the sun.
Fred is not a mongoose or a bird.

The problem is that we are using very detailed, complex predicates (such as LaysEggsInWater) without defining them. (Incidentally, the conclusion being derived — that Fred does not live in the desert — is correct, but the chain of reasoning is invalid! Fred, a male frog, does not lay eggs.)

Why is it a bad idea to use complex predicates without defining them? *Informally*, it's disturbing because for us to "understand" something means that we can answer questions about it, can relate it to most things to which it ought to be . . . er, *related*. If you hear that Fred LaysEggsInWater then you ought to be able to answer questions like "Does Fred lay eggs?" and "Is Fred sometimes in the water?"

Formally, it's a bad idea because it's explosive, as follows. (We'll make a very simplistic argument.) Suppose we have a thousand primitive properties of objects that we can perceive; and let a complex property be composed of three primitives. Then we have a billion (1000^3) complex properties. If we represent everything in terms of complex properties rather than primitives, then we may require up to a billion billion rules to represent their interrelationships — that is, 10^{18} rules. If instead we defined each complex property in terms of its primitive components, we would have a billion definitions and a million rules relating primitives. This is the same argument in favor of planning islands in a search, where again an exponential search has its exponent cut by a factor of 2. If we define a series of levels of decreasingly primitive relations, we can chip away more and more at this exponent.

Basically, what we're saying is that we need to relate things by virtue of the relations between their constituents. This is what happens in the world too, it's just that human beings are so good at abstracting to just the right level of abstraction that we aren't conscious of the mental "work" we're doing.

For instance, when you rent a car, you figure out how to drive it by dealing with the various parts of the car: the door lock, the door handle, the seat adjuster, the headlights, the wipers, the turn indicators, etc. You have and use a few rules for each of those types of car parts, rules that help you quickly locate them in a new car and operate them. You *don't* have a thousand scripts like "how to drive a Camaro," "how to drive a Prelude," etc. (Of course, if we do happen to get into a type of car we are familiar with, we can draw on our already-cached script for that kind of car.)

With only one narrow class of problem to solve, such as getting ready to drive a Honda Prelude, and only a (relatively) small set of facts to represent, however, we can always get away with cheating. In the driving-a-Prelude case, we could program the specific arm motions that would turn on the car's headlights.

In such cases the representations developed reflect more the structure of the problem than the structure of the world. The narrower (and smaller) the task, the worse this problem, this trap, becomes.

In knowledge representation, therefore, narrow domains are misleading. And small KBs likely won't scale up easily into huge KBs. This, then, is the representation trap, the trap that has snared (or even *characterized*) expert systems to date: choosing a set of long, complex primitives (predicate names) that have a lot of knowledge compiled within them, and writing rules that are also tailored to the program's domain (omitting premises that needn't be worried about in that particular task). The bait in the trap is the fact that it works — at least within the narrow domain for which that particular program was designed. The catch is that the resultant system is isolated and brittle.

1.6. Ontological versus Knowledge Engineering *or* Why Building a Huge KB Is Different from Building *n* Small KBs

Cyc needs a deep, well-organized ontology of real-world knowledge. This is in contrast to, say, the latest special purpose Expert System.

1.6.1. Why Expert Systems Don't Display Synergy.
What's special about having just a narrow range of problems to solve? It allows you to cut corners in two ways. The first way is pretty obvious — you need to encode only a sliver of the world's knowledge.

The second way to cut corners is much less obvious: having a narrow task allows you to represent — and reason about — a simpler world, not just a smaller one. (See also "The Representation Trap," Section 1.5.) The point is, even if your problem touches on some "tough" knowledge — belief, substances, events, time, space, structure and function, etc. — you can usually get by with capturing just a few selected aspects of them. Let's give a few examples of what we mean:

Decreasingly simple views of time: (a) Your task might allow you to forget about time entirely — treat each "case" as if it occurred in a single instant of time (for example, MYCIN). (b) Or you might have to represent only a distinct "before" and "after" snapshot for each problem (for example, STRIPS). (c) Or your task domain might allow you to do linear interpolation between "cusp" snapshots. (d) Or you might have a "time-line" data structure in your program, with knowledge tied to whatever intervals during which it is relevant or true (for example, HearSayII, STRADS).

Decreasingly simple views of structure: (a) You might be able to ignore structure entirely, and just use a "feature-vector" representation. (For example, MYCIN can decide which kind of meningitis a person has, without knowing that people have two arms and two legs.) (b) MYCIN does presume that there is a single spinal cord and brain, but this is woven into the program at the level of global variables, not explicitly, declaratively "understood" by the program. (c) There may be a few specific joints, or compound assemblies, whose internal structure matters in doing your chosen task. If so, you can model each such structure in your program idiosyncratically, after learning what level of detail you'll need. (d) Your program might contain a whole vocabulary of task-related types of combiners or joints, plus a "grammar" of their legal uses, that allows more dynamic analysis of structures and synthesis of new ones.

Now we're getting to the source of incompatibility between different expert systems. Even if the two ES's were written in the same language (tool, shell), and even if their domains seem related (for example, medical diagnosis), still there's almost no chance of being able to usefully dump rules from one ES into the other. There are two types of almost-unavoidable incompatibility:

INCOMPATIBILITY 1.   Each rule, each piece of knowledge, has implicit in it the various assumptions and simplifications that were present implicitly in its ES. If you take a rule from a system that presumes "just one instant of time," it's going to have predicates that check whether the patient "has" symptoms x, y, and z. Even though we understand that this means "did the patient have them all at the same time," that's not stated in the rule — it's implicit in the way the ES was designed. Now dump that poor rule into an ES in which time is handled differently, and it might fire at inappropriate times.

INCOMPATIBILITY 2.   What's even more likely to happen is that the rule will never fire, because the various ways that ES#1 carved up the world — the predicates used to state the rules — are not quite the same as the ways that ES#2 carved up the world. One system's rules might talk about the presence of the attribute Feverishness, the other might talk about the magnitude of the parameter BodyTemperature. One might have Headache value categorized as Mild or Severe, the other might use three terms like Slight, Moderate, Extreme. The first ES would have other rules that would conclude "Severe" about some condition, and other rules that might be triggered by a "Severe" condition. But none of the rules from the second ES would ever conclude, or be triggered by, a "Severe" value.

1.6.2.   The Path to Fertile Co-mingling.   So either the rules collide with each other, or they pass in the night without interacting at all. No wonder ES's aren't "inter-combinable"! What can we do to ensure a more fertile co-mingling?

To answer that critical question, let's think about how we are able to look at either of those ES's and understand what it's saying. How do we understand that Low/Medium/High corresponds to a dividing up of the scale of responses, as does Mild/Severe, or Slight/Moderate/Extreme? We have knowledge — the "right" knowledge — of how to interrelate them: namely, we can visualize the linear scale that is their common generalization. The ES's don't have that knowledge, but they don't *individually* "need" it, either, except when faced with some unusual, unexpected circumstances.

We now can see more clearly what each ES's task is. It isn't to do medical diagnosis, or design chips, or whatever, it's to help humans do those things, to input and output symbols that are largely meaningless to it but that will mean something to the people who are using the system.

At some level, people also choose to respond mechanically — we don't always drop down one level in detail, but the key difference is that, generally speaking, we *could* if the situation warranted it. When we are vague, when we omit details, it is generally a choice we've made; it is voluntary simplifying from a position of strength, a situation wherein we *could* be precise if we need to.

What would it mean for a program to operate from such a "position of strength" rather than to operate by the illusion of competence? It would mean a program that had an over-arching framework for the world's knowledge and that had its detailed knowledge — predicates, frames, slots, rules, or whatever — related to that global ontology. In addition, the program would need the general knowledge that connects together the specific areas' expertise and allows them to combine synergistically.

The "Mild" or "Severe" classes are a low-to-high partitioning of the continuum of Strengths. So is "Low, Medium, High," so is "Slight, Moderate, Extreme," and so on. An intelligent agent, be it human or machine, would know this common generalization, and would be familiar with these three special cases.

The "Feverishness" parameter would have links that relate it to — indeed, define it in terms of — an atypically high value for the

BodyTemperature parameter. That in turn would be related to Temperature in general, so that, for example, either Fahrenheit or Centigrade scales could be used, and (if any detailed piece of knowledge is needed) body temperature, skin temperature, and environmental temperature could be interrelated.

This makes it sound like we're advocating a set of translation tricks, a set of useful transformations. Well, in a way that's right. But it's not so much "a set of . . ." as "an *adequate, global* set of . . . ." What do we mean by that? We mean that everything that humans can easily conceptualize ought to be easily, naturally tied in to this over-arching framework for knowledge. The sort of translations we listed above (converting among temperatures, or from fever to temperature, or from one way of breaking up a Low-to-High scale to another way) ought to be typical applications of the framework. How many such typical things would there have to be, then, in this "top layer"? The bad news is that we believe the answer is millions. But the good news is that it should be only a few million (at least if you count only "things" like frames that each have a lot of content to them).

Given that expert systems can't co-mingle today and will require something like Cyc to serve as the "semantic glue" among them before they can effectively cooperate, how are we to construct Cyc? Sections 1.7.3 and 1.7.4 present a similar chicken-and-egg situation with respect to machine learning (ML) and with respect to natural language understanding (NLU). Efforts in these three areas (ES, NLU, ML) have finessed the problems that we must solve in order to get Cyc built, so we can't just use any of them as a model and "scale them up."

1.7.   Building Cyc

The previous subsections have argued for building a huge KB; that is the effort under way as Cyc. There are two parts to our task:

- Do the top layers of the global ontology correctly

- Relate all the rest of human knowledge to those top layers

This is where we diverge from philosophers and, frankly, previous AI work (yes, even our own). Instead of talking more about this, and making forays here and there as needed to gather a few examples, we set out to actually do it. Well, almost. We figured that if we could get pretty far on setting up the top layers, everyone would pitch in and help us relate the rest of human knowledge to them.

Is it possible? Who knows? But let's get started and see! That was our attitude in 1984; we gave Cyc a 10–20 percent chance of succeeding. Now it looks like our original guess about the size of the task was about right, and we'd give us a full 50–60 percent chance of succeeding.

The first task involves on the order of ten million entries. (As Marvin Minsky observed, that's about the same order of magnitude as the number of things a human being acquires — burns into long-term memory — during ages 0 to 8, assuming one new entry every ten seconds of one's waking life.) The second task is unbounded, but probably another ten to fifty million entries would suffice for general intelligence (for example, the intelligence required for acquiring knowledge in school and in extra-curricular conversations). Quite a bit more may be needed for qualitatively super-human intelligence.

The most easily foreseen mode of failure was — and is — that the knowledge enterers might diverge, either by stepping on one another's toes (misusing each other's terms) or by passing one another in the night (re-entering already-existing concepts, giving those units slightly different names).

If the latter duplication is ever noticed, then it may be fairly easy to fix (either by relating the units to one another, or, in extreme cases, just merging them), so the failure mode would lie in never realizing that this duplication occurred in the KB.

One interesting tool that helps in identifying such duplication is to have Cyc actively search for new analogies. Some of them are genuine, interesting analogies; some of them are mappings between non-analogous concepts A and B, which signifies that we haven't yet told Cyc enough about A and B to differentiate them properly; and a third class of apparent analogies are between concepts that are really just different formulations of the same knowledge — that is, passings in the night.

Since 1984, we've been building and organizing and reorganizing our growing consensus reality KB in Cyc. We now have about a million entries in it, and we expect it to increase by a factor of 4 by mid-1990. Thanks to an array of explicit and implicit methods for stating and enforcing semantics, they appear to be converging, not diverging. The following sections discuss what it means for semantics to converge; they also cover various tactics that might have been used for building the Cyc KB. The chapter ends with a brief sketch of the method we've settled on and the anatomy of the current Cyc system.

1.7.1. Convergence. Naturally, we must build up the Cyc KB from *some* sort of primitives. We have claimed that it must be built from deeply understood knowledge rather than from complex "impenetrable" predicates (or slots or whatever).

At first, doing this just made life difficult; having a deep but small KB didn't pay off. Fortunately, as we built Cyc ever larger and larger, we found that the set of primitives began to converge. That is, it requires less and less work to enter each new fact. This phenomenon is not surprising (it was, for example, predicted in Pat Hayes' *Naive Physics Manifesto*), it is merely very important. And it was quite comforting to see it really happen!

Let's illustrate how convergence can occur. Consider a legal reasoning system that must advise someone whether to sue someone else. Say your car has been scratched, and there are plenty of witnesses. With little common sense, the system might fire a rule like

> IF your property has been damaged by X, and there is little doubt as to the facts of the case, and monetary recompense is not forthcoming,
> THEN sue X

But if your car is scratched by a bag lady, litigation may be a bad idea. A clause like ". . . and the perpetrator is not a bag lady" might be added to solve this problem. For more generality, the new conjunct might be phrased ". . . and X is not destitute."

The Cyc approach would be different. We would describe what the process of suing is (a way of getting money from a defendant) and what money is, and we would give very general rules about the process of transferring some X from Y to Z, including the precondition that some X must exist at Y in order to be transferred from there, the fact that there is some overhead cost to running a transfer process, and perhaps some special knowledge about who does what to whom and who pays what to whom during and after the suing activity that would take place in America today.

From this, Cyc could generate the appropriate behavior in this case. But more importantly, the system would now be able to exhibit robust behavior in an unimaginably large number of other cases also. For instance, it could reason that if someone drops a few coins into a beggar's cup, then they had (at least) those coins on their person just prior to the charitable act; it could reason that the world's consumption of resources will eventually have to cease; and it could reason that one usually doesn't borrow money from bag ladies.

To solve the specific "car-scratching" problem, it's tempting to put in special case knowledge. But as you widen the definition of the problem domain (for example, "acting intelligently in interpersonal situations involving money or property"), it becomes more economical to opt for the deeper, more spread out approach. In the limit ("acting intelligently in general"), such a policy is wildly cost-effective.

1.7.2. Tactics for Ontological Engineering.

So we must build a good global ontology of human knowledge (that is, one that spans current human consensus reality) if we are to avoid the representation trap. Choosing a set of representation primitives (predicates, objects, functions) has been called *ontological engineering* — that is, defining the categories and relationships of the domain. (This is empirical, experimental engineering, as contrasted with *ontological theorizing*, which philosophers have done for millennia.)

More than just having a good ontology, however, we must also build up a large knowledge base organized according to that ontology, a KB of millions of (frame-sized) pieces of consensus reality knowledge. How many millions? We hope and expect it's about 5 million frames, each with several dozen "fact-sized" slot entries; but we'll find out! This project is mankind's first foray into large-scale ontological engineering.

Well, what about encyclopedias and thesauruses?

Encyclopedia writers have been able to finesse 90 percent of the ontology issue because of three factors:

1. An encyclopedia is largely a linearly ordered sequence of articles, so the main decision to make is "grain size," not organization.

2. People learn early in life what sorts of topics will and won't have articles dedicated to them.

3. To the extent that 1 and 2 are insufficient, a peppering of cross references will help a person jump from an almost-correct place to the correct place.

Thesaurus writers have been able to finesse 99 percent of the ontology issue. Go take a look at the table of contents of a thesaurus, and you'll see an interesting phenomenon: it's terrible! For instance, the leading thesaurus was developed a couple centuries ago; one of the top-level divisions of knowledge is Theology, Physics is a sub-sub-part of Chemistry, and so on. And yet, the thesaurus works fine. Its job is not to be a good global ontology, but rather to be good locally, to clump together words with similar meanings. Thesauri have to be only *locally* good.

So both Cyc and its ontology must be built almost from scratch. The question, then, is: How should such a gargantuan knowledge base be constructed? What methodology, what tactics, will suffice? We'll examine a few possible short-cut methods, and then describe the method we finally chose.

1.7.3. Free Lunch Try 1: Natural Language Understanding.

It would be super to get a program to speak English, after which we could sit back and watch as it "went to school." That works well for people, but there's an awful lot that kids know long before they enter school, before they can even begin to speak coherently. It's not clear how that knowledge gets into their heads and is organized in the 0–2 year time period; some of it probably has a head start (that is, is "wired in") as a result of the way we've evolved over the eons. But the bottom line is this: *You can't seriously expect to do natural language understanding until you already know most of consensus reality!* Recall the following pair of sentences:

> *The ink is in the pen.*
> *The pig is in the pen.*

The first sentence's "pen" is a writing implement, the second is a pig-sty or corral. How do you know that? It's not English that tells you, it's your knowledge of how big things are, what it takes to serve as a container for liquid, what sorts of things ink goes in, what sorts of things pigs go in — and why. That is, you disambiguate the word "pen" by drawing on your knowledge of the real world. Here's another example:

> *The little girl saw the bicycle in the window. She wanted it.*
> *The little girl saw the bicycle in the window. She pressed her nose up against it.*

What does the word "it" refer to in each of those sentence pairs, the bicycle or the window? How do you know that? You know because of your knowledge of the real world, of human emotions and capabilities and anatomy, of physical and mental and physiological limitations, and so on — *not* because of English grammar and syntax. If the girl collected glass, the first sentence's "it" might refer to the window; if she were fabulously wealthy, "it" might even refer to the whole store! But those would be one-in-a-million situations (or jokes); all the rest of the time, "it" would refer to the bicycle. In the second sentence, even more real-world knowledge is required to fully understand why she would press her nose against the store window: for example, to see more details (which in turn presupposes a good understanding of the relative locations of nose and eyes), or to get as physically close to the bike as possible (which in turn presupposes an understanding of the socioeconomic implications of actually entering a store as opposed to merely window-shopping).

Fred likes ice cream, candy, etc.

What does "etc." mean in the sentence above? Looking at the common properties in the two given items to induce from, we infer the general category "sweets." So ellipses ("etc.," "and so on," ". . .") can be understood only if the listener already knows enough of the properties of the items to be able to search for the commonality.

Dogs are on my front lawn.
Dogs are mammals.
Dogs are widely distributed on Earth.

Clearly, "Dogs are X" can mean many different things. The first sentence means "Each member of some specific set of dogs is on my front lawn." The second sentence means "Each member of the set of all dogs is also a member of the set of all mammals." The third sentence means "The areaDistributedOver of the set of all Dogs is a large fraction of the land area of the Earth."

The Columbia University School of Journalism collects humorous examples of ambiguous phrases from real newspaper headlines. While these are admittedly extreme, the average reader has no trouble understanding them on, say, the second or third reading:

British Left Waffles on Falklands
Sharon to Press His Suit in Israel
More Silverware Stolen — Police Seek Pattern

One day (hopefully in this century), natural language understanding will be the most important mode of knowledge acquisition into the growing Cyc KB. In that vision, Cyc reads texts, novels, journals, newspapers, and so on, and holds discussions with human beings to help clarify the difficult parts (or the unintelligible parts such as a transliterated accent or "dialect" woven into text) and to help check its assimilations.

One day, we hope Cyc will read those humorous headlines and understand them (and also understand their obvious misinterpretations). Before that day arrives, however, a lot of material must already be in the KB.

So, to summarize Free Lunch Try 1, we believe that Cyc and NLU will mature synergistically, each requiring the other. But NLU alone is not a short-cut to building Cyc, at least not in its first half-decade of existence.

1.7.4. Free Lunch Try 2: Machine Learning.

It would be super to get a program to discover the needed knowledge on its own, just by its observing the world, noticing regularities, doing simple experiments to verify them, and so on. Lenat spent his youth (1973–1983) pursuing this dream. The AM and Eurisko programs were surprisingly successful, and are partially responsible for catalyzing the renaissance of learning as a subfield of AI. But . . .

But they rely on a trick: having a representation so well chosen that *syntax mirrors semantics*. In such a situation, one can go far just by doing syntactic mutation and exploration. [See Lenat & Brown, 1984.]

The better understood the domain is, the more likely it is that such a representation can be found. Unfortunately, this is a lot like burning coal: after a while, the energy is released, the fire dies, and you have to go out and manually dig up some more fuel. We kept hoping that we'd ignite a positively reinforcing cycle, but we never even came close.

Machine-learning researchers are working on ways to actually generate a bootstrapping process, by using existing and newly acquired knowledge to guide and improve the learning process, but an effective system is a long way off.

In the final analysis, we succumbed to "the more you know, the more and faster you can learn." More precisely, the inverse of this statement bit us:

> If you don't know very much to begin with,
> Then you can't learn much right away, and what you do learn
> you probably won't learn very quickly.

What was holding those programs back was the lack of a large knowledge base to use as a substrate for the learning process. And given current peripherals, it would be hard for Cyc to go out on its own and acquire a sufficient experiential base from which to induce the required common sense.

1.7.5. Try 3: Hard Work (No Free Lunch).

The limited success we had with automatic program synthesis from examples and dialogues [Green *et al.*, 1974] in the early seventies led us to the AM research (automated discovery of domain concepts). Its limited success led us to Eurisko, which tried to discover new heuristics as it went along. *Its* limited success led us to believe that there is no free lunch; that is, that we had to apply the tactic of last resort — hard work — and thus Cyc was born. We are building the needed KB manually, one piece at a time, at least up to the crossover point where natural language understanding begins to be a more effective way of further enlarging it.

This task looked — and still looks — just barely possible. We estimated that it would take about two person-centuries to build up that KB, assuming that we don't get stuck too badly on representation thorns along the way. In real time, our schedule was — and still is — to complete the project (reach that crossover point) in the ten-year period that ends in late 1994.

Naturally, there were — and are — a lot of hard problems (or, depending on how you look at things, interesting issues). Some of them are: how we decide what knowledge to encode and how we encode it; how to handle the "thorns" (how to represent substances, parts, time, space, belief, and counterfactuals); how Cyc can access, compute, inherit, deduce, or guess answers; and how we're going to squeeze two person-centuries into a decade of real time, without having the knowledge enterers' semantics fatally "diverge."

Back in section 1.5, "The Representation Trap," we spotlighted the need to choose a good set of primitives. That will be one of our "keys" to achieving convergence: defining knowledge in each area in terms of knowledge in other (often more general) areas. For example, when baseball is explained to Cyc, it is in terms of generic actions like running, hitting, catching, competing, cooperating, taking turns, and so on. This is also the source of power behind modularity in programs, primitives in programming languages, and grammatical structure rather than monolithic messages in natural languages.

The other "keys" to semantic convergence are (a) to have a sufficiently large KB that one can tell it something new by plucking a similar piece of knowledge and making some small editing changes to it, (b) to have a good enough global ontology to make that easy, and (c) to have Cyc function as an intelligent agent whose first important task is to help with its own continuing enlargement (including policing the KB, building and using user-models to accelerate their actions, making guesses that semi-automate the copy-and-edit process, and so on).

A few years ago, shortly after we began, we published our initial plans [Lenat, Shepherd, et al., 1986]. Our schedule was to have enough of the KB built to transition to natural language understanding as the dominant knowledge entry mode in 1994. By now, we've gotten pretty far along. Not surprisingly, there have been unexpected problems and unexpected discoveries. Perhaps the biggest surprise is that we're still on schedule. The thorns we had to deal with — time, change, the overall ontology, and so on — have been faced up to and trimmed, rather than avoided. In more detail, . . . , well, that's what the rest of this book is about.

2. Overview of Cyc

Cyc comprises three "pieces":

1. The knowledge base itself (Cyc KB)

2. The environment: the interface editing/browsing tools (UE and MUE), the multi-user knowledge server, the binary KB dumper, and so on

3. The representation language (CycL)

The boundaries between these pieces are not as sharp as they are in most systems. For example, much of CycL is represented in the KB, and some of it is *only* represented that way; so the border between the KB and CycL is hazy. Similarly, much of the user interface is represented in (and *only* in) the KB, blurring the border between the KB and the environment.

The sections in this chapter answer a few basic questions about each of the three pieces of Cyc.

2.1. The KB Itself

The Cyc knowledge base is to be the repository of the bulk of the factual and heuristic knowledge, much of it usually left unstated, that comprises "consensus reality": the things we assume everybody already knows.

WHAT WILL Cyc'S KB CONTAIN?   As a broad "driving force" or "forcing function," we chose to encode the knowledge required to understand a one-volume desk encyclopedia and a newspaper — including editorials, advertisements, advice columns, and so on. This does *not* mean the contents of such works (though, frankly, we often add some of that as well!); rather, it means ferreting out and representing the underlying common sense knowledge that the writers of those articles assumed that their readers already possessed.

Another good "forcing function" is to examine articles that we disbelieve and introspect on why we find them incredible. (For example, one article tells of an Indian guru who sat underwater for seven days and seven nights. One of its great internal details: "Skeptics claim he came up at night for air.")

Introspection, although a good tool, is not the only one used. Knowledge editors pose questions about a piece of text just "explained," questions that "anyone" should be able to answer having just read that text, and Cyc is further augmented until it, too, can answer those questions. The newly added knowledge is generalized, both to make it more broadly applicable and to help test — and push us into extending — Cyc's ontology.

WHAT IS THE TIME SCALE FOR THE CONSTRUCTION OF Cyc? During 1984–1989, a small team of AI researchers has been encoding mutually dissimilar articles and pieces of knowledge. Much of their time has been spent figuring out adequate work-arounds for various representation "thorns," such as time, space, belief, causality, substances, intelligent action, mind versus body, and so on.

Beginning in 1989, a growing cadre of knowledge editors has begun to use machine-assisted copy&edit procedures to encode the final 99 percent of the Basic KB. At the same time, Elaine Rich, Jim Barnett, and other natural language understanding researchers have begun building a system that interacts synergistically with Cyc: calling on Cyc to do semantic disambiguation, anaphoric reference resolution, ellipsis interpretation, etc.; and being used by Cyc as a front-end knowledge acquisition mechanism.

Anecdotal successes have been achieved in each "direction" during 1989, and the hope is that by late 1994, this combined system will make obsolete the current manual method of knowledge entry. Gradually, the role of the humans will shift to resemble that of teachers or tutors: recommending what to read next and explaining difficult passages. That phase (Cyc *qua* voracious reader) will never quite end, but after some number of years — perhaps around the turn of the century — Cyc should be as well fleshed out as the "person on the street," and as flexible. That is, Cyc will be increasingly "usable" during the 1990s.

HOW WILL Cyc'S KB BE USED? As performance programs get "stuck," they can fall back on more and more general knowledge, and/or rely on analogy, to cope with their predicament. Those same techniques should also speed up knowledge entry.

As described in chapter 1, we believe that this KB will enable the next generation of AI work and achievements in expert systems, machine learning, and, of course, natural language understanding.

HOW IS Cyc'S KB ORGANIZED?   This is the issue of the "global ontology of human knowledge." We are not claiming that we have the correct organization, just a more or less adequate one — or maybe even less: one that is *correctable* and *extendable* into an adequate ontology. Subsequent sections will have a lot to say about the organizing principles that underly the knowledge base: what are the basic categories, why have categories at all, etc.

2.2.   The Interface

WHAT TOOLS ENABLE A KNOWLEDGE EDITOR TO RAPIDLY BROWSE AND EDIT THE KB?   The tools we've built so far include a "symbolic spreadsheet" frame editor (UE), whose commands are structural and textual, and a spatial "museum room" editor (MUE) that maps frames metaphorically into floorplans of rooms. See figures 2–1 and 2–2; also see chapter 8, which discusses these editors in more detail.

Beginning back in 1984, we also developed a node&link semantic net graphing and editing/browsing interface, but this soon became too cluttered and tangled to be useful. To avoid the "spaghetti" phenomenon, we tried having just local (instead of global) placement of nodes, but that lost the valuable kinesthetic memory, the "feel," of the KB (for example, remembering that emotions are just over to the left of hobbies).

ARE THEY TOOLS FOR THE NOVICE OR THE EXPERT?   Unlike most "human interface tools," these tools have been built to help already-fluent knowledge editors — not naive users. They are power tools to navigate around knowledge space and to resculpt the knowledge. They are intelligence amplifiers for the most talented knowledge editors, not mental prostheses to hold the hands of neophyte editors.

Developing these tools has led us to consider and experiment with various exotic I/O technologies: speech synthesis, speech understanding, on-line visual dictionaries to point to, sound-space navigation, animation, color, pedals, 3D helmets, etc. Very little of that technology-dependent material will be covered in this book, because of its ephemeral and experimental nature and its general unavailability (or, at least, nonstandardization) outside our laboratory.

normal slot allInstanceOf

Lock ☐ Legal ☐ Filters ☒ Expanders ☒ Previous ☐

More above

overrideLocalDefault?   (7)
remotelyDependentOn   (allGenls)
remotelyDependentSlots   (showName imageArray edito
slotBeingDisplayedOf   (HKESlotValueDisplay8-Sere
specSlots   (+instanceOf +generalizati
toCompute   (ComputeByComposing allGe
toTest   (FUNCTION (LAMBDA (U VI &
unitDisplayedBy   (HKESlot-UnitDisplay2-Sere

More below

unit Person

Lock ☐ Legal ☐ Filters ☒ Expanders ☒ Previous ☐

Top of unit

instanceOf   (PersonType)
allInstanceOf   (AgentType CompositeTang&I
instances   (Cohen Person-2 PersonSVS-
allInstances   (Cohen Person-2 PersonSVS-
performsDaily   (+Sleeping)
constraints   (@ConstraintOnPerson_age @
genls   (LegalEntity SentientAnima
allGenls   (RepresentedThing Animal I

More below

Top of object

Use Next ☒   Lock ☐   Memory ☐   Previous ☐

Justification for Lenat.hasIdeologies.RepublicanIde
Entry: RepublicanIdeology, Net CF=I
   Source: RepublicanParty, path:
   (memberOfThisPoliticalParty) CF=T
   †Properties: I-TYPE=InheritanceInference.

Bottom of object

Layout Unit   Show Unit   Copy Unit
  Undo   Tell   TCVSP

⇧⇧⇧
Control-G Show Unit
Unit to display: allInstanceOf
Control-G Show Unit
Unit to display: Person

Unit Editor

Mannuthus: connection down (deaf/mute) Queues: Net: 0; BG: (0 4 Await Command); Untransmitted: 2.

[Thu 27 Jul 12:00:00] doug (+Lenat)   CL ZHEI: Menu Choose   Shandra

---

unit Lenat

Lock ☐ Legal ☐ Filters ☒ Expanders ☒ Previous ☐

More above

hasIdeologies   (RepublicanIdeology)
hasInstMemDetail   (ProfessorAtUniversityData
languageSpoken   (EnglishLanguage)
&+likedBy   (DFoster Lenat Jones Huhns
&likes   (Shepherd Gumby Derthick L
memberOfPoliticalParty   (+RepublicanParty)
likesMechanicalEngineer   (Guha Wobel Yasath)
mechanicalEngineerLikedBy   (Wobel Yasath)

More below

unit @ConstraintOnPerson_age

Lock ☐ Legal ☐ Filters ☒ Expanders ☒ Previous ☐

Top of unit

english   ("The age of a Person is b
instanceOf   (SeeUnit)
allInstanceOf   (IndividualObject Stuff In
entryIsA   (Number)
constraintInheritedTo   ()
overrideLocalDefault?   (7)
slotConstraints   ((Lisp< (U age) 100) (Lisp
slotsConstrained   (age)

More below

Top of object

Use Next ☐   Lock ☐   Memory ☐

unit allInstanceOf.toCompute:
(ComputeByComposing allGenls InstanceOf)
++++++++++++++++++++++++++++++++

Bottom of ...

Change PW
  Server

Operations on: Jones
   Start new rule entry <control-sh-Mouse-M>
   Create slot entry detail <meta-sh-Mouse-M>
   Change entry's certainty <hyper-sh-Mouse-M>
   Delete this entry <control-meta-Mouse-L>
   Lower Entry's Certainty <hyper-sh-Mouse-L>
   Raise Entry's Certainty <hyper-sh-Mouse-R>
   Print justification for entry <hyper-meta-Mouse-R>
   Print English for entry <hyper-Mouse-R>
   Show Source of Entry <hyper-super-shift-Mouse-L>
   Display this unit <hyper-meta-Mouse-R>
   Similar Units Functions <hyper-super-meta-Mouse-M>

EDIT: Lenat.likes
Hyper-<END> to finish: Hype

100

☐ #2Derthick #2Guha

#2Shepherd #2Gumby
#2Loeffler #2Lenat
#2Gooch

☐ #2Crowley

8
Znacs 3 (LISP) *-*
Menu Operations on: #2Jones

Figure 2-1: The Default Frame Editor (UE) Configuration

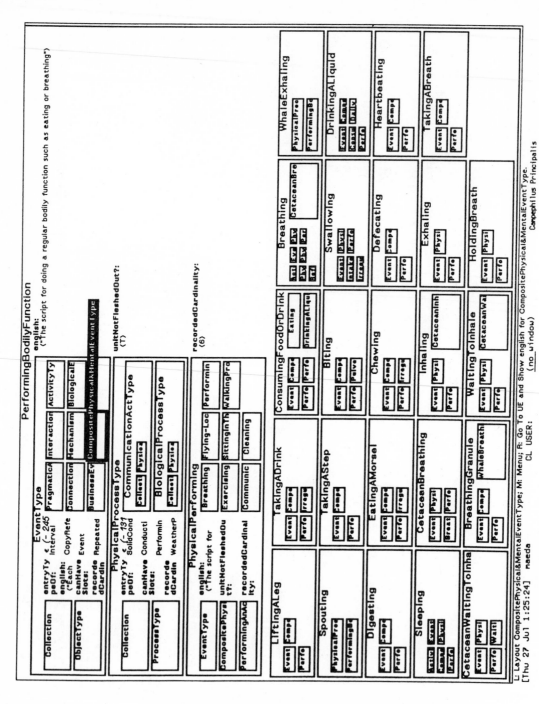

Figure 2-2: The Default Museum Editor (MUE) Configuration

WHAT IS THE RELATIONSHIP BETWEEN THESE EDITING TOOLS AND THE OTHER PARTS OF Cyc? The UE and MUE tools are front ends, interfacing between the human user and the CycL Representation Language (described below). Each UE/MUE operation gets converted into a CycL command (or, occasionally, a sequence of CycL commands) that is then run and that changes the Cyc KB.

Although CycL is written in CommonLisp, UE and MUE cannot be, because there are no CommonLisp standards for windows, debugging, network protocols, etc. The 1988 versions contained much code that was idiosyncratic to ZetaLisp, to SCL (Symbolics Common Lisp), to the Symbolics Lisp machine, and even to the then-current Symbolics software release (Release 7.2). During 1989, we decided it was worth developing a set of equivalent customized interfaces for other machines (such as Suns, TI Explorers, DEC 3100s, and Mac IIs).

HOW CAN MORE THAN ONE PERSON WORK ON THE SYSTEM AT A TIME? Several dozen users (knowledge editors) currently work simultaneously on the Cyc KB. Under the present scheme, each user has his own full copy of (each piece of) Cyc, and each is connected by a "thin wire" to a central machine called the Cyc Knowledge Server (KS). Each user runs UE and MUE, viewing and modifying his own local copy of the KB.

Each editing change performed by a knowledge editor is checked locally, to see if any constraints are violated (see section 2.3.2); if no errors are found, the change is broadcast to the KS. There it is checked again, and if, once more, it causes no errors, it is broadcast to all the other users. Each of these high-level editing operations will generate a number of primitive changes on each machine (anywhere from one primitive operation to millions, but usually about a hundred).

If an error is detected, a dialogue is initiated to resolve it. In the case of a constraint violation, for example, the user might be asked if this is an exception, or if the constraint needs to be weakened or modified. In the case of one user directly undoing something that another has recently done, Cyc mediates a "discussion" by online menus to resolve the problem. (If one party has already logged off, a provisional decision is reached, but the discussion still occurs, just over a longer time period, by electronic mail messages.)

DOESN'T EACH USER HAVE LONG WAITS, THEN, AS HIS (AND OTHER USERS') OPERATIONS TAKE PLACE? Originally the answer was Yes, so we had to take steps to correct the problem. The solution we chose is to have a separate foreground process (talking to the user) and background process (doing the rippling, talking to the Knowledge Server, and attending to other users' operations). That way, the user can continue, usually editing as quickly as desired, letting the background catch up asynchronously. This is not error-proof, of course, but in practice it almost never leads to collisions.

On a larger scale, any operation that might take a long time to propagate (for example, several minutes) is maintained as backward-only until an off-time (such as the middle of the night), at which point Cyc takes the time to forward-propagate it through the KB.

Several types of accretive operations are distributed among those machines that are currently idle (given a distribution of users and machines such as our present one, there are often as many idle machines as there are those in active use):

- Checking for policy conflicts and cases of two knowledge editors "stepping on each other's toes." These conflicts are typically more subtle than one KE's directly undoing a recent action of another.

- Detecting inconsistencies or unlikelihoods in the KB.

- Looking for analogies, which may turn out to be genuine, valuable new analogies; false analogies that point out omissions in the KB (X and Y are not analogous, Cyc just wasn't told enough about them to know that); or trivial analogies that point out missing links (or, in extreme cases, full duplication of effort) in the KB.

HOW COULD Cyc EVER BE "DISTRIBUTED," IF ITS VERY RELIANCE ON ANALOGY MEANS THAT ITS CALCULATIONS WILL BE VERY NON-LOCAL? Yes, we want to split Cyc up across multiple machines, in a more thorough fashion than the opportunistic ways mentioned in the previous paragraph, and yes, Cyc is inherently non-local: one of its major precepts is that it should reason analogically — that is, by rapidly accessing and matching against far-flung knowledge base entries.

To solve this problem, we took the same sort of pragmatic approach we took to the previous problem (and to most of the others, come to think of it.) Namely, don't worry about database collisions, timing, etc. More particularly, don't worry about the "race" that develops if P and ¬P are asserted almost simultaneously on two machines. Why? Because we're building a consensus reality KB, and think how rarely a statement and its direct negation both get asserted, let alone nearly simultaneously. In those rare cases in which it does happen, one of the two will "win," and the loser will eventually find out (perhaps minutes or even hours later), when the system gets around to checking various machines' agreement on that part of the KB. At that time, the winner and the loser will be invited to add some additional conditions (or at least, indicate which group of folks believed each "side" of the controversy, and when), thereby resolving the temporary contradiction.

Many of the ideas woven into Cyc's interface are based on the Knoesphere work [Lenat *et al.*, 1983], Hypertext, Smalltalk, Balance of Power, and other pioneering Human Interface (HI) work, which in turn owes a debt to Alan Kay, Ted Nelson, Chris Crawford, Nick Negroponte, and other HI pioneers.

2.3. The CycL Representation Language — Introduction

Before discussing the representation issues involved in building Cyc's KB, let us take a brief look at some of the details of the language in which we will be representing the world.

Think of this section as a summary of what can be expressed in CycL and what types of inference are done for you by CycL. It should give you enough background to understand the later discussions and examples.

2.3.1. CycL Is Frame-Based. Superficially, CycL is a frame-based language; that is, it's based around triples like "the *capital* of *Texas* is *Austin*." All the assertions about Texas are gathered together into one data structure called the Texas *frame* or the Texas *unit*:

```
Texas
    capital: (Austin)
    residents: (Doug Guha Mary)
    stateOf: (UnitedStatesOfAmerica)
```

The unit representing Texas is depicted here as having three *slots*, each of which has a corresponding *value*. The value of a slot of a unit is always a list of individual *entries*. Even a slot like *capital*, which should have only one entry, is assumed to have a singleton set as its value.

(An aside for purists: The semantics of the list (v1 v2 . . .) appearing as the value of the s slot of unit u is: $s(u,v1) \wedge s(u,v2) \wedge$ . . . Thus, the order of entries, and the number of times they occur, do not convey any meaning. So to be more precise about it, a slot's value is just a mathematical *set*, not a bag, list, oset, poset, or multiset.)

2.3.2. **On Top of the Frames Is a Predicate-calculus-like Constraint Language.** Why did we say that CycL is only *superficially* a frame language? Because the expressive power of frames by themselves is insufficient to represent concisely all that we would like to say. For instance:

"Bill is either a terrific fisherman or a terrific liar."
"Siblings almost never have the same first names."

In order to overcome this deficiency, another language, the *CycL constraint language*, sits on top of the basic frame language and provides the requisite expressiveness.

The constraint language is essentially predicate calculus. We can have expressions like "For all slots s and s', if s is transitive and the inverse of s is s', then s' is transitive." Considering the slots as our "predicates," this means that our constraint language is at first sight at least second-order.

Pragmatically, expressions above first order are almost never actually used. Also, an explicit set over which any quantified variable could possibly range is almost always known. There are some optimizations that are performed in those cases: in case the statement is only first-order, in case it can be easily first-orderized, in case it has variables x that range over a given set X, in case it has some "constants" in it, and so on. For example, a few special constructs have been added, such as TheSetOf (e.g., (TheSetOf $\times$ PerfectNumber (IsA $\times$ OddNumber))). See the later subsection 2.3.6 for details.

Why bother having two languages — frames and predicate calculus constraints? Why not just use the more powerful one (predicate calculus)? Though the constraint language is more powerful, the frame language makes inference (deduction) much simpler and faster. It turns out that many of the things we need to say about the world *can* be said compactly in a simple, efficient frame language. So, although we could just adopt the constraint language, as it is more powerful, we would still want to add the cross-indexing that makes frames so efficient — and adequate — in most cases.

2.3.3. **The Kinds of Frames That Exist in Cyc.** Each Cyc unit represents something — a real-world object, a type of process, a particular event, an abstract idea. Often we'll just say *Fred*, in this document, to mean either the person Fred or the Cyc unit representing Fred. In potentially ambiguous cases, we'll preface unit names by #%. So if we were being precise here, we'd say that #%Texas has three slots, but Texas has no slots (only frames can have slots — #%Texas is a frame in Cyc, but Texas is a state in the U.S.A.).

Four basic kinds of frames exist in the system: "normal" ones, SlotUnits, SeeUnits, and SlotEntryDetails.

"NORMAL" UNITS

Ninety percent of all frames fall into this category; they are the frames that represent various real-world concepts and things such as Fred, the set of all Dogs, the process of Walking, the English word *red*, and so on.

SLOTUNITS

These are frames that represent types of slots. For example, the *unit* called #%residents is a full-fledged Cyc unit, and describes that type of slot. It contains information such as "only a geopolitical region can be said to have residents; each of those residents must be a person; if residents(x,y) then residentOf(y,x); all lifelong residents of a region are residents of that region." A SlotUnit represents the *whole relationship* — not just a particular instance of that relationship, like residents(Texas,Doug), or one small class of instances, like residents(Texas,{Doug,Mary,Guha}).

   Having a frame representing each type of slot is a big win; it lets us state facts about them, lets us interrelate them, and lets us define and constrain them. Consider:

```
residents
    instanceOf: (Slot)
    inverse: (residentOf)
    makesSenseFor: (GeopoliticalRegion)
    entryIsA: (Person)
    specSlots: (lifelongResidents illegalAliens
        registeredVoters)
    slotConstraints: ((coTemporal u v))
```

   This says that #%residents is a kind of slot ("instanceOf" is like "member of" or "element of"); and *x* is on the #%residents slot of *Y* if and only if *Y* is on the #%residentOf slot of *x*; and only geopolitical regions should have a #%residents slot; all the entries on a #%residents slot had better represent individual people. The next slot — specSlots — indicates that if *x* is known to be a lifelong resident of *Y* (or an illegal alien living in *Y*, or registered to vote in *Y*), then *x* can be assumed to also be a resident of *Y*. The final slot — slotConstraints — says that if *u* is a resident of *v*, then they'd better both exist at the same time. That's how Cyc would know, for example, that Julius Caesar couldn't be a resident of NewYork.

These are units that serve as "footnotes," providing metalevel information about a particular slot of a particular unit. Consider the residents slot of the Texas unit above. We might want to say that this slot's value has about 10 million entries — though we certainly don't know exactly what they all are! Or we might want to say that the rate of change is low in the number of residents of Texas, even if we don't know how many residents it has. SeeUnits enable us to express these facts:

```
Texas
    capital: (Austin)
   ◊residents: (Doug Guha Mary)
    stateOf: (UnitedStatesOfAmerica)

SeeUnitFor-residents·Texas
    instanceOf: (SeeUnit)
    modifiesUnit: (Texas)
    modifiesSlot: (residents)
   ◊rateOfChange: ( )
    cardinality: (10000000)

SeeUnitFor-rateOfChange
        ·SeeUnitFor-residents·Texas
    instanceOf: (SeeUnit)
    modifiesUnit: (SeeUnitFor-residents·Texas)
    modifiesSlot: (rateOfChange)
    qualitativeValue: (Low)
```

The first "diamond" on the residents slot of the Texas unit points to the second unit. The second diamond, which is on the rateOfChange slot of that second unit, points to the third unit.

SeeUnits are full-fledged units in Cyc and hence can themselves have SeeUnits. In the above example, for instance, we don't know the true (absolute) rate of change of the residents slot of Texas, but we do know something *about* that value, namely that it is qualitatively Low.

These are similar to SeeUnits, but instead of "talking about" a whole slot of a unit, they modify a single entry on a slot of a unit. Suppose we want to say something about *Guha* being an entry on the *residents* slot of the *Texas* unit — for example, that this relationship became true during 1987 and has been a never-ending surprise both to him and to Lenat. To do that, we'd create a SlotEntryDetail unit:

```
SeeUnitFor-Guha∈residents·Texas
    instanceOf: (SlotEntryDetailTypeOfSeeUnit)
    modifiesUnit: (Texas)
    modifiesSlot: (residents)
    modifiesEntry: (Guha)
    becameTrueIn: (1987)
    surprisingTo: (Guha Lenat)
    moreLikelyThan:
       (SeeUnitFor-PickupTruck∈ownsA·Mary)
```

. . . and that unit would be pointed to by the Guha entry in the residents slot of the Texas unit:

```
Texas
    capital: (Austin)
    residents: (Doug ◊Guha Mary)
    stateOf: (UnitedStatesOfAmerica)
```

SeeUnits and SlotEntryDetails are similar to the "reified objects" suggested in [McCarthy 81].

2.3.4. The "Fields" Stored for Every Slot of Every Unit. (Warning: You should probably just skim over this section on first reading, until you have looked over the rest of this chapter.)

In addition to just storing a *value*, CycL maintains half a dozen other fields as well, for every slot of every unit. These fields contain such information as:

- A truth value (TV) for each entry in the value

- A symbolic justification for why that entry is present in the value

- Bookkeeping information used by the truth maintenance facility (for example, other unit/slot values that this value depends on and other unit/slot values that depend on this value)

- Some of the properties that each entry v1 on the value inherits just by virtue of its being there

- Information pertaining to the attitudes of agents toward this proposition (beliefs, desires, etc.)

Notice that the TV field could in principle be handled by just having lots of SlotEntryDetails; and most of the other fields could in principle be handled by just having lots of SeeUnits. But by examining and codifying the most frequent — and highly optimizable — kinds of bookkeeping remarks we needed to make about a value or an entry, we were able to obviate the need for SeeUnits and SlotEntryDetails; at present, they are very rare in the KB.

2.3.5. Inference in CycL: What Does Cyc "Do"?

We've already discussed frame/slot/entry triples, SlotUnits, SeeUnits, and SlotEntryDetails. Coupled with the details of our scheme for handling non-numeric certainty factors, alternate worlds, etc., these elements make up the "Statics" of Cyc. In this section, we'll discuss the "Kinematics" of Cyc: What sorts of inference does it actually do, as it runs?

Rather than have a single general-purpose inference scheme (such as, say, Resolution), CycL has a number of special-purpose inference schemes (currently 24 of them), each of which is optimized for dealing with "inference rules" of a particular kind.

Some of these inference mechanisms include:

- Inheritance (simple propagation along any type of arc, not just A-KIND-OF)

- Automatic classification (recognizing something that satisfies a certain definition)

- Maintenance of "inverse links" (for example, keeping likes in sync with likedBy)

- Maintenance of "definitions" (for example, grandparents $=_{df}$ parents ∘ parents)

- Maintenance of "dependencies"

- Maintenance of "genlSlots," "refinements," and "inContextVersions" of a slot

- Firing of demons (for example, afterAdding methods on slots)

- Checking constraints (constraints can be absolute or just usually "true by default")

- Using general wffs (well-formed formulae)

- Agenda-based best-first search (metalevel guidance)

- Finding and using determinations and structural analogies

- Gathering and combining multiple constraints

- Guessing, based on making a *nearly*-closed-world assumption

- Guessing, based on "illegal" but metaphorically sensible leaps

A metalevel agenda is used to decide which inference scheme is to be used when. Each task on the agenda is a full-fledged Cyc unit that can be reasoned about in much the same way as can "object level" units.

The inference schemes in the language are divided into several levels, with each level depending on (and freely "calling") the previous level.

Get0 Simply access the data structure; akin to GETPROP

Get4 Try some of the simpler, faster CycL inference mechanisms: toCompute, genlSlots, demons, and inheritance that is temporarily backward (and eventually will be forward)

Get6 Try the above, plus the more costly CycL inference mechanisms: slotValueSubsumes, classification, slotConstraints, structures, slotValueEquals, and full backward inheritance

Get8 Try some plausible guessing mechanisms, such as determinations, constraint-resolving, closed world assuming, analogy, metaphor, and metonymy

(CycL inference features such as *inverses* are never "called" by the Get. . . functions because there is a guarantee that these are always forward propagated. Hence, even Get0 should find the entries (if any) added by these inference mechanisms. The same goes for forward inheritance — its contributions are always cached, so even Get0 will find them.)

The metalevel information at levels 0–4 is almost completely calculated *at the time of assertion* of facts, and simply cached. That makes retrieval at those levels fast.

Almost all the reasoning done by the system can be considered a kind of *defeasible* reasoning. As we shall see later on, almost any "assertion" can be overridden by, or combined with, any more certain information.

CycL has a truth maintenance system (TMS); there are five types of truth values attached to — and symbolic justifications for and against — each entry on each slot of each unit. This system is not a general TMS: each optimized inference scheme is largely responsible for ensuring that the inferences drawn by it are still valid. So, for example, when a conflict arises, very customized control can be exerted to resolve it.

2.3.6. Salient Aspects of the Constraint Language.   The constraint language supplements the basic workhorse — the language of frames and slots. It is a real boon, enabling us to easily state:

- Disjunctions (Jim's father is either Sam or Bill or a Chinese fisherman)

- Quantified statements (Some of Fred's older siblings got higher grades)

- Relationships among slot values (People are younger than their parents)

- Negations (Fred isn't a Dane; Brothers rarely have the same first names)

We had the choice of not allowing such statements to be made, forcing them to be done by making a "statement" unit for each of these, or just biting the bullet and adopting an additional language in which it's easy to make such statements. Given the need for expressiveness, the choice was quite obvious.

This is not to say that the frame language is completely useless. As it turns out, a vast majority of the statements we would like to make about the world *can* be stated in the form of binary predicates with both the arguments being constants; hence, these statements can be directly represented as simple unit/slot/entry triples. As stated earlier, this is a feature of the real world (that is, of the two *aspects* of the world we're usually interested in: tangible objects and intelligences). So we may as well make use of this in order to make our language more efficient. Hence, the constraint language is simply an addition to the basic frame language.

The constraint language has a syntax similar to that of predicate calculus. Just as each kind of slot has a unit representing it, so each kind of predicate has a unit representing it. Any slot may be viewed as — and, in our constraint language, actually used as — a predicate. For example, we could say (residents Texas Doug).

There are modified versions of the universal and existential quantifiers; in our system, they're predicates called ForAll and ThereExists. The modification is that one must specify the set over which quantification is done (either explicitly or by a functional form). This is at least as good as standard ∀ and ∃, because this set can be specified to be the universal set. And, in most real-world cases, we will know a limiting set for the variable to possibly range over, so it is computationally much better to be able to supply that set.

For example, consider the following expression:

```
(#%ThereExists y (#%AfricanCountry #%allInstances)
    (#%ThereExists x (#%WorldLeader #%allInstances)
      (#%And (#%presidentOf x y)
             (#%firstName x #%Samuel)))))
```

This might be a worse search, if it weren't clear that we were looking for a world leader. In other words, presidentOf and firstName are both legal slots for all people, so Cyc might (in the worst case) otherwise have had to look through all the units representing people in order to find out whether such a person existed. (Because presidentOf can be filled with any organization, not just a country, a person can be president of some group and not be a world leader.) Instead, Cyc can now look through the relatively tiny set of known world leaders. See [Green *et al.*, 1974]. So the addition of an extra argument to the two quantifiers is only to improve the efficiency and has no effect on the semantics of the quantifiers.

Propositions in the constraint language can have a whole unit representing them. Associated with these propositions are a number of Lisp functions (generated automatically by the system), each of which is optimized for a particular task (such as checking the truth of the proposition at some point or translating it into the frame language for some set of bindings). So most of the time CycL can ignore the proposition and use only these functions. This is largely for reasons of efficiency; it recoups some of the efficiency that would otherwise be lost by having such an expressive representation.

Expressions in the constraint language are used for different purposes in Cyc. For instance:

- Stating constraints on slot values (to signal errors and violations)

- Specifying which units can legally possess a certain type of slot

- Stating the definition of a collection (for automatic classification)

- Stating the premises and conclusions for different kinds of "rules"

Constraints on slot values may be "soft" — i.e., only defaults. That's useful in the real world, where many things, though possible, should cause Cyc to raise its metaphorical eyebrows: a person over 110 years old, an armadillo with a job, or twin sisters who have the same first name.

The constraint mechanism is tightly coupled with the inheritance mechanism: constraints get inherited along various arcs (allInstances, parts, allSpecs) and end up in the inheritedSlotConstraints slot of many "lower" units, where they actually apply and are maintained.

Thus, the Inheritance part of CycL is being exploited by the Constraints part of CycL. Basically, inheritance provides a means of efficient indexing, so that it is always easy to figure out which rules and constraints affect a given unit.

We will discuss the Constraint Language in much more detail in chapter 3.

3. The CycL Representation Language

Chapter 2, section 2.3 provided enough detail about CycL to allow you to understand the rest of the examples in this book; this chapter goes into much more detail.

3.1. The Rationale Behind the Design of CycL

This section describes the design elements of the dynamics of the CycL language. This discussion is intentionally at a high level of abstraction and hence does not concern itself with most of the implementation details (such as the data structures used).

CycL is intended to be a language for representing various aspects of common sense/consensus reality (namely for use as representation language for Cyc). Based on this are two major motivating concerns:

- Because the size of Cyc is expected to be very large, the computational efficiency of the system should be fairly high.

- Because a large fraction of common sense seems most easily expressible as a set of default rules, it is important that it be easy to state such rules (especially the most commonly needed kinds), and it is important that the default reasoning abilities of the system be reasonably sophisticated (at least those kinds of default inference that are most commonly called for).

The language can be conceptualized as being formed by four important modules (of vastly varying size):

- *The inferencing module* that is responsible for interpreting the rules available in Cyc (both monotonic and default "rules"). In other words, given that a "rule" *might possibly* be relevant, this module sees if it is indeed relevant in the current state of the KB. If it is relevant, this module "runs" it to produce some conclusion, some new assertions.

- *The stripped-down truth maintenance system (TMS) conceptual module.* Suppose a rule ran, and concluded u.s.v1. Since then, we've learned some more things, the KB has changed, and now it turns out that that rule would no longer have run. If u.s.v1 is still around, it has become "stale"; all its support has gone away. This TMS module ensures that u.s.v1 is retracted if there is no other support for it. This module is referred to as a *conceptual* module because as we shall see later, this module has been partially unified with the inference module. However, for purposes of understanding the design of the language, it is convenient to regard this as a separate module.

- *The contention resolution module* that compares the conclusions of different rules and, in case of conflict, attempts to resolve the conflict.

- *The contradiction detection and resolution module* that detects situations when the conclusions of monotonic (absolutely certain) rules have been overridden by those of other monotonic rules. The only way to resolve this kind of contradiction, short of retracting or weakening one of the rules, is to change the KB so that the antecedent of one of the contradictory rules is not satisfied. This module detects such contradictions, and, when it is possible and reasonably safe to do so, automatically modifies the KB to preserve consistency.

Before we go into some of the details of each of these modules, because a large fraction of the design of CycL has been heavily influenced by its non-monotonic nature, it makes sense to take a look at the intuition behind the default reasoning scheme chosen.

3.1.1.   The Intuition Behind CycL's Default Reasoning Scheme.   Consider a default rule R1: P→Q, that is, a rule called R1, whose antecedent is P and whose consequent is Q. The meaning of this rule in CycL is as follows.

If P is true,
and there does not exist any other rule R' such that the antecedent of R' is true and the consequent of R' is either (not Q) or (unknown Q) and the relation (overrides R' R1) is known to be true,
Then Q is assumed to be true.

(*Note:* a Domain closure assumption is made when looking for R'. That is, we consider only the rules currently known to exist at that moment.)

In the case where no other applicable rule has anything to say about Q that disagrees with what R1 is concluding, things are quite simple and it seems reasonable to conclude Q.

Let us consider the case where there *is* some other rule R that wishes to conclude something else about Q — that is, something that disagrees with rule R1. In this case, there are two possible extensions (as generated by a standard monotonic inference procedure) of the facts in our KB; one in which we believe R1, and conclude Q, and one in which we believe R instead, and conclude whatever it says to — either (not Q) or (unknown Q). What we would like to be able to do is to specify some kind of preference criterion to enable a selection of one of the two extensions.

When we consider a fact Q, we can place the contending extensions into three classes: those that assert that Q is true, those that assert that it is unknown, and those that assert that it is false. The process of deciding which one to select could be viewed as comparing the justifications for each of these extensions, and choosing the most plausible one.

The justification for each of these three extensions could be viewed as a tree of the rules used to generate these extensions from the original KB. Hence, the process of comparing these justifications is equivalent to comparing these trees. As a first approximation, the comparison of these trees could be done by comparing the rules at the topmost node (that is, the last rules) of these three trees.

This is precisely what CycL does. The comparison itself is done using the *overrides* relationship. That is, CycL checks to see if (overrides R1 R), in which case it listens to R1, or if (overrides R R1), in which case it listens to R.

This conclusion (about Q) is non-monotonic in nature. Why? Because at some later time, some new fact (or rule) might get added, which in turn might cause some rule Ri to have its antecedent satisfied — and suppose Ri would disagree with R1 about Q and Ri is capable of overriding R1. In such a situation, it's important for CycL to retract its first statement about Q (whatever R1 concluded) and add the statement that Ri wants to conclude about Q.

This simple scheme — comparing the topmost nodes in these trees — seems to work most of the time, possibly because the "depth" of the inference chain in most common sense reasoning tasks is rather small. Of course, it does fail in certain cases. For example, it is possible that the last step in two trees (called *arguments* henceforth) is the same rule; however, these two instances of the use of this rule could be based on entirely different premises and yield contradictory answers. In such cases, doing a comparison only up to depth 1 is going to keep us from preferring one over the other, because how can we prefer R87 to R87? (In cases where there is no known relationship between these different rules, a scheme for combining these supports is used; this scheme is discussed later.)

As of now, there seem to be two ways to resolve such situations to obtain the desired answer:

1. The first scheme involves comparing these two trees to a greater depth. In this scheme, however, the problem of comparison becomes not only more expensive but also less precisely defined. There are times when this is still the best way out. CycL, however, does not support this scheme, at least not in its current implementation.

2. The other option is to introduce additional default rules to get over the inherent symmetry at the top of these justification trees. This is the scheme currently used in CycL to resolve such problems. It is likely, however, that in the future we will move to some more desirable/robust scheme for comparing extensions. That is, more schemes besides these two are being investigated.

It should be noted that this scheme for default reasoning is very similar to prioritized circumscription. To obtain an "equivalent" circumscriptive theory we do the following.

(a) For every sentence Ri: P→Q, we add $\neg$ ab$_i$ v P→Q.

(b) If Ri overrides Rj, we minimize ab$_i$ before minimizing ab$_j$.

The current CycL implementation however is not guaranteed to find the minimal extensions.

If we have a default rule P→Q and P is true, then Q is "default" true. If we have a monotonic rule P→Q and P is "default" true, then Q is default true and if P is monotonically true, then Q is "monotonically" true. If we have "arguments" for Q, some of which claim that P is true, others which conclude P is false etc., and where none of these overrides the others, the following table is used to combine contradictory claims. (T = default true, 100 = monotonically true, 0 = monotonically false, − = default false, ~ = unknown)

```
         TV from argument        0    —    ~    T   100
                               _____
                             |
         TV from         0   |  0    0    0    0    x
         argument            |
                         —   |  0    —    —    ~   100
                             |
                         ~   |  0    —    ~    T   100
                             |
                         T   |  0    ~    T    T   100
                             |
                        100  |  x   100  100  100  100
```

(In this matrix, the "x" represents a genuine monotonic contradiction that must be dynamically resolved.)

The next sections take a closer look at each of Cyc's modules — the inferencing module, the TMS module, the contention resolution module, and the contradiction detection and resolution module — and examines some of the issues that have affected their design. Further details on the Default Reasoning Scheme are given in section 6.5.4.3.

3.1.2. The Inferencing Module.

This module is the heart of the system. It is the one responsible for drawing conclusions from the rules and facts in the knowledge base.

Most systems use a uniform inferencing strategy, which usually means an inference engine that uses exactly one kind of inference rule (e.g., modus powers, the resolution principle). In CycL, however, the inferencing module is divided into a number of "features," each one being capable of handling a particular syntactic category of sentences in a relatively efficient fashion.

Why? There's an 80/20 at work here. Most of the rules that Cyc needs to have can be categorized in one of a couple dozen syntactic categories, and each category can be handled in a very efficient fashion — certainly more efficiently than a general If/Then rule can be handled. And overall, such a strategy will increase the overall efficiency of the system.

A more detailed account of some of the important inference features is given later. There are a number of features that differ in complexity and form a partial order (in terms of complexity).

A few observations can be made about the inferencing module:

- Cyc has dozens of separate inference features purely for efficiency reasons. Each feature isolates a commonly occurring syntactic category of rules. All that is done by each specialized feature can easily be accomplished by the most general feature (wffs), albeit slowly. So the presence of these features does not have any effect on the actual inferential ability of the system (in terms of what can be inferred).

- The representation of the rules varies in the different syntactic categories. This is done to allow easy access to the relevant rules by the different features. Ways of overcoming the problems that arise because of this are dealt with later in this book.

- The code required to efficiently implement a wide category of these features is quite simple. Consequently, we were recently able to build a facility that inputs a description of a desired new inference feature (that is, it is given the formal schema for the rule type being implemented) and generates all the code required to implement the new feature.

- This module can be smart about the order in which different rules are considered, by making use of the partial order induced by the relationship *overrides*. In other words, if there are two rules R1 and R2, where R1 overrides R2, then R1 may as well be tried first. That way, if it does conclude something, we need not even try R2. Again, this is merely an efficiency issue; evaluating R2 first should not produce different results.

The sense in which the term 'rule' is used in this document is more like a wff than as a production rule. Stating $P \rightarrow Q$ not just allows the system to conclude Q when P is true, but also allows $\neg P$ to be concluded when $\neg Q$ is true.

3.1.3. The TMS Module. The truth maintenance system (TMS) is responsible for ensuring that if we have inferred Q (from P and R1: $P \rightarrow Q$) and we find that the rule R1 is no longer true, or we find that P is no longer true, then this particular support for Q is retracted.

We make use of the notion of having a hierarchy (in terms of efficiency — in this case, efficiency of both time and space) of special-purpose procedures to deal with this problem. Because we already have a hierarchy of inference features, this same hierarchy is used for the TMS purposes.

In practice, the TMS routine for each of the inference features is closely related to the routine implementing the inferencing for that inference feature. This avoids a duplication of search, for instance.

Also, the TMS routines have full access to the knowledge base itself, so that the knowledge of the structure of different rules, etc., can be exploited to do certain tasks more efficiently. One interesting application of this is the way that CycL can analyze the sentences in the KB to determine possible circular justifications and use this information to speed up the real-time search for these.

In addition to the TMS routines implemented for the forward inferencing by the inference routines themselves, there is a generic set of TMS routines that can be used by any of the inference features for doing the TMS-related work for backward inferencing. (Almost any of the features can be asserted in either a forward (cached) or a backward (on demand) direction.)

3.1.4. The Contention Resolution Module. This module is responsible for comparing the different arguments in favor of and against concluding something, and for adding the conclusion supported by the strongest argument. As explained earlier, this involves checking for the presence of the *overrides* relationship between the various rules that are concluding contradictory things.

Because rules are first-class objects in our ontology, this relationship may be stated in a declarative fashion like any other assertion. That is, there can be a unit (frame) in the KB representing R82 and another unit representing rule R201, and R82.overrides can contain R201. Because *overrides* is just a slot in Cyc, like any other slot, rules of all sorts can *conclude* assertions of the form x.overrides.y. [The notation u.s. refers to the s slot of u. Similarly, u.s.v1 is another notation for s(u,v1)]

In the absence of such a declarative overrides relationship, a procedure is invoked to check for certain standard overrides relationships. For example, the inheritance feature checks to see if one rule is "closer" to the subject of the conclusion than the contending rule, and if so, lets the closer rule override the more distant rule. See [Touretzsky, 1984]. To reiterate, this is only in case there is no explicit overrides relationship between the two rules asserted in the KB.

3.1.5. The Contradiction Detection and Resolution Module. This module is responsible for ensuring that the conclusions of monotonic (100-percent certain) rules hold when their antecedents are true.

Because the facts used to prove the antecedents of a rule may be defaults, it is possible that the conclusions of a monotonic rule are not monotonically true. As a result, the conclusions of a monotonic rule can legally be — and often are — overridden.

In such cases, however, because the *rule* was monotonic, it is necessary to make sure that the antecedent of the rule is not satisfied. This involves applying the monotonic rule in a "backward" direction. What does that mean? Suppose the rule were P→Q, and P had been asserted as "true by default." So Q was asserted as being "true by default." Now we're given (not Q), with absolute certainty. So we infer (not P), with absolute certainty.

In the case of rules with multiple antecedent terms, there may unfortunately be many different default facts whose truth values could be changed. In that case, a preference criterion may be imposed upon these using the partial order induced by the predicate moreLikelyThan, which holds between default facts (u.s.v1 assertions) and indicates that one is more likely to be true than another.

For instance, one could assert that Hell.temperature.BelowFreezing is more likely than Carter.termsInOffice.2. That's easily done in CycL, because each u.s.v1 can be explicitly represented by a unit, if there's a need to do so. So those two units would be created, and the second one would be listed as an entry on the first one's moreLikelyThan slot.

3.1.6. The Epistemological Level / Heuristic Level Translator.

Before concluding this brief overview of the basics of the design of CycL, we cover one more issue — the epistemological level. As mentioned earlier, the representation of the different rules in CycL could be vastly different based on the syntactic category they fall in. Also, it is possible that new useful syntactic categories will be discovered, and hence, new representations will be invented for the corresponding new inference features.

Most of these, however, will add to the efficiency but not the inferential ability of the system. Because these representations are purely for efficiency reasons, they should be hidden from users — both human users and other programs who are calling on CycL. Users should worry about issues relating to things such as the ontology to use, the default rules to enter, etc.; they should not have to worry about using and choosing among dozens of specialized inference features.

In order to make this possible, there is a level of CycL that contains a representation of the material in the knowledge base in a syntax that is independent of the inference mechanisms that will use them. This level is called the epistemological level.

This level could be thought of as a window into the KB, a uniform interface that hides the variation that's seething internally "below the surface" — the dozens of different inference features and their corresponding different representations. The epistemological level supports a number of facilities, such as:

1. Queries to Cyc may be addressed to the epistemological level in terms of the language used in the epistemological level. That language is (at present) essentially the CycL constraint language, which in turn is essentially predicate calculus. These queries are then translated into the deeper CycL languages and processed; the answers are translated to suit the user.

2. Facts may be asserted in the language of the epistemological level.

3. Rules may also be asserted in the language of the epistemological level. They are then analyzed, to see which inference feature best implements them, and converted to run internally most efficiently.

4. Any rule stated as one of the specialized inference features may be entered, and the epistemological level will translate it into its own general language.

5. By combining features 3 and 4, the epistemological level can look over users' shoulders as they enter a new rule in some form; this level can then convert the rule to the general language and then reconvert it to whichever inference feature most efficiently implements it.

6. Facts, rules, etc., in the epistemological level that refer to some concept may be accessed. Other sorts of pattern matching are provided as well.

As of now the language used by this level is the CycL constraint language. It should be possible to add other languages in the future.

It is important to note that the epistemological level is not merely an interface layer that consists of some translating functions. It has a static aspect that consists of the set of all the statements asserted through it into the KB. In the case of feature 5 above, it also keeps the original way in which the rule was stated by the user.

Why bother storing these intermediate and initial states? Why not just discard them and keep the final state of each rule? The rationale behind this is that it is desirable that the syntactic form of a sentence (rule, fact, etc.) presented to a user be (as far as possible) identical to the form entered by the user.

Also, in the case of representation languages, where understanding is much easier than generation, it is important to store the original representation provided.

In brief, this is the rationale behind the design of CycL. Many issues have not been covered here (they are covered elsewhere in this book). However, the basic concepts stated here are the ones that have driven the design (and this implementation) of CycL.

3.2. Details of the Frame Representation and the CycL Constraint Language

This section continues the discussion of the frame system, and the constraint language, far beyond that begun in earlier sections. You may prefer to skim or skip over this section. However, every knowledge editor — every Cyc KB builder — should become familiar with the syntax as detailed here.

3.2.1. Details of the Frame Language.

The basic concepts of the frame language, discussed briefly earlier, are enlarged upon here, with different examples and much more detail.

3.2.1.1.
TERMINOLOGY
AND
CONVENTIONS

We said that CycL is (at least superficially) a frame-based language. Here, for instance, is part of the frame or *unit* that represents Guha:

```
Guha
  instanceOf                   (MechanicalEngineer LispHacker
                                  HumanCyclist GraduateStudent)
  computersFamiliarWith        (SymbolicsMachine)
  age                          (23)
  languageSpoken               (EnglishLanguage TamilLanguage
                                  HindiLanguage GermanLanguage)
  programsIn                   (Lisp)
  screenForUnitEditor          (:monochrome)
```

The above frame has six *slots*. The types of slots that are present are: instanceOf, computersFamiliarWith, age, languageSpoken, programsIn, and screenForUnitEditor. Each slot is structured; for now, consider it as comprising a pointer to the type of slot (for example, languageSpoken) and a pointer to the *value* of that slot for that unit. The value of a slot is always a list representing a set; for instance, the value of the age slot of Guha, is the singleton list (23). Later we'll see other fields of slots besides the type of the slot and its value (for example, some justification for the entries in the value.) Each element of a value is called an *entry*; for instance, :monochrome is the only entry on the screenForUnitEditor slot of the Guha unit.

By convention, the name of a (unit representing a kind of) slot begins with a small letter; units representing non-slots begin with a capital letter. (Actually, the CycL language strictly *enforces* these naming conventions at the present time, so they're more than just conventions.)

Another reminder: #%Fred means "the unit called Fred." Thus, #%Get4 is a Cyc unit, whereas Get4 is a Lisp symbol. In this book, we often omit the #% prefixes, for readability. It should be clear from context which apparent atom names really are atoms, and which are units. For example, we could have written the Guha unit as follows:

```
#%Guha
  #%instanceOf              (#%MechanicalEngineer #%LispHacker
                                #%HumanCyclist #%GraduateStudent)
  #%computersFamiliarWith   (#%SymbolicsMachine)
  #%age                     (23)
  #%languageSpoken          (#%EnglishLanguage #%TamilLanguage
                                #%HindiLanguage #%GermanLanguage)
  #%programsIn              (#%Lisp)
  #%screenForUnitEditor     (:monochrome)
```

Recall that CycL is primarily a set of Lisp functions. Most of those functions have arguments that were chosen using the following mnemonic:

u = unit
s = slot
v = value
v1 = one entry on the value

Also, we will often write a unit name and a slot name, separated by a dot, to indicate that slot of that unit. Thus, Guha.programsIn is a slot whose sole entry is Lisp. When discussing a CycL function, or when speaking generically, we might talk about "u.s", meaning "some slot s of a unit u." We also use the notation "u.s.x" to mean that "x is an entry on the s slot of unit u" (for example, Knuth.programsIn.Pascal).

3.2.1.2. SLOT VALUES ARE SETS OF ENTRIES

Every slot value really is no more nor less than a mathematical *set* of entries. It doesn't matter what order the entries are in, and no entry can ever be present more than once in a value. This is crucial, so let's restate it:

1. **You should never depend on entries of a slot being in any particular order,** such as the order in which you inserted them, or the order they were in ten minutes ago. CycL is free to reorder the entries

however it wishes. If you really want the *list* of U.S. Presidents in order, then you can't just use the slot #%instances; use a slot like #%instancesInChronOrder:

```
USPresident
  instances: (TJefferson GBush RNixon
    GWashington RReagan . . . )
  instancesInChronOrder: ((GWashington
    TJefferson . . . ))
```

Notice that the second slot value has just a single entry, but that that one entry itself is a long ordered *list*. This proliferation of types of slots is not a problem, because you create new types of slots only when you have some real reason for needing them, and they explicitly define themselves and state their relationships to other slots. Therefore the slot instancesInChronOrder would have slots that, for any unit *u*, constrain it to have just one entry, constrain the entry to be set-equal to the value of the instances slot of *u*, and constrain *that* list to be sorted by startingTime.

(The sorting really would be done "by startingTime," but the entries would be temporal subabstractions of GWashington, TJefferson, etc., representing them while they were President: PresidentWashington, PresidentJefferson, and so on. Or, equivalently, the sorting would be "by earliest startingTime of any temporal subabstraction that was also a USPresident.")

CycL will not rearrange the order of *the members of the members* of a value. That would be factually incorrect in the USPresident.instancesInChronOrder case, but it would be downright disastrous in the case of an entry which was a Lisp function. Consider:

```
PrimeNumber
  defn: ((LAMBDA (x) (EQUAL (LENGTH
    (DivisorsOf x)) 2)))
```

If CycL were free to rearrange the elements of that single entry — say, into ((EQUAL (LENGTH (DivisorsOf x)) 2 LAMBDA (x)) — imagine how unhappy that would make the Lisp interpreter!

2. **No entry can occur more than once in a value.** If we had a slot called firstNamesOfParents, and Fred's parents were both named "Bobby," then there would only be one string "Bobby" as an entry in that value. Of course, one could define a slot theListOfFirstNamesOfParents, and that could have the value (("Bobby" "Bobby")) on the unit representing Fred. More likely,

one would have a slot called parents, and it would have the value (BobbyJaneSmith BobbyJackSmith). Each of those two entries would be full-fledged units as well, and might have a slot called firstName, and each of their firstName values would be ("Bobby").

One view of frames is that placing an entry v on the s slot of unit u is really just asserting s(u,v). So the Guha frame is equivalent to asserting the following:

```
age(Guha,23) ∧
    languageSpoken(Guha,EnglishLanguage) ∧
languageSpoken(Guha,TamilLanguage) ∧
    languageSpoken(Guha,HindiLanguage)
∧ languageSpoken(Guha,GermanLanguage) ∧
    programsIn(Guha,Lisp) ∧
screenForUnitEditor(Guha,:monochrome). . .
```

If we take this view, then the two "rigid requirements" discussed above fall right out as reasonable restrictions:

Assertion 1 really just means that if we assert P(u,v) and P(u,v'), it doesn't matter in which order we do the asserting. This is something we'd better be prepared to live with, because we all know the tautology: $P(u,v) \wedge P(u,v') \leftrightarrow P(u,v') \wedge P(u,v)$.

Assertion 2 really just means that if we assert P(u,v) more than once, that's no better or worse than just asserting it once. Again, this is something we'd better live with, because we all know the tautology: $P(u,v) \wedge P(u,v) \leftrightarrow P(u,v)$.

So *that's* why we require that every value be a set — with no repeated entries and with no "meaning" attached to the order of the entries.

3.2.1.3. KINDS OF FRAMES

A number of different "kinds" of frames (units) are allowed by the CycL language and are present in the Cyc knowledge base:

- Frames that represent kinds of slots — for example, instances, age, parents. Each kind of slot that is used on any unit in Cyc is in turn represented by a frame. This has several benefits: it allows us to give explicit intensional definitions of slots (if we didn't have such units, the semantics of a slot would be defined only by its use: by its occurrences throughout the KB and through its being mentioned in rules); it allows us to give explicit constraints and relationships on the slot (for example, that parents have up to two entries, can legally be specified for any instance of Animal, must have Animals as entries, etc.); and it allows us to give explicit constraints and relationships among slots (for example, that the grandparents of u are always the parents of the parents of u; or that the interestingRelatives are always a subset of the allRelatives of u; or that the parents of u contains v1 if and only if the children of v1 contains u, etc.).

- Frames for "normal" units: individuals (such as Fred, collections (such as Person), substances (such as Wood), processes (such as Sailing), events (such as WashingtonCrossingTheDelaware), functions (such as Plus), and so on. The vast majority of the units in the Cyc KB belong to this category, because it is primarily these units we wish to reason about.

- Footnote-like frames for saying something (some metalevel information) *about* either a slot value or a particular entry on a slot value. See [McCarthy, 1979], [Greiner and Lenat, 1980]. They're used for:

  - stating constraints on slot values

  - stating the relative values of numerical slots (such as height, age, and color)

  - stating the qualitative values of numerical slots (such as color)

  - stating things such as the number of entries on the slot value

  - stating historical information (who last placed this entry here, and when)

3.2.1.4. OTHER FIELDS OF EACH SLOT, BESIDES THE VALUE

As we said earlier, each frame consists of a number of slots, each with a value. Each slot s of each unit u is not just a list of entries; rather, it is a full-fledged data structure with several fields, just one of which happens to be the *value* of u.s. In addition to the value, the u.s data structure contains information pertaining to the following:

- The justifications for the presence of each entry that occurs

- The certainty of each entry (we will come to this in a moment)

- Record-keeping information stored by (and used primarily by) the truth maintenance system. For instance, which other slot values does this determine, and which slot values is this u.s in turn dependent upon?

- Inheritance information: What defaults should be propagated to all entries on u.s? To all entries on the s' slot of any entry on u.s? To all entries on the s" slot of any entry on the s' slot of any entry on u.s? And so on. This allows us to say things like: "by default, the IQ of one's grandchildren is VeryHigh," or: "by default, the integrity of the mother of the fiancée of a mother's son is Low." There, u = HumanMother (the set of all human mothers), s = allInstances, s′ = sons, s″ = fiancée, s‴ = mother, and s″″ = integrity.

- Beliefs about this slot of this unit. First, we record who believes the particular information specified for a given u.s on the slot descriptor. By default, of course, this is just Cyc itself! Second, we record new slot descriptors (whole structures as outlined above) with the alternative beliefs for this slot, in the cases when we (or rather, the system) knows about other peoples' beliefs.

So, when we say that "Guha.age" refers to "the age slot of the Guha unit," we don't just mean that it refers to "the singleton list (23)." Guha.age really signifies "that whole place" — the "age" part of the "Guha" data structure — with all its various fields (the value, justification for the value, etc.), of which one field happens to be the value field, and that field happens to have the value (23). We will sometimes blur this distinction, though, in this book, and say "23 is a member of Guha.age," when we really ought to be more precise and say "23 is a member of the value field of Guha.age."

3.2.2. Details of the Constraint Language.
At the beginning of the previous section, we said that CycL is only *superficially* a frame language. Many of the interesting features of CycL utilize what has now come to be known as the *constraint language*. Let us first look at the language itself and then see how it has been "unified" with (deeply interwoven with) the frame language.

3.2.2.1. SYNTAX OF THE CL
The syntax of the constraint language (CL) is similar to that of prefix predicate calculus. The kinds of predicates that are allowable are discussed below:

1. Every kind of slot may be used as a predicate. So if we wanted to say that the unit u has the entry v1 on the slot s, we would write that as (s u v1). To say that Fred's parents include Sam and Jane, we'd write the two expressions (parents Fred Sam) and (parents Fred Jane).

2. A large fraction of the useful predicates in the world have arity 2 or less, and can therefore be represented as a type of slot. For example, parents, age, instanceOf, and the thousands of other slots in the system. Some useful predicates, however, happen to have an arity greater than 2. In such cases, we create a unit representing them in Cyc, indicate that they are an instance of Predicate, provide

them with some sort of definition (there are various ways to do this), and then can use them freely as predicates in the constraint language.

Here's an example. We decided long ago we needed a predicate that would take two arguments, a set X and a slot s, and that would return T if all the elements of X had the same value for their s slots. To do this, we created a unit called AllHaveSame, made it an instance of NonSlotPredicate, and gave it the slot *expansion*. The expansion slot of a NonSlotPredicate contains an expression in the constraint language that defines the predicate. CycL then converted this expansion into a Lisp function, which it stored in the lispDefun slot of AllHaveSame. The expansion, by the way, was:

```
(#%ForAll X v1
   (#%ForAll Y v1
      (#%Equal (X v2) (Y v2))))
```

The predicates' expansions follow the convention that their arguments are called v1, v2, v3, . . . So, in this case, v1 is the first argument, corresponding to the set X, and v2 is the second argument, corresponding to the slot s. So to state the proposition that all the MichiganGears have the same gear module, we'd write

```
(#%AllHaveSame (#%MichiganGear #%allInstances)
               #%gearModule)
```

Some of the useful non-slot predicates and logic symbols include #%LogAnd, #%LogOr, #%Unknown, #%Unknown or False, #%LogNot #%LogImplication, #%Equal, #%Member, #%GreaterThan, #%DoesIntersect, #%Subsumes, #%AllHaveSame, etc. The "expansion" of a relation is a formula that defines the relation.

A later section discusses predicates of arity greater than two at length.

3. Just as non-slot predicates may be used, it is possible to use functions that return a value that's not just treated as T/NIL, as a truth value. For instance, the function might return a set that is then mapped over. There must again be an explicit unit in the knowledge base that represents the function. Suppose we define ChristmasPresentsReceived as a function of two arguments: the recipients and the year. It returns a list of the items the recipient got that year for Christmas. We define that unit, give it a definition (a lispDefun, an expansion, . . .), record its being an instance of Function, and then we can use it. Using it means that we can write expressions in the constraint language like

```
(#%ForAll x (#%ChristmasPresents
                (#%Bill #%father) #%TheYear1987)
  (#%ForAll y (#%ChristmasPresents
                (#%Bill #%father) #%TheYear1986)
    (#%GreaterThan (x #%cost) (y #%cost)))))
```

This is the proposition that every single present that Bill's father got in 1987 was more expensive than any present he got in 1986.

Notice how father and cost are also being used as if they were functions. Every slot may be used as a function in this fashion. However, when this is done, a special syntax is used.

In order to refer to the value of the s slot of u, we'd write (u s). If we wanted to refer to the union of all the values of the s2 slot of all the values of the s1 slot of u, we would say ((u s1) s2). So that's like defining a new slot that is the composition of s2 ∘ s1 and then asking what its value is for u.

We could write, for example, (((u s1) s2) s3), or replace u (or s1 or s2 . . .) by any expression that evaluated into one or more units (or, respectively, slots). In the example below, we've replaced u by (ChristmasPresents u #%TheYear1987), which evaluates into a list of units, and we've replaced s2 by (s2 genlSlots), which evaluates into a list of slots.

```
((((ChristmasPresents u #%TheYear1987) s1)
    (s2 genlSlots)) s3)
```

4. Variables and quantification. Two very important units, #%ForAll and #%ThereExists, are used for quantification. Unlike standard logic syntax, these units take an additional argument, which is the set over which the quantification is done. The idea behind this is that very rarely is it necessary to make universally quantified statements without having some bound on what "universe" the variable can possibly range over. If we say "For all x, x > 1 → NumberOfDivisors(x) > 1", x clearly ranges over only numbers, so we might as well say "For all x *in the set Number*, x > 1 → NumberOfDivisors(x) > 1". In CycL, we'd write this

```
(#%ForAll x #%Number
  (#%LogImplication
    (#%GreaterThan x 1)
    (#%GreaterThan (x #%numberOfDivisors) 1)))
```

If there were no numberOfDivisors slot, but instead there were a NumberOfDivisors function, then we'd write that last line as:

```
(#%GreaterThan (#%NumberOfDivisors x) 1)
```

If we wanted to say that all of Fred's friends are artists, we would write: (#%ForAll x (#%Fred #%friends) (#%allInstanceOf x #%Artist)). [Notice that we used *all*InstanceOf, not instanceOf. We don't care what type of artist they are; all we care about is whether they're any type of artist at all. So they could point to Artist directly (through a single instanceOf link), or point to it by a long path (one instanceOf link and then several genls links) — we don't care, so we use allInstanceOf.]

The unit #%ThereExists is pretty much like #%ForAll, but it tests whether any one of its domain satisfies the test. If we wanted to say that some (at least one) of Fred's friends are artists, we would write:

```
(#%ThereExists x (#%Fred #%friends)
  (#%allInstanceOf x #%Artist)).
```

In addition, there is a third special construct, called #%TheSetOf, whose syntax is (#%TheSetOf *variable1 collection* (P *variable1* . . .)), which evaluates to the set of all members of *collection* that satisfy the predicate *P*. So, to retrieve the set of Fred's friends who are artists, we'd write

```
(#%TheSetOf z (#%Fred #%friends)
  (#%allInstanceOf z #%Artist)).
```

This construct also may be used to specify the set over which a universally or existentially quantified statement ranges. Suppose we wanted to say that all of Fred's friends who are artists live in the U.S.A. We'd write

```
(#%ForAll x (#%TheSetOf z (#%Fred #%friends)
              (#%allInstanceOf z #%Artist))
            (#%countryOfResidence x #%USA))
```

The constraint language is not strictly first-order. A predicate appearing in one of these expressions might be a quantified variable. For instance, here is how we would say that Fred has the entry Red for at least one of the slots that are instances of the category #%ColorSlot:

```
(#%ThereExists z (#%ColorSlot
  #%allInstances) (z #%Fred #%Red))
```

Here, z might be bound to #% hasSlightTintOf.

When we use an expression of the form (#%ForAll x C P), all the occurrences of x within expression P are considered *bound*; we say that x is an explicitly quantified variable. In addition to such explicitly quantified variables, a constraint expression can have some "free" variables. The variables that may "legally," meaningfully occur freely in the expression are determined very precisely by the context in which these expressions are used and in practice additional conjuncts can be added and the free variables can be universally quantified. We shall explain in detail what these variables are when we talk about the use of these expressions. For now, one example is an *expansion* of a predicate. Recall that the #%expansion slot of #%AllHaveSame was filled with the following entry, in which v1 and v2 are free variables:

```
(#%ForAll X v1
  (#%ForAll Y v1
      (#%Equal (X v2) (Y v2))))
```

CycL expects — demands — that each predicate's and function's expansion contain its *n* arguments as free variables that must be called v1, v2, . . . , v*n*.

3.2.2.2. WHY HAVE BOTH A CONSTRAINT LANGUAGE AND A FRAME LANGUAGE?

Why do we need the constraint language in addition to the frame language? We touched on this earlier, in Section 2.3.1. Given that we would like well-defined semantics for slot values, etc., it becomes difficult/expensive to state a number of things, such as disjunctions (Fred's middle name is either Bruce or Bertrand), negations (Fred's middle name is not Bob), quantifications (all of Fred's cars are expensive, and at least one of them is imported), expressions of arity three or greater (Fred received trains for Christmas in 1986), etc. The later sections of this book give many examples of the need for the constraint language.

A more interesting question is, "If we have a language whose expressiveness is far more than that of the frame system, why use frames at all?" The answer is that Cyc is a representation of the world, and it turns out that there are a large number of basic propositions (no disjunctions or variables) that happen to hold in a reasonable representation of the world. That is, it so happens that a large fraction of what we want to represent *can* be quite naturally expressed as u.s.v triples. This being the case, it is computationally useful to have a well-defined, simple language that is sufficient for that large number of cases. In other words, the frame language is more efficient, so let's use it whenever we can. In a sense, this "economic" argument for having and using frames is not much different from our argument for having and using the various inference templates we've been discussing in this document: it's a question of finding an efficient means to do most of what you want done, be it representing situations or drawing conclusions.

We said earlier that the various non-slot predicates and functions are defined by (a) creating a unit with the predicate or function name to represent it — let's call it P for purposes of example, (b) giving P an instanceOf that makes it a NonSlotPredicate or a Function, as the case may be, and (c) defining P by giving its *expansion*. There are other slots, such as lispDefun, expressionArity, and so on, which CycL will then automatically calculate and cache on P. So the real trick is how to fill in the #%expansion slot of P — that's where the bulk of the semantics is specified. What should that entry be? The short and aesthetic solution is: just write an expression in the constraint language there, and let it have v1, v2, . . . vn as free variables representing its n arguments. You don't happen to like v1, v2, . . . vn? Just provide a SeeUnit on P.expansion, and on that SeeUnit provide a slot called variableNames that contains a list (that is, a single entry that is a list) of the free variable names in the order in which they are arguments to P. So if we wanted, the entry in the #%expansion slot of #%AllHaveSame could have been the following:

```
(#%ForAll X theListL
  (#%ForAll Y theListL
    (#%Equal (X s) (Y s))))
```

as long as we provided a SeeUnit on #%AllHaveSame.#%expansion, and as long as we provided on that SeeUnit a #%variableNames slot whose *entry* would be (theListL s); that is, that slot's *value* would be ((theListL s)). Thus, it's only if such a slot is absent that the default (v1 v2 . . .) is assumed.

3.2.2.3.
INFERENCE USING
THE CL

This section takes a brief look at the inference CycL can do using these expressions. Obviously, with a language as general as the one explained here, we can't hope to have any reasonably efficient *complete* inference scheme. (This is partly the reason why we retain the frame language in addition to the constraint language.) So aiming for either completeness or a single general-purpose "constraint interpreter" would likely result in failure or something that was terribly slow. Instead, our basic approach has been to develop a series of special-purpose interpreters for executing special classes of tasks involving constraint expressions.

For instance, one special kind of task is to take a given constraint expression and a list of bindings for its free variables, and then *evaluate* the constraint expression. If it's a true/false type of expression, determine whether it's true or false; if it's the kind that returns some other kind of value, find that value. For example, take the expression (#%AllHaveSame (#%Fred #%children) #%lastName), and actually see whether or not, in the current KB, all of Fred's children have the same last name. To do that, CycL would recursively *evaluate* (#%Fred #%children), which is easy to do — it becomes a call on Get4: (Get4 #%Fred #%children). Let's say the answer was (#%Bob #%Tim #%Sue). Then, to evaluate the #%AllHaveSame predicate, CycL would access the #%*expansion* of #%AllHaveSame, with the first argument bound to the list (#%Bob #%Tim #%Sue), and the second argument bound to #%lastName. That would end up evaluating

```
(#%ForAll X' (#%Bob #%Tim #%Sue)
    (#%ForAll Y' (#%Bob #%Tim #%Sue)
        (#%Equal (X #%lastName) (Y
            #%lastName))))
```

That, in turn, would end up iterating in nested fashion down the list, nine times evaluating (#%Equal . . . . . .). Thus, a unit's #%lastName would be accessed 18 times, and the 9 equality tests would be done. If all of that succeeded, then the final value would be T, otherwise NIL. What if one of the children didn't have a lastName recorded? The answer is that the evaluator must be told whether to treat such cases as true or false. When *checking constraints,* the evaluator would just skip over the missing information — unrecorded data is treated as "don't care." So a NIL result means "it's definitely false," and a T result means "it might be true." At other times, the evaluator is told to return T only if "it's known to be true." (In practice, two evaluators are used, one that would return NIL and one that would return T for this case.)

Let's take a closer look at the evaluation of these constraint expressions. Consider a constraint C that we are interested in evaluating. Let this constraint have the form (P a1 a2 . . . an). Let us assume that P has a procedural attachment F such that when (a1 a2 . . . an) is applied to F we get the truth value of C. If P were a slot, then C would be of the form (P u v1) and F would be of the form (memx u P v1), and if C were of the form (u s), F would be of the form (getx u s). (The functions memx and getx are the two basic classes of query functions in CycL. They can make use of any of the features mentioned in this document.)

Because we can't expect every function and predicate to be provided with a procedural attachment, we are interested in computing the procedural attachments for these from their expansions. Once this has been done, we could consider the given constraint to be a new function/predicate that has as its arguments the free variables referred to in the constraint; the procedural attachment for this function/predicate could then be generated.

A crude approximation of this is quite simple, because all we have to do is to walk down the constraint and substitute every function and predicate with its procedural attachment (possibly invoking this procedure recursively to obtain the procedural attachments for these). Then, when we want to evaluate the constraint for some set of variable bindings, all we have to do is to funcall this Lisp function on the given set of arguments. However, this scheme of evaluating constraints seems quite weak.

For example, suppose there were a rule that said $A(u) \wedge G(u) \rightarrow P(a1,a2 \ldots an)$. If this rule were to apply here, there seems to be no apparent scheme by which we would utilize this rule in proving $P(a1,a2 \ldots an)$.

Let us consider a partial solution for this problem. As mentioned earlier, the procedural attachment generated to compute C breaks down into a combination of a number of queries that try either to prove that some entry is on a slot value or to find the net slot value.

Let us now make a couple of assumptions. Suppose $(P\ a1,a2 \ldots an)$ can be translated into a unique set of ui.si.vi — that is, given the set of bindings we have, the frame language can represent our constraint. In this case, we could translate the conclusions of our rule into a set of slot values; we could then run our procedural attachment, which would query these slot values, find the appropriate values, and enable us to find the value of C. As of now, this is the basic scheme for determining the value of constraints in CycL.

Why does this scheme for proving constraints seem even remotely justifiable and what are its primary shortcomings? The justification of this scheme makes an appeal to the basic hypothesis mentioned earlier that a vast majority of knowledge is expressible in the form of units slots and entries on these. Given this, the assumption we made should hold a large fraction of the time.

In some cases, however, the assumption of the constraint being translatable into some set of ui.si.vi does not hold. The first case is when we do not have the bindings for all the variables mentioned in the constraint. The second case is when the constraint is not translatable because of the lack of expressive power in the frame language (existentials, disjunctions, etc.). Enabling CycL to solve the first class of cases is one of the research problems being worked on today. The major shortcoming of this scheme is that it does only extensional theorem proving (by making appropriate domain closure assumptions). A number of special purpose intensional theorem proving strategies are being added to overcome this shortcoming.

A second special task is to take a given constraint and a set of bindings for the free variables used in that constraint and make it true (at least try to — it might not be possible to express it in the constraint language). This in turn means translating (pieces of) the constraint into the frame language. In the case above, if some of Fred's children had their lastName recorded, but some didn't, *achieving* the constraint would be done by filling in all those missing lastName slots with that same lastName.

For each of these special tasks, we ended up writing a "compiler" in addition to the "interpreter"; the compiler takes a constraint expression and generates a CommonLisp function that tests (or achieves) that constraint. For instance, in the case of the constraint expression we discussed above (#%AllHaveSame (#%Fred #%children) #%lastName), the following piece of Lisp code is synthesized by CycL and run whenever the constraint is to be tested:

```
(EVERY
  '(LAMBDA (x) (EVERY '(LAMBDA (y) (EQUAL (#%Get4 x #%lastName)
                                          (#%Get4 y #%lastName)))
                      (Get4 #%Fred #%children)))
  (Get4 #%Fred #%children))
```

Every time a new constraint expression is entered into the KB, the constraint compilers are run on it; they generate Lisp code, and that code is cached. When a task requires some constraint to be tested (or translated, etc.), the appropriate piece of Lisp code is retrieved and run.

Now that we've given a brief overview of the constraint language, we're ready to describe all the different features (inference templates) provided by CycL. The first eight or so (for example, inverse slots, transfersThro) pretty much depend only on the frame-like part of CycL. The final dozen or more features, however, depend crucially on the constraint language. The idea is that we noticed special classes of constraint expressions (or special classes of use) and we have coded into CycL a set of sufficiently complete and efficient ways of handling these common special classes. But that's what the section 3.3 is all about.

3.2.3. Predicates of Arity Greater Than Two.   First, a quick note on notation. Below, we use several notations to represent the fact that, say, Fred's daughter is Ann:

Fred.daughter.Ann
daughter(Fred Ann)
daughter(Fred,Ann)
(daughter Fred Ann)
Ann ∈ Fred.daughter
Ann ∈ (daughter Fred)
Ann ∈ (Fred daughter)

The ambiguity in the last pair of notations will — as you might hope — cause us to shun them, however. (In truly ambiguous cases, the very last notation is the least likely to be used.)

3.2.3.1. PREDICATES OF ARITY GREATER THAN 2

It is a nuisance being stuck with just binary predicates; often we want predicates that take an arbitrary number of arguments:

• Unary Predicates: [These are slots with T or NIL as legal entries.]

married(Fred)
¬hiddenInUE?(instanceOf)
even?(28)

The first assertion could be made in Cyc as married?(Fred T). That is, we would have T be the entry on the married? slot of the Fred unit. The second one would be hiddenInUE?(instanceOf NIL). That is, NIL would be placed as the entry on the hiddenInUE? slot of the unit instanceOf. For the third assertion, we might create the unit TheNumber28, which represents 28, and assert even?(TheNumber28 T).

A unary predicate p(x) is equivalent to defining a new collection Things-that-satisfy-p. For example, we could define the three collections MarriedPeople, HiddenInUESlots, EvenNumbers. Those x which satisfy the predicates are now precisely those which are instances of the corresponding collections. For example, allInstanceOf(Fred MarriedPeople), and allInstanceOf(TheNumber28 EvenNumbers). In the latter case, we could also have represented this as allActualInstanceOf(28 EvenNumber).

• Binary Predicates: these are the usual sorts of slot in Cyc. For example,

wife(Fred,Jane)
inverse(likes,likedBy)
isSuccessorOf(34, 33)

In a situation where we have a slot with n entries, we have in effect n separate assertions. For example, children(Fred Bobby), children(Fred Susie), etc. We say "in effect," however, since sometimes we want to state assertions about *the whole set of entries* for Fred.children. For instance, without knowing exactly who all the children of Fred are, besides Bobby and Susie, we might still want to make a constraint that Fred has at least 4 children (and place that on the see-unit for the children slot of Fred), or we might state that each child of Fred inherits a default noseLength: Enormous.

• Ternary Predicates: [These have been awkward to represent in Cyc, hitherto.]

saw(Fred, Joe, Thursday)
introduced(Sam, Jane, John)
between(Chicago, NewYork, LosAngeles)
isSumOf(12, 3, 9)

- Quaternary and Quinary (and higher-arity) Predicates:

rectangleCorners(A,B,C,D)
pointsFormingSubPathOf(Austin,SanAntonio,MexicoCity,Dallas)
famousLatitudeLinesFromNorthToSouth(ArcticCircle,
    TropicOfCancer, Equator, TropicOfCapricorn, AntarcticCircle)

As you can see, the ternary predicates are pretty important, but we're clearly beginning to "reach" a bit to come up with some of those quaternary and quinary predicates. Why is that? The next section begins to probe at that question. Then, in section 3.2.3.3, we discuss in detail the way Cyc now handles (represents, accepts, displays, and reasons about) assertions of arity ≥3.

3.2.3.2. THE PREDOMINANCE OF LOW-ARITY RELATIONS: NATURAL OR ARTIFACTUAL?

It is very useful to be able to state ternary assertions in Cyc, and sometimes useful to be able to state higher-arity assertions as well. *The lower the arity, the more common and crucial such predicates are.* In the extreme case of arity = 0, we have "True" and "False"; in the nearly extreme case of arity = 1, we have the special conceptual construct of "a collection"; in the slightly less extreme case of arity = 2, we have standard frames (associative triples); in the case of arity = 3, we can think of lots of very important predicates (e.g., "between"); in the case of arity = 4, we can think of some; . . . in the case of arity = 14, we probably can't think of any.

Why are there fewer common higher-arity predicates? Does this reflect the loosely coupled nature of the world we live in? Well, not exactly; we believe it mostly just reflects human cognitive limitations (er, *features*). It reflects the loosely coupled and hierarchical nature of the mental world we think in. For example, we could use a quaternary predicate to assert that the Austin-to-SanAntonio highway segment is a sub-path of the route you might take when driving from Mexico City to Dallas. Namely, we could assert:
pointsFormingSubPathOf(Austin,SanAntonio,MexicoCity,Dallas)
This seems a bit contrived; why not create the separate Austin-to-SanAntonio and MexicoCity-to-Dallas paths as separate concepts, represented by separate units, and then just assert a binary predicate (normal slot!) between them?
subPathOf(AustinToSanAntonioPath, MexicoCityToDallasPath). And that is the point of this paragraph: most (not all) quaternary and higher-arity predicates are contrived and unnatural in just this fashion.

The famousLatitudeLinesFromNorthToSouth would be more naturally split up into four assertions, each of the form famousLatLineToMySouth(x,y).

To the extent that we have several useful things to say about a sub-structure (say, the AustinToSanAntonioPath), then it's good to break a higher-arity assertion into a nested set of lower-arity relations — that is, a lower-arity relation between more structured arguments. To the extent that there is nothing else to say about a sub-structure, though, all we're seeing is an artifact of human memory and information processing architecture limitations.

Two additional comments are needed. First, for those with minimal Latin: in case you wondered, the adjectives for arity 1–10 are: unary, binary, ternary, quaternary, quinary, senary, septenary, octonary, nonary, and denary. The unfamiliarity of the latter ones underscores our point about the decreasing utility of higher-arity predicates.

Second, for those concerned with computer science theory: If a first order language has only monadic/unary predicates, then its proof theory becomes completely decidable. This also supports the importance/utility of predicates being inversely proportional to their arity. If we have only unary predicates, even though we are working in a decidable language, it is still NP-hard (non-polynomial) and P-space complete. If you go one step further and have only 0-ary predicates this reduces to propositional logic; and now it becomes easier, going from NP-hard (and P-space complete) to NP-complete.

3.2.3.3.
REPRESENTING
TERNARY AND
HIGHER-ARITY
ASSERTIONS IN Cyc

We now have a scheme for representing predicates of any arity in Cyc, for displaying them, for reasoning with them, etc. To describe it in detail, let's consider the example "Fred saw the Leaning Tower of Pisa on Thursday." So we're using "saw" here as a ternary predicate: saw(Fred LeaningTowerOfPisa Thursday).

There are five important properties or details of these new beasts; as we shall see in the following five subsections, each of the five is analogous to (or a generalization of) a similar property that already exists in Cyc for plain old slots.

1. **Typing of Arguments:** In defining a binary relation such as "likes," we would state the domain (makesSenseFor) and range (entryIsA) of the slot. In the case of "saw," there are analogues of entryIsA and makesSenseFor. Namely, "saw" relates a triple of things: a person (who did the seeing), a thing (that was seen), and an interval (the time during which the seeing took place), that is,
   saw : Person x Thing x Interval
   So we have the following slots — #%argumentOneType

#%argumentTwoType #%argumentThreeType and so on. (Note that #%makesSenseFor is the analogue of #%argumentOneType.) So in this case we have:

argumentOneType(saw Person)
argumentTwoType(saw Thing)
argumentThreeType(saw Interval)

2. **Inverses:** In defining a *binary* relation, such as "likes," we could define a unique inverse relation, in this case "likedBy". (Although, in Cyc, in cases where the entries on a slot might not be units, no inverse slot is explicitly defined and maintained.)

   In the case of *ternary* or higher-arity predicates, however, there are many possible inverse-like relations one could define (on the order of n!, for a predicate with n arguments). Of these, we are interested in at most n of these.

   In the case of "saw," the *legally* possible inverse-like slots are:

saw: Person x Thing x Interval
saw2: Person x Interval x Thing
saw3: Thing x Person x Interval
saw4: Thing x Interval x Person
saw5: Interval x Person x Thing
saw6: Interval x Thing x Person

   And what we're claiming is that we'll want to explicitly define and maintain at most 3 of these 3! relations: at most one of saw or saw2; at most one of saw3 or saw4; and at most one of saw5 or saw6. In the case where n = 2, we have the standard case of a binary relation — a slot — and its inverse slot; since 2! = 2, there is no ambiguity or choice. We represent both of them in Cyc.

   Consider p(a1 a2 a3 a4 a5), a quinary predicate. There is no reason to have a new relation equivalent to p but with a1 as its first argument and just a permutation of a2-a5 as its next 4; similarly, we expect there to be at most one useful predicate equivalent to p whose first argument is a2, in which case the a1, a3, a4, a5 will appear in whichever (single!) order they seem most natural in; and we expect that there is at most one useful predicate equivalent to p whose first argument is a3; etc.

   Now let's return to "saw"; recall we were about to choose 3 of the 3! inverse-like slots, to represent explicitly. Suppose we choose saw, saw3, and saw5. How do we tell Cyc how exactly they correspond to each other? We use a slot called #%variantPredPattern, and on it we place an expression involving the special symbols arg1, arg2, arg3, . . . Note that arg1 is not a unit name; it is a special atomic symbol that is "parsed" (understood) by the #%variantPredPattern slot.

```
#%saw
    #%variantPredPattern: ((#%saw3 (arg2 arg1 arg3))
                           (#%saw5 (arg3 arg1 arg2)))
```

Of course, we'd probably rename #%saw3 to something like #%seenBy, etc. And we might not even want #%saw5 explicitly represented at all.

When we state inverse(s1 s2), Cyc immediately asserts inverse(s2 s1) for us. In the n-ary case, a similar thing happens. When we state the above #%variantPredPattern assertions, Cyc also asserts the proper four *additional* #%variantPredPattern assertions: two each on the units #%saw3 and #%saw5. For instance, on saw3:

```
#%saw3
    #%variantPredPattern: ((#%saw (arg2 arg1 arg3))
                           (#%saw5 (arg3 arg2 arg1)))
```

3. **UE Interface:** First, let's consider how we display binary (and unary) relations in the UE unit editor — assertions like u.s.v1, u.s.v2, . . . [In the prefix notation, rather than the "dot" notation, these would be the assertions s(u,v1), s(u,v2), . . .] We devote a unit edit pane to unit u, and a line in that pane is devoted to slot s (for unit u). On that line, on the left, we print the name of s, and on the right part of the line we print the list v1, v2, . . .

Now let's generalize this, and see how higher-arity predicates can be displayed in the UE. Consider again our example — saw(Fred LeaningTowerOfPisa Thursday).

We'll still have a unit edit pane devoted to Fred, and a line devoted to the slot "saw," but now one of its entries will appear as a list of length two: (LeaningTowerOfPisa Thursday).

In general, each entry on each n-ary predicate slot will appear as a list of length n-1. If you want to edit this, say to retract saw(Fred LeaningTowerOfPisa Thursday) and add saw(Fred Austin May), you would edit the slot value normally, rub out the (LeaningTowerOfPisa Thursday) entry, and type in (Austin May).

Since the arity of each slot is explicitly recorded, there is no ambiguity here. Each and every entry on any unit's #%saw slot *must* be a list of precisely two elements.

4. **CycL Interface:** There is a single CycL level interface for predicates that works for normal slots as well as for those with arity greater than two. The interface functions are as follows:

- *(pget* proposition &optional (access-level 6))

  Example:

  (pget '(#%saw #%Joe #%LeaningTowerOfPisa #%August1989))

→ true or false [actually, what's returned is either (((T.T))) or NIL]

(pget '(#%saw #%Joe x #%August1989)) → a binding list for x, of all the things that Joe saw during August, 1989. E.g., The value might be: (((x . #%Table12)) ((x . #%Pencil9)) ((x . #%LeaningTowerOfPisa)))

(pget '(#%saw r #%LeaningTowerOfPisa s)) → a long list of (person time) pairs. Namely, all the people who've seen the tower (possible bindings for r) and when they saw it (corresponding s bindings). E.g., (((r . #%Joe) (s . #%#%August1989)) ((r . #%Abe) (s . #%1950)))

(pget '(#%saw a b c)) → a very long list of (person thing time) triples. Namely, all the particular instances of the #%saw relationship that are in Cyc's KB! For instance, the start of that list might be: (((a . #%Joe) (b . #%LeaningTowerOfPisa) (c . #%August1989)) ((a . #%Abe) (b . #%MonaLisa) (c . #%March1975)) . . .)

"pget" stands for "proposition-get".

The required argument, "proposition," is of the form (<predicate> arg1 arg2 . . .).

arg1, arg2, etc. may be symbols (rather than unit names, lists, numbers, or strings). Each such symbol is construed to be a free variable. If there are such variables, a set of binding lists that satisfy the proposition is returned. If none of the arguments are variables, then the value returned is either (((t . t))) or NIL, depending on whether or not the given arguments satisfy the predicate <predicate>.

The "access-level" corresponds to the "level of getting," hence the current legal values are 0, 2, 4, 6, and 8. [As described elsewhere, get0 does essentially no work whatsoever, get4 will run various features such as eliminating redundant entries and will run "backward" inference templates to acquire entries, and get8 typically produces a whole new task to add to the agenda to come up with a better slot value!]

- (*prop-in4* proposition truth-value source)
  Example:
  (prop-in4
  '(#%saw #%Joe #%LeaningTowerOfPisa #%August1989)
  100
  #%Sam)

"proposition" must have one of these two forms:
  (#%LogAnd (<predicate1> <arg11> <arg12> . . .)

> (<predicate2> <arg21> <arg22> . . .) . . .)
> (<predicate> <arg1> <arg2> . . .).

None of the arguments "arg . . ." may be variables. The example prop-in4 above would result in the proposition (#%saw #%Joe #%LeaningTowerOfPisa #%August1989) being asserted with the truth value of 100 and the source of (#%Sam).

- (*prop-out4* proposition source)

This is identical to prop-in4, only the proposition is retracted. If it is a conjunction such that only some of the conjuncts are currently true, those that are true are retracted. Note: if you do a (get4 #%Joe #%saw), you will simply get the already-present entries (#%LeaningTowerOfPisa #%August1989), (#%Paris #%Summer1989), etc.

So before going on, let us take a look at how the unit #%saw looks:

```
#%saw
english:          ("A relation holding between some
                   person, something they saw, and the
                   time interval during which they saw
                   it.")
instanceOf:        (#%TertiaryPredicate)
argumentOneType:   (#%Person)
argumentTwoType:   (#%Thing)
argumentThreeType: (#%Interval)
variantPredPattern: ((#%seenBy (arg2 arg1 arg3)) (#%saw5
                   (arg3 arg1 arg2)))
myCreator:         (#%Guha)
arity:             (3)   ← inherited from TertiaryPredicate.allInstances
    .
    .
    .
```

5. **Inference:** Inference related to predicates of arity greater than 2 will be restricted for now to horn clauses (discussed in 3.3.16).

So, if you want Cyc to *conclude* #%saw(#%Joe #%LeaningTowerOfPisa #%August1989), then that exact assertion — or some generalization of it — must be asserted by some horn rule (that is, by a horn rule whose right hand side is either #%saw(#%Joe #%LeaningTowerOfPisa #%August1989) or a generalization of that. For example, you might have a horn rule whose lhs (left hand side) referred to the variables x and y, and whose rhs (right hand side) said #%saw(x #%LeaningTowerOfPisa y); and that rule might, in some circumstance, "fire" with x bound to #%Joe and y bound to #%August1989.

And if you want to conclude something *based on* #%saw(#%Joe #%LeaningTowerOfPisa #%August1989), then you will have to write a horn rule which has this assertion (or some generalization of it) as (part of) its left-hand side.

3.2.3.4. OTHER ISSUES IN REPRESENTATION RELATED TO THE CHOICE OF BINARY VERSUS HIGHER-ARITY PREDICATES

It is well known that a proposition of the form P(a,b,c,d, . . .) can be converted to a set of assertions, each of which uses only binary predicates by creating some new objects. Namely, one way to do it is to create object m which corresponds to "a and then b in the context of first and second arguments to P," and object n which corresponds to "c and then d in the context of third and fourth arguments to P," and then making a series of assertions, each of them binary:

P1(a, m),
P2(b, m),
P3(c, n),
P4(d, n),
P5(m, n),
etc.

Let's look at an example. We want to state that the distance between Austin and Palo Alto is 1700 miles. This could be stated using a *quaternary* predicate

```
distanceBetweenAndHowMeasured(Austin PaloAlto
    1700 Miles),
```

which takes two places, a number, and a unit of measure.

Alternatively, we could create a new object, the concept 1700Miles, and use a *ternary* predicate:

```
distanceBetween(Austin PaloAlto 1700Miles)
```

As a third alternative, we could create two new objects — 1700Miles and AustinPaloAltoPath — and state only *binary* assertions:

```
hasPathDetail(Austin AustinPaloAltoPath)
hasPathDetail(PaloAlto
AustinPaloAltoPath)
lengthInThoseUnits(1700Miles 1700)
unitsOfMeasure(1700Miles Miles)
pathLength(AustinPaloAltoPath 1700Miles)
```

Note that making these assertions may of course trigger various "rules," the simplest of which might just make "inverse" assertions, such as:

```
pathBetween(AustinPaloAltoPath Austin)
pathBetween(AustinPaloAltoPath PaloAlto)
pathLengthOf(1700Miles AustinPaloAltoPath)
distancesInTheseUnits(Miles 1700Miles)
```

In our notation,

```
P = distanceBetweenAndHowMeasured
a = Austin
b = PaloAlto
c = 1700
d = Miles
```

and the new objects are:

```
m = AustinPaloAltoPath
n = 1700Miles
```

and the new predicates are:

```
P1 = hasPathDetail
P2 = hasPathDetail
P3 = lengthInThoseUnits
P4 = unitsOfMeasure
P5 = pathLength
```

Given their conciseness, and naturalness, we tend to prefer the last two ways of representing the assertion: either using the ternary predicate or the "meaningfully chosen" binarized form. "Naturalness" means that there is a nice interpretation of, for example, the ternary distanceBetween predicate, and of the binary predicates P3 and P4 that lets us create the unit 1700Miles, and of the binary predicates P1 and P2 (in this case, they're both just hasPathDetail) that lets us create the unit AustinPaloAltoPath, and of the binary predicate pathLength that lets us connect the two new objects (i.e., to relate AustinPaloAltoPath to 1700Miles).

But the various objects m, n, . . and predicates P1, P2, . . . are not always so "natural." Sometimes, they don't really make much sense independently of the example for which they're created; they're spurious "formal" constructs whose only reason for existence is to avoid using ternary (or higher) predicates in some situation!

In cases where they *do* have a nice interpretation (such as AustinPaloAltoPath), we might want to state other information; that is, besides its length, we know that this path is usually travelled by air, that there are no nonstop commercial flights along that path today, that no water body needs to be crossed to traverse this path, etc.

At first glance it seems tempting to add simply more arguments to the predicate distanceBetween. But this will not work out since the arity of a predicate is a constant, and can't be changed on the fly. So if we decide to add a new type of information regarding the path, we would have to go and redo the entire distanceBetween relation (in which case we'd probably want to change its name, besides!)

In contrast, in our preferred ("natural") binarized version it is simple to just add another slot to AustinPaltoPath. So in the event that we might want to state such extra information, and there could be an arbitrary amount of such extra information, it seems better to adopt the "binarized" version. On the other hand, if in a large number of cases we are not going to be stating this extra information (that is, we *just* state the length of the distance between the two places), it seems to be a waste to create these extra units.

An even clearer example of where we doubt we'll be stating more information is the LengthInThoseUnits relation, used in this example to connect 1700 and 1700 Miles. One could imagine a #%1700 unit, and a #%pathsWhoseLengthIsThisManyMiles slot, and then the entries would be all the 1700-mile-long paths in existence. Yes, one can imagine it, but not without shuddering. Here is a clear case where we want some special constructs to hold (magnitude, unitsOfMeasure) pairs, rather than having to create explicit units for each of them.

In an attempt to eat our cake and have it too, we use the following scheme:
* Allow the use of the ternary (or quaternary) predicate.
* Also allow the slots for the natural binarized version (more on these slots in a minute), and in the event we have extra things to say (as in the above example), we create this new object and add the appropriate slots to it.

Since there may be rules that are based on the ternary version, we do the following. If there exists a unit for the binarized version, Cyc keeps the ternary and binarized versions in sync. What does this mean? Let us look at the earlier example again. Let us assume that we initially have distanceBetween(Austin PaloAlto 1700Miles). Now we decide that there are some extra things we want to say about the path between the two cities. So we create a new object called AustinPaloAltoPath. Now if we change the binarized representation *or* the ternary version, the other is kept automatically updated. So any rules that assume (that is, trigger off) one will still "work."

How do we specify the set of slots that are to be used to "binarize" a ternary predicate s? This is done by giving the s unit a #%binaryTranslation slot. s.binaryTranslation must contain just a single entry which is itself a list of three slots (s1 s2 s3) each of which must be an instance of the collection BinarisingSlot (that is, #%BinarisingSlot must appear as an entry in the #%allInstanceOf slot of s1, in the #%allInstanceOf slot of s2, and similarly of s3). The meaning is that, for all x, y, z,

$$s(x\ y\ z) \leftrightarrow$$
$$(s1(a\ x) \land$$
$$s2(a\ y) \land$$
$$s3(a\ z))$$

The final technical detail concerns the slots for the binarized version. Given a quaternary predicate we may need five new slots (P1, P2, P3, P4, P5, above) to implement the binarized version of it. Given a ternary predicate, we might need four new slots to implement a binarized version of it. If we had to define a whole new set of slots for each ternary and higher-arity predicate, we could get swamped with an explosion of these "binarizing" slots.

Luckily, it is not necessary to have a separate set of four slots for each ternary predicate, a separate set of five slots for each quaternary predicate, etc. In fact we can use the same set of these binarizing slots for a number of n-ary predicates. In fact, one extreme would be to use a *standard* set of slots to do this job! After careful consideration, we have made this the *default*.

What are these four "universal binarizing slots" for ternary predicates? Interestingly enough, three of them aren't new slots at all! They are the slots that relate a (s u v1) triple to a slot entry detail for this triple, namely:

slotsDetailed
unitsDetailed
entriesDetailed

In addition we add a couple of slots: argumentThreeDetailed and (to binarize quaternary predicates) argumentFourDetailed. The binarizing slots for a ternary (or quaternary) predicate are stated using the slot binaryTranslation. The default is the set of slots mentioned above. If you want a different set, the binarizing slots you use must be instances (i.e., in the allInstances slot) of the collection BinarisingSlot.

Let us clarify this in the context of our previous example. Using the default binarizing slots, we would state our binary representation of the fact by creating a new unit (let's call it AustinPaloAltoPath) and asserting:

entriesDetailed(AustinPaloAltoPath Austin)
unitsDetailed(AustinPaloAltoPath PaloAlto)

slotsDetailed(AustinPaloAltoPath distanceBetween)
argumentThreeDetailed(AustinPaloAltoPath 1700Miles)

[Note how entriesDetailed serves the role of P1; unitsDetailed serves the role of P2; slotsDetailed relates the new object to the slot we were going to have to make ternary, otherwise. And, lastly, note that we don't have the slot pathLength here; instead, we use the more general slot argumentThreeDetailed.]

As another example, suppose we want to say that Berkeley and Texas have a treaty that allows extradition. We might already have the slot hasTreatyWith, which is binary (it connects two political entities); the *urge* is to just make a ternary version of it (with the third argument being the type of action that the treaty allows) and assert:

```
hasTreatyWithThatAllows(Berkeley Texas
    Extradition).
```

However, we can state this using our binary scheme, without having to create hasTreatyWithThatAllows. To do this, we would create a new unit, say Treaty56, and assert:

```
entriesDetailed(Treaty56 Texas)
unitsDetailed(Treaty56 Berkeley)
slotsDetailed(Treaty56 hasTreatyWith)
argumentThreeDetailed(Treaty56 Extradition)
```

Notice how the new object is "defined" by the first three assertions, and the extra argument that we wanted to stick onto the old binary slot hasTreatyWith is "placed" by the fourth assertion.

One of the interesting things about this translation from the ternary version to the binary version was our using SEDs — *slot entry details* — (and their corresponding special #% . . . Detailed slots) to do the job.

What exactly *are* these slot entry detail units? One way to view them is as follows — given a proposition p(a1, a2, . . .) we can consider the proposition itself as a first-class object in our ontology. We can do the same with function terms of the form s(u) where s is a slot and u is a unit and s(u) is the "value" of the slot s on the unit u. s(u) *considered as an object* is called a "see unit" in Cyc.

There are two ways of making propositions into first-class objects. One of them first appeared in the RLL paper [Lenat&Greiner 80] and the other one first appeared in Jon McCarthy's "First order theories of common sense . . . " paper. The latter has better properties when dealing with things like referential opacities, etc., but the former is computationally far more tractable.

There are a couple of interesting aspects to this kind of translation.

We discuss both of them briefly (entire books have been written on each of these issues):

Let us take a look at some of the things we can say about these propositional objects (called SEDs from now on). We can (and *do*) have slots to denote the following:

the truth value of the proposition,
the justifications for the system's belief in the proposition, etc.

So we could have the proposition canPerform(Tweety, Flying) with the truth value T (that is, default true) and the source (that is, the justification for our belief) being (#%Bird (#%allInstances)). So if we had the SED @SED_Tweety_canPerform_Flying, we can have the following slots on that unit:

@SED_Tweety_canPerform_Flying
 unitsDetailed: Tweety
 slotsDetailed: canPerform
 entriesDetailed: Flying
 entryTruthValue: T
 entryJustification: (#%Bird (#%allInstances))

Cyc keeps the values of these slots in synch with the truth value, etc., of the proposition. (We won't elaborate here on some of the neat things we can do with this kind of stuff; we'll just remark that it can be useful in distinguishing between proof traces and explanations, solving the old problem of rescuing the princess from the railroad, etc.). But we will elaborate a little on one *negative* implication of doing this (having these slots, having these SEDs, etc.).

What we are doing is in effect trying to reflect the meta-theory of our language in our language. That is, we construct a language of propositions, and assign these things truth values, and so on. We then construct a proof theory and talk about justifications. Note that things like truth values and justifications are not things "in" our language but are things "about" our language. Now we make these things *parts* of the language, i.e., we put them *in* the language. The basic result of this is that it now becomes relatively easy (i.e., without resorting to something fancy like *Godelization*) to construct paradoxes in the language.

This is more than just a theoretical issue, since it means that we might need to do more work, we could easily have contradictions, etc. However, rather than shy away from all this stuff because of paradoxes (or construct something like type theory) *we have decided to wing it and live with the prospect of allowing possible paradoxes in the language.*

To be more precise, we handle this by assigning the truth value of "unknown" ("~") to these paradoxes. So if we take a sentence such as "this sentence is false," its truth value is not false or true but unknown; that is, in Cyc, given the choice of five truth values 100, T, ~, -, 0, paradoxes would have a truth value of ~.

RICH OBJECTS.   The term *rich objects* was coined by Hayes and McCarthy to describe objects about which there could be an arbitrarily large number of things to say. They made use of this concept in defining *situation calculus*, where situations were rich objects and actions were not rich objects.

If an object is not rich, and there are only some small number of things to say about it, we can actually convert the object into a proposition or function term. For example, consider the notion of "the distance between Austin and PaloAlto." If we decided that this was not a rich object, we could simply use a ternary proposition to describe this object in its entirety, and be done with it.

Unfortunately there are very few things that are (a) worth talking about at all, yet (b) are really not rich. The option of making everything rich is not a nice option either — it's too computationally expensive, e.g., 1700Miles is a good example of a locally useful but non-rich object. This is exactly the problem we faced with the binarization of predicates earlier.

We can see a general solution to this problem in our approach, that is, we have the propositional representation of the "semi-rich" object, and as more information about that thing comes along, we make the proposition into a full-fledged object and thereby allow it to become rich.

This rich versus poor representation issue crops up very often under different guises. To illustrate that, let's conclude with a seemingly unrelated example:

Consider the slot authorOf; as in authorOf(Shakespeare TwelfthNight). Suppose Ullman writes a new AI textbook, and we assert authorOf(Ullman, AITextBook905). Then we decide that we want to talk about *where* he wrote it, how *fast* he wrote it, etc. So we create a unit corresponding to Ullman writing that book; a unit called UllmanWritingAITextBook905, which would be an instance of WritingEvent, and then we assert various things about it (such as location and duration, which we can assert about any event). This construction is identical to our taking a proposition and creating a new unit @SED_Ullman_authorOf_AITextBook905; that unit would be an instance of SlotEntryDetail. So that is the other way to make the proposition into an object.

This suggests that SEDs are not the only kind of units to binarize propositions or to make propositions into objects. This was the basic motivation to allow for alternate binary translations.

3.3. Details of Inferencing in CycL

This section goes into much more detail about inferencing than was done in earlier sections. You may prefer to skim or skip over this section. However, every knowledge editor — every Cyc KB builder — should become familiar with all of the inference templates described here.

The knowledge represented in most AI programs can be divided into the following two classes:

1. Basic propositions. These are simple facts about the world. For example:
   "Fred ate Chicken43 for dinner last night."
   "Fred is an American."
   "The set of all people is a subset of the set of all mammals."
   "Joe believes that Fred is an American."

2. Templates for inference. These allow us to conclude additional facts. For example:
   "Everyone's grandparents are (precisely) their parents' parents."
   "Most Americans like to eat chicken."
   "Every living creature is older than its children."
   "x is a senior citizen if and only if x is human and over 65 years old."
   "When it rains hard, people without umbrellas usually walk more quickly than people with umbrellas."

Isn't inferencing a pretty simple topic to cover, for a single system? After all, in most languages, there is one way of handling knowledge in the second class above, one single inference engine that operates by resolution, by rule firing, etc. In such a system, we would just specify, for example, the single general "rule language" and be done with it. So don't we simply have to explain how to state If/Then rules in CycL? No, there's more to it than that.

We've made an attempt in CycL to identify and classify the standard kinds of rules that need to be stated in a KB like Cyc. For each of these clichéd types of rules, we've developed a streamlined means of stating such rules and (as much as possible) an optimized way of running them. We've also implemented an optimized TMS for maintaining each of them.

This section goes into the details of the various inference mechanisms (knowledge in class 2 above) that are built into CycL. As of late-1989, CycL contained a couple dozen different such templates for inference. Some of these are: recording the inverse of a slot; stating how toCompute one slot in terms of others; inheriting facts along some arc (which could be — but needn't be — the allInstances type of slot, the simplest type of inheritance), sufficient definitions that automatically classify individuals into appropriate categories; placing constraints on slots; demons; Horn clause rules; and toTestExpressions. Then we come to the least efficient but most general "sound" mechanism, full-fledged general If/Then rules. Another mechanism to discuss is metalevel procedural attachment, which is done in CycL via an *Agenda* mechanism.

The final few inference procedures are unsound "guessing" functions, aimed at producing "merely plausible" inferences: finding and using determinations (functional dependencies); combining multiple constraints (both numeric and symbolic); and computing the plausibility of a particular "situation" involving some units having certain slot/values. (This latter mechanism is useful for guiding Cyc in making plausible closed-world assumptions, for semantic disambiguation of natural language, for deciding which "illegalities" are metaphorically meaningful, etc.)

3.3.1. Inverses. BASIC IDEA.   Often, we'll know a relation P and its inverse P'; we might assert P(x,y) or we might instead assert P'(y,x), but those *mean the same thing*, so it shouldn't matter to the system which of those we assert — the other one should get asserted automatically.

EXAMPLES.   The inverse of parents is children; the inverse of murdered is murderedBy; the inverse of children is parents. Recalling that our notation for "v1 is an entry on the slot s of unit u" is u.s.v1, we could write this parents.inverse.children. Also recall that u.s means "the s slot of the unit u."

Note that whenever s is an inverse of s', then s' is an inverse of s. Thus, the *inverse* of *inverse* is *inverse*. Also notice that inverses are (in CycL) "total"; the inverse of *parents* does not include *sons*, or *daughters*, just *children*; the inverse of *father* is *fatherOf*, not *children*. Because inverses are total, inverse is of necessity a single-valued slot (s.inverse cannot have more than one entry).

Every slot s that takes only units as its entries may have an inverse slot. We go one step further, and say that every such slot *should* have an inverse slot. In fact, as soon as you create a new kind of slot, CycL will automatically create its inverse for you if it possibly can.

IN ACTION.   Suppose someone asserts Fred.parents.Tom. That is, someone adds Tom as an entry to the parents slot of the Fred unit. What happens then? CycL immediately enters Fred on Tom.children. This in turn might cause other inferences, of course.

If we weren't careful, one of those additional inferences would be to place Tom as an entry on Fred.parents! That infinite loop would get nipped in the bud, but in this case CycL knows about inverses, so it knows not to even start to propagate the inverse of an inverse like that. That kind of built-in knowledge is a simple example of what we mean when we say that the various inference templates are built into CycL in an optimized form. If, instead, CycL were just running If/Then rules, we could still produce this same effect (see the If/Then rule right below here), but it would be much less efficient.

CLASS OF RULE ENCOMPASSED. $\forall x, y.\ s(x,y) \leftrightarrow s'(y,x)$

CycL SYNTAX.   Place s' as the sole entry on s.inverse.

SIGNIFICANCE.   We need this template because in Cyc, as in traditional frame systems, the indexing is done solely on the objects and not on the entries of the slots. So if Fred.father contains the entry Bill, and someone asks us if Bill is someone's father, in order *not* to have to search the whole KB to answer this question, we need an inverse pointer from the entry (Bill) back to the unit Fred. In this case, fatherOf is the inverse slot of father, so Bill.fatherOf would contain the entry Fred. Some slots (e.g., siblings) can be their own inverses.

Similarly, if we decide to kill (obliterate) the Bill unit, we would like a way to quickly find all the places in the KB that refer to it, rather than having to exhaustively search through the KB to find and purge all those references to Bill.

3.3.2. Genl Slots.

BASIC IDEA.   The idea here is that certain slots, for any unit u, are just naturally going to contain a subset of some other slot's entries. If I say that Joe's *best*Friend is Sam, then you also know immediately that Sam is one of Joe's *good*Friends, and you also know he's one of Joe's friends&acquaintances.

EXAMPLES.   For all people, the set of their goodFriends is always a subset of their friends&acquaintances. So goodFriends.genlSlots contains the entry friends&acquaintances. The inverse of genlSlots is specSlots, so friends&acquaintances.specSlots contains the entry goodFriends. Other examples of this relationship are:

specs is a specSlot of allSpecs
instances is a specSlot of allInstances
genls is a specSlot of allGenls
presidentOf is a specSlot of citizenOf

Note that whenever s is a specSlot of s', then s.inverse must also be a specSlot of s'.inverse.

IN ACTION.   Suppose bestFriend.genlsSlots contains goodFriends, and suppose goodFriends.genlSlots contains friends&acquaintances. Now, when Joe gets entered as Fred.bestFriend, CycL immediately records Joe as a new entry on Fred.goodFriends; that in turn causes CycL to immediately add Joe to Fred.friends&acquaintances.

Alas, friendship is not always symmetric, so these slots are not their own inverses. The inverse of bestFriend, for example, is bestFriendOf. Because the three "friends" slots *do* have inverses (see the section above on inverses), CycL also automatically records Fred as an entry on Joe.bestFriendOf, Joe.goodFriendsOf, and Joe.Fred.friends&acquaintancesOf.

There is an additional "direction" in which entries sometimes can get propagated: from a slot to its *spec*Slots! How can this be?

If we learn that Betsy is not Fred's child, we can also conclude that she is not Fred's son, nor his daughter, nor his eldestSon, nor his favoriteDaughter, etc.

CLASS OF RULE ENCOMPASSED. $\forall x,y.\ s(x,y) \rightarrow s'(x,y)$

CycL SYNTAX.   Place s' as an entry on s.genlSlots.

SIGNIFICANCE.   We want to allow slots to proliferate, yet we do not want the KB to fall into isolated little pockets. For example, we want to have slots like grossIncome, alternativeMinTaxableIncome, adjustedGrossIncome, netIncome, afterTaxIncome, and so on, yet we still want to be able to state a general rule like "If someone's *income* is very high, Then he probably has someone else do his taxes." The solution is to use the genlSlots mechanism.

In particular, we make all those various slots entries on income.specSlots. That way, when anything asserts that Jane has very high alternativeMinTaxableIncome, CycL will also immediately record that she has very high income, and that in turn will trigger the rule. (The preceding argument applies to triggering any type of inference template, not just an If/Then rule. In the following sections, we'll often use the term *rule* in a generic sense, such as this, to mean any of the couple dozen inference templates CycL incorporates.)

3.3.3.   Refinements.   BASIC IDEAS.   The slot famousFather is what we call a *refinement* of father. The concept of refinements is closely related to that of genlSlots. When we say s.genlSlots.s', we mean that ($\forall$u) u.s is a subset of u.s'. Of course, this is pretty trivial if u.s is empty, so the only interesting case is where u.s is nonempty. "Refinements" goes this one better. It says that if the more specific slot s is nonempty for a unit u, then u.s and u.s' must be *equal* in value.

EXAMPLES. Consider the slots famousFather and father. For example, AmyCarter.famousFather contains JimmyCarter as its only entry. But AmyCarter.father must also be the singleton (JimmyCarter). How do we know that? Well, if someone has a famous father, that person is also their father. Period. You may not have a famous father, but if you *do*, that person is also your father.

Another example: malePresident and femalePresident are refinements of president. If a country has a value for malePresident, that value must be the same as its president slot value. The same goes for femalePresident: if a value exists for it for some country, that person is also the country's president.

IN ACTION. Add father to famousFather.refinementOf. Or, equivalently, add famousFather to father.refinements. (Whichever one you do, CycL will do the other for you.) Now if you record AmyCarter.famousFather.JimmyCarter, CycL will immediately record AmyCarter.father.JimmyCarter. Moreover, if anyone ever alters AmyCarter.father, the system will alter AmyCarter.famousFather in exactly the same way. This will continue until AmyCarter.famousFather again becomes empty, at which point this "slaving" of the two values halts.

Recall that genlSlots always draws inferences in one direction (if the CF is high enough) or the other (if the CF is low enough). *Refinements*, however, can draw inferences in both directions.

CLASS OF RULE ENCOMPASSED.

$$\forall x, y, z.\ s(x, y) \rightarrow (s(x, z) \leftrightarrow s'(x, z))$$

Or, equivalently:

$$\forall x.\ (\exists y.\ s(x, y)) \rightarrow (\forall z.\ s(x, z) \leftrightarrow s'(x, z))$$

CycL SYNTAX. Place s as an entry on s'.refinements.

SIGNIFICANCE. As above, the motivation here is proliferation without divergence. Note that if x.s is null, then x.s' can be anything; just because Joe doesn't have a famousFather doesn't mean he has *no* father.

3.3.4. In-context Versions. BASIC IDEA. InContextVersion slots are yet another breed of genlSlots; they're even more specialized than refinements are. In the case of refinements, the "more general" slot is slaved to equal the more specialized one, in cases where the specialized one has a non-null values. In the case of inContextVersion slots, the two slots must have identical values whenever they're both *legal* for a unit.

EXAMPLES. famousFather is *not* an inContextVersion of father: both slots are legal for all people; everyone has a father, but not everyone has a famousFather.

By contrast, emperor *is* an inContextVersion of headOfState. The former makes sense for Empire; the latter makes sense for the much broader collection GeopoliticalEntity. In the case of empires — such as, say, TheRomanEmpireIn50BC — both slots are legal. Because they're both legal, and emperor.inContextVersionOf.headOfState, the same individual *must* be both the empire's headOfState and its emperor. Whenever anyone gets recorded as one of those, or removed from one of those slots, CycL will know that the same action has to be taken on the other slot, as well.

IN ACTION. Record emperor.inContextVersionOf.headOfState. For any unit that is in the intersection of the makesSenseFor of the two slots — that is, any unit that is both an Empire and a GeopoliticalEntity — CycL will maintain the two slots as equal to each other. Anything added to or removed from one slot will be added to or removed from the other slot.

Unlike refinements, this will occur even if both slots are empty to start with, and a new entry is made into TheRomanEmpireIn50BC.headOfState. If we'd declared emperor to be merely a refinement of headOfState, then, in this situation, TheRomanEmpireIn50BC.emperor would have stayed null.

CLASS OF RULE ENCOMPASSED.

$$\forall x,y.\ \text{legalSlots}(x,s) \wedge \text{legalSlots}(x,s') \rightarrow$$
$$(s(x,y) \leftrightarrow s'(x,y))$$

Note that *legalSlots* is a slot just like any other. It in turn is defined by:

$$\forall x,C.\ \text{legalSlots}(x,s) \leftrightarrow \text{makesSenseFor}(s,C) \wedge$$
$$\text{allInstanceOf}(x,C)$$

(Actually, things are a little more complicated, given the existence of s.makesSenseForSpecsOf, s.doesNotMakeSenseFor, and the even more general s.slotConstraints. Each of these conditions is conjoined to help form the complete definition of the predicate legalSlots(x,s).)

CycL SYNTAX. Place s' as an entry on s.inContextVersionOf.

SIGNIFICANCE. The significance of the inContextVersion mechanism is the same as that for refinements. For instance, the musicians in a concert script are the performingProfessionals; so are the footballPlayers in an NFL football game script and the robbers in a bank robbery script.

Part of the significance is to help with human interfacing: the person who has to enter in the details of the next bank robbery will have an easier time of it if he just has to fill in a value for robbers rather than the more encompassing, more general slot performingProfessionals.

But this is not the end of the story. There is a true inference-motivated reason for this mechanism as well. We often might have some special rules (or templates) that apply to robbers, some special rules that apply to musicians, etc., as well as some general rules and facts that apply to all performingProfessionals.

3.3.5. TransfersThro(ugh).

The parenthesized letters in this section's title, "(ugh)," refer to the fact that transfersThro is short for transfersThrough; they also reflect our reaction to choosing that particular abbreviation rather than, say, transfersThru.

BASIC IDEA. CycL needs to have a compact, efficient way of representing inferences of the form "a person usually has the same last name as his sons do." Or: "a trilogy is written in the same language as one of its books."

EXAMPLES. In CycL, we would represent those two examples by specifying that lastName.transfersThro.sonOf and languageWrittenIn.transfersThro.subTexts. The first example tells CycL that "if the lastName of x is ln, and x is the sonOf y, then the lastName of y is also (probably) ln." The second example says "if a text is written in language L, and one of its subtexts is ST, then ST is also (probably) written in language L."

Here are some examples from the existing system:

slot	transfersThro
languageWrittenIn	subTexts
accessibleTextFile	subTexts
subEventsList	specStructures
sufficientPreconditionConstraints	specStructures
necessaryPreconditionConstraints	specStructures
finalStateConstraints	specStructures
criterialStructureConstraints	specStructures
structureConstraints	specStructures
relevantTexts	containsUnits

```
physicalExtentType              specs
constraintToSatisfy             subTasksOfProblemWithSameGoals
unitForWhichToFindSlotValue     subTasksOfProblemWithSameGoals
unitAffectedByOperation         subTasksOfProblemWithSameGoals
```

IN ACTION.   Let's say we assert that lastName.transfersThro.sonOf, that Michael is the sonOf Kirk, and that Michael's lastName is Douglas. Then CycL would conclude that Kirk's lastName was also Douglas.

CLASS OF RULE ENCOMPASSED. $\forall x,y,z.\ s(x,y) \wedge s'(x,z) \rightarrow s(z,y).$

CycL SYNTAX.   Place s' as an entry on s.transfersThro.

SIGNIFICANCE.   This is just one more common type of rule that now needn't be written as a bulky rule, but rather as a single slot entry (see CycL syntax above) and that therefore should be much easier to learn, modify, and analogize to automatically. This mechanism has been optimized in CycL for efficient truth maintenance.

3.3.6.   makesSenseFor, entryIsA, and entryFormat.   BASIC IDEA.   Every slot has various constraints on when and how it can be used. The most common sorts of constraints are: what collection of units is this slot legal for, and what sort of entries can fill it? That is, what is its domain and range? A third common question is: how many entries can this slot take? The answer to that question is usually either "just one" or "any number."

EXAMPLES.   lastName makes sense for people and is filled with a string; ageInYears makes sense for tangible objects and is filled with a non-negative real number; instanceOf is legal for every unit in the system, and its entries must be collections; genls makes sense for collections and in turn is filled with collections; inverse makes sense for (units representing kinds of) slots and in turn is filled with the same kinds of units; colorOfObject makes sense for tangible objects and is filled with Colors; physicalExtent makes sense for composite tangible/intangible objects and is filled with tangible physical objects.
   Most slots (for example, instanceOf, genls) can take any number of entries, but some of those mentioned can only take a single entry (for example, lastName, ageInYears, inverse). The slot physicalExtent is interesting in that a composite object such as Fred can have several physicalExtent entries (FredsBodyAsAKid, FredsBodyWhileHeJogs, FredsBodyDuring1988, . . .) so long as they are all subabstractions of a single entity (namely FredsBody). By the way, that entity may or may not be an entry of that slot. Another example in which subabstractions are important is the parents slot; it can have any number of

entries so long as each one is a subabstraction of one of two entities. Thus, Fred.parents might be (Sam SamAsARetiree JaneWhileWorkingInTexas JaneDuring1988).

IN ACTION.   Given that we assert all the various makesSenseFor (domain) and entryIsA (range) and entryFormat (number of entries & entities allowable) constraints as specified in the examples from the last few paragraphs, CycL will enforce them.

Whenever someone tries to assert x.s.y, CycL checks to see whether s is a legal slot for x, and whether y is a legal entry for s. If you try to assert Red.age.Fred, CycL will complain that Red can't have an age slot (because it's not a tangible object), and anyway, Fred is not a valid entry for age (because it's not a number). Although CycL merely signals an error in this situation, it is expected that most interfaces built on top of CycL will choose to catch these errors and turn them into nicely phrased queries to the user, such as "Excuse me, but should Red be a tangible object? Or should we broaden what age makesSenseFor? Or was that just a mistake?" The UE interface, which is discussed elsewhere, does this sort of thing. Naturally, the same sort of error would be generated if someone tried to give Fred a second lastName, as that would violate lastName.entryFormat. The same sort of error would occur if you tried to give Fred a second entry on his mother slot, unless the unit you were adding and the unit already there were both subabstractions of the same entity (the same person). In addition, if a set of assertions can be added to ensure that the constraints are not violated, CycL will do so.

CLASS OF RULE ENCOMPASSED.
s.makesSenseFor.D: $\forall x,y. \; s(x,y) \rightarrow$ allInstanceOf(x,D)
s.entryIsA.R: $\forall x,y. \; s(x,y) \rightarrow$ allInstanceOf(y,R)
s.entryFormat.SingleEntry: $\forall x,y,z. \; s(x,y) \wedge s(x,z) \rightarrow y = z$
s.entryFormat.SubAbs: $\forall x,y,z. \; s(x,y) \wedge s(x,z) \rightarrow$
    IntersectS(allsuperAbstrac(y),allSuperAbstrac(z))

CycL SYNTAX.   (See the section above called "Class of Rule Encompassed" for the meaning of s, D, and R.) Place the unit D in the makesSenseFor slot of s, place R in the entryIsA slot of s, and place an instance of Format in the entryFormat slot of s.

The current allowable formats are: SingleEntry, SetTheFormat, and SubAbs. If s can take only one entry, place SingleEntry in the entryFormat slot of s. If s can take any number of entries, place SetTheFormat in the entryFormat slot. If s can take any number of entries, but they must all be subAbstractions of the same entity, place SubAbs here. (The SubAbs format might be called "SingleEntity," but that's too easily misread as "SingleEntry," so we changed the name.)

All three of these slots — makesSenseFor, entryIsA, and entryFormat — make sense for slots and are single-entry slots. Here is a more detailed listing of each of these slots' instanceOf, makesSenseFor, entryIsA, entryFormat, and inverse:

```
makesSenseFor.instanceOf.MakesSenseforSlot
makesSenseFor.makesSenseFor.Slot
makesSenseFor.entryIsA.Collection
makesSenseFor.entryFormat.SingleEntry
makesSenseFor.inverse.canHaveSlots

entryIsA.instanceOf.SlotValueConstrainmentSlot
entryIsA.makesSenseFor.SlotOrConstraintOnASlot
entryIsA.entryIsA.Collection
entryIsA.entryFormat.SingleEntry
entryIsA.inverse.entryTypeOf

entryFormat.instanceOf.EntryFormatConstrainmentSlot
entryFormat.makesSenseFor.SlotOrConstraintOnASlot
entryFormat.entryIsA.Format
entryFormat.entryFormat.SingleEntry
entryFormat.inverse.entryFormatOf
```

SIGNIFICANCE. If you examine the instanceOf of the various slots above, you'll see the following three collections: MakesSenseforSlot, SlotValueConstrainmentSlot, and EntryFormatConstrainmentSlot. As you might guess, these contain many other sorts of slots that help to constrain the legal uses — and to signal an illegal use — of other slots. Let's examine each of those three classes in turn.

MakesSenseforSlot currently has the following instances:

`#%makesSenseFor`	← *s.makesSenseFor.C: we just discussed this*
`#%doesNotMSF`	← *instances of C can't have s slots*
`#%msfSeeUnitType`	← *SeeUnits modifying instances of C can have s*
`#%makesSenseForSpecs`	← *all specs of C can legally have s slots*
`#%msfSuperPartType`	← *anything having a C as a part can have slot s*

New types of MakesSenseforSlot can easily be defined by providing a value for the new slot's *expansion* slot. In fact, that's how most of the above ones were defined. For instance, the makesSenseForSpecs was created by giving it its instanceOf value (namely MakesSenseforSlot), its entryIsA (Collection), it makesSenseFor (Slot), its entryFormat (SingleEntry), and an expansion slot filled with:

```
(#%allGenls u constraint-entry)
```

Note

Details of how to read/write such expressions will be provided below, late in section 3.3.10.

Most of this unit-creation was done very quickly, by copying from makesSenseFor and editing a bit here and there. CycL also created the inverse slot for this slot, something the user named specsCanHaveSlots, and CycL filled in all the relevant slots for it automatically.

EntryFormatConstrainmentSlot currently has the following instances:

```
#%entryFormat              ← we just discussed this
#%slotCardinality          ← the exact number of entries s
                             should have
#%noOfEntriesLessThan      ← s can have at most this many
                             entries
#%slotEntityCardinality    ← the exact number of entities s
                             should have
#%noOfEntitiesLessThan     ← entries of s can be subabstractions
                             of at most this many distinct
                             entities
```

These, too, are defined by their expansions, and new instances can be created and defined that way. #%noOfEntriesLessThan, for example, has the following expansion:

```
(#%LessThan (#%LispLength v) constraint-entry).
```

As explained later, the free variables 'v' and 'constraint-entry' have certain special constraints on their domain.

SlotValueConstrainmentSlot currently has the following instances:

```
#%entryIsA
#%entryIsGreaterThan
#%entryIsLessThan
#%qualitativeValueOfSlot
#%slotValueSubsumes
#%myEntryContainsTheEntryOn
#%entryIsAnInstanceOfEntryOn
#%myEntryHasAGenlOn
#%entryIsASpecOfEntryOn
#%negationSlot
```

```
#%nonReflexive
#%slotValueEquals
#%inverseToCompute
#%coveredByValues
#%partitionedIntoValues
#%mutuallyDisjointEntries
#%thereExistsAnEntryWIA          ← WIA stands for "Which
                                  — Is A"

#%entryIsAPartOf
#%entryIsOneOf
#%entryHasAPartWhichIsA
#%entriesHaveDifferent
#%entryIsNotA
#%entryIsASpecOf
#%slotConstraints                ← the most general one; a
                                  — "last resort"
```

These also have their expansion slots (sorry, not at all like those on a PC). #%The expansion of #%thereExistsAnEntryWIA is:

```
(#%ForAll X constraint-entry
(#%ThereExists y V (#%allInstanceOf y X)))
```

In addition to specifying constraints on the entries and the number of entries on the unit corresponding to the slot itself, which thereby apply to all the occurrences of the slot, users may also specify additional constraints on the entries and number of entries that apply to sets of units that are subsets of the makesSenseFor of the slot. Let's take a look at an example of this.

SIGNIFICANCE.   An early section in this book addressed the significance of having each kind of slot represented by a full-fledged unit. Given the usefulness of that, it's clear that we need to specify the domain, range, and number of entries for each kind of slot.

Those three types of constraints (makesSenseFor, entryIsA, entryFormat) enable the system to catch most of the simple errors that occur during knowledge entry. In the future, we expect they will help guide the system's analogical reasoning process as well — for example, by gradually weakening these constraints rather than treating them as absolute.

In addition to all this there are three special constrainment slots that make sense for collections. These are #%mutuallyDisjointWith, #%covering, and #%partitionedInto.

3.3.6.1.
#%MUTUALLY-
DISJOINTWITH

A quick example of this is
BaleenWhale.mutuallyDisjointWith.ToothedWhale. Not only does this slot make sense for Collection, its entryIsA is also Collection. Here's what the slot means: If a collection is asserted to be *mutually disjoint with* another collection, no unit can be made an instance of both. So nothing can be an instance of BaleenWhale and also an instance of ToothedWhale. If you try to assert that something is an instance of both, CycL will complain. The default CF of this type of constraint is 100 — that is, typically it is an absolute constraint and may not be violated. Some examples of the use of this slot in Cyc at present are:

```
collections that must be disjoint from each
    other
(InternalMachineThing RepresentedThing)
(FemaleAnimal-Physical MaleAnimal-Physical)
(IndividualObject Collection)
(PrivateInformation PublicInformation)
(InorganicSubstance OrganicSubstance)
(NonIntervalBasedQuantitySlot
    IntervalBasedQuantitySlot)
(DifferenceChange PrimitiveChange
    ReplacementChange)
(SomethingNotExisting SomethingExisting
    NotYetExisting)
(ClosedCategoryWord DerivedWord)
(MajorSyntacticCategoryNoun
    MajorSyntacticCategoryAdverb
  MajorSyntacticCategoryAdjective
    MajorSyntacticCategoryVerb)
(Non-LivingObject BiologicalLivingObject)
(ToothedWhale BaleenWhale)
(MalePerson FemalePerson)
(MaleAnimal FemaleAnimal)
(ArtificialTangibleObject
    NaturalTangibleStuff)
```

3.3.6.2.
#%COVERING

An entry on u.covering is *a list of collections* whose union contains (is a superset of) u. There's no requirement that says that the members of that list have to be mutually disjoint, and there's no requirement that says that each of the members of the list is a subset of u.

   Thing.covering contains (RepresentedThing InternalMachineThing) as well as (IndividualObject Intangible Collection).

   Person.covering might contain this entry: (MaleAnimal FemalePersonOver18 FemalePersonUnder21)

Notice that those sets aren't disjoint (Sally is a female person aged 20), and MaleAnimal isn't a subset of Person. But the union of the three sets does indeed contain Person as a subset, so it's a valid entry on Person.covering.

The way this is used by CycL is as follows. Suppose we find out that Fred is not a FemalePersonOver18 nor a FemalePersonUnder21, but is a Person. Then, thanks to this Person.covering entry, CycL can conclude that Fred must be an instance of MaleAnimal — which he is.

3.3.6.3. #%PARTITIONED-INTO

This slot also takes lists of sets as its value. Each entry (each list of sets) on u.partitionedInto is recorded as an entry on u.covering, and all the members of that entry are recorded as being mutually-DisjointWith each other.

For example, Person.partitionedInto contains the entry (MaleAdultPerson FemaleAdultPerson Child). As soon as we assert that, Person.covering also gets that as an entry. Also, CycL immediately asserts that MaleAdultPerson.mutuallyDisjointWith contains both FemaleAdultPerson and Child; and Child.mutuallyDisjointWith both MaleAdultPerson and FemaleAdultPerson; etc. So as soon as we find out that Fred is a MaleAdultPerson, CycL will conclude that he is a Person, he is not a FemaleAdultPerson, and he is not a Child.

3.3.7. Inheritance.

BASIC IDEA. When a particular sort of "chain" is formed in the knowledge base, we can conclude that that particular known (fixed) entry belongs on a certain slot s^n of a certain unit Um (which is the "end" of the chain). The chain would look something like this:

$$\begin{array}{ccccccc} S0 & S1 & S2 & S3 & Sn\text{--}2 & Sn\text{--}1 & Sn \\ U0 \rightarrow & U1 \rightarrow & U2 \rightarrow & U3 \rightarrow & \ldots \rightarrow & Un\text{--}1 \rightarrow & Un \rightarrow & C \end{array}$$

U0 and C and all the Si are "given"; the other Ui are "to be found." The idea is that if the first n links are present, CycL should add the final one — that is, add C as an entry to the Sn slot of unit Un. (The meaning of the chain is that U0.S0 already contains U1 as one of its entries, U1.S1 contains U2, and U2.S2 contains U3, and so on.)

EXAMPLES. If $n = 1$ and S0 = allInstances, this collapses to what most people in AI refer to as *inheritance*. That is, it then just says "All instances of U0 should by default possess the entry C on their S1 slots." For example, in this extreme case, if U0 = Person and S1 = IQ and C = 100, the inheritance says that all instances of Person should get a default IQ of 100.

An example of a less degenerate chain, one in which $n = 3$, is: "If

JoeTheJinx works on a project, and that project uses a computer that is manufactured by some company, then that company's future outlook is dark." Here, U0 = JoeTheJinx, S0 = worksOnProject, S1 = computerUsed, S2 = manufacturedBy, S3 = futureOutlook, and C = Dark.

IN ACTION.   CycL can use each inheritance template either in an opportunistic (forward) "direction" or in a demand-driven (backward) "direction." Typically, this is fixed at the time that the template is entered into the system. A single slot s of a single unit u can contain several inheritance "templates" — remember, these aren't *entries* on u.s, — and each template can have its own forward/backward "setting."

Let's suppose we enter the default iq = 100 template to be *forward* inherited to Person.allInstances. Immediately, forward propagation is done; CycL visits all instances of Person and gives each one's iq slot a default entry of 100. (Anyone who has a stronger reason for thinking his IQ is something else will note this default but immediately override it with the more "local" information.) Also, whenever in the future CycL notices an assertion of the form Person.allInstances.x, it immediately gives x a default IQ of 100. If any unit y ever *stops* being an instance of Person, CycL immediately removes this template's particular support for iq = 100 (though there still may be some local information to that effect, or some default coming from other places, such as MiskatonicUniversity.graduates, etc., that keeps y.iq set to 100).

Suppose instead that we entered the iq = 100 template as a *backward* inheritance on Person.allInstances. Nothing at all (except a little bookkeeping) happens immediately. Later, if someone asks for Fred.iq, and Fred happens to be an instance of Person, this piece of knowledge is found and used, and the default value of 100 is returned for Fred.iq. Backward inheritances are sought if the "level" of the asking is 6 or higher (that is, backward inheritances are not sought when calling functions like Get0, Get2, Get4, Mem0, Mem4, etc., but they *are* sought when calling Get6, Mem6, Get8, etc.).

There is a third inheritance "setting," besides forward and backward: forwardEventually. This *simulates* forward inheritance; very little work is done at the time the inheritance template is entered; the massive exhaustive forward propagation is simply not done. The price for not doing this is to slow down retrievals on that slot in the future — even a low-level retrieval such as (Get4 #%Fido #%iq) — because CycL must check to see if this template *would have* caused a default entry to be placed there on Fido.iq. Although it's up to "the environment" (the knowledge server, the user interface, etc.) what to do about this, the *intention* is that during long periods of idle time (say, at night), the exhaustive forward ripplings will get carried out, and the forwardEventually templates will be converted into vanilla forward templates.

The above discussion dealt with the simplest sort of inheritance, a chain of length $n = 1$, but the same procedure and options hold for inheritance chains of any length. The bookkeeping chore gets worse, but let CycL worry about that.

CLASS OF RULE ENCOMPASSED.   See the "Basic idea" paragraph above.

CycL SYNTAX.   Visually we depict this (both in this book and on screen using our UE editor) by repeated indentation — n levels deep for a chain of length n. There is a particular CycL function to call, inh-in4, to bring about the creation of a new inheritance template; that function is given as arguments U0, the chain of Si, and the final entry C that is being inherited.

SIGNIFICANCE.   Inheritance has always been the bulwark of frame-based reasoning. Its usefulness is expanded by the generality of the inference type that CycL calls "inheritance" — that is, by allowing chains of any length, and by allowing any slots at all (not just allInstances) to comprise the chain.

Because C is constant, and because U0 and all the Si are known at the beginning, CycL is able to handle this type of inference fairly efficiently.

The importance of inheritance in CycL, however, is lowered a large degree because of the existence of all the other inference mechanisms! So users should not hesitate to use inheritance in CycL, but they should use it only when no more efficient inference mechanism is applicable.

3.3.8. toCompute.   BASIC IDEA.   The toCompute mechanism provides a way to define one slot in terms of other slots. For example, uncles $= df$ brothers ∘ parents. Once a slot is so defined, CycL will automatically calculate it as needed.

EXAMPLES.   To compute uncles(u), we can find the parents(u), and then find their brothers. In CycL, we would effect this definition by recording the following expression in the toCompute slot of uncles:

```
(#%ComputeByComposing #%brothers #%parents)
```

We could also define slots in terms of other slots that are themselves computed; for example, we could define uncles' Sons as (#%ComputeByComposing #%sons #%uncles).

Besides ComputeByComposing, there are several other ToCompute functions. Let's consider ComputeByStarring. This defines a slot as the Kleene star of another. For example, ancestors(u) are parents(u), their parents, *their* parents, and so on. Mathematically, we'd write this as ancestors $=_{df}$ parents.* In CycL, we'd write the following expression: (#%ComputeByStarring #%parents) and place it on the toCompute slot of the unit ancestors.

Caveat

As with the mathematical definition of Kleene starring, the meaning of ComputeByStarring is "any number of link-followings," and this includes 0 and 1. Hence, Fred and Fred's parents will also be listed among Fred's ancestors. If this isn't what's wanted — say we don't mind Fred's parents but we do mind Fred himself being considered one of his ancestors — then use ComputeByDifferencing to define a new slot, trueAncestors, which won't include Fred; alternatively, you could use ComputeByKleenePlussing from the beginning. That is, either

```
trueAncestors =df
(ComputeByKleenePlussing parents)
```

or

```
trueAncestors =df
(ComputeByDifferencing ancestors self)
```

Another useful ToComputeFunction is ComputeByUnioning. For example,

```
siblings =df
(ComputeByUnioning brothers sisters)
```

Actually, in cases where we know for certain that the two slots' values must be disjoint, we can use ComputeByAppending instead of ComputeByUnioning. So we could have said:

```
siblings =df
(ComputeByAppending brothers sisters).
```

IN ACTION. After placing the above definitions on the appropriate units' toCompute slots, we can ask CycL for the value of the siblings slot of Fred, or the uncles of Fred, or whatever, and it will retrieve the correct value. It does this in two ways:

1. The defined slot (say, siblings) is cached. (This is the default for all slots.) In this case, CycL propagates the definition "forward," ex-

haustively and continually, keeping all units' siblings slots up to date. So if we were to do even a (Get0 #%Fred #%siblings), the correct value would already be there. If Fred got (or lost) a brother or a sister, his siblings slot value would be adjusted accordingly.

2. The defined slot is not cached, but only calculated upon demand. To make this happen, we would place a dontCache? slot on the unit siblings and give it the entry T. Now, no big search is done at the time we define siblings. Moreover, no bookkeeping is done when, say, Fred gets a new brother. However, the cost for this laissez-faire scheme is that every time we want to find Fred's siblings, the definition is looked up, Fred's brothers and sisters are found, and the resultant lists are appended. Also, (Get0 #%Fred #%siblings) would return NIL — as it always will for non-cached slots — and we would have to call (Get4 #%Fred #%siblings), or Get6, or Get8, etc., to get the right value returned.

On the other hand, functions such as Mem4 (and higher) can be clever about how they return their answers, not bothering to assemble the full Fred.siblings value, but rather walking around the proper nodes until they know enough to return their answer. For example, for ComputeByUnioning or ComputeByAppending, Mem4 just needs to independently search each tree, and return T if any of those searches pay off. For more details of this "trick," see the later section on toTestExpressions.

CLASS OF RULE ENCOMPASSED.   Each separate ToComputeFunction captures a separate type of rule:

• Suppose that s3 is defined as (ComputeByComposing s2 s1). This covers:

$$\forall x, z. \ s3(x,z) \leftrightarrow (\exists y. \ s1(x,y) \wedge s2(y,z))$$

• Suppose that s3 is defined as (ComputeByUnioning s1 s2). This covers:

$$\forall x, y. \ s3(x,y) \leftrightarrow s1(x,y) \vee s2(x,y)$$

• Suppose that s3 is defined as (ComputeByIntersecting s1 s2). This covers:

$$\forall x, y. \ s3(x,y) \leftrightarrow s1(x,y) \wedge s2(x,y)$$

• Suppose that s2 is defined as (ComputeByStarring s1). This covers:

$$\forall x, y. \ s2(x,y) \leftrightarrow x = y \vee s1(x,y)$$
$$\vee (\exists z. \ s1(x,z) \wedge s1(z,y))$$
$$\vee (\exists z, z2. \ s1(x,z) \wedge s1(z,z2) \wedge s1(z2,y))$$
$$\vee \ \dots$$

$$\vee \; (\exists z, z2, z3. \; s1(x,z) \wedge s1(z,z2) \wedge$$
$$s1(z2,z3) \wedge s1(z3,y))$$
$$\vee \; \ldots$$

- Suppose that s2 is defined as (ComputeByPlussing s1). This covers:

$$\forall x, y. \; s2(x,y) \leftrightarrow s1(x,y) \vee (\exists z. \; s1(x,z) \wedge$$
$$s1(z,y))$$
$$\vee \; (\exists z, z2. \; s1(x,z) \wedge s1(z,z2) \wedge$$
$$s1(z2,y))$$
$$\vee \; (\exists z, z2, z3. \; s1(x,z) \wedge s1(z,z2) \wedge$$
$$s1(z2,z3) \wedge s1(z3,y))$$
$$\vee \; \ldots$$

- Suppose that s3 is defined as (ComputeByAppending s1 s2). This covers:

$$\forall x, y. \; ; \neg(s1(x,y) \wedge s2(x,y)) \wedge (s3(x,y) \leftrightarrow$$
$$s1(x,y) \vee s2(x,y))$$

- Suppose that s3 is defined as (ComputeByDifferencing s1 s2). This covers:

$$\forall x, y. \; s3(x,y) \leftrightarrow s1(x,y) \wedge \neg s2(x,y)$$

CycL SYNTAX.   To define siblings, we place the expression (#%ComputeByAppending #%brothers #%sisters) as an entry in the toCompute slot of the unit #%siblings. Other ways of computing slots, such as ComputeByComposing, ComputeByUnioning, etc., work similarly.

SIGNIFICANCE.   This mechanism is much less general than many of the others; it handles a much smaller set of circumstances. However, it is very efficient. (The same could be said, to an even greater degree, for the inverse slot mechanism.)

To achieve this efficiency, we have imposed three limitations on the use of this mechanism:

1. There may be at most one toCompute for any kind of slot. That is, the entryFormat of toCompute is SingleEntry.

2. The toCompute specifies the complete value of the slot. It is not directly editable "by hand." To be safe, this toCompute should be the only way of concluding the value of that kind of slot.

3. The *"defined in terms of"* ($=df$) relation is a strict partial ordering. That is, three slots must never all be defined in terms of one another, such as:
   $s1 =_{df} s2 \cup s3$

$$s2 =_{df} s1 - s3$$
$$s3 =_{df} s1 - s2$$

Any *two* of those definitions could be present without any problems, but not all three.

A later section (3.3.11) will deal with another mechanism — slotValueSubsumes — for concluding the value for a slot s where these three constraints do not hold but s is still "sort of" defined in terms of others. toCompute is more efficient.

3.3.9. Coextensional Sets. BASIC IDEA AND EXAMPLE. Coextensional sets have been provided to make some of the implications of the ontology of Cyc easier to implement. Consider the collection Event. As explained later, every Process must be an Event, and every Event must be a Process. That is what we mean when we say that they are coextensional: their all-Instances must be equal. We use this feature to assert that two sets are coextensional; thereafter, CycL enforces that property.

CLASS OF RULE ENCOMPASSED.

```
(∀x) allInstanceOf(x C1) ↔ allInstanceOf (x C2)
```

CycL SYNTAX. Place C1 on C2.coExtensionalSets. The slot coExtensionalSets is its own inverse, so CycL will immediately place C2 on C1.coExtensionalSets.

IN ACTION. Suppose we assert that C1 and C2 are coExtensionalSets; that is, we assert C1.coExtensionalSets.C2. Let's also assume that C1.specs.C2. Now, if C1 is placed on the allInstanceOf of some unit u, C2 is placed on the allInstanceOf of u (actually, it is placed on u.instanceOf, and is removed from there if it's already on u.allInstanceOf). If C1 is removed from the allInstanceOf of u, C2 is removed from the instanceOf of u.

3.3.10. Constraints on Slots. BASIC IDEA. Earlier, we talked about the slots #%entryIsA, #%makesSenseFor, and #%entryFormat. We saw how they help to define various slots by imposing constraints on what can fill that kind of slot, what sort of unit can legally have it, and how many entries it can take. We also discussed dozens of other slots that also constrain and help define kinds of slots (for example, #%doesNotMSF, #%entryIsASpecOf, etc.). Together, these are all that's needed in about 95 percent of the cases. Here we finally get down to the mat, and talk about how to handle that final 5 percent.

If we are trying to constrain the value of the s slot of the unit u, we add what is called a *constraint unit* to u.s. This constraint unit — let's call it CU — has the following important slots:

- #%slotsConstrained — This usually contains just s.

- #%constraintInheritedTo — This contains a list of the units to which this constraint applies. It will certainly contain u. The same constraint might very well apply to many different units' s slots, in which case all those units would be listed here. If the constraint is a popular one, there might be tens of thousands — or, one day, billions — of entries here! Hence, it's proven cost-effective not to bother caching this particular slot. The inverse of this slot is #%inheritedSlotConstraints, which points from a unit to the constraints that apply to it. That slot *is* cached.

- #%slotConstraints — This is the "important slot." Its entries are expressions in the constraint language that are supposed to be true for the slot value to which they refer. These expressions may have the following free variables (variables appearing in the constraint expression that are not explicitly quantified in that expression):

  u — This is assumed to be bound to one of the units for which this constraint is supposed to hold true. That is, the constraint will be *evaluated* only while u is bound to some unit that has CU on its #%inheritedSlotConstraints slot.

  s — This is assumed to be bound to the slot being constrained.

  v — This is assumed to be bound to the value of u.s.

EXAMPLES. In practice, when we state some interesting and useful constraint, it's likely that we want it to apply to a whole class of units, not just a single unit u. For example, "Everyone must be younger than his/her parents" or "Neighbors of FredTheDrummer are bleary-eyed."

We state this by inheriting (or inferring through some other means — see all the subsections in 3.3) the appropriate *constraint unit*. Let's look at some examples. "Everyone must be younger than his/her parents" is done as follows:

```
Person
   allInstances
      inheritedSlotConstraints:
      (YoungerThanParentsConstraint)

YoungerThanParentsConstraint
   instanceOf: (#%SlotConstraint)
   slotsConstrained: (#%age)
   constraintInheritedTo: ( )    ← this isn't cached!
```

```
slotConstraints: ((#%LessThan v
  ((u #%parents) #%age)))
```

IN ACTION.   Suppose we declare Fred to be a person. For example, we place #%Austinite in his #%instanceOf slot. Then his #%allInstanceOf slot gets a large set of entries, including #%Texan, #%American, #%Person, #%Mammal, #%Animal, and #%Thing. In particular, note that now Person.allInstances.Fred. So the inheritance from Person.allInstances kicks in, and Fred automatically gets an inheritedSlotConstraints slot, with the entry YoungerThanParentsConstraint. Thus, as soon as we created a unit called Fred, and gave it instanceOf: Austinite, the Fred unit would get two more slots automatically:

```
Fred
   instanceOf: (Austinite)
   allInstanceOf: (#%Texan #%American #%Person
                     #%Mammal #%Animal #%Thing ...)
   inheritedSlotConstraints: (YoungerThanParentsConstraint)
```

Now suppose we put some entries on Fred.parents, on their ages, and on Fred.age. If we use real (or reasonable) values for all these things, there's no problem. But what happens if we assert Fred.father.Sam, Sam.age.40, Fred.age.50? (By the way, because father.genlSlots.parents, Fred.parents.Sam is added by CycL.) Whenever the last of the three contradictory assertions is made, CycL will notice that YoungerThanParentsConstraint is violated, and it will generate an error message.

Essentially, the last of the three assertions (whichever order you do them in) won't be completed and propagated throughout the system. Instead, you would have to abort that operation, or (preferably via a user interface) fix the problem — for example, you could remove the constraint, weaken it by rewording it, lower the truth estimate of the constraint (thereby possibly allowing a violation of the constraint that would then be recorded on Fred as an unusual slot entry); in addition, you could alter Fred.instanceOf (or Austinite.genls, or . . .) so that Fred wouldn't end up being a Person after all, or you could correct Fred's father's age to be a number larger than 50, or. . . . You get the idea.

More details   In practice, there seemed to be a small number of "types" of constraints that were stated very often. That is, they exhibited certain syntactic regularities. In order to facilitate their representation, we added a number of new slots that these Constraint Units may now have; we refer to these as "slotized" constraints. These slots include

#%entryisOneOf, #%entryHasAPartWhichIsA, #%doesNotMSF, #%makesSenseForSpecsOf, #%entryIsASpecOf, etc. These are just the "special" constrainment slots we studied earlier.

The semantics of each of these slots is again expressed through their #%expansion. That is, every one of these slots has the slot #%expansion, which contains an expression in the constraint language that explains the semantics of the slot.

Earlier in this chapter (section 3.3.6), we said we'd explain the details of how to write such expansions. Well, we've already covered the constraint language, so all we have left to do is to explain that these expressions may have the following four free variables in them:

- u — the unit where this slotized constraint is being used

- s — the slot whose value this slotized constraint is constraining

- v — the value this slotized constraint is used to constrain (= u.s)

- *constraint-entry* — the value of the slotized constraint as it appears on the constraint unit

Notice that slots like entryIsA, entryIsNotA, and all the various slotized constraints, seem to be as meaningful for a unit representing a slot as they are for a unit representing a slot constraint. Therefore, any unit representing a kind of slot may also have any of the slotized constraints, as well as a truthEstimate. This is why, in our earlier discussion, we saw that entryIsA.makesSenseFor was not Slot, but rather SlotOrConstraintOnASlot.

One of the implications of the previous paragraph is that any unit representing a kind of slot may have a slotConstraints slot. Hence, slotConstraints.makesSenseFor.SlotOrConstraintOnASlot.

Also, although our examples so far have shown just a single constraint on a u.s, any given u.s may have any number of constraints applying to it. Whenever the value of u.s is updated (for example, when some entry gets added or removed or has its cf changed), all the constraints on it are checked. Constraints are also checked when a new inheritedSlotConstraint is added or when some slot is referred to in a constraint for that unit (or a related unit) is updated. This includes the constraints placed on the unit s itself and the different entries of u.#%inheritedSlotConstraints that constrain s.

It should be noted that these 'constraints' are really just like any other kind of assertions (inheritance etc.) and lead to drawing conclusions etc. So if we have entryIsA(s C) and s(u vi), this allows us to conclude allInstanceof(vi C).

3.3.11.   slotValueSubsumes.   Earlier in this chapter (section 3.3.8), we discussed CycL's toCompute mechanism, a means of computing the values of slots. Near the end of that discussion, we listed three restrictions imposed by the toCompute mechanism and said that later we would show what to do if those conditions didn't hold. At this point, we are ready to talk about this issue.

Constraint #1 was: There may be at most one toCompute for any kind of slot. That is, the entryFormat of toCompute is SingleEntry. Well, it would be really nice if we could provide multiple means of computing the slot value (or parts thereof). CycL could then try them in sequence or in parallel; some might work in one situation and not in another, some might be fast in some situation and slow in another, etc.

Constraint #2 was: The toCompute specifies the complete value of the slot. Well, it would be nice if we could compute *some* entries on that slot, without having to guarantee that we had the one true method that delivers all of them at once.

Constraint #3 was: The "defined in terms of" relation is a strict partial ordering. That is, we must never see three slots that are all defined in terms of one another, such as: $s1 =_{df} s2 \cup s3$; $s2 =_{df} s1 - s3$; and $s3 =_{df} s1 - s2$. Any *two* of those could be present without any problems, but not all three. Well, it would be nice to be able to specify some simple antecedent that must be satisfied for this means of computing the slot value to be valid (for example, that the other two slots already have known values). This would enable us to provide a means of computing the slot value for subsets of the domain of the slot, or for various situations that occur dynamically (such as two particular other slots having values).

For our purposes, it's most useful to talk about constraint #2 first. This constraint is overcome as follows. Instead of giving s a toCompute slot, we give it a #%slotValueSubsumes slot. The expression (which, by the way, may freely use the variable u) is interpreted as meaning "when you evaluate this for a unit u, you'll get some of the u.s entries it ought to have."

To overcome Constraint #3, create a constraint unit on u.s. On that unit, place a #%slotValueSubsumes slot filled with some constraint expression (which uses the variable u freely.) CycL interprets that to mean "the value of this constraint expression is a subset of the entries that belong on u.s". Unlike the case in the previous paragraph, this applies just to a single unit u, not to all units that legally can have slot s. To make this useful, therefore, it's likely that this will be an inheritedSlotConstraint on a set of units; to make it different from the previous paragraph's case, it's likely that this set of units will be a spec of (that is, a *proper* subset of) s.makesSenseFor.

And now, we simply wave our magic wands and dispel Constraint #1, at least for the case of #%slotValueSubsumes; it takes any number of entries, not just one. Also, in addition to specifying a slotValueSubsumes that applies to the whole domain of the slot, users may specify slotValueSubsumes for a subset of the domain of the slot. This is done by treating the slot slotValueSubsumes like any constrainment slot (such as slotConstraints or entryIsA); slotValueSubsumes is placed on constraint units, which then go on the slot inheritedSlotConstraints of the units for which this slotValueSubsumption holds.

With what cf should the entries concluded by a #%slotValueSubsumes expression be asserted? This can be specified by making the slotValueSubsumes a default or monotonic rule.

The #%slotValueSubsumes expression not only acts as a means of computing the slot value, but also is treated as a constraint on the value of the slot! So CycL will signal a constraint violation if u.s is changed so that it no longer contains the values given by the slotValueSubsumes expression.

When a slotValueSubsumes expression is entered, CycL asks (if it's not told at the time) whether or not it must keep the value of the slot updated (as we just described) whenever possible, or whether it's okay for it to compute the value of the slot only when demanded. In the latter case, the constraint expression is evaluated only when the value of the slot is asked for (that is, in a backward direction) with a strength of 6 or greater. The slotValueSubsumes is treated as a constraint except that the slotValueSubsumes can be maintained in a backward direction.

Another slot, #%slotValueEquals, is a slight variation of slotValueSubsumes. #%slotValueEquals is a specSlot of slotValueSubsumes and, in addition, inherits a constraint that says that the value generated by this expression must be equal to the value of the slot. This slot may have only one entry.

3.3.12. Automatic Classification.

What exactly do we mean by *classification*? As with *inheritance*, we mean something quite a bit more general than the term's usual meaning in AI. In CycL, "classification is any inference where a *sufficient defining predicate* for u.s is used to determine some entries for u.s. If s = allInstances, this is "plain old" automatic classification.

This is done by providing a constraint unit (let's call it SD1) for u.s. It's a special sort of constraint unit of a type known as SufficientDefiningSeeUnit. SD1 has all the usual slots that a constraint unit can have, plus three special ones:

1. #%definesSlotEntry — This contains the slot for which we are providing a sufficient defining condition

2. #%modifiesUnit — This contains the unit for whose slot we are providing this predicate

3. #%sufficientCondition — This is the important one! It contains an expression in the constraint language that is a predicate (interpreted as evaulating either to NIL = false, or non-NIL = true) and that is the "sufficient defining predicate for u.s". This expression may refer to the entry that we are trying to place on this slot value; it may refer to the entry that is being classified into the unit.slot on which the SufficientDefiningSeeUnit occurs as u.

```
Citizenship Guessing Rule 16
instanceOf: SufficientDefiningSeeUnit
definesSlotEntry: #%citizens
modifies Unit: #%USA
sufficientCondition: (#%LogAnd
                        (#%livesIn U #%USA)
                        (#%LogNot (#%ownsA U
                          #Passport)))
```

This default rule says that people living in the U.S. who don't own a passport are probably U.S. citizens. Thus can be asserted in either a forward or backward direction.

If the constraint expression is not merely a sufficient condition for something sitting on u.s, but a *necessary and sufficient* condition, the predicate is entered on the slot #%necessaryAndSufficientCondition on SD1. (By the way, doing so will cause CycL to immediately enter it also on SD1.sufficientCondition, because sufficientCondition is on necessaryAndSufficientCondition.genlSlots.)

Every #%SufficientDefiningSeeUnit — such as SD1 — may have a number of more specialized sufficient defining see units; they would be placed on its #%specSufficientDefinition slot. The semantics of this slot are such that the following key relationship holds: *#%sufficientCondition and #%necessaryAndSufficientCondition transferThro the #%specSufficientDefinition slot.*

3.3.13. ToTestExpressions. BASIC IDEA. Sometimes we would like to provide a procedural attachment to a slot (either holding on its entire domain, or holding on some particular subset of the domain) for determining whether an entry may be placed on a slot value.

Automatic classification (3.3.12) was originally intended to do this, but there are a couple of drawbacks to that method: the classifying expression does not allow us to refer to the unit on which the slot sits, and users are not allowed to specify an arbitrary Lisp function as the classifying function.

The first flaw is obviously undesirable, and we are in the process of getting rid of it. The second problem is more subtle, in that the truth maintenance for the inference done using these classification rules depends heavily on an analysis of the classification expression. If there were a piece of Lisp code sitting there instead, it would not be possible to carry out this kind of analysis. So we never cache the results obtained from these procedural attachments.

CycL SYNTAX. Suppose the satisfying condition for v1 to sit on u.s is given by F (where F is a unit, F is an instance of Function, and F represents the Lisp function f), such that when f(u s v1) returns True (non-NIL), u.s.v1 may be assumed to be True. Then on the slot s (or on a constraint unit constraining s for some part of its domain), you place the slot #%toTestExpression with the entry (F u s v1).

ACTION. Whenever a query is made that tries to find out if a given entry v1 is on u.s, we run the function f with the arguments u, s, v1, and, if this returns a non-NIL value, we return True. However, because F can represent an arbitrary function and we have no idea about the other slot values on which this conclusion is dependent, we have no means for doing the truth maintenance. That is why *the result obtained by this inference scheme is not cached.*

3.3.14. Demons. BASIC IDEA. The purpose of this feature is to allow us to specify a function to be run whenever a slot is modified.

CycL SYNTAX. If we want the function F to be run whenever a modification is made to the slot s (for any unit), we place the function F on s. #%afterAdding on the slot. F is allowed to be either a Lisp function or a unit representing one. (Of course, we recommend the latter!)

ACTION. Whenever any unit's s slot is modified, the function F is called with the following arguments:

- u (the unit being modified)
- s (the slot being modified)
- oldv (the old value of the slot; i.e., the old value of u.s)
- newv (the new value of the slot, i.e., of u.s)
- deltav (the entries that have gone in or out of u.s)

Caveat

The use of these demons is strongly discouraged for any inference! In many ways, they represent "mysterious side effects," and it is hard for

Cyc to reason about the consequences of its actions if there are demons firing off all the time. As of now, they are used largely by CycL
itself for tasks such as adding some appropriate set of indexing pointers (whenever constraint expressions are added), recompiling
CycL-generated functions when the expression from which they were
generated is changed, etc.

3.3.15. Other Uses of Constraints: Structures and Scripts.

Constraints are also used in
the representation of structures and scripts. The ontological issues related to this are dealt with later, in chapter 6. The following discussion
is quite terse; you may want to return to this subsection after having
read section 6.6.

In the following paragraphs we shall attempt to cover only *some* of
the detailed language-level points, such as exactly which slots must be
used and what semantics they require.

3.3.15.1. STRUCTURES

The *structure* of an object is the set of constraints that hold between its
parts. The term *parts* is used to refer not just to physical parts but also
to temporal parts and other kinds of parts. So in principle there is
nothing really unique about the representation of structures — they're
just bundles of related constraints. However, in their current CycL implementation, three aspects in the representation of structures merit
special attention:

- There is some significance to the clustering of sets of constraints that
  apply to objects. So, rather than represent these constraints using
  the usual constraint units, constraints that apply to a single object
  should be collected together on a single unit, which should be made
  an instance of #%Structure.

- Because it is likely that certain standard sets of relations apply between different objects repeatedly, we introduce a new class of
  NonSlotPredicate called StructurePredicate. These are just like the
  normal NonSlotPredicates except that whereas the typical
  NonSlotPredicate is purely syntactic, these predicates are not. A special class of StructurePredicates is #%RepeatedStructurePredicate.
  These are used to represent repeated sequences of relations. These
  predicates take a list as their argument, and their units have the slot
  #%interRepeatedStructureExpansion, which contains that relationship between the nth and $n+1^{st}$ element of the list. Also, given an object with n repeated elements, the slots #%lastRepeatedElement and
  #%firstRepeatedElement are used to refer to the last and first element of the sequence, respectively.

- The representation of the structure requires some means of referring to the parts of the object. Sometimes, each part sits on a separate slot of the unit. Often, however, this is not the case. We need some means of referring to *the part of the object that is an X*. This is done by having the slot #%partsList on the structure. This contains a listing of the different parts of the individual. The syntax for this is as follows: (. . . (symbol Type number) . . .), where *symbol* is the symbol used to refer to that part (for example, X), *Type* is the collection of which that part should be an instance (for example, TableLeg), and *number* is the number of occurrences of that kind of part (for example, 4). If we had an already-existing slot in the KB where this type of part is listed (such as #%legsOfThisTable), the *symbol* would be substituted by, say, (u #%legsOfThisTable). In addition, the structure must have the slot #%structurePartSlot, which contains the name of the slot on which the different parts referred to by symbols sit. The #%structureConstraints slot is perhaps the most important slot on the whole structure unit — it contains all the constraints on the structure! This slot has a specSlot called #%criterialStructureConstraints, which has the constraints that are considered absolutely essential to defining this structure. See Section 6.6 for examples of structures.

Every structure may also have the slot #%specStructures. This slot points to more specialized structures and has the following semantics: *the slots #%structureConstraints, #%partsList and #%criterialStructureConstraints transferThro this slot.*

IN ACTION.   CycL can do two kinds of inference using these structure descriptions:

- Instantiate these structures — This involves creating the unit that is going to have this structure on its hasStructure slot (usually an instance of some class that inherits this structure down to its instances); it also involves creating the different parts and placing the appropriate relations between these parts (that is, the relations specified by the structure constraints). (It is also possible to ask for the recursive creation of the parts of the parts and so on (up to a specified depth)).

- Given that an individual has a structure Str1, the structure constraints that are present on the Str1 could be treated as if they were slotConstraints on the different slots of the individual and its parts. This means that we could have CycL add the relationship between the different parts of the individual, either in the forward or backward direction. The certainty with which these assertions are made is indicated on the structure unit. Also, additional slots are present on the structures (such as #%structurePredicatesInvolved) that we believe could prove useful to perform tasks such as structural analogies.

3.3.15.2.
EventStructures —
STRUCTURES OF
SCRIPTS

EventStructures are a subset of the static structures described above. The special things we have to handle for these structures are as follows. (This section assumes that you have already read the section on scripts later in this book, namely Section 6.6.)

Every script has a number of actors. However, given that the ontology has this "subabstraction" view of the world, there are three subabstractions associated with every actor: before, during, and after. Because the actor in the script is just an appropriate subabstraction of the entity that plays that role (usually the minimal superabstraction of the three subabstractions involved in that script), little can be inferred about the actor based on this information. However, it is still convenient to refer to "the actor," and yet to talk about the actor in its three different stages, without needing four explicit symbols for these different concepts or three explicit slots for the different subabstractions for the different actors.

As explained later in this book every role may have a slot (e.g., robber, loot, victim); or we could group actors together on the slot given in the #%structureActorSlot); all the before, after, and during subabstractions of the actors may be located on the slots #%beforeActors, #%afterActors, and #%duringActors. In order to refer to the subabstraction of the actor X that occurs on the s slot of u, we say (#%SubAbsOfActorIn X (u s)). However, even this is only a last resort. All this is explained in Section 6.6.

Given that any specific abstraction of a script has three interesting regions — before, during, and after — we can almost always infer the right subabstraction based on the context. So there are three important slots: #%initialStateConstraint, #%duringStateConstraints, and #%finalStateConstraints. Any reference to an actor on these slots is supposed to refer to (respectively) the before, during, or after subabstractions of that actor in that script. Suppose we want to say that the performer in a CriminalAction is a Criminal after the event (we don't want to say anything about whether he is a criminal before or during). On the finalStateConstraints of CriminalActionStructure, we would say ((#%allInstanceOf (u #%performer) #%Criminal).

In addition, we might like to state a number of constraints that relate the values of slots on before and after (or during) subabstractions of actors to each other. That is, sometimes in the "after" context, you'll want to refer to the way some actor was "during" and the way some actor was "before" the event took place. This is done by making use of the slot #%changeConstraints. These are constraints that use a special class of predicates called #%ChangePredicate. These predicates are defined by the slot #%changeExpansion; the special symbol u may be used to refer to the event in which the change is taking place. A categorization of the change predicates and some examples is given in chapter 6, section 6.6.

If all this fails, we can just state the constraint we want to state by using the #%SubAbsofActorIn predicate, as described above, and we then place that constraint on the structureConstraints slot.

Two additional differences exist between normal structures and event structures:

- The slot #%partsList has a specSlot, #%subEventsList, that makes sense for EventStructure. It contains the list of subevents. The slot #%structurePartsSlot also has its analogue, #%structureSubEventSlot.

- Four slots transferThro the slot #%specStructures; they are: #%changeConstraints, #%finalStateConstraints, #%initialStateConstraints, and #%duringStateConstraints.

The relations implied by these constraints (those on the slots #%changeConstraints, #%finalStateConstraints, #%initialStateConstraints, and #%duringStateConstraints) are kept enforced by CycL. That is, as soon as the bindings for the variables used in these expressions are known, these expressions are translated (if possible) from the constraint language into the frame language.

3.3.16. **(Simplified) Horn Clause Rules.**   BASIC IDEA.   This feature corresponds to a simplification of Horn clause rules. This was supposed to be intermediate in complexity between inheritance and constraint language features like slotValueSubsumes and automatic classification. And it often is intermediate in terms of, for example, CPU time consumed. In some cases, however, it is more efficient to use slotValueSubsumes rather than this Horn clause rule feature.

CycL SYNTAX.   Each horn rule is a "sentence" which has the schema: (#%LogImplication <lhs> <rhs>).

A Cyc unit is created for each horn rule and place the whole sentence into the slot #%hornClause on the unit corresponding to the horn rule. Note that #%hornClause is a SingleEntry slot.

Before discussing the legal syntax for a horn rule's lhs and rhs, we need to make two more definitions:

Definition: A function or predicate is said to have an *attachment* if there is some way to "evaluate" it; that is, to check its satisfiability in a given model (part of which resides inside the machine). In Cyc, this means having a #%lispDefun slot, whose entries are Lisp functions that *compute* that predicate, for example, the #%lispDefun slot of #%Equal contains EQUAL, the #%lispDefun of #%GreaterThanOrEqualTo contains $\geq$, and so on. (Note that EQUAL and $\geq$ are executable Lisp functions.) Examples of predicates *without* attachments are: #%likes, #%saw, etc.

Definition: A *legal function term* (note: not a legal lhs) is defined as follows. It must be of the form (<Function-unit> <arg1> <arg2> . . .); "Function-unit" must be a Cyc unit that has an attachment; and each of "arg1", "arg2", etc., must either be a variable that was referred to earlier in the lhs or must itself be a legal function term.

    * Now we can define a *legal lhs* for a horn rule, as follows

- An expression of the form (<predicate> <arg1> <arg2> . . .) is a legal lhs, so long as "predicate" is any unit whose #%allInstanceOf contains #%Predicate, and each argument "arg1", "arg2", . . . is either

    a constant (e.g., #%Paris or '(:in :out) or 42 or "the end")
    or a variable (e.g., q or r)
    or — if "predicate" has an attachment — a legal function term

    So, if "predicate" has no lispDefun, hence cannot be evaluated, then the various "arg1", "arg2", . . . may not be function terms.
    If the predicate *does* have an attachment (for example, #%GreaterThan), then "arg1", "arg2", . . . *may* legally be function terms; but all the variables occurring in the arg$i$ expressions must have been referred to earlier in the rule's lhs. That is, these arg$i$ terms cannot be used to *generate* bindings for variables. They can be used only to *eliminate* candidate bindings.

- An expression (<logical-connective> <form1> <form2> . . .) is a legal lhs, so long as "form1", "form2", . . . are each legal lhs terms and the "logical-connective" is one of these three:

    #%LogAnd
    #%LogOr
    #%FalseOrUnknown

    * And we define a *legal rhs* for a horn rule as follows:

- (<predicate> <arg1> <arg2> . . .) is a legal rhs, where each "arg$i$" is one of the following:

    a constant
    a variable referred to (hence bound) in the rule's lhs

a skolem function term in a subset of the variables referred to in the rule's lhs (more on skolem function terms later).

- (#%LogAnd <term1> <term2> . . .) is a legal rhs, where "term1", "term2" . . . are all legal rhs terms.

The semantics of these rules should be obvious. Each of these horn rules can be either forward or backward, and can be either at level 6 or 8.

SIGNIFICANCE. Almost all the classification rules and many of the slotValueSubsumes rules that involve some logical connective are now handled by this class of rules. It fills a gap that was sorely noticed — namely, bridging the large gap in complexity and generality between inheritance on the one hand (efficient but limited) and slotValueSubsumes and automatic classification on the other hand (general but inefficient).

3.3.17. General If/Then Rules (or Rather, Their Absence). Consider the 16 inference "features" we've talked about so far and how they relate to the standard rules of the form $P(x) \rightarrow Q(y)$.

The basic idea here has been to recognize standard syntactic categories of rules, and then provide specialized means of handling them; those specialized mechanisms can and should be (and, we hope, *are*) both easier to enter (at least they're terser!) and more efficient to run (they exploit various regularities that can be guaranteed to hold in that subtype of rule). We also exploit a constraint we impose on the user — that of determining whether a constraint/rule should always be in the forward direction — to optimize the TMS for this constraint/rule.

For instance, consider CycL's maintenance of inverse slots. Yes, we could write a pair of rules like

```
∀x,y. children(x,y) → parents(y,x)
∀x,y. parents(y,x) → children(x,y)
```

It is easier, however, just to assert children.inverse.parents, and let CycL do the rest of the work. Moreover, CycL can exploit various aspects of inverses: the fact that each slot will have only one inverse, whose inverse will be the original slot; the fact that the entryIsA of the inverse is the makesSenseFor of the original slot and vice versa; the fact that. . . . You get the idea.

The preceding subsections — at least all of the sections discussed before the constraint language — fall into a special category: each of those features is nothing more than a specific type of rule (which happens to be very useful).

How did we isolate those various special cases of P(x) → Q(y)? What sort of regularities have we looked for and which ones were we able to non-trivially exploit?

Clearly, we've looked for and exploited regularities in the syntactic form of the antecedent and/or the consequent. The regularity we want is of the form s(u, C), where *C is a constant* (this is related to the definition of inheritance in CycL).

From this perspective, the slotValueSubsumes feature encompasses the class of rules where the antecedent has the form s(u, C).

The classification feature falls into the category where the consequent is of the form s(u, C).

The other features are really just special cases of those two features. Between these two classes (and their useful subclasses), most of the rules that we would like to state are handled. In theory, we could use slotValueSubsumes and classification to handle all the inference features described in 3.3.1–3.3.9 too. Again, we *don't* do that because that would mean not using knowledge we have about the regularities in these rules.

But what about rules designed to allow us to state very general things where neither the antecedent nor the consequent has the form s(u, C)? There are two options in these cases.

- Option 1: Sometimes such rules really ought to be broken down into two inference steps, one consisting of a classification rule (or inheritance) and the second consisting of a slotValueSubsumes.

  It is a purely syntactic trick to show that this break-up is always possible. It is akin to introducing a new unit C with the slot s'. Then you say that one rule recognizes C.s' (classification) and one rule acts on entries of C.s' (slotValueSubsumes). Big deal. In keeping with the entire spirit and aims of Cyc, we recommend this course of action only if the two "halves" of the rule make sense intuitively; that is, if the new unit C is a meaningful one.

- Option 2: Consider a general rule of the form P(u) → Q(x). Almost always, we would like to provide some constraint on the bindings for u in P(u). Because of this, we could reformulate the rule as s(u C)^P'(u) → Q(x).

  Now if s were to be the slot #%inheritedSlotConstraints and C were to be a constraint unit, we are left with P'(u) →Q(x), which is something easily expressible as a constraint that is placed on the slot #%slotConstraints. So *the third distinct category of rules comprises those expressed in slotConstraints.* Again, these could be either forward or backward.

  In practice, however, it has been observed that there are really very few cases in which we would want to have a rule stated in this form. In most cases, it turns out that a better representation would involve a combination of inheritance, constraints, classification, etc.

3.3.18. Procedural Attachments (via the Agenda). BASIC IDEA. In certain cases, we would like to specify some arbitrary script, the execution of which is capable of providing the answer for some query: for example, looking up a database, asking the user, etc. This feature provides a mechanism for providing such "hooks" into CycL.

CycL SYNTAX. If we want the script X to be considered for obtaining the value of the slot s of the unit u, either on the slot s or on one of the entries of u.inheritedSlotConstraints (which constrains the slot s) we place the slot #%problemSolvingMethodsToUse, with the entry X.

IN ACTION. If an attempt to obtain the value of u.s is made using a get level of 6 or higher, the agenda is invoked and an instance of X is created and placed on this agenda, with the X.#%unitForWhichToFindSlotValue being the unit u and the slot s being the entry on X.#%slotForWhichToFindValue. The script X is responsible for placing its conclusions in the appropriate place with the appropriate justifications, etc. Details of the agenda mechanism are provided in a later section, 3.4.5.

3.3.19. Plausible Inference by Determinations. Determinations correspond to inference rules of the form

```
((P determines Q) → (∀ x y
  (P(S,x)∧P(T,x)∧Q(S,y) → Q(T,y))))
```

Basically, what this says is that if two things have the same value for the set of properties defined by P, they are likely to have the same value for the set of properties defined by Q. Some examples of this include

```
a gem's type determines its color
a person's age and nationality determines his
  politicalParty
```

Let's consider an example of a determination found by Cyc:

```
#%historicIncarnationOf determines
  #%physicalExtent
```

This implies that if two things are historical incarnations of the same entity, they are likely to have the same physical extent. So if we were to take two subabstractions of an entity (Malta), say the Roman Colony of Malta and the British dominion of Malta, and we know the physical extent of one of them, we could make a guess about the physical extent of the other.

Reasoning using determinations could be thought of as a simple kind of reasoning by analogy.

Determinations can be discovered by CycL (on its good days), can be asserted by users (any day of the week), and can be used by CycL (whenever Get8 is asked to get — or we should say, "guess at" — a value for u.s).

To assert that s is determined by s1 and s2, say, we create a new unit D1, make D1 an instance of Determination, and give it a determinationPredicate slot with the entry (s1 s2). We also give D1 a slotDetermined slot, with entry s. That's it. Well, if we *want* to do more work, we can specify an entry matchFactor, which must be a number in the 0 to 1 range. This number represents the fraction of the s1 and s2 entries that must be shared in common on both u93 and u105 for example, before CycL will conclude (using this determination) that u93 and u105 are likely to have equal s slots. The default for matchFactor is .5; we expect that time will tell what a good default is, in general and for specific classes of slots. Another highly optional slot for D1 is determinationCondition. If the slot is present on D1, it must be filled with a predicate that can return False (NIL) for various systematic exceptions to the determination.

More complicated expressions for determinationPredicate are permitted and are synthesized by CycL. We will not go into the syntax of such expressions here.

3.3.20. Plausible Inference by Resolving Constraints. We often don't know a slot value, u.s, but we do know a set of constraints that apply to it. If this set of constraints is sufficiently constraining, we can guess at the value u.s by finding possible entries that satisfy all the constraints. There are two common and important special cases of this:

- All the entries in u.s must be numbers
- All the entries in u.s must be units

Let's consider an example of the first case. If s is single-valued, and numeric, we can use arithmetic to resolve the inequalities.

Note for purists   Yes, in the general case, especially if s is multiple-valued, this could be arbitrarily complex. However, we are trying to identify classes of constraint sets that can be fairly easily "resolved."

Let's look at an example. Consider the age slot of the Fred unit. We may have several constraints on this, picked up here and there from various miscellaneous other things we know about Fred:

```
Fred.age >4          (from hobbies: Bowling)
Fred.age >17         (from childrens' ages
                        being 3 and 4)
Fred.age <26         (from mother's age being
                        39)
Fred.age =2(mod      (from just missing voting
  4)                    age once)
Fred.age >20         (from having voted
                        sometime)
```

If we add the assumption that the age must be an integer, we can resolve these inequalities (using simple linear programming) to get the result that Fred must be exactly 22 years old.

As an example of the second case, assume we have the following set of constraints on u:

```
(#%IsA u #%Woman)
(#%stageOfExistence u #%Dead)
(#%landsControlledBy (u #%nationalLeaderOf)
  #%Britain)
```

Using these different constraints, we could make a guess at the value of u by finding out the different values of u that could satisfy this set of constraints. In this case, there are not too many.

3.3.21. Computing Plausibility of Scenarios.

This is not strictly an inference scheme, in that it is rarely used for finding the values of slots. Instead, this scheme is used for purposes such as computing the plausibility of a given scenario, or more specifically some u.s.v1.

This involves doing the following:

1. Check the different constraints on the slot value and, for every constraint that is violated, reduce the plausibility of the given proposition.

2. In case a constraint is violated, try to find possible extensions to the

given unit, slot, and entry. This process of finding extensions involves the following:

2a. *Traversing instances links:* If the assertion u.s.v1 can't be true for u (or if v1 is a wrong entry) but instances of u (or v1) could fit the bill, we assume that the intended meaning was to state a general rule about the instances of the class as opposed to the class itself. Human knowledge enterers, authors, etc., often make this sort of "error."

For example, suppose someone asserts #%Person.#%height.5.8Ft. Though Person (being the set of all people) can't have a height, *instances* of Person can have a height. So CycL assumes that the intended meaning was that "people are usually 5.8 ft tall" and allows *that* as the plausible meaning. (That is, it takes the assertion to be an inheritance — to wit, that 5.8 gets inherited to Person.allInstances.)

2b. *Traversing different generalization and specialization links:* Often, though the given unit, slot, or entry is illegal, an appropriate generalization or specialization of it is legal. We assume then that this generalization/specialization was the intended meaning and accept this as a plausible answer. Of course, the plausibility ought to be decreased a lot if it is an extreme generalization (for example, Thing). This happens automatically, as we step away from u (or s or v1) one "step" at a time, as described later on in this section, weakening the plausibility estimate each time.

2c. *Traversing metonomical links:* Often, a user might refer to u' when they actually mean v', where v' is an entry of u'.s'. For example, they say that "the culprit was the USA," when they mean "the culprit was some agent of the USA." Yes, we're really saying here that sometimes an assertion mentions x (x can be u, s, or v1) when what's really intended is (some entry on) x.s'. Wow! What an opportunity for explosive search.

Because the unit x may have any number of slots, what is the basis for deciding which slots we must consider while doing this kind of traversal? For deciding this we use the slot #%metaphorSensibility. Every slot s' may have this slot, and the entry is a number between 0 and 1. This slot gives us the plausibility of a reference to x actually meaning some entry on x.s'.

Most slots have no metaphorSensibility, and the default is assumed to be 0. Some slots, such as #%controls and #%physicalExtent, have a high metaphorSensibility and can be used for this kind of link traversal.

As a simple example, consider the headline "United States Sinks Ship." Now, it is not possible for the United States to sink a ship (it is a CompositeTangible&IntangibleObject, and only a tangible object can sink a ship). Well, #%physicalExtent has high metaphorSensibility, so maybe the speaker meant that the PhysicalUnitedStates got up and landed on the poor enemy ship. Not too likely, Cyc says, since the size of the PhysicalUnitedStates is much larger than that of a Stadium, which is about the largest mobile weapon or weapon-carrier it knows. Well, #%controls also has high metaphorSensibility; maybe the UnitedStates controls some other agent who sank the ship. For instance, the USNavy, which in turn controls a number of ships whose physicalExtents are quite capable of the act. So after these various link traversals, CycL concludes that there is that particular plausible meaning to the given sentence. One final example: "Mary read Shakespeare."

2d. *Similar values:* When a slot takes qualitative values as its entries, even if the given value is not legal, it is possible that a similar value is legal. How do we find "similar values"? The value might be a number, in which case similarity is pretty obvious. Or it might be a qualitative value, such as Hot, which points to adjoining qualitative states (Warm, VeryHot).

For example, consider the statement "Indians are Red." This is not true, because there is a constraint that says that humans can have only colors that are the legal skin colors. However, one of the colors that is similar to Red is FleshRedColor, which *is* a legal skin color, thus allowing us to accept this as a plausible statement. Similar knowledge is brought to bear to understand "the red conductor," given the various possible meanings of "red" and "conductor."

Given a proposition, we start off with the u.s.v1 given and, one by one, test all the constraints; when some constraint fails, we start extending the given proposition in all directions. Associated with each extension scheme is a plausibility reduction factor. So we keep extending the given statement along a "sphere of roughly constant plausibility," with the search in any direction being cut off as soon as the plausibility in that direction falls below a certain threshold. If a solution is found before the plausibility in all directions drops below the threshold, that solution is reported as a plausible meaning of the given statement along with its plausibility. If no solution is found in this way, we lower the threshold and continue expanding the sphere. Eventually, the threshold gets unacceptably low and we quit.

One of the uses for this kind of inference is to help in the process of disambiguating natural language sentences. The idea is to create the different scenarios derived from the syntactic parsing of the sentences and choose the one that seems most reasonable.

Another use is to guide the making of "closed world assumptions" (CWA). For example, some rule might fire if only we knew that X was a subset of Y. X appears to be a subset of Y — that is, extensionally. CWA says "Well, go ahead and assume it's not a coincidence and go on with the reasoning." As you might imagine, indiscriminate use of CWA can lead to staggering errors! On the other hand, with even a smidgin of common sense behind it, it can lead to quite reasonable guesses. Let's look at a particular example.

The problem is to try to guess whether Jim speaks quietly. (Let's assume that "speaks" is a slot, and "quietly" is an acceptable qualitative value for that slot.) We call Get8, and it is on the verge of giving up. Lots of resources yet remain, so it goes ahead and considers CWA. It notices the following rule, which, in principle, might conclude that Jim.speaks.quietly:

```
Rule83:
    IF (all shirts a person u owns are
       non-loud in color)
    THEN (u speaks quietly)
```

Assume that Jim.owns contains three shirts: (Shirt1, Shirt2, Shirt3). Shirt1.color is a PastelColor; the other two are of completely unknown color.

First, we assume (by CWA) that these are the only shirts Jim owns. We don't know if Jim owns any other shirts. By the CWA, we don't worry about this — we act as if these are his only three shirts.

So the goal now is to show that these three shirts have non-loud color. Gee, that wasn't so bad, was it! Read on.

Next, we do the best we can (that is, we try the other 19 inference techniques) to get the colors of Shirt2 and Shirt3. Suppose that this leads to the conclusion that the color of Shirt2 is a PastelColor. At this point, a Determination kicks in: shirt color is often determined by the color of the other shirts one owns! Therefore, even though we don't know exactly what color Shirt1 or Shirt2 is, we can conclude that Shirt3 is probably a PastelColor, because the other two are.

Now that Cyc has (with some plausibility) concluded that all three shirts are PastelColors, it tries to show that the sets PastelColor and LoudColor are mutually disjoint. Let's say this isn't already in the KB.

However, there are several instances of each set, and the sets have, at present, no common instance. So — we invoke CWA to conclude that the sets really (intensionally) are disjoint. That means that each of Jim's shirts is a non-loud color, hence the rule can fire, and we conclude that Jim speaks quietly.

On the good side, this method is very general. Given any relation, we can see if it holds in the KB at present, and, if so, we can assert that it always will hold. That is, if it holds extensionally, assert it intensionally.

On the bad side, to use this method all the time is lunatic. This method, like abduction and astrology, must be used in moderation. In the coming year or so, we hope that a body of heuristics to guide the use of this inference technique will be codified and entered in Cyc.

3.3.22. Conclusions about Inferencing in CycL. CycL has a lot of inference schemes. The reason is that when you want to do defeasible reasoning, truth maintenance, etc., and you just use a single "clean" inference mechanism (such as resolution rules), the complexity of the computation becomes high. However, if a large number of the statements in the knowledge base have a particular well-defined syntax, it is possible to exploit this regularity by using special-purpose algorithms to handle the inference, TMS, etc. We believe this to be the case in CycL. Actually, we've stacked the deck in our favor, because we *developed* each mechanism only as it was needed!

To make this scheme work, the user must employ the simple inference schemes (for example, inverse, toCompute) whenever possible, rather than always using the general ones (for example, If/Then rules).

On the other hand, to get a lot of people to use the system, we have a compromise solution: namely, we have a piece of code (and eventually, part of the KB) that examines each new inference rule and sees if it can be transformed into one of the other, more streamlined, inference schemes and this is what the "epistemological" level mentioned earlier is for.

- The categorization of the different inference templates described in this document has largely been based on the *syntax* of these "rules." It may be possible to have a similar classification of inferences on a *semantic* basis (some possible classes could include: design, diagnosis, configuration, etc.).

- Other than statistical induction of different kinds done in "batch mode," CycL does not yet include much in the way of learning schemes. We need to add explanation-based generalization (chunking), AM- and Eurisko-like learning, and so on.

- More of CycL should be represented in the KB. Following the RLL dream [Greiner&Lenat, 1980], one of the interesting things about the CycL language is that we hope one day to fully represent it in terms of itself, that is, as a set of units in the Cyc KB. This could prove to be useful, and even necessary, if Cyc is to monitor itself and (based on what it discovers) modify itself. Unfortunately, we do not have infinite resources, and this remains one of our lower priority goals at the moment.

(There has to be some set of code that "starts off running," but even that code can be described in the KB. Of course, there may be multiple interpretations, as in a Lisp interpreter being described in Lisp, with OR being described as (OR evaluate-args-left-to-right evaluate-args-right-to-left). Depending on how OR happens to start out being coded, it concurs with its description. So, because we must start off with some code running, we can't guarantee that there won't be more subtle versions of that multiple-interpretation bug.)

3.3.23. Skolemization in Cyc. We mentioned above, when we discussed horn rules, that *skolem terms* may appear in the rhs (right-hand side) of horn rules. What are skolem terms? First we'll give a motivation for having them — some idea of what purpose they serve in Cyc. Second, we'll introduce their semantics. Finally, we'll give their syntax.

Example: Consider the statement (which we'll call S, below): *"every person has some female and some male as their parents"*.

You know a lot of people, and probably — for at least some of them — you haven't ever consciously thought about their parents. If I ask you about their parents (for example, your first grade teacher's parents' names), you'd draw a blank. Of course, you'd still be able to answer questions like "Do you think your first grade teacher had parents? How many? How many of her parents were male? Female? Might their birthdates have been 100 years apart?"

In Cyc, when we do a Get0, we retrieve only the already-cached information. In this case, (Get0 #%Lenat #%firstGradeTeacher) returns #%MrsMoore, but (Get0 #%MrsMoore #%parents) returns NIL, since I (and Cyc) know nothing about them. Yet if we evaluate the expression (Get6 #%MrsMoore #%parents), we want two units to be created, filled in as entries on the #%parents slot of #%MrsMoore, and that list of those two units — say (#%MrsMooresMother #%MrsMooresFather) — to be returned as the value of the Get6 expression.

Somehow, statement S, above, should be statable in Cyc, and should cause MrsMooresMother and MrsMooresFather to get created, when the Get6 is done, the first being given gender: Female, and the second being given gender: Male.

The skolemization facility is there in Cyc to enable such unit creation.

Let us consider how we would state this example. First consider the normal fopc (first order predicate calculus) version of statement S:

```
(ForAll x
  (ThereExists y z
    (instanceOf(x Person) →
    (And instanceOf(y MalePerson)
         parent(x y)
         instanceOf(z FemalePerson)
         parent(x z)))))
```

We remove the ThereExists by skolemizing (creating two functions f and m) and we remove the ForAll (all free variables are considered universally quantified) to get:

```
(instanceOf(x Person) →
    (And instanceOf(f(x) MalePerson)
         parent(x f(x))
         instanceOf(m(x) FemalePerson)
         parent(x m(x))))
```

where m and f are skolem functions that take a person to his mother and father, respectively. [Note that it is purely a fortuitous property of this example that f and m have nice interpretations like father and mother. In a lot of cases they don't; i.e., the skolem functions don't "deserve to have names," they don't warrant being represented explicitly in Cyc.]

The above rule is now almost in our horn clause form. However, we don't allow arbitrary functions like f and m. Rather, in Cyc, terms such as f(x) and m(x) would be denoted using *skolem terms*. In the case of f(x) and m(x), these would be (#%SkolemFunction (x) 1) and (#%SkolemFunction (x) 2), respectively. The "(x)" indicates that we're talking about some function of x, and the final "1" and "2" are tags (indices) to keep the two functions-of-x separate.

So in this case, in Cyc, we would denote our rule S by:

```
(#%LogImplication (#%instanceOf x #%Person)
  (#%LogAnd (#%instanceOf (#%SkolemFunction (x) 1) #%MalePerson)
          (#%parent x (#%SkolemFunction (x) 1))
          (#%instanceOf (#%SkolemFunction (x) 2) %FemalePerson)
          (#%parent x (#%SkolemFunction (x) 2))))
```

Notice we've explictly marked in all the "#%"'s, so the reader can see that the only non-unit references in the whole horn rule are to the variable x and the integers 1 and 2.

Note

More generally, suppose there are n such functions g1, g2, . . . g$_n$ in the rhs of a rule (in the example above, n = 2 and g1 = f and g2 = m). The arguments to function g$_i$ — suppose they're x$_i$1, x$_i$2, . . . — will depend on the ForAlls enclosing the ThereExists in the original statement. We then denote g$_i$(x$_i$1, x$_i$2, . . .) in Cyc by
(#%SkolemFunction (x$_i$1 x$_i$2 . . .) i).

Let us see what the S rule will do, in Cyc. If MrsMoore is a person (that is, #%MrsMoore.#%allInstanceOf.#%Person) and we evaluate the expression (Get6 #%MrsMoore #%parents), then rule S will get accessed and run, and Cyc will create two units, say #%Person809 and #%Person810, and then assert all of the following:

#%instanceOf(#%Person809 #%MalePerson)
#%instanceOf(#%Person810 #%FemalePerson)
#%instanceOf(#%Person809 #%SkolemUnit)
#%instanceOf(#%Person810 #%#%SkolemUnit)
#%parent(#%MrsMoore #%Person809)
#%parent(#%MrsMoore #%Person810)

Of course they in turn will trigger other "rules"; for example, all instances of #%MalePerson get the entry #%Male for their #%gender slot, and so on.

If we next ask for Fred's parents it creates two more units, and so on. Now what if #%MrsMoore *stops* being a #%Person? Then those 2 units that were created (#%Person809 and #%Person810) stop being her parents, and also stop being a #%Man and a #%Woman (hence stop having gender: male and gender: female, etc.). Cyc does not instantly kill those units, though; they remain around, at least for a while, in case #%MrsMoore again becomes a #%Person one day, and they remain instances of #%SkolemUnit.

At first sight this seems to be just a reworking of what can already be done using structures. There are two points in this regard.

• The Structures will create units only when you call the Lisp function make-complete-instance-of. It will not create units when you do a get6. Though it seems tempting to simply force get6 to call make-complete-instance-of, the TMS issues and the issues mentioned below get way too complex.

- The Structures stuff is not very good for saying things of the form (*if* <some complicated condition> *then* (ThereExists . . .)). The left-hand side for Structures is implicitly just of the form *hasStructure(x StructureFoo)*. True, one could have this expression: (*if* <some complicated condition> *then* hasStructure(x StructureFoo)) in Cyc, but it seems nicer to have a more direct construction and avoid spurious structure units.

There are a number of issues that crop up here. They arise as soon as one considers a few example scenarios:

SCENARIO.   We create the two units for Mrs. Moore's father and mother (#%Person809 and #%Person810) and then we find that Joe is her father. The obvious thing to do is to say that #%Person809 (which is an instance of #%Man) is the same as #%Joe, and maybe merge these two units. But wait a minute. S didn't actually state that Fred can only have one father. Maybe Person809 and Joe are two of several fathers Joe has! (For example, consider S': "*Every person has two close-relatives, including a male close-relative and a female close-relative*".) So we need a way to state in Cyc that a person has *exactly* one father and take care of the merging of the two units (and possibly the un-merging if, later on, Joe turns out not to be Mrs. Moore's father after all).

SCENARIO.   What if we say that some person — #%Person999 — is one of Mrs. Moore's parents. (Perhaps #%Person999 was itself created by skolemization, as some other rule fired sometime.) Now we don't even know which of the two earlier units (#%Person809 or #%Person810) we should merge with #%Person999. Well, maybe we can go ask the user.

We mentioned earlier that we would end this section by giving the syntax of skolem terms. And here it is:

A *skolem term* has the following syntax: (#%SkolemFunction (<var1> <var2> . . .) <tag>) where each "var_i" is a variable referred to freely in the lhs of the rule, and "tag" is an integral index used in case there are a number of different skolem functions (having the same argument lists) in the rule.

3.4.   Getting, Putting, and Metalevel Inference

3.4.1.   Getting and Putting u.s Values.   Let's now take a look at what gets done when by CycL, and how the user (or other intelligent agent) can provide to CycL some information regarding what gets done when. Following this, we will examine some of the different utilities provided by the CycL language.

Getting and *Putting* are the two major classes of operations in CycL. Roughly speaking, Getting includes the following kinds of actions:

- Retrieving the current stored value of u.s

- Carrying out some inference to find the value of u.s

- Checking whether or not some item is an entry on u.s.

  A few important "extreme cases" of this are:

- Retrieving all at once all the slots/values of u (this is currently trivial in CycL, because of the way units are stored internally)

- Checking whether u.s is empty. This is not handled separately in CycL at present — that is, one does (NOT (Get . . . . u s)) — but it might one day be considered worth optimizing.

- There are CycL functions for getting other attributes, such as

  - The justifications for the entries in u.s

  - The entries that get inherited to the value of u.s

  - The beliefs other agents hold about the value of u.s

  - The units that have some value for the slot s

  - The units that have the same value as u for slot s

  Roughly speaking, Putting includes the following kinds of actions:

- Adding or removing an entry on u.s (changing the certainty of u.s.v1)

- Propagating the aftereffects of those changes throughout the KB

- Adding and/or removing several entries "in parallel" on u.s (meaning that the propagation of the effects of the net change are carried out simultaneously)

  A few important "extreme cases" of this are:

- Creating a new unit

- Obliterating a unit

- Renaming a unit

- Asserting a rule

CycL is organized into a number of language levels, each designating a level of complexity greater than the previous level. Each level can have its own Getting functions; (Get8 u s) might do much more work than (Get0 u s) would in searching for entries of u.s. What does "more work" mean? Each higher-numbered level allows some additional CycL features to be used. Get6, for instance, will invoke backward inheritance templates, whereas Get0 never will.

As we said earlier in this book (in Section 2.3.5), the different Get levels and the features they use are as follows (don't worry about the numbers; they're historical):

Get0 — Simply access the data structure (forward rules)

Get4 — Try some of the simpler, faster CycL inference mechanisms: toCompute, genlSlots, and temporary backward inheritance

Get6 — Try the above, plus the more costly CycL inference mechanisms: slotValueSubsumes, classification, slotConstraints, structures, and full backward inheritance

Get8 — Try even the unsound, plausible guessing mechanisms, such as determinations, constraint-resolving, and closed-world assuming

In every case, the user (or calling program) must decide which level of Get function is appropriate. That decision is based on factors such as:

• The amount of resources available (if you have to make a guess right away, don't expend a lot of time on minor sub-sub-sub-tasks)

• The CycL features that might want to "run" when you do this kind of operation to u.s. (some of them are likely to be slow, or unsure, or might disturb parts of the KB you aren't willing to "touch" now . . .)

What are the "CycL features"? They are the couple dozen different inference mechanisms available in CycL: inverse slots, genlSlots, toCompute, slotConstraints, rules, inContextVersions, inheritance, automatic classification, and so on, as described in Section 3.3.

To reiterate: each of the various CycL features (such as backward inheritance) are only performed at and above a certain CycL language level. (In the case of backward inheritance, by the way, it's level 6.) Therefore, the user can choose from many levels of Getting functions. For reasons we'll see below, there is only a single level of Putting functions.

3.4.2. Putting. Most of the Putting operations involve asserting some entries on u.s. Each entry on u.s has a number of sources (justifications), each with its own certainty factor. When adding an entry x to u.s, we may specify the truth value (IV) with which we are asserting u.s.x. If it is not specified, CycL will access the default truth value for s and will take that to be the truth value of u.s.x.

Although each entry may have a source, the user may *not* specify the source. This is not a restriction, really, just a sort of safeguard, because the user should never want or need to specify the source of u.s.x. Why is that? The default source for u.s.x is u.s — that is, the default is that it is *local,* that the x term originates at the slot value u.s where it was placed. For u.s.x to have anything other than this as its source would say "this entry was inferred from somewhere else, by some CycL inference mechanism." And all such statements are generated automatically by those inference mechanisms; they should never be "forged" by hand. What the user *can* do is to cause some particular inference mechanism to be invoked, and then *it* will make the proper bookkeeping notations as to the source of the entries it propagates.

Similarly, users may "really" remove only local entries. If they want to remove u.s.x, and it's not local, they have three options:

- Option #1 is to add a new local u.s.x entry, with a TV that is "Unknown". Because local justification terms always override non-local justification terms, the resultant TV of u.s.x will be Unknown. This is treated the same by CycL as "the entry is simply absent from u.s — we have no evidence in favor of its being there or against its being there, any more/less than any random legal entry's being there."

- Option #2 is to go to the rule R that asserted the u.s.x entry, examine what it says, and try to decide why it's wrongly placing x on u.s. Then alter the rule R that led to u.s.x, or alter the "triggering entries" elsewhere in the KB that allowed that template to "fire" in this case. As a result, u.s.x will be automatically retracted by CycL.

- Option #3 is to add some new inference rule (inheritance, etc.) and/or some additional entries on various slots of various units, so that some negative evidence is concluded about u.s.x. Or assert a new rule R' that concludes u.s.x with TV Unknown and assert R'.overrides.R.

Option #1 should be used if the absence of u.s.x is just a special case, a hard-to-explain exception to a general rule that is worth keeping around just the way it's currently stated. Option #2 should be used if CycL never should have even *dreamed* of asserting u.s.x — that is, if the inference path it used is simply broken somehow. Option #3 should be used if asserting u.s.x is superficially plausible, but common sense would lead us to realize that there are extenuating circumstances in this case and u.s.x shouldn't really be there.

Unlike the Getting operations, all the Putting operations *that the user may invoke* take place at only one "level." The system decides internally which internal level of Putting is appropriate.

3.4.3. Why "Putting Levels" are Invisible to the User (Optional).

Okay, why *shouldn't* the user decide which Putting "level" to invoke? As explained earlier, the reason for having many *Get* levels is to allow the user to give a coarse resource level specification. It does not usually matter to later Getting/Putting operations whether that previous query was done using a low Get level or a high Get level. But this is not true for the various operations carried out as soon as u.s.x is asserted; they are *propagations* upon which later operations could critically depend. Consider the automatic maintenance of inverses. If we say Fred.children.Bobby, and children has an inverse slot, parents, then the "choice" of whether or not to bother asserting Bobby.parents.Fred is no "choice" at all — CycL must do it. If, later, you ask for Bobby's parents, CycL will assume that it's not worth scouring the whole KB looking for units whose children include Bobby, because all such entries would have immediately propagated entries onto Bobby.parents. CycL must be able to make these assumptions, or else every inference becomes staggeringly time-consuming. Again, this all comes down to an economic, not a "theoretical," argument: some operations (like the maintenance of inverses) have a branching factor of 1 in the forward direction and zillions (okay, five billion in the case of Bobby.parents) in the backward direction. So it's a negligible cost to do the propagation at Putting time, and a vast cost to do it instead at Getting time. This same sort of argument extends to most of the CycL features; it's proven to be always better to let CycL decide for itself what propagations to do when a Putting operation occurs.

Warning

The remainder of this subsection, even more than what you've read so far, is full of very low-level details and is, therefore, optional reading.

One interesting issue is: how does CycL quickly decide, in each case, what those propagating operations are? That is, which operations should it even *consider* executing when u.s.x is asserted? Well, it could use its various inference mechanisms to dynamically *infer* which operations to carry out, and to decide which mechanism to use it could recursively use its various inference mechanisms . . . yes, that could get awfully slow. Instead, we adopted the following policy:
The operations that should be done are cached on the unit s.

Let's assume that somewhere in the KB is a fact that would imply that we might need to perform an operation (OP) when an assertion about a unit's s slot occurs. Then, on s.level4PutFeatures, CycL stores some information that tells it to do just that. There is an assumption here that it is sufficient to characterize "the set of features to be considered when u.s changes" as a function of s. Though we might possibly get an even better guess at this set of features by considering u too, the evaluation and caching of this information itself could consume a lot of time and space. Therefore, we consider only s, not u, when obtaining this set of features.

As an example, consider the following kind of slot: biologicalFather. On biologicalFather.level4PutFeatures we find this list of OPs:

```
(#%InverseMaintenance
#%RemoveRedundantRemoteEntriesForSingleEntry
#%ToComputeExpressionDependency
#%SimpleInheritancePropagation
#%HigherLevelsTMS)
```

Because biologicalFather.inverse exists, InverseMaintenance should certainly be done any time anybody adds or removes entries (or alters some of the CFs) on any unit's biologicalFather slot.

Because everyone has but a single biologicalFather, biologicalFather.entryFormat is SingleEntry. Because of *that*, RemoveRedundantRemoteEntriesForSingleEntry is one of the OPs that should be done whenever any unit's biologicalFather slot is altered.

Because Cyc is told that biologicalParents are the union of biologicalFather and biologicalMother, then u.biologicalParents should be updated to reflect alterations in either u.biologicalFather or u.biologicalMother. Therefore, CycL records ToComputeExpressionDependency as one of the OPs in biologicalFather.level4PutFeatures (and also, of course, in biologicalMother.level4PutFeatures).

Hair color, eye color, skin color, race, height, blood type, tendencyToBaldness, and many other attributes are inherited (both biologically and in CycL terms!) from a person's biological father. If you find out who Fred's biologicalFather is, for example, you can make a whole class of new guesses about his physical attributes, and vice versa. Therefore, because such "simple inheritance" links exist, SimpleInheritancePropagation is one of the OPs that has to be performed whenever we find out something about somebody's biologicalFather.

Because biologicalFather is used in a complex backward inference (a backward inference using the constraint language), and because there could be *other* inferences I, J, K . . . that depend on u.biologicalFather, as soon as u.biologicalFather changes, this assertion's support for (justification of) those conclusions I, J, K . . . has to be retracted. (The sd-implications field of u.s points to these conclusions.) This automatic retracting is handled by the feature HigherLevelsTMS, which is why it's one of the OPs that appear on biologicalFather.level4PutFeatures.

Okay, now here's the good news: you, the user, never need to worry about these things! When you give biologicalFather an inverse slot, CycL will, all by itself, place InverseMaintenance as one of the OPs in biologicalFather.level4PutFeatures. When you give biologicalParents its toCompute slot, and that involves biologicalFather, then, again, CycL automatically places ToComputeExpressionDependency as one of the OPs in biologicalFather.level4PutFeatures. And so on. So you should never place an entry manually in any slot's level4PutFeatures. That's why this subsection was labeled "optional." That's really good news, because if you had to manually choose the OPs to place into each new slot's level4PutFeatures, you'd be selecting from quite a long list: at present, CycL has about 29 different types of OPs and 137 problem-solving-related task-types.

In case you wondered why the slot is called level4PutFeatures, that's a carryover from earlier days, when (a) Putting operations had level numbers on them, as Getting functions still do, (b) Putting operations were really called Put (that is, Put0, Put2, Put4, Put6), and (c) most of the CycL features "kicked in" all at once at level 4.

By the way, biologicalFather.level4PutFeatures contains one single entry, which is the *ordered list* of OPs to carry out whenever a biologicalFather slot is altered. The order in which the OPs are listed is the order in which they should be executed; this order is carefully chosen by CycL (using information on the slots precedingFeatures and followingFeatures on the units corresponding to the OPs). There is a partial ordering among the various kinds of possible OPs, so that they won't "interfere" with each other, and CycL embeds this in a linear ordering as needed for each slot.

The problem with the OPs scheme we've discussed so far is that the operations to be performed when u.s.x gets asserted/removed/modified are purely a function of the slot s, and all other state variables are ignored. A later subsection tells how to obtain more control over this process. Only time will tell how rarely or frequently such finer-grained control is necessary.

In addition to operations that specifically alter some particular u.s (In . . . and Out . . .), there are a number of less widely used Putting operations. The names of these functions, and the list and meaning of their arguments, are given out to users of Cyc. Here is what one important class of such operations does:

make-complete-instance-of. *This function creates a brand new instance of a class, along with its parts, and also asserts the appropriate relations between those parts. We can also specify the depth of the instantiation — that is, we can indicate whether we want to create the units corresponding to the parts of the parts, etc.*

3.4.4. Getting. There are currently two basic types of Getting operations: Get . . . functions that find the value of u.s (that is, that return a list of its entries), and Mem . . . functions that find out whether some given entry is or is not on u.s. Obviously, the latter kind of operation could, in many cases, be significantly faster and easier than the former.

As you might expect, there are extra arguments that can be passed to these Get . . . and Mem . . . functions that indicate:

- What TV range of entries is desired

- Which "field" of u.s or u.s.x to get (for example, justifications or TVs). (The default is the value field — the list of entries. Generally, in the current CycL, there are completely separate Getting functions for each field, because it is easier for humans to write — and read — separate Getting functions than it is to supply an extra "field" argument to a single Getting function.)

- What "filters" (constraints) the entries must pass in order for them to get collected into the final value returned. For example, suppose we wanted to get the set of those U.S. presidents whose first names were John; we could do

```
(Get6 #%USA #%presidents
      '(:satisfying-constraint (#%firstName
        u "John")))
```

The CycL inference features that are tried by (Get4 u s) are those listed on s.level4GetFeatures. Similarly, (Get6 u s) would try all the features listed on s.level6GetFeatures, and so on.

The Mem . . . operations work slightly differently. Mem6 first tries Mem4, which first tries Mem2, which first tries Mem0. If the lower-level Mem . . . operation fails, then the higher-level Mem . . . operation tries out the features that become available to Mem . . . at that language level.

As in the case of the level4PutFeatures, all the level*n*GetFeatures slots are maintained automatically by the system.

In addition to the Get . . . and Mem . . . query operations, there are dozens of less widely used query operations. Here is what three important classes of such operations do:

- *Units-having*: This class of operations covers the following queries:

  - Finding all the units having some value for a given slot

  - Finding *n* units having some value for a given slot

  - Finding units having some set as a subset of their value for some given slot

- *Units-satisfying*: This class of operations covers the following sort of query: given a constraint C(u), where there is one and only one unscoped variable, u, find the set of units (currently in the KB) that satisfy this constraint

- *Find-similar-units*: Each of these operations is a specialized (but often useful) form of *units-satisfying*. The idea here is to locate units similar to u. The "constraint" would be nightmarish to write out in detail. Instead, we may specify a set of slots to consider in the match (find-units-matching-on-slots) or we may not specify any slots (find-subsumed-units, find-similar-units). The first method specifies whether to try for perfect matching or imperfect matching up to some match-factor (a number in [0,1], representing the fraction of entries in common); the other method specifies the conditions that must be satisfied by the units found (for example, find-similar-entities).

3.4.5. The Agenda — Control Over the Inference — The Metalevel.   Knowledge in the KB should drive, or at least strongly affect, the inference process that CycL goes through in trying to solve a problem (for example, trying to get the value of u.s). In 3.4.3 and 3.4.4, we saw how the sequence of actions tried by CycL is influenced by slots such as level4GetFeatures. In this section, we'll see how to obtain even greater metalevel control (that is, reasoning about, and control over, the inference process) by using the *CycL agenda mechanism*.

Think of the CycL agenda mechanism as a simple scheduler: it has a priority-ordered queue of "Tasks," and its basic action is — over and over again — find the first task on the queue that satisfies a set of given conditions and "execute" it (work on it for a while).

So let's examine what we mean by a "task" and what it means to "execute" a task, and let's see what the selection "conditions" mentioned here are all about.

3.4.5.1. WHAT IS A TASK?

A *task* is a script that can be performed by the system. Each kind of task must be an instance not just of Script (= EventType), but of a much more restrictive collection: ProblemSolvingType. Moreover, it must be a spec of SolvingAProblem. Given the system's current lack of robotic sensors/effectors, it is pretty much restricted to tasks that (try to) carry out some sort of computational procedure. So, for example, FindingPrimeNumbers is something it might be able to do, or PlanningACircumnavigationRoute, but not CircumnavigatingTheGlobe (at least, not until it gets lots of additional peripherals!).

3.4.5.2. WHAT DOES IT MEAN TO EXECUTE A TASK?

Every task may have a slot called howToRunTask. The entry of this slot, if it exists, must be a Lisp function of one argument. "Executing task X" is equivalent to running the X.howToRunTask. function with X as its argument. CycL places the result of executing X on X.problemSolution. Most tasks don't have their own special howToRunTask function, of course — if they did, they wouldn't need to take X as an argument! Rather, a few broadly applicable "interpreters" end up filling most of the howToRunTask slots. The most general of these, the *default executrix*, is a function that does the following:

1. Check to see if task X is *primitive*. That is, *can* and *should* it be carried out just by calling a known Lisp function? To test whether it *can* be carried out that simply, the executrix looks at X.lispFunctionToUse. If there's anything there, it'll be such a Lisp function. That function should be capable of executing the task all by itself — though possibly in a brute-force fashion. The executrix *could* just call it, with argument X. But *should* it, or is there some extenuating circumstance? Before running that function, the default executrix examines the slot X.expandTask?, to see if it's T or NIL. If it's NIL, the executrix just runs X.lispFunctionToUse and returns the result.

2. If the task does not have subtasks, and the executrix has never tried to find subtasks for it, then it tries to do so now, and it records, on X.taskStatus, whatever progress is made. In more detail, CycL does the following:

    2a. If there is a special means of finding the subtasks — that is, if there is some value for X.howToFindSubTasks — this slot is used; else

    2b. If X.structure exists, the structure is instantiated for X; else

    2c. Call (Get6 X #%subTasks). If this returns NIL, then

2d. Create a new task X′ and put it on the agenda; X′ will try to find subtasks for task X. Also, assert X.tasksToBePerformedBefore.X′. This causes the current task X to be "suspended" until X′ finishes.

3. If an attempt has been made to get the subtasks, but there are still no subtasks, then things are looking sort of bleak. At this stage, if there is a lispFunctionToUse, the executrix will use it even if the X.expandTask? is NIL. If there is no X.lispFunctionToUse, it will report failure and exit.

4. If there *are* subtasks, and X is being executed again, that must mean that an appropriate set of its subtasks have been completed. That is, X is being executed again so as to allow it to combine the results of the subtasks (that is, to compute the value of X.problemSolution). The information regarding how to combine the results from the subtasks can be provided in the following ways:

   4a. X.howToCombineSubtasks exists. If so, it contains an instance of HowToCombineSubtasksExpression, which represents (and contains on its constraintExpression slot) an expression in the constraint language (which refers to the task as "u"). So these constraint expressions are evaluated, with u bound to the task (in our case, X), and the value of this expression is returned as the "value" of X. (Recall that X might be a task trying to get some unit/slot value.)

   4b. Any of the other CycL inference mechanisms (such as genlSlots, slotValueSubsumes, inheritance, . . .) can be employed to infer X.problemSolution from known slots of the subTasks of X. For example, if X.structure is known, the structure description scheme can be used to relate the values of the slot problemSolution to X and its subtasks.

   Once step 4a or 4b is finished, the executrix (part of CycL) records the fact that X is complete by asserting X.taskStatus.TaskComplete. It then exits.

5. If you get to this stage, you are in pretty bad shape, and there's probably not much that the system can do. Perhaps someone hit an ABORT during the running of the combining function? The executrix just passes over the task for now and hopes for the best. Maybe one of the "eternal" tasks on the agenda should keep an eye out for tasks that seem to be perpetually suspended in this fashion, and should try to take more radical action on them.

3.4.5.3.
CONDITIONS FOR
CHOOSING THE
NEXT TASK TO
WORK ON

The above five steps explain how CycL executes a task X that's been chosen. But how did X get chosen? What are the conditions under which a task X gets to be the next one executed? The following two criteria are applied:

- X must be *executable*.
- There must be no executable task that is *preferred* to X.

For a task X to be *executable*, it has to meet all three of these criteria:

- The task is not yet complete. That is, X.taskStatus does *not* contain the entry TaskCompleted.

- There is no reason *not* to run the task. This is determined by examining X.taskNonExecutabilityPredicate. Does it have some entries? If so, they represent constraints that had better not be true (or else this task is nonexecutable). Each entry will be an instance of ProblemTaskExecutabilityPredicate; more specifically, it will have a constraintExpression slot filled with a constraint expression having the single free variable u. If any of these constraints hold (when u is bound to the task — in our case, X), the task is considered to be nonexecutable. There are a number of default entries for this slot. For instance, one default reason not to run a task is that there aren't enough resources — that is, if X.resourcesUsed is larger than X.resourcesAllocated. Another reason not to execute a task is if any of the entries of the slot tasksToBePerformedBefore is not complete.

- There *is* some reason to run the task. How is that determined? Look at X.taskExecutabilityPredicate. Are there some entries there? If so, each one of them is a predicate; just check to see if *any* of them is true. (By the way, those predicates must all be units that are instances of ProblemTaskExecutabilityPredicate.) Some high-level default entries exist for this slot. For example, there is one that says that if no attempt has been made to run a task, it is executable. Another default is "X has subtasks, and they're all now complete."

When is one task X *preferred* to another task Y? When either:

- Y.morePreferredTasks.X, or
- Neither X nor Y is listed on the other's morePreferredTasks slot, and X.taskPriority is greater than Y.taskPriority.

Incidentally, because there is an explicit unit representing each task X, any of the CycL features (inheritance, classification, etc.) can be used to infer entries on slots on those "task units." That is, a number of slots on the tasks, such as taskGoals, can be used to infer entries on some of the important slots of X, such as taskPriority and morePreferredTasks — those slots are important because the CycL agenda uses them (as described above) to decide what to do next. It is also possible for inferences to be drawn from nontask units to slots on task units. So, if Fred is the user who posted task T83, and Fred is currently late for an important meeting, then perhaps we'll give him a break and increase T83.taskPriority a little bit.

Because there is no real distinction between "inferences aimed at concluding stuff about MikeDukakis" and "inferences aimed at concluding facts about the task units," *all of the inference features available in CycL can be used to control the agenda.* Well, this has to bottom out somewhere. What about the inferencing required to find out the values of the slots morePreferredTasks? In principle, these could again make use of the agenda. In practice, this is almost never done. However, when this *is* done, CycL does not use the same agenda — rather, it spawns off a new agenda, runs that to completion (until that agenda becomes empty), and then uses the value returned by that agenda as the value of X.morePreferredTasks. (That value helps to run the original agenda.)

Also, it is not necessary that all the *subtasks* spawned by task X on agenda A be run by agenda A! In principle, there can be a large number of more or less permanent agendas — for example, one for each machine that's networked to a single knowledge server. In that case, each machine would know about all the machines' agendas (and all the tasks on all the agendas). Even though a machine would usually work on its own agenda's tasks, any one agenda could pick a task of any other agenda and choose to run it (for example, if its own agenda was empty). At least one of the other machines would then be grateful! This is the scheme we are using among the Cyc group's Lisp machines at MCC, by the way. As you might expect, a number of meta-metalevel tasks sit on agendas and decide how to share the load between different agenda.

The CycL function that "runs" an agenda is called run-cyc-agenda. Given an agenda unit A (a Cyc unit representing an agenda), several instances of this function could be running A simultaneously. The value of the variable *agenda-unit-for-this-machine* is bound to the agenda A being run when a task is being executed. This means that one of the tasks could do a Get6, which might need an agenda, which would result in Get6 "taking over" this agenda, running it, and then exiting (that is, returning control to the previous call of run-cyc-agenda).

However, these features are (typically) used only when the agenda is used to carry various introspective tasks — tasks that are potentially very time-consuming.

Having presented a rough idea of what the agenda is all about, we're ready to illustrate how it can be used to exercise control over CycL's inferencing.

3.4.6. Metalevel Guidance of CycL Inferencing.

Suppose we have represented in CycL the full computational procedure involved in the different CycL inference templates (inverse slots, genlSlots, refinements, horn rules, inContextVersions, slotized constraints, inheritance, automatic classification, and so on). Essentially, this would mean describing the various subtasks (steps) in each inference procedure, relating the subtasks, specifying their order of execution, etc. Of course, at some point in this representation of the inference procedures, we would be able to go no deeper and would have to "bottom out": some of the tasks would have a lispFunctionToRun slot instead of having a list of further subtasks.

Once we have done this, invoking a CycL inference procedure would be equivalent to executing the task corresponding to that inference procedure. During the execution of that task, there are going to be certain "opportunistic" decision steps that take into account the fact that, although from a logical soundness perspective it does not matter which path is taken, from the perspective of computational efficiency, choosing certain paths could be enormously preferred.

Metalevel inference could be defined as inference directed at choosing preferred paths in precisely these conditions. In general, metalevel inference would make its choices by drawing upon knowledge the system already has. If we were really executing our inference procedure by running these tasks, the order (and, hence, speed) of execution would be heavily influenced by such "relevant" knowledge in the KB. That knowledge enables the task to be performed more efficiently. This information could be called metalevel information. But notice that it is also "object level" information — it's used for lots of different purposes, presumably, and it just so happens that it sometimes also helps with metalevel control. (E.g., Fred is late for his meeting.)

In order to exercise control over an inference procedure (say inheritance), it is not imperative (though it would be nice) to have that inference mechanism *completely* represented. If we are interested only in the "short-term speed-up" benefits of intelligently guided inferencing, then we need not represent the parts of the inference process in which no intelligence can be exercised, no hard choices need to be made. Such subprocedures can be coded as lumps of Lisp code. (But don't say we didn't warn you about the long-term paucity of a system that can't fully introspect.) What we're saying here is that it is *sufficient* (a) to represent just the decision steps with the "opportunistic" property mentioned earlier (that is, decision steps such that, although all the paths are logically sound, some are preferred from the standpoint of computational efficiency); and (b) to write the different relations affecting those steps.

The representation of these inference procedures is somewhat influenced by the structure and nature of their interpreter, which is the agenda. How and why? The agenda's flow of control is determined by the values of various slots on various units — for example, by the morePreferredTasks slots sitting on the various tasks on the agenda. Hence, to represent the flow of control, we write rules, inheritances, etc., for such slots.

3.4.7. Metalevel Control in Getting.

Each type of Getting function (Get . . . , Mem . . .) has a corresponding task type. Suppose you call (Get6 Fred diagnosis). It might be a task that runs quickly and returns a value, or it might take a huge amount of time, or there might be a large number of paths to search.

In those latter cases, a best-first (agenda-based) search might be useful. CycL decides whether this is likely to be the case, and, if it is, it not only executes (Get6 Fred diagnosis) but also adds a task — let's call it T1 — to the agenda. T1 will try to find Fred.diagnosis. In the course of the execution of this task, new tasks T11, T12, T13, . . . , T1n are created, corresponding to the n different features that might be tried for obtaining the slot value. Each of these will be recorded on T1.subTasks. E.g., T14 might be GetFred.diagnosisByInheritance.

If we were just to execute all these different subtasks, one after another, exhaustively (until each one finished), there could be no win, because that's exactly what CycL would have done if it had just executed the Get6 in the non-agenda-based fashion to begin with! The potentially big improvement would be if we had some rules that (based on the slot and unit being considered) helped give us a preference ordering of these subtasks or helped rule out certain orderings.

How do we write these rules? Well, this is syntactically no different from writing rules at the base level — rules about Swimming and ApplePie and nextPresident. It's just that, instead of writing "rules" that tell us how to find the value of the slot nextPresident for a country, we're writing "rules" that deal with slots of tasks — slots such as lessPreferredTasks, morePreferredTasks, expectedRunningTime, expectedNumberOfQueriesToTheUser, maxAmtOfStorageConsumed, etc. (By "rule," we mean all the various inference schemes in CycL).

But now we have just generated a whole bunch of additional Getting tasks, such as (Get4 T11 morePreferredTasks). These in turn might be set up as tasks on the agenda! So isn't there an infinite recursion here? No; even though we could, in principle, invoke the metalevel (agenda) to help with those tasks, in practice it's almost never worth doing. So the chance of recurring two levels is very very small; the chance of recurring three levels is very very very small, etc.

The careful reader will have observed that there is one generated task T1*a* for which the default interpreter *does* use the metalevel itself. This is the task of determining the subtasks for T1. (This particular kind of task, in turn, has an interpreter that *doesn't* use the metalevel to decide *its* subtasks.)

3.4.8.   An Example of Metalevel Information.   Let's consider a simple example of how we'd represent some metalevel piece of information about some simple inference. Suppose our goal is to see whether or not Fred.acquaintances.Joe — that is, to see whether or not Joe is one of Fred's acquaintances.

We look at acquaintances.slotValueSubsumes and find several different expressions, all of which will (when evaluated) generate entries for u.acquaintances:

1. (u relatives)

2. (u coWorkers)

3. (TheSetOf x (Person #%allInstances) (sendsChristmasCardsTo x u))

4. (u houseMates)

5. (u valet)

.

.

.

So, we could plug in "Fred" for "u" in those expressions, evaluate them, and keep doing that right down the line until either Joe appeared or we exhausted the list of expressions. But to just go through them in some random order (say 1, 2, 3, 4, 5) could be terribly inefficient; for example, expression 3 might take hours to evaluate, whereas 4 and 5 would be almost instantaneous. Surely we ought to try the quick methods before the slow ones, don't you think?

That's the "rule" that we wish to encode. That is, the metalevel piece of knowledge we want to add is:

"Try the simpler expressions before the harder expressions."

So, for example, the third acquaintances.slotValueSubsumes entry should be the last one we try to evaluate, because it maps through all people in the KB!

To make all this more precise, let's assume that Fred.inheritedSlotConstraints contains five entries — the units U1 . . . U5. Each U*i* would have acquaintances as its slotConstrained, and its slotValueSubsumes slots would contain the five constraint expressions above. Each U*i* has a slot called simplerRules, which would list some others of the U*i*. So, for example,

U1.simplerRules = (U4 U5)
U3.simplerRules = (U1 U2 U4 U5)
U5.simplerRules = ( )
and so on.

We create a task type TT1 corresponding to "finding whether or not u.s.v1 using slotValueSubsumes rules," and we create an instance of TT1, t1, which corresponds to "finding whether or not Fred.acquaintances.Joe using slotValueSubsumes rules." The five t1.subTasks (let's call them t11, t12, . . . t15) would correspond to "applying the single slotValueSubsumes rule U1 with u = Fred to see whether or not Joe is one of the values," plus the same sort of task for U2, . . . , U5.

Each of these subtask units would be an instance of the following task type (TT2): "Applying a single slotValueSubsumes rule," which in turn is a spec of (TT3): "Applying a single inference template."

In order to indicate that we prefer simpler rules, we inherit:

```
TT3
  specs: (TT2)
  allInstances: (t11 t12 t13 ...)
    inheritedSlotConstraints: (SC93 ...)

SC93
  slotsConstrained: (taskPreferred)
  toTestExpression: ((#%simplerRule
    (u #%ruleBeingApplied)
    (v1 #%ruleBeingApplied)))
```

This constraint, SC93, would get inherited to the subtasks of the task t1 — that is, to t11, t12, . . . t15, which in turn would cause the simpler t1.subTasks to be preferred to (hence executed before) the less simple ones. Thus, t13 (the least simple one) would be performed last.

(We should probably mention that you shouldn't have to explicitly add all the simplerRule entries — you have a task on the agenda for computing them.)

3.4.9. Metalevel Control of Mem . . .

When running a task for (Get6 Fred diagnosis), we wanted to explore every means of getting the slot value, *because they might all contribute some entries*. But consider the Mem . . . class of operations; for example, suppose we were doing (Mem6 Fred diagnosis Measles). Here the situation is different; we'd like to stop searching if *any* of the schemes we try succeeds.

The example in this subsection will show part of the declarative "definition" of Memming; to wit, the following metalevel piece of knowledge that it contains:

> "*As soon as one inferencing operation* (whose goal is the same as the original Mem) *succeeds, you can stop!*"

In such a situation, the overall task has succeeded, and hence must be run again, so it will "record," and "react" to, its success. In the case of the previous example, task t1 can stop as soon as any one of the five slotValueSubsumes entries succeeds in producing Joe.

How can that piece of metalevel knowledge be represented in CycL? On the executability conditions for Mem, we state an expression that says "one of the subtasks (having the same goals as the original Memming operation) has succeeded." When that expression is satisfied, the original task should be rerun, because it will also have succeeded.

There is another general metalevel heuristic that says that "a task is preferred to all of its subtasks." Thus, as soon as the previous paragraph's "rule" fires successfully, the original Mem task will be run again, and it will report success and exit.

3.4.10. CycL Syntax for Invoking the Agenda.

Now, what are the magic words to be uttered to get CycL to use the metalevel in order to answer a query such as (Get6 u s)?

The flow of control in answering this query is as follows: the first thing Get6 does is to determine whether or not it should run "directly" or "through the agenda." If it is determined that this query is one that should make use of the agenda, an instance of the task-type corresponding to Get6 is created and placed on the agenda, and it will eventually run. As soon as the result is obtained, it is returned to the caller.

So we still have to tell you two things: how to tell Get6 to use the agenda (or not to use it) and how does CycL figure out what task type corresponds to Get6?

3.4.10.1.
DETERMINING
WHETHER TO USE
THE AGENDA

How does Get6 determine whether it should run through the agenda? Let's suppose the actual "function call" was (Get6 Fred diagnosis). (For the moment, we'll assume that CycL already knows that GetSlotValueUsingGet6 is the unit representing "Using the Get6 methods to get some u.s." See section 3.4.10.2 for an explanation of how it knows this.)

To see whether or not to use the agenda, CycL funcalls the function that is bound to the global variable *possibly-use-agenda?*. The *default* value of this variable is a function that:

1. Gets the entry F on
   GetSlotValueUsingGet6.whenToUseAgendaFunction

2. Ensures that F is a valid Lisp function

3. Funcalls F with the task type (that is, GetSlotValueUsingGet6) as the first argument and the arguments to Get6 (in this case, #%Fred and #%diagnosis) as the other arguments

This function F could have been either handwritten or synthesized automatically by CycL from the expression E on GetSlotValueUsingGet6.whenToUseAgendaExpression. This expression E may refer to the task unit freely, using the variable "u." Here u refers to the unit that will be created to do the Get6. That is, u is to be a new unit that will represent a particular one-time-only task, namely this call on (Get6 Fred diagnosis).

Warning

Most readers should now just skip down to section 3.4.11 — or at least to section 3.4.10.2. The bottom line of this section is that CycL might not be able to *perfectly* translate E into F.

In principle, E could refer to any slot of this task unit u. Now here's the problem. The whole point of evaluating E is to see whether or not to use the agenda to tackle (Get6 Fred diagnosis) — that is, *whether or not to go to the trouble to make u exist!* So how can E be evaluated if it refers to u and has subexpressions like (u expectedRunningTime)?

The solution is a bit of a kludge. What CycL does is to preprocess each kind of Getting function — such as Get6 — so as to produce a snazzy Lisp function for that type of Getting; it then stores it on the whenToUseAgendaFunction slot of (in this case) GetSlotValueUsingGet6. How is this preprocessing or "compiling" done?

In essence: for each reference to some slot of u — say (u #%expectedRunningTime) — we will find some way to calculate or estimate the value of this slot of u if it were to exist. In some cases, such as (u #%unitForWhichToFindSlotValue), this is easy to evaluate "in closed form" — its value is just #%Fred. Similarly, (u #%slotForWhichToFindValue) would be replaced by #%diagnosis. In other cases, the "simulated evaluation" or "compilation" would not be so easy to do; in those cases, CycL temporarily (just during this "compilation" phase) allows a hypothetical instance of GetSlotValueUsingGet6 to flicker into existence.

3.4.10.2.
IDENTIFYING THE
TASK TYPE
CORRESPONDING
TO THE QUERY

How does Get6 know that GetSlotValueUsingGet6 is the task type corresponding to Get6? When we define the Lisp function GET6, we do it not by using DEFUN but rather by using a special macro called DEFINE-AGENDA-FUNCTION. Part of this definition involves specifying the task type, the relationship between the arguments of the function and the slots on an instance of the task type, etc. In principle, all the functions in which we might want to break away into the agenda will be defined using this macro. Note — this is *not* the way we define all the functions in CycL, because only a small number of these functions are such that metalevel information can be used for them.

3.4.11. Metalevel Control in Putting.   Before explaining how the metalevel might be used to guide the Putting process, let us first see how CycL behaves when no attempt is made to exert any kind of control over the Putting process. The control structure in that case is as follows:

Assume that the operation being done (either by the user or by some CycL function) involves a set of simultaneous insertions and deletions from u.s. Let's call the inserted entries x1i and the deleted entries x2j.

The first thing CycL does is to make the actual stated changes to the s slot of the unit u. That is, the x1i get inserted and the x2j get deleted. This is done by calling some level 0 Putting functions.

At this point, CycL calls the function execute-features, which is responsible for all the forward propagation that needs to be done based on the changed entries — that is, based on all the x1i and x2j. How does execute-features work? It looks at s.level4PutFeatures and, for each of those features OP, in the order in which they occur, the OP.lispFunctionToRun is funcalled with a standard set of arguments. These features are units representing classes of operations. Some of these features are things such as maintaining inverses, propagating genlSlot relations, and firing forward rules.

Now where does the issue of control come in? Basically, the operation over which we wish to exercise control is this forward propagation; that is, the change will have something to do with the way the function execute-features works.

In order to exert some metalevel guidance, we must have some means by which we can talk about the act of performing these different features — that is, the act of carrying out these various propagation operations. To this end, we have a unit explicitly represent the task of executing features. Its subtasks can then be things such as the handling of forward rules, inheritance, etc. These in turn can have subtasks, such as the firing of individual "rules." Now, because the tasks of executing features (and its subtasks) are going to be tasks on the agenda, we can exercise control over what gets executed by the agenda by controlling the task parameters the agenda looks at: the executability of tasks, the preference, etc. Doing this is straightforward, because these tasks are first-class objects, just like MickeyMouse or GeorgeBush. All we do is write "rules" that apply to these tasks. (Again, by "rules" we mean any of the two dozen inference templates available in CycL.)

As you have probably realized, having explicit units corresponding to all these different tasks could potentially add a large overhead to the inference process. Therefore, we would like to provide another piece of metalevel control information: a predicate (or heuristic) for deciding when it might be cost-effective to actually try using the metalevel. Could this be done by stating an inference rule for the slot expandTask?

This would still require CycL to create a unit for each occurrence of execute-features. The way in which we avoid even *this* expense is by using the variable *meta-level-activation-predicate*. This variable should be bound to a function F. F is funcalled for every OP we are trying to execute — that is, for each entry on s.level4PutFeatures. In each case, if it returns a non-NIL value, the task unit corresponding to that specific sort of inference feature is instantiated and placed on an agenda, and the agenda is run. Some possible entries for s.level4PutFeatures are #%ToComputeDependency, #%SimpleInheritancePropagation, and #%UpdateGenlSlots.

The actual control that can be exerted over the inferencing in Putting is less than the control that can be exerted over the Getting. This is because there is a set of operations that must always be carried for overall KB consistency and such. After all, you can't just "choose not to maintain inverse slots" sometimes. Moreover, you can't even "choose to maintain inverses after maintaining inheritance." The order in which these operations may be performed is highly restricted. So the main reason one might want to exert control over the Putting is not to exert control over things the normal Putting would have done, but to do additional things. For example, for some backward rules, you might like to provide a condition under which, when it holds, the rules are forward propagated. (Say, the condition that Cyc's future funding is at stake in this instance.)

3.5. Neats versus Scruffies: A Digression

Before moving on, we'd like to make a brief digression into an issue of the philosophy and methodology of AI. The basic hypothesis behind symbolic AI is that it is possible to simulate intelligence in a particular "world" by manipulating a set of symbols that represent that "world."

One approach is to pick a particular task domain and then solve the problem by doing the following in that "microworld":

1. Define the appropriate symbol-manipulation techniques

2. Build an adequate symbol set for representing that tiny "world"

The opposite approach is to try to be completely domain-independent, to find some general-purpose reasoning mechanism and build a reasoner that uses it, independent of any starting set of knowledge.

We believe that neither of these extremes is what's needed. On the one hand, formal logic trivializes the second approach. It does not take advantage of the myriad natural constraints that the real world is forced to live by; for example, it has little to say about the continued identity of an individual object over time. On the other hand, expert systems trivialize the first approach. An expert system for a narrow task can — and inevitably does — make a huge number of assumptions and choices implicitly (such as, that each "case" can be assumed to occur at a single moment in time).

Neither of the two approaches is exactly right. We agree that the steps involved in both approaches have to be done, but we believe that neither can be "ignored" if a proper job is to be done on the other. In particular, we want to use the regularities in the real world to help us develop a powerful set of reasoning mechanisms. That is, the "power" will come from the fact that the mechanism is used frequently in many situations and optimized for most of the uses that actually crop up. Without the guidance provided by real-world regularities, the set of possible mechanisms we could write is virtually infinite (and that's before we even begin to worry about what data structures and algorithms we should use to implement them!).

3.5.1. Distinguishing Cyc from Expert Systems. Cyc's chosen "microworld" is more or less *every particular task domain, down to some (pre-expert) level of detail.* As with expert systems, the "symbol set" that we need to build the Cyc KB can and should be biased by, perhaps largely driven by, all those special cases. And the symbol-manipulation techniques we need can and should make use of properties of that particular symbol set.

The difference is that the breadth of the task domain forces that latter set — the symbol manipulation techniques — to be much larger and more sophisticated than in any particular narrow-domain expert system. Also, the task itself is often largely specified in advance in the case of an ES, so Cyc needs a much more use-neutral representation; since no such thing exists, Cyc supports multiple representations and ways of automatically mapping among them.

(No, we don't believe in use-neutrality, but we do believe in the "Be Prepared" motto. As in house-building, in building a KB, no one tool is universal, but almost the same effect is achieved by having a large tool kit. The tool kit for Cyc is of course less elegant, more costly to assemble and cart around, etc., than that for an ES. Tough. Some people might argue that this reflects our inadequate understanding of the elegance of the real world, that this project exceeds the limits of human cognitive abilities, or even that the existence of one general multi-use toolkit is theoretically impossible. Until some objection has been proved (which we believe is unlikely), we'll continue to be happy with our toolbox.)

3.5.2. Distinguishing Cyc from First-order Predicate Calculus (FOPC) Theorem Proving Systems.

Cyc is also quite different from FOPC systems that use some single inferencing mechanism, such as resolution. Differences exist at two levels. First, many powerful special concepts help define/constrain the real world: spatial substanceness, causality, communication, memory, modeling, movement, time, and so on. It is "fair" and "proper" for such concepts to be handled specially by Cyc; that is, to treat them such that representing and reasoning about them becomes easier. Second, because we have some idea of the syntactic structures that are/must be present in the Cyc knowledge base, the inference schemes can be optimized to make use of whatever regularities happen to manifest in those symbol structures. (See Section 3.3.)

4. Representation: What and Why?

In any knowledge base, and for any intelligent agent, it is essential to make the right distinctions in order to be able to organize and cope with the complexity of the real world. In order to know what constitutes a good set of individuals, categories, attributes and relations, we have to understand how the possession of, for example, a *category* in one's vocabulary assists in making appropriate decisions . . .

In addition to enunciating a policy for representation, the Cyc project also had to find ways for dealing with human fallibility in executing that policy. The vexing question of crime detection and subsequent punishment or rehabilitation is dealt with in section 7, below, entitled *Mistakes Commonly Made When Knowledge Is Entered.* In the current section, we will simply lay down the law."

> — from Lenat *et al.* (eds.), *The Ontological Engineer's Handbook, 2nd ed.*, Addison-Wesley, 1997, pp. 1 and 9,814, respectively.

4.1. Who Gets To Be Somebody? *or* The Cosmic Cookie Cutter

Even without waxing metaphysical or political, this question can be tricky. What does it mean to identify a distinct concept, a *thing* like Fred, Eating, Happiness, or the number 42? It means taking the formless void (or not so void) and applying a cosmic cookie cutter, drawing a boundary around what thereby becomes a *something*. Only once this is done can we decide on what categories are worth having and what attributes and relations are worth defining, because these are all parasitic on a universe of distinguishable things.

Syntactically speaking, a *thing* is anything *about which* you can state a fact, and *to which* you can ascribe a name. Any *thing* can be represented by a unit in Cyc, and each Cyc unit (that is, frame) represents one *thing*. So extensionally, *unit* and *thing* are synonymous.

(Of course, lots of *things* aren't explicitly represented (yet) in Cyc; that just means that there aren't (yet) *units* representing them in the KB. But any *thing* that can be conceptualized and named could then have a *unit* created and added to the KB to represent it.)

A category, attribute, or relation can itself also be a distinguishable thing. One can state (second-order) facts about it:

"The inverse of the eats relation is eatenBy"
"The extension of the category Dog (the set of all dogs) is Fido, Rover, RinTinTin, Lassie . . ."
"The cardinality of the category USState is 50"

A particular instance of a slot can also be a distinguishable thing. For example, I know that SteveDouglas has three sons, though I can never seem to recall their names; that's a fact about the *thing* that is "the value of the sons slot of the SteveDouglas unit."

Even a single entry on a value of a slot of a unit can be a distinguishable thing. For example, I know that the residents slot of Texas contains Doug, and that that unit/slot/entry assertion has been true since 1984. That's not a fact about residents, or about the whole value of the residents slot of the Texas unit, it's just a fact about one single unit/slot/entry triple.

So where should we cut our cookies? Simply put, our answer is that a *thing*, as part of the universe, should possess some interesting properties, and should be capable of playing a direct role, as a whole, in some situation for which Cyc, or some application client, might be interested in solving a problem. Each *thing* should, therefore, not only be able to have a name, but should also *deserve* to have a name.

Oddly enough, there have been several ontological proposals at odds with this approach, but our experiences (including those of trying other ways and failing) indicate that we're on the right track.

To make this airy proposal more concrete, we'll examine seven examples, and see whether or not each is a *thing*, and, in some cases, what sort of thing it is:

• Is SteveDouglas a *thing*?

• Is Person (the set of all people) a *thing*?

• Is 428,914,563 a *thing*?

- Is DiningAtARestaurant a *thing*? Is it an IndividualObject or is it a Collection? How about LenatDiningAtJoesBar&GrillOn4July1988?

- Is TheMetsOutfield a *thing*? Is it an IndividualObject or a Collection?

- Is the substance Gold a *thing*? Is it an IndividualObject or a Collection?

- Is Meningitis a *thing*? Is it an IndividualObject or a Collection?

4.1.1. Example 1: Is SteveDouglas a *Thing*?   *Answer:* Yes. We know some things about this IndividualObject, such as who portrayed him (Fred MacMurray), his epistemological status (fictional character), and his number of sons (three).

4.1.2. Example 2: Is Person (the set of all people) a *Thing*?   *Answer:* Yes. We know its cardinality (to the nearest billion), the rate at which members appear and disappear from it, who its members are (or at least who some of its members are), its Linnaean rank (species), and so on.

4.1.3. Example 3: Is 428,914,563 a *Thing*?   *Answer:* Now it is. Until we made up this example, no one on Earth probably ever saw that particular number written out or used anywhere, nor had anything to say specially about it. We always *could* have created a unit called TheNumber428914563, but until now we had very little to say about it. Now we could at least say

```
TheNumber428914563
   instanceOf: PositiveInteger
   actualReferent: 428914563
   usedAsExampleIn: Lenat&Guha'sCycBook
```

So the number of potential units in Cyc is infinite. There are that many possible instances of PositiveInteger alone! At any moment, Cyc contains only those units about which we have something special to say. For example, TheNumber0 and TheNumber1 and TheNumber2 certainly deserve to exist; that is, it's worth having named units representing 0, 1, and 2.

What's the smallest integer about which we have nothing interesting to say? That's sort of a joke because we would then have one interesting thing to say about it. The pragmatic answer is that somewhere around 100, we begin representing every tenth number, and somewhere around 1,000 we begin representing every hundredth number, and so on. (Numbers larger than, say, a googolyplex ($10^{10^{100}}$) will only be represented explicitly if there is something special to say about them.) These can be considered all the elements of the category RoundNumber. Of course there will be other special numbers (for example, 256 and 42 and 666) and categories of numbers (PrimeNumber, PerfectNumber, PowerOf2) that we know and love and that we represent explicitly in Cyc.

This is just an application of the general philosophy we stated above, which should apply to the KB as a whole: represent all — but only — those *things* that are interesting, important, unusual, or that otherwise need to be represented.

4.1.4. Example 4: Is DiningAtARestaurant a *Thing*?

Answer: Now we're starting to get into a tricky area. The trickiness is that DiningAtARestaurant is not a single event, but rather a large category of events: all the times that anyone has, or will, or could imaginably dine at any restaurant. Including any events that are hypothetical, counterfactual, believed, feared, etc. For example, we can imagine an event in which J.F.K and Aristotle are dining together on Mars. That is an event and can have a unit representing it, even though it's fictitious.

If Lenat ate dinner at Joe's Bar and Grill on July 4, 1988, we might represent that event in Cyc by LenatDiningAtJoesBar&GrillOn4July1988. This unit would be *an instance of* DiningAtARestaurant. That is, it would be a member of that category, an element of that set.

It wasn't hard to decide that LenatDiningAtJoesBar&GrillOn4July1988 should be a unit. We can think of plenty of things to say about it:

```
LenatDiningAtJoesBar&GrillOn4July1988
   instanceOf: DiningAtARestaurant
   diner: Lenat
   restaurant: JoesBar&Grill
   date: "4-July-1988"
   typeOfFoodsEaten: Chicken, Peas,
      ChocolatePie
   durationInMins: 120
   costInUS$: 14
```

It also wasn't hard to decide that DiningAtARestaurant should be a unit, a *thing*. There are some useful things to say about that unit, though we have to be a little careful:

```
DiningAtARestaurant
  instanceOf: ProcessType
  instances: LenatDiningAtJoesBar
      &GrillOn4July1988  ← lots more!
  genls: ReceivingService  ← "genls" is like "supersets"
  interestingness: High
  canHaveSlots: diner, restaurant,
      typeOfFoodsEaten
  allInstances: LenatDiningAtJoesBar
      &GrillOn4July1988  ← lots more!
    durationInMins: 60
    costInUS$: 8
    interestingness: Low
  frequencyPerWeekPerPerson: 2
```

Notice that some of what we have to say is default information about the typical instance of DiningAtARestaurant (namely, how long it would take and how much it would cost and how interesting it is). That information is *inherited* (as defaults) to all instances of DiningAtARestaurant — including the event of LenatDiningAtJoesBar&GrillOn4July1988. Throughout this book, inherited information is denoted by *indentation*, as in this case.

Notice also how we represent the fact that the category DiningAtARestaurant is very interesting (it's often used as an example in AI, for instance!), but the typical instance of it — each dining event itself — is (by default) not very interesting.

Also notice that the defaults generally apply to allInstances of DiningAtARestaurant, not just to direct instances. That means that if there's an intermediate category, beneath DiningAtARestaurant, then the defaults continue on through that (unless it overrides them). For example, suppose that one of the specs of DiningAtARestaurant is DiningAtAnItalianRestaurant. That latter unit might introduce some new defaults (such as the menu items, the kind of tablecloths, costInUS$, etc.), but most of the old defaults from DiningAtARestaurant would still be valid for, and inherited to, instances of DiningAtAnItalianRestaurant (for example, the durationInMins, interestingness, etc.).

Notice that we are assuming that the default costInUS$ of a DiningAtAnItalianRestaurant event supersedes — overrides — the default costInUS$ from the more general category DiningAtARestaurant.

The hard part, the tricky part, is to realize that DiningAtARestaurant is a category of events, but LenatDiningAtJoesBar&GrillOn4July1988 is just one event. It's tricky because in English we can just smoothly slide to ever more specialized versions of the Dining category:

Dining
DiningAtARestaurant
DiningAtJoesBar&Grill
LenatDiningAtJoesBar&GrillDuringJuly
LenatDiningAtJoesBar&GrillOn4July1988

Why isn't each of these a category — that is, just a subset of the preceding one? In other words, where did we cross the line from a category of events to a single event? The answer is that we didn't; that last "category" — which has only one event in it — should really be called something like TheCategoryOfEventsInWhichLenatDinesAtJoesBar&GrillOn4July1988. It would then have TheEventInWhichLenatDinesAtJoesBar&GrillOn4July1988 as its one and only instance. It is this latter, single event that we named LenatDiningAtJoesBar&GrillOn4July1988 a few paragraphs ago, and for which we sketched out some slots. We never bothered defining the singleton collection of which that event is the only instance, because there is nothing interesting to say about that singleton category.

This is very important, so we'll repeat it. We normally wouldn't have TheCategoryOfEventsInWhichLenatDinesAtJoesBar&GrillOn4July1988 as a unit in Cyc, because it doesn't "deserve" to exist. Also, we probably should, for clarity, call the other categories by more crisp names, such as

TheCategoryOfDiningEvents
TheCategoryOfEventsInWhichSomeoneDinesAtARestaurant
TheCategoryOfEventsInWhichSomeoneDinesAtJoesBar&Grill
TheCategoryOfEventsInWhichLenatDinesAtJoesBar&Grill
TheCategoryOfEventsInWhichLenatDinesAtJoesBar&GrillDuringJuly
TheCategoryOfEventsInWhichLenatDinesAtJoesBar&GrillOn4July1988

Now it's easy to see that LenatDiningAtJoesBar&GrillOn4July1988 is an *instance* of that last category. It's probably the *only* instance of that category, of course. (If Lenat ate there for both lunch and dinner, it would have two instances; if news commentators and historians and novelists later speculate about various alternative forms that historic meal might have taken, each of those could also be an instance of the category.) But having those long names for categories is unpleasant in English — and in Cyc — so we usually shorten them.

Since we human beings all have common sense, we have no trouble disambiguating DiningAtARestaurant as a set (a set of events), and LenatDiningAtJoesBar&GrillOn4July1988 as a noncollection (it's just an event).

This tendency of English to gloss over type-token distinctions has been discussed in greater depth and at much greater length by philosophers (see, for example, Davidson, 1980).

So long as the correct relations (instanceOf, which is like "element of," and genls, which is like "subset of") are used to relate the various concepts in Cyc, we permit this same sort of shortening in their names; of course, in principle, the names could all be mechanically generated symbols like G000001, G0000002, anyway. Having more evocative names is mostly for the benefit of the human user. (One day, when Cyc powers a natural language understanding program to an acceptable level of performance, we could go back and safely replace all the unit names by randomly generated symbols.)

So to go back to our list, we see a series of "subset" relationships (*specs*) and one single "element" relationship (*instances*):

```
Dining
  -specs->
  DiningAtARestaurant
      -specs->
      DiningAtJoesBar&Grill
          -specs->
          LenatDiningAtJoesBar&GrillDuringJuly
              -instances->
                  LenatDiningAtJoesBar&GrillOn4July1988
```

4.1.5. Example 5: Is TheMetsOutfield a *Thing*?

Answer: Sure. But the trickier question is: Is it an individual object whose *parts* are people, or is it just a collection whose *elements* (that is, whose instances) are people?

Having read example 4, you might suspect the trap here. Namely, there are two different concepts, and *each* potentially could be represented by a unit. The unified individual object might be called

```
TheMetsOutfieldAsAWhole
    instanceOf: Mechanism
    parts: Darryl, Mookie, Kevin
    typeOfPart: MetsOutfielder
    errorRate: .004
    degreeOfSynchronization: .92
    analogues: AutomobileEngine
    favoriteTactics: TwoManRelaying
    interestingness: High
    age: 41
    english: "The well-oiled machine that is the
       Mets outfield"
```

The set of people might be called

```
MetsOutfielder
  instanceOf: CollectionOfPeople
  allInstances: Darryl, Mookie, Kevin
    errorRate: .0013
    heightInMeters: 2.03
    interestingness: Moderate
    english: "A person who is an outfielder
      for the Mets"
    age: 27
  typeOfPartOf: TheMetsOutfieldAsAWhole
  genls: Outfielder, MetsPlayer
  interestingness: Low
  english: "The set of all Mets outfielders"
```

Note on syntax:
The syntax

Unit1
s1
s2:(c)

is equivalent to $\forall x$ (s1 Unit1 x) $\rightarrow$ (s2 x c).
That is, *inherit*, to all entries on Unit1.s1, the entry c for their s2 slot.

We've intentionally given some of the same slots to these units, to show how they differ. Notice that TheMetsOutfieldAsAWhole has existed for more than forty years; also notice that the category MetsOutfielder has no age because it's a timeless mathematical entity (of course, for untold eons it was an empty set); and, finally, notice that all instances of that category inherit, by default, an age of 27 (that's how old Cyc believes the typical Mets outfielder is).

We just raised a very tricky issue: the instances of the set MetsOutfielder change from year to year. We'll see presently how Cyc represents this; the basic answer is that a unit can represent a temporal "slice" of an entity. So there could be several temporalSubabstractions of TheMetsOutfieldAsAWhole, each of them listing a different set of *parts* — that is, a different set of IndividualObjects who comprised the Mets outfield during that period of time. Similarly, there could be several specs of MetsOutfielder, such as MetsOutfielderIn1983, each with its own set of *instances*.

4.1.6. **Example 6: Is the Substance Gold a *Thing*?** *Answer:* Let's apply our criterion: Is there something you can say about the substance gold? Sure, there are defaults we can state for all instances of gold (density, melting point, etc.), there are relationships to other types of stuff (liquid gold, metal), there is a known "granule size" beneath which something is no longer gold (gold atom), there is an overall interestingness of this concept, and so on. So the answer is yes.

```
Gold
   instanceOf: StuffType
   allInstances: GoldRing837, GoldRing838,
      GoldTooth5347,...
      density: 8.3
      meltingPtDegreesCentigrade: 653
      color: Yellow
      interestingness: VeryHigh
   genls: Metal, ChemicalElement,
      GoldMoreOrLess, Stuff
   specs: LiquidGold, GoldNugget,...
   granule: GoldAtom
   interestingness: High
```

As with the last two examples we've discussed, the danger here is that of confusing "being a thing" with "being an individual object." In example 4, we saw how a singleton set might easily be confused with its lone element. In example 5, we saw how an object might be confused with the set of its parts.

We could — by stretching — imagine all the lumps of gold scattered throughout the universe as being subparts of the single cosmic distributed individual object called AllTheGoldInTheUniverse. That's of dubious use, though; that sprawling, massive object rarely if ever enters into any real problem-solving situation. Normally, we just have one or two particular gold lumps, rings, necklaces, or teeth. So the individual objects are the discrete pieces of gold that interest us. "Gold" itself is best viewed as a category, or collection, of all the pieces of gold.

To reiterate: In this example, the possible confusion is between the set of all gold objects and the single big piece of all the gold in the universe. That cosmic piece of gold is, we must admit, an individual object, even though some part of it is in Texas, and some part of it is in Alaska, and some small part of it is inside Alpha Centauri. But that's okay, it's still just an IndividualObject — we have no problem treating a baseball team in the field as a single object, after all.

(Unlike the baseball team, though, each piece of gold is more or less the same stuff. That's what it means to be a type of *stuff* after all: if you take some Wood, and break it into several smaller portions, each of them is still a piece of Wood. The same goes for Water, Air, Earth, Fire, Time, Energy, Walking, Owning, and Gold. We'll have a lot more to say about Stuff later on.)

All categories can have the slots *instances* (members, elements) and *genls* (supersets). Most categories can have a meaningful *cardinality* slot (number of instances), but that slot doesn't really make sense for categories, such as "Gold," that represent a type of stuff. Any type of stuff can have a *granule* slot that says how fine-grained a portion can be before the stuff-like nature breaks down (for example, for Walking, the granule is TakingAStep; for Gold, the granule is GoldAtom).

Some categories — again, like Gold — represent not just stuff but a type of *physical,* material substance. Can Gold have slots like melting point, density, and color? Not really; either those characteristics should be inherited to allInstances of that category or a different kind of slot — say colorOfTypicalInstance — should be defined and used. That is, strictly speaking no category can have a mass or color slot — only (or at least partially) tangible individual objects can possess such slots.

So Gold can't have a massInKG slot, but AllTheGoldInTheUniverse could. If we ever did want to talk about that multipart tangible object — for instance, to say that its mass is 8.2 trillion kilograms — we could name that IndividualObject and give it some slots. For example, we'd create a unit like:

```
AllTheGoldInTheUniverse
    instanceOf: Gold
    massInKg: 8,200,000,000,000
    parts: GoldRing837, GoldTooth5347,...
    slotsKnownToBeNull: spatiallyContinuous?
```

Each unit in the KB must be either a Collection (a category that can have instances) or an IndividualObject (a category that can't have instances). In terms of Cyc KB terminology, IndividualObject is a spec of Thing, and Collection is a spec of Thing, and Thing is *partitioned into* IndividualObject and Collection. That means that every unit in the system must be either an instance of IndividualObject or an instance of Collection, but must not be an instance of both.

(A *partition* of a collection C is a set of subsets of C, such that (a) each pair of the subsets is disjoint and (b) the union of the subsets covers all of C. A set of subsets of C that satisfies the first of these conditions is a *mutualDisjoin* of C, and a set of subsets of C that satisfies the second of these conditions is a *covering* of C. So the partitions of C are always those things that are in the intersection of the mutualDisjoins and the coverings of C.)

```
Thing
    instanceOf: Collection
    specs: Collection, IndividualObject
```

```
Collection
  instanceOf: Collection
  genls: Thing
  complement: IndividualObject
  canHaveSlots: instances, genls, specs,
    cardinality
  cantHaveSlots: parts
  instances: Thing, Collection,
    IndividualObject, Stuff,...

IndividualObject
  instanceOf: Collection
  genls: Thing
  complement: Collection
  canHaveSlots: parts
  cantHaveSlots: instances, genls, specs,
    cardinality

Stuff
  instanceOf: Collection
  genls: IndividualObject        ← we'll have more to say about
                                             this later.

  canHaveSlots: portions
  cantHaveSlots: parts, cardinality
```

4.1.7. Example 7: Is Meningitis an IndividualObject or a Collection? Let's look at this one last case. Once more, there is a danger of being misled if we are speaking in English (and/or some expert system language that fails to make all the relevant distinctions).

- "Did *Meningitis* cause Frank's death?" No, an individual infection event *involving* meningitis bacteria caused his death.

- "Does *Meningitis* last around three months?" No, collections last forever (in their Platonic universe), but each bout of the disease — each instance of Meningitis — lasts about three months. In other words, Meningitis is a *collection* of infection episodes, each of which is an event (and, thus, an individual object). The Meningitis unit inherits to all its instances a default value (three months) for their *duration* slots.

What the expert system MYCIN does, in effect, is to pretend that there is only one patient in the world, and it pretends that there is just one moment hanging in time as well, so that it doesn't matter if that patient suffers from the only instance of *Meningitis* or has the set of meningitis episodes all to himself. Cyc, on the other hand, can't be sure *what* task it's going to have to cope with, so it must handle a more general class of temporal situations. Hence, Cyc must be *more precise* both about individual objects and about time.

4.2. Why Are Categories Useful?

So now we have some distinguishable units, and we assign some attributes and values to them. Why bother with categories? We could, in theory, carry out all our inferences in terms of attributes and relations of IndividualObjects (non-Collections). But categorizing has proven to be a useful efficiency technique for people.

(For instance, that last sentence is hard to state unless you can state the concept of *people* (the category of all the people in the world). In Cyc, we allow categories to exist; that particular one might be represented by the unit #%Person. And the point of Cyc is to act intelligently, not to play the game of seeing how little it can start with and still not collapse.)

However, we have already seen that borrowing directly from natural language can lead to grave category errors — very grave indeed. In deciding whether or not to distinguish (create a separate unit representing) a particular category, the knowledge enterers (and Cyc) need some standard for judging its utility that is more objective than "well, it intuitively sounded right to me," or "it's a common English word."

So: *Why are categories efficient?* They provide a single place to bundle together several implications:

- What default properties do (most of) its members exhibit?

- How can we recognize a member of this category?

- What special heuristics should we use in dealing with a member?

- How many members are there?

- What do you call somebody who studies these things for a living?

- What questions can you meaningfully ask about the members of this category?

- How often does this category's list of members change?

Suppose we want to assert that people are very emotional. The way to do that in Cyc is to place a note to that effect on the Person unit. More exactly, what one does is to place an inheritance entry of

"#%emotionalLevel: #%High" on the #%allInstances slot of the unit #%Person.

```
     Person
genls: (Primate LegalEntity IntelligentAgent Biped)
specs: (American Women Criminal...)   ← lots more!
canHaveSlots: (occupation nativeLanguage...)   ← lots more!
allInstances: (Guha Lenat...)   ← billions and billions more!
   emotionalLevel: High
   iq: 100
```

Logically, instead of having the collection Person, we could just write a rule with a complex antecedent:

```
"If x is warm-blooded and bipedal and has an
opposable thumb and a brain and hair and...
Then x has High emotionalLevel."
```

It doesn't matter *theoretically*, but it does matter *pragmatically*, economically. It saves a lot of time to have one place to bundle together in one data structure all the various implications of X being human: defaults (being able to guess X's IQ and height and weight), legal slots (knowing you can meaningfully ask about X's occupation and native language), and so on. In addition, by naming the category, we provide an efficient way to state new properties that apply to all the members of the category. The choice is between saying that *"Humans are susceptible to AIDS"* and saying that *"Warm-blooded, bipedal individuals with opposable thumbs and . . . are susceptible to AIDS."*

Perhaps even more important, in all this, is the difficulty in precisely defining some important categories (for example, LivingThing, EthnicGroup, BookkeepingSlot). Even if we don't have a perfect characterizing function for those sets, we still can use them: there are rules to conclude that x belongs to the set; other rules that fire based (partially) on membership in the set; and so on.

Another, but less important, reason to have explicitly represented collections is that we sometimes have attributes of the set as a whole — for example, its cardinality. We ought to be able to represent the fact that "the category American has 200 million elements" without having to extensionally list them all!

Often, we have a choice of whether to define a new collection or a new slot instead. For example, suppose we want to say that fire engines are red. We could define RedThing (the set of all red things) and FireEngine (the set of all fire engines), and list the second on the specs slot of the first. Or, we could define a true/false attribute like red? and say that FireEngine inherits to its allInstances the default value True for their red? slot. Or, we could define a slot like colorOfObject and say that FireEngine inherits to its allInstances the default value TheColorRed for their colorOfObject slot. We like the third solution the best, intuitively . . . but why? In all three cases, we'd have to define one unit for each color; in scheme one, we'd have to define BlueThing, GreenThing, etc.; in scheme two we'd have to define blue? green?, etc.; in scheme three we'd have to define TheColorBlue, TheColorGreen, etc. So why prefer the third scheme? The answer is that we'd have to define those colors anyway: to talk about their placement on the spectrum, for instance. If there were just two colors — say red and non-red — defining red? would be a good idea; but having to define scores of true/false slots like that is inefficient, because we'd want to interrelate them anyway.

4.2.1. Summary: A Policy for Deciding When To Make a Category.   Let's collect the above points together and try to come up with a policy for when to group a bunch of IndividualObjects into a category. We'll have more to say about red? versus RedObject versus TheColorRed in section 4.3 below.

We say that we should explicitly define the collection if:

1. We have several interesting things to say about it. Those "interesting things" could be assertions about the collection as a whole (for example, cardinality), defaults to inherit to members of the collection, metalevel information about it (for example, how various cultures have disagreed about the boundary of the category), etc.

2. The collection has a nonempty canHaveSlots (that is, a list of slots that make sense only for instances of this collection). This is one of the most important, perhaps even essential, types of "interesting things to say," and it should almost always be present.

3. At least some of the things that can be said about this collection could not be said equally well about some larger group (some superset that is also worth explicitly defining).

4. The definition of the category is imprecise (the "boundaries" are questionable), very long, or very costly to compute.

5. The number of "siblings" (for example, complementary sets whose union is the natural generalization of this one) is low.

In any case, the nub of the matter is that:

The decision to have named categories is largely one of utility, not reality.

4.2.2. Categories of Slots. As an *application* of the precepts just espoused, let's consider when we should and shouldn't bother defining a new slot category — things like Slot, DefiningSlot, TaxonomicSlot, BookkeepingSlot, Actor&RoleSlot, CountrySlot. These are Collections whose members are each a kind of slot (for example, instanceOf is an instance of TaxonomicSlot; myLastEditor is an instance of BookkeepingSlot; and nationalPopulation is an instance of both NumericValuedSlot and CountrySlot).

A new slot category XSlot is worth defining when some or (even better) most of the following four conditions hold:

1. *XSlot* has a non-empty canHaveSlots slot. That is, there are some slots that only *XSlot* type slots can legally possess. For example, all instances of NumericValuedSlot can legally have the slot meanValue. (The meanValue for nationalPopulation might be 10000000.) So meanValue is an entry on the canHaveSlots slot of the unit NumericValuedSlot. And that's one argument supporting the decision to allow NumericValuedSlot to exist as a separate unit in Cyc.

2. The definition of *XSlot* is not simple. If there *is* a clean, simple definition, and neither reason 1 nor reason 3 applies, then it's quite possible that there is no need at all for *XSlot* to exist as a separate unit in Cyc. For instance, consider DogSlot. This collection might include such fascinating slots as #%dogShowsWon. The definition of DogSlot is simply "slots that make sense for dogs" — that is, precisely the entries listed on the canHaveSlots slot of Dog. Anything we might have to say about DogSlot — any slot/value pair — could just as easily be stated as an inherited slot/value pair placed on the canHaveSlots slot of the Dog unit. Conversely, consider the collections TaxonomicSlot or IntensionalSlot. In cases like those, any definition we might make would be very slippery indeed, or very complex, or both. We'd better allow those units to exist — that is, allow them each to have a Cyc unit that represents that set of slots.

3. There are several slot/value pairs sitting on *XSlot*, besides the taxonomic ones like instanceOf and the defining ones like makeSenseFor. Or, there are some SeeUnits (footnotes) on some of *XSlot*'s slots. Consider the collection ProcessSlot, whose instances include such slots as actors, rateOfProcess, and granule. There's something "special" about slots like those: if you take any temporal slice of any process, that slice would have the same values for all those slots (consider the process of walking; a "piece" of any walking event, say Fred walking home one afternoon, would have the same rateOfProcess as the overall event, namely four miles per hour; it would have the same granule, namely TakingAStep; and it

would have the same actors, namely Fred). The way to represent that in Cyc is to place a special kind of SeeUnit or footnote on the allInstances slot of ProcessSlot; that SeeUnit expresses the desired constraint. The point here is that, because we have several such "special things" to say about ProcessSlot, it's worth allowing it to exist.

4. Human beings think of it as a natural kind of slot to define. This is the weakest of the four reasons, and the most dangerous. It's dangerous because it can be overused, especially in ways that over-stress the common taxonomic slots like *instances* and *specs*. We've allowed ourselves only about a dozen "chits" for making slot categories with this justification — all the other slot categories in Cyc have to stand on their own merits, supported by one or more of the first three reasons. An example of this "justification" being invoked is in the existence of the unit called PersonSlot — that is, the set of slots that make sense for people. There are of course lots of elements of this collection (iq, spouse, passportNumber, . . .), but what is there to say that's *really* unique to such slots as a whole? What couldn't you also say about slots (such as hairiness) that make sense for Mammal? The answer is: "Well, nothing, really, but we intuitively like to think of ourselves as special, and part of that ego trip is to think of PersonSlot as an important category of slots." Okay, so we use up one of our dozen "chits" there, and allow it to exist. Perhaps one day, Cyc may use up another "chit" to create AIProgramSlot; who knows?

4.3. AttributeValues versus Categories

In general, the values stored on each and every slot on each and every unit in the system is a set. If we look at the Fred frame and examine the children slot, we would see the list (Sam Janet FredJunior) — that is, a set with three elements. Should we have a separate unit in the knowledge base for each of these collections — for example, a separate unit for the set {Sam, Janet, FredJunior}? No, clearly, that way lies only the madness of infinite loops and the *appearance* of having more knowledge.

So each slot of each unit — let's call it u.s for short — is *implicitly* representing an instance of Collection (the set of all sets), even though u.s is not a full-fledged unit in Cyc.

But sometimes there are things we need to say about u.s; how do we do that? For instance, suppose we know that Fred has five children, but we don't know all their names; or suppose we know that the list of Fred.kids seems to be growing at the rate of one new entry every two years; or suppose we know that the Fred.kids data (the list of kids we think are Fred's) was supplied by the IRS on 8/3/89, etc. We'd like to be able to talk explicitly *about* these "implicit sets" without having to make them full-fledged separate units.

Before we go on, let's consider an example to see what we really mean by an alternate representation of these sets. Consider the notion of hilliness. We might want to inherit a large number of properties to some region based on the fact that it is hilly (for example, its soil is likely to be rocky). There are two ways of representing the notion of hilliness:

1. Create the unit HillyRegion, which represents the set of all hilly regions. State that allInstances of this unit — for example, Appalachia — will inherit various properties (such as "soilRockiness: High").

   ```
   HillyRegion
      english: ("The set of all hilly geographic
         regions")
      allInstanceOf: (Collection...)
      allInstances: (Appalachia...)
        soilRockiness: (High)
   ```

2. Create the unit Hilly, which represents a type of topography; indeed, it might be an element of the collection TopographyTrait. (Note: Hilly is *not* a collection!) Create a pair of units called topography and topographyOf, which are new types of slots, and are inverses of each other. The slot topography is meant to point from a region to its topography type (and vice versa for topographyOf). So the topography slot of Appalachia would contain Hilly, and the topographyOf slot of Hilly would contain Appalachia. Then state that Hilly.topographyOf inherits various properties (such as soilRockiness: High). Whatever entries are filled in — now or later — as entries on the topographyOf slot of Hilly (for example, Appalachia), those entries would then inherit the default value High for their soilRockiness slot.

   ```
   Hilly
      english: ("A rolling sort of terrain")
      allInstanceOf: (TopographyTrait....)
      topographyOf: (Appalachia...)
        soilRockiness: (High)
   ```

Although method 2 *sounds* more complicated than method 1, that's really just because we're all used to inheritance down "is-a" links, but not along other arbitrary slots. The tradeoff between methods 1 and 2 is really the question of whether we should define (1) a new collection (HillyRegion) or (2) a new pair of slots (topography and topographyOf) and a set of TopographyTraits. So which is preferable?

If we had something to say about the *set* of hilly regions (for example, its cardinality) or if there were some legal slots that originated from HillyRegion (for example, avgHillHeight), then we would advise strongly in favor of creating the collection HillyRegion. But assume for the moment that neither of those conditions is true. Then which of (1) or (2) is preferable?

We can't answer the question in full generality, but the basic answer is that to take the first option — that is, to create HillyRegion — would overwork the instance/instanceOf hierarchy. Let's see what this means.

Recall why we wanted the collection in the first place: to inherit some default values for certain attributes (for example, soilRockiness). But why not make those attributes into collections, too — why should we stop with HillyRegion? We could create the collection RockySoilRegion (and, also, LoamySoilRegion, and SandySoilRegion, and ClayishSoilRegion, and . . . zzzSoilRegion for each legal entry zzz that could exist on a soilRockiness slot). It would be tempting just to record that RockySoilRegion is a subset of HillyRegion, but that would be much more absolute, much more than just a default value. So what we'd have to do is to say

```
HillyRegion
   instanceOf: (RegionType)
   allInstances: (Appalachia...)
     allInstanceOf: (RockySoilRegion)
```

That is, each instance of HillyRegion will *inherit the default value* RockySoilRegion on its allInstanceOf slot. Inheriting a default allInstanceOf value in this way seems a bit overtaxing of the instance/instanceOf hierarchy. It's not just that inheritance would all reside in those two slots, but in a way most of the representation would reside there. That really would be overworking those two slots!

Overworking your system's "is-a" slots (instance/instanceOf) is bad for the following two reasons:

- First, you'd suffer a loss of clarity and precision, as the meaning of is-a is rather fuzzy:

  - Must all instances of HillyRegion be explicitly represented?

  - Is every item listed on HillyRegion.instances *guaranteed* to be a true instance? Or are the items listed there merely *likely* to be true instances of that category? (A "true instance" is one that satisfies the definition of the collection.) Or are the listed entries each expected to be somehow *close to* a true instance?

It seems safer to use a wider range of slots, each with narrower but more well-defined semantics.

- The second reason it's bad to cram so much into instance/instanceOf slots is that such an excessive dependence on one slot-pair could lead to computational inefficiency. The instanceOf slot of a unit might eventually contain many entries — some of which were there just to specify what type of soil the region had, some of which were there just to specify its topography, some of which were there just to specify what nation owns the land. . . . If you keep going down that path, you lose the real power, the efficiency, of frame systems: the cross-indexing and teasing apart of diverse attributes. So, we argue, it would be better to have separate slots for soilRockiness, topography, and controllingCountry.

In other words, instead of having:

```
Texas
    instanceOf: (RockySoilRegion,
      DesertTopographyRegion,
      RegionControlledByUSA...)
```

we'd slightly prefer to have:

```
Texas
    instanceOf: (GeopoliticalRegion)
    soilRockiness: (High)
    desertnessOfTerrain: (High)
    controllingCountry: (USA)
```

But now we might be a bit bothered by the proliferation of types of slots. How often in your life have you used the concept of soilRockiness, after all?

(This is an example of the proliferation of slots when the semantics of slots is hidden in the slot name. We're relying here to a large extent on personal introspection to set the "level of proliferation" initially, and we're relying on empirical testing to adjust it from that initial setting.)

So, like Goldilocks, let's back off to a middle position, and have a slot like soilQuality, which could have a value like Rocky, and a slot like topography, which could have values like Desertlike, Hilly, or Mountainous.

So we'd much prefer:

```
Texas
    instanceOf: (GeopoliticalRegion)
    soilQuality: (Rocky Sandy)
    topography: (Desertlike Hilly)
    controllingCountry: (USA)
```

(The "soilQuality: Rocky" entry is inherited here from Hilly.topography, and the "soilQuality: Sandy" entry is inherited here from Desertlike.topography.)

Now that we have justified the use of things like Rocky and Hilly instead of collections like RockySoilRegion and HillyRegion, let us see where to place them in the hierarchy of *things*.

They fall into a category referred to as AttributeValue. There are many different subsets of this category, such as physical attribute value (of which Red is a member), mental attribute value (of which Happy is a member), etc.

The different AttributeValues, such as Hilly, Rocky, Desertlike, and Red (that is, TheColorRed), are related by slots such as genlAttributes and specAttributes that point to (respectively) more general and more specialized members of the same category. For example, BrightRed is one of the specAttributes of Red.

```
Pink
    instanceOf: (ColorOfObject)
    allInstanceOf: (ColorOfObject
            PhysicalAttributeValue
            AttributeValue RepresentedThing
            IntangibleStuff IndividualObject
            Intangible Stuff Thing)
    genlAttributes: (ReddishColor)
    specAttributes: (HotPink DullPink)
```

The various named subsets of AttributeValue include the collections TopographyTrait, SoilQuality, ColorOfObject, etc. Hilly is an instance of the first, Rocky of the second, and Red (which we called TheColorRed) is an instance of the third. Each of those subsets of AttributeValue is, usually, the entryIsA (class of legal fillers for) of some slot. For instance, the set of legal fillers for the slot topography is TopographyTrait. The set of legal fillers for color is ColorOfObject. And the set of legal fillers for the slot soilQuality is the collection SoilQuality. (The names of slots begin with small letters, and the names of non-slot units begin with capital letters.)

Various default values are often inherited through those slots — such as the inference "Hilly topography → Rocky soilQuality."

```
Hilly
   english: ("A rolling sort of terrain")
   allInstanceOf: (TopographyTrait...)
   topographyOf: (Appalachia...)
     soilQuality: (Rocky)
```

Now, as soon as we place "topography: Hilly" on any unit, that unit will instantly inherit the default slot/value pair "soilQuality: Rocky." We discuss this type of inheritance elsewhere.

Before leaving the subject of attributes, let's take a brief look at an alternate view of the ontological status of these things. Consider the AttributeValue Red. The notion of Red does not really make sense unless we're in a world where there are some colored physical objects. Note that we could have replaced the AttributeValue Red with a unary predicate such as red? — a slot whose legal entries are just True and False (T and NIL). In this fashion, Red is very different from Fred: Fred makes sense whether or not any other IndividualObjects (as opposed to Collections) exist around him. Fred could well exist as the only object in the world, but it would make little sense to talk of Red if there were no objects in our world.

Some other specs (subsets) of the class AttributeValue are: Mass, Velocity, Momentum, and so on. All *instances* of those sets (for example, MassOfTheEarth, SpeedOfLight, etc.) are — just like Red — merely attributes of objects. From the point of view of this analogy between AttributeValues and slots, we could consider each AttributeValue as the defining predicate of some set; that is, as the characteristic function of a set that may or may not be explicitly represented. If there is also an explicit representation of the set, the set and the AttributeValue are related by the slot definingAttributeOf. If we wanted to have both #%red? and #%Red in Cyc, they might look like the following:

```
red?
   instanceOf: Slot
   allInstanceOf: Relationship,
        SlotOrConstraintOnASlot,
        IntangibleObject, Intangible,
        IndividualObject, Thing...
   entryIsA: TruthValue
   makesSenseFor: TangibleObject
   definingAttributeOf: Red
   interestingness: Low
```

```
      english: "A T/NIL-valued slot that indicates
               whether or not an object is colored
               red. See Red."

  Red
    instanceOf: ColorOfObject
    allInstanceOf: AttributeValue,
          ScaleOfValues, Thing,
          IndividualObject...
    nextScaleState: Orange
    prevScaleState: Infrared
    genlAttributes: ReddishColor
    specAttributes: BrightRed, DullRed...
    definingAttribute: red?
    interestingness: Moderate
    english: "One of the possible
          AttributeValues for the color slot."
```

5. A Glimpse of Cyc's Global Ontology

Fortunately, there appear to be several categories of interest in the world, several worthwhile ways of dividing up the set of IndividualObjects. Here are some of the more familiar, useful ones:

• Tangible versus intangible

• Actual instances "inside" the machine (for example, the string "Fred") or instances not actually "in there" (for example, Fred himself)

• Static thing versus dynamic process

• Collection versus individual object

• Distinct entity versus an aspect/slice/subabstraction of one

   Based on that, we might start out our ontology as shown in Figure 5-1.

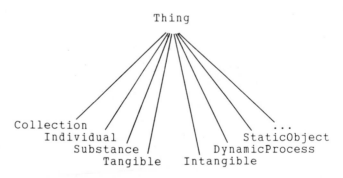

Figure 5–1: First Ontological Diagram

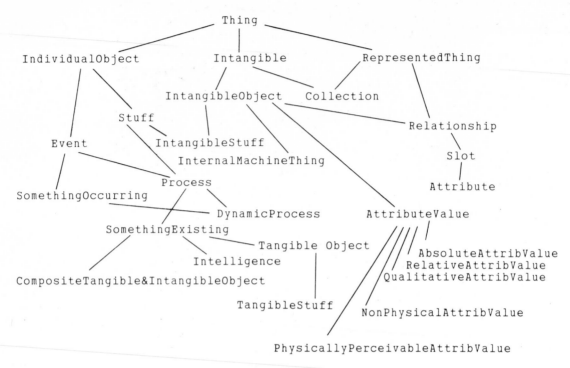

Figure 5–2: Second Ontological Diagram

Some of those categories, however, are actually specializations (subsets) of other categories. Once the dust settles, the diagram looks more like Figure 5-2.

Caveat 1

Figure 5-2 is still but a caricature of the rich web of interrelationships in Cyc. It displays only one kind of slot (specs), even though Cyc now contains several thousand types of internode relationships (kinds of slots). It doesn't show any of the other information present at each node, and it doesn't show the information about partitioning, mutual disjunction, and covering. For instance, it doesn't reflect the fact that every Thing is either an IndividualObject or a Collection. There are slots in Cyc, such as *disjointFrom*, which we haven't drawn in Figure 5-2, that communicate the fact that TangibleObject and Intangible are related to each other. There are slots, such as *instances*, that relate Collection to every single one of the drawn nodes! And, of course, the diagram displays only a few of the roughly ten thousand categories that are already in Cyc.

Caveat 2   We will see later that IndividualObject and Stuff are coextensional; hence, Event will turn out also to be a spec of Stuff. We will also see later that Event and Process are coextensional; hence, SomethingOccurring will turn out also to be a spec of Process. You may wish to draw in those arcs on Figure 5-2.

Caveat 3   As in a thesaurus, much of Cyc's power is in the details, not the top-level ontology. Sure it's worth hearing about these top-level categories, but in a way it's like trying to study a company by examining an aerial photograph of the office building that houses it.

Despite its shortcomings, the diagram in Figure 5–2 will help us "walk through the top level" of the Cyc KB. We'll now discuss what these different categories represent, and why we've organized them into this particular hierarchy.

5.1. The General Categories in Cyc

The world according to Cyc is conceived of as being composed of a number of *things* related to each other. Each unit (a Cyc frame) represents a thing, and each thing worth talking about is represented by a unit.

These things are grouped into different collections. This section describes the most fundamental (high-level) collections in Cyc, and the relations among them. In the process of this exposition, then, you will find out about not only many of the important collections but also many of the important types of slots.

5.1.1. A Few Basic Slots (and Ideas).   Each collection (except one — the universal set, called Thing) must have some entries on its genls slot. That is, every named set except Thing is a proper subset of some other named set.

By the way, we'll use the terms *members*, *elements*, and *instances* more or less interchangeably in this book, just as we'll intermix the usage of *collection*, *set*, and *category*. Another important set of synonyms is *frame*, *unit*, *thing*, and *concept*, to signify something that is represented explicitly in Cyc by a set of slot/value pairs; that is, something that is worth naming and has indeed been named.

Every thing — every unit — must be a member of at least one named collection; at worst, it belongs to the most general of all collections, Thing. This notion of "belonging to," or "being a member of," is denoted using the instanceOf slot in Cyc.

The notation u.s.x means "x is an entry on the s slot of unit u." So Fred.daughters.Sue means that Sue is one of the entries on the daughters slot of Fred. Sometimes, we'll write u.s to denote the entire s slot of unit u; that is, the whole (implicit) set of entries. For example, "Fred.children is a superset of Fred.daughters, which in turn contains Sue and Janet."

Almost all slots in Cyc have inverses. The *inverse* of specs is genls; if Mammal.genls.Animal, then Animal.specs.Mammal. The inverse of instanceOf is *instances*. So if Fred.instanceOf.MovieStar, then MovieStar.instances.Fred. The inverse of inverse is inverse; hence, the inverse of genls is specs, and the inverse of instances is instanceOf.

Inverse links such as these are maintained automatically in Cyc; the user doesn't have to enter that redundant information. Altogether, Cyc draws on about two dozen different built-in inference mechanisms such as this "inverse slot maintenance" mechanism.

Most transitive relations have both "immediate-only" and "transitive-closure" forms. For instance, let's consider *ancestors*. It's a transitive relation; that is, if x.ancestors.y and y.ancestors.z, then x.ancestors.z. We can usefully distinguish (1) the slot ancestors, and (2) the slot immediateAncestors. The immediateAncestors of x are precisely those members z of x.ancestors for which no intermediate ancestor y exists (for which x.ancestors.y and y.ancestors.z). In English, of course, we call that immediateAncestors relationship "parents." In Cyc, then, there is a parents slot and an ancestors slot; ancestors is the KleeneStar of parents, which is represented by:

```
ancestors
    instanceOf: (Slot)
    toCompute: ((ComputeByStarring parents))
```

Another transitive relation is superset; if A ⊂ B and B ⊂ C, then A ⊂ C. So in Cyc we have the two slots genls (immediate supersets of a collection) and allGenls (all supersets). Person.genls might contain just the two entries Primate and IntelligentAgent, whereas Person.allGenls would contain those plus many more (such as Mammal, Animal, Thing, and, degenerately, Person itself). Cyc also has the two slots specs and allSpecs, which incidentally are the inverses, respectively, of genls and allGenls.

The slots instanceOf and allInstanceOf are a bit more subtle, though. "Element-of" is not transitive. 7 is a PrimeNumber, and PrimeNumber is an InfiniteSet, but 7 certainly isn't an infinite set. However, we can usefully distinguish between the "immediate" sets to which x belongs and their "more distant" supersets. To look at it another way, consider x.allInstanceOf to be the full set of all the explicitly-represented Collections in Cyc to which x legally belongs. Then x.instanceOf is a subset of x.allInstanceOf; namely, it's just those sets that have no subset also in x.allInstanceOf. For example, suppose Fred.allInstanceOf contains

```
(Driver UnitedStatesPerson-1989
UnitedStatesPerson AmericanPerson
Person LegalEntity SentientAnimal
IntelligentAgent Affector
IndividualAgent Animal Agent
CompositeTangible&IntangibleObject
SomethingExisting SomethingInSomeState
NorthAmericanPerson
SocialEntity Thing IndividualObject Event
Entity RepresentedThing Stuff
Process Golfer Man Sportsman Person Primate
Vertebrate Mammal...)
```

Most of those are redundant — supersets of other entries on the same list — and so Fred.instanceOf would just contain

```
(Driver UnitedStatesPerson-1989 Golfer Man)
```

That defines instanceOf in terms of allInstanceOf. We could equally well do it the other way around; for example, in Cyc, on allInstanceOf.toCompute, is the following entry: (ComputeByComposing allGenls instancesOf). That is, given the instanceOf entries of x, we union together their allGenls, and the result is precisely x.allInstanceOf. Finally, as you might expect, the inverse slots instances and allInstances exist. Throughout this book, we will sometimes colloquially say "Fred is an instance of Person" when (to be precise) we mean Fred.allInstanceOf.Person.

Readers can view allInstanceOf as the "real" relation, and instanceOf merely as an efficiency/economy convenience. However, from the point of view of knowledge *enterers*, they just keep on adding entries to Fred.instances; redundant ones are pruned away automatically, and Fred.allInstances is continually kept properly up to date.

Now let's turn to some of the top-level collections in the system.

5.1.2. Partitionings of Thing. *Thing* — This is the universal set. Its defining predicate is "True"; so if you ask Cyc whether something is an instance of *Thing*, the answer is always "sure!" Anything you can imagine — and, more particularly, anything Cyc does imagine — is an element of this set.

Thing is partitioned in three ways:

- RepresentedThing versus InternalMachineThing

- IndividualObject versus Collection

- Intangible versus TangibleObject vs CompositeTangible&IntangibleObject

The next several sections cover these three partitionings of the world.

5.1.3. RepresentedThing versus InternalMachineThing. Every Cyc unit must be an instance of one, and only one, of these two sets: RepresentedThing and InternalMachineThing. This is one of the *trickiest* partitionings, but not one of the most *powerful*, so feel free to skip down to the next section if you get lost or bored here.

InternalMachineThing includes data structures within the machine that is (at that moment) running Cyc. That is, these are the things that Cyc can directly point at: list structures, numbers, ASCII strings, and so on.

For example, consider the unit #%TheNumber42. This is a unit that represents the integer 42. #%TheNumber42.instanceOf is *not* InternalMachineThing, however, it is Represented-InternalMachineThing. No Cyc *units* are instances of InternalMachineThing; they are, at most, representations of such things. One could, however, have the unit #%EvenNumber, which would be a collection and a subset of InternalMachineThing. #%EvenNumber would then not have an instances slot at all, but it could have a slot called actualInstances, whose value would be a list of numbers containing, for example, 42 (*not* #%TheNumber42). A distinct collection, called #%Represented-EvenNumber, would exist, which would have instances (including #%TheNumber42) but no actualInstances. These two collections point to each other via the slot actuallyRepresentsType (and its inverse).

```
EvenNumber
    allInstanceOf: Collection...
    allGenls: Integer Number,...,
        InternalMachineThing, Thing
    allSpecs: PositiveEvenNumber,...
    allActualInstances:...-2, 0, 2, 4,...,42...
    actuallyRepresentsTypeOf:
        Represented-EvenNumber

Represented-EvenNumber
    allInstanceOf: Collection...
```

```
allGenls: Represented-Integer....
   Represented-InternalMachineThing,
   RepresentedThing, Thing
allSpecs: Represented-PositiveEvenNumber...
allInstances:...MinusTwo, Zero, Two...
   TheNumber42...
actuallyRepresentsType: EvenNumber
```

So no units in the system are instances of InternalMachineThing, and very few units are instances of Represented-InternalMachineThing. For example, if #%GeorgeBush were a Represented-InternalMachineThing, it would have an actualReferent slot whose entry would have to *be* (literally!) the real flesh-and-blood person George Bush! It's not that GeorgeBush has no actualReferent, it's just that there's no way for the machine to contain a "real pointer" to it. And that's the crux of the InternalMachineThing versus RepresentedThing partitioning.

When you *represent* a thing, you're choosing a (hopefully judicious) set of attributes to capture, but there's always that danger that you've omitted some important details. That's why it's important for physicists to do experiments in the real world. Similarly, Cyc can be 100-percent sure about, and do any sort of unanticipated experiments on, only the actualInstances of the collection InternalMachineThing. This is unfortunate, because there are relatively few important, interesting instances of InternalMachineThing. Most of the time, Cyc is dealing with instances of RepresentedThing, so all it can do is to manipulate the *descriptions* of those things. That is, Cyc spends most of its time drawing inferences based on slots other than actualInstances.

InternalMachineThing and its specs are the only collections in the system that can have actualInstances and allActualInstances slots on them. But all collections can have allInstances slots, which point to units representing members of that collection. So USPresident can't have an actualInstances slot, but it can have an allInstances slot, and on that slot might sit the entry GeorgeBush, the unit representing our current president.

Cyc is written in a representation language called CycL, which is in turn written in Common Lisp (at present). We have also made an attempt to have the details of the CycL language explicitly represented in the Cyc knowledge base. Because CycL is written in Lisp, it follows that Cyc will need to know a lot about Lisp; hence, somewhere inside its knowledge base, it will need to distinguish between Lisp and non-Lisp things. As a result, an explicit distinction is made in Cyc's KB between them; that is, Thing is partitioned into LispEntity and NonLispEntity.

LispEntity is a spec of InternalMachineThing. Unfortunately, every RepresentedThing is guaranteed to be a NonLispEntity, which forces us to assert RepresentedThing.genls.NonLispEntity. That is, NonLispEntity is "higher in the tree" than RepresentedThing. Even though the LispEntity versus NonLispEntity partition is not "important," it nevertheless *visually appears* to have an important role when a person glances at the genls/specs hierarchy.

We did not have the heart to draw LispEntity and NonLispEntity on the diagram we presented in Figure 5-2. If you want to, you can pencil in NonLispEntity between Thing and RepresentedThing; and you can pencil in LispEntity below InternalMachineThing.

The other thing that is often remarked on, when looking at the top levels of the genls/specs tree, is that RepresentedThing and InternalMachineThing are not placed symmetrically; similarly, NonLispEntity and LispEntity are not placed symmetrically. This is just a special case of the following general observation:

A set and its complement may reside on very different levels of the overall hierarchy; as one is enlarged, it rises higher and higher, while its complement moves down and down toward the leaves of that tree. So the complement of a very small, very specific set of things will of necessity be a huge subset of Thing, hence will be very high up in the genls/specs hierarchy, probably right below Thing. Moreover, in such cases, the smaller set is the more interesting one.

That explains why NonLispEntity is so high up in the hierarchy. And so dull.

Let's look at this asymmetry phenomenon in a little more detail. Why is RepresentedThing so high up in the genls/specs hierarchy compared to InternalMachineThing? RepresentedThing includes everything that is tangible, or that at least has a tangible part (for example, Fred), all events (such as running, or running a Lisp program), every purely theoretical construct, such as the set of all prime numbers, and several other types of things.

That is, we can be sure that

1. No tangible object can be an InternalMachineThing

2. No real-world event can be an InternalMachineThing

3. No collection can be an InternalMachineThing

So what? From 1, we conclude that InternalMachineThing is a spec of Intangible; from 3, we conclude that it is also a spec of IndividualObject. That's why InternalMachineThing is so much "lower down" in the genls/spec hierarchy than its complement, RepresentedThing. By contrast, the only other named sets that we know of as being proper supersets of RepresentedThing are our old friend Thing plus a lot of big dull sets like NonLispEntity, NonFortranEntity, NonBlackNonRavens, etc.

5.1.4. IndividualObject versus Collection (Part 1). *Collection* — This is the set of all sets. Its instances are all the various and sundry categories that are *explicitly mentioned* in Cyc.

Here are some sample instances of Collection:

Person (the set of all people)
MetsOutfielder (a smaller set of people; this is a spec of Person)
DiningAtARestaurant (each instance of this collection is one event)
Jelly (each instance is a particular piece or portion of this stuff)

Here are some units that are not instances of Collection. Each of them is an instance of IndividualObject; each of them has no elements:

```
Fred, TheNumber42, TheJellyOnSandwich830415
LenatDiningAtJoesBar&GrillOn4July1988,
EnglishLanguage, UnitedStatesOfAmerica,
```

Every actualInstance of InternalMachineThing is also a non-Collection, of course; for example, the number 42, or the string "5-August-1989".

Let's consider MetsOutfielder. Because Thing represents the universal, all-encompassing set, every Mets outfielder — every instance of the category MetsOutfielder — is an instance of Thing. That is (by definition) what it means for MetsOutfielder to be a subset of Thing. This same argument applies for any category: *each instance of Collection is a subset of Thing.*

5.1.5. Those Basic Organizing Slots Again. How do we represent, in Cyc, the fact that MetsOutfielder is a subset of Thing? Earlier, we mentioned the slots genls and specs, which seemed to capture this relationship. That is, there would be a specs slot on Thing, pointing to MetsOutfielder — one of its entries would be MetsOutfielder. In our notation, Thing.specs.MetsOutfielder.

In addition, there would be a genls slot on MetsOutfielder pointing to Thing. Actually, of course, there would be lots of "intermediate" collections, so it would really be the allSpecs and allGenls slots that connect Thing to MetsOutfielder.

Sets of Sets: if a collection X has the property that each instance of X is also a collection, it is "a set of sets." In that case, X is not just a subset of Thing, it's a subset of Collection. Looked at another way, X is a set of sets if and only if it is a subset of Collection.

These sets of sets are important units, as we'll see later; they include ObjectType, EventType, PersonType, SubstanceType, and so on. The *instances* of PersonType include AmericanPerson, Monarch, Secretary, and hundreds of additional collections. The point here is that the instances of these . . . Type units are themselves each a collection; they have instances of their own. GeorgeBush is an instance of the AmericanPerson collection, which in turn is an instance of PersonType; that is, PersonType.allInstances.AmericanPerson, and AmericanPerson.allInstances.GeorgeBush. Similarly, Zero is an instance of RepresentedEvenNumber, which is an instance of InfiniteSet.

5.1.6. IndividualObject versus Collection (Part 2).

IndividualObject — An IndividualObject is anything other than a collection. In other words, the category Thing is *partitioned* into Collection and IndividualObject.

Only an IndividualObject can have *parts,* just as only a Collection can have instances, genls, and specs.

Don't confuse parts and instances; they are quite distinct relationships: Your head is a *part* of your body, and it is an *instance* of the category HumanHead (the set of all human heads). GeorgeBush is an *instance* of Person, and a *part* of USGovernment.

Can't any IndividualObject be regarded as a set, namely the set consisting of all its parts? We believe that it's a little more than just nomenclature. Here's the idea: Two separate concepts exist for, say Fred's car:

```
TheSetOfPartsOfFredsCar   ←   a collection
TheStructuredIndividualThatIsFredsCar   ←   an indiv.
```

The former is a collection and the latter is an IndividualObject. The *instances* of the former are the *parts* of the latter. The crucial observation is that almost always, in real life, one of these two units is important, and the other isn't.

Here are some of the slots and values for those two units:

```
TheStructuredIndividualThatIsFredsCar
   instanceOf: Camaro
   allInstanceOf: Camaro, Chevy, AmericanCar,
      Automobile, Vehicle, Device,
      IndividualObject, Thing
```

```
owner: Fred
yearOfManufacture: 1988
originalCostInUS$: 15000
parts: Fred'sCar'sSteeringWheel,
    Fred'sCar'sLeftFrontTire...
setOfParts: TheSetOfPartsOfFredsCar
```

TheSetOfPartsOfFredsCar
```
instanceOf: Collection
allInstanceOf: Collection, Thing
genls: CamaroPart
allGenls: TheSetOfPartsOfFredsCar,
    CamaroPart, CarPart, DevicePart,
    ManufacturedProduct, PhysicalObject,
    IndividualObject, Thing
setOfPartsOf:
    TheStructuredIndividualThatIsFredsCar
```

We said it's important, so let's repeat it: You often have the choice of viewing X as a set (having members) or as an individual object (having parts); in real life, one of these two views is generally vastly better than the other.

If many key relationships hold among the parts, we usually focus on the thing as an IndividualObject. If the parts don't really interrelate much, we usually focus on the thing as a Collection. Occasionally, we might want to flip back and forth among the two views, in which case we maintain both units, but that's a rarity!

For instance, we sometimes talk about the American public as a set of individual people, and we sometimes talk about the American public as a single reified "whole" in which each person plays a part. So both units would deserve to exist in Cyc: AmericanPerson (a set of people) and AmericanPublic (a massive individual that has hundreds of millions of complex, heavily interrelated parts).

See if you can spot the error in the following sentence: "Vandals disassembled Fred's car one night, and in the morning all he found was the set of his car's parts, there in his driveway."

The problem is that Fred can't find or perceive a collection, a set. Sets are intangible, imperceivable things; they are mathematical constructs. Fred could perceive each of the car parts, and he could perceive various attributes of them (for example, their orientation and relative location). And that would be enough for Fred to get angry; he would appreciate the fact that that his car's parts now lack most of the interrelationships that, the night before, they held to each other — interrelationships that enable the car to carry out its intended function.

This distinction — partOf versus instanceOf — may seem a bit vague, but it's actually a fundamental one we make all the time. If we look at Fred's car, we all admit that we can say "It is an automobile"; that is, FredsCar is an instance of the collection Automobile. But if we look at his car's muffler, we would never say "It is a Fred's car"; that is, it would be wrong to claim that FredsCarsMuffler is an instance of FredsCar. To begin with, FredsCar is not even a collection, it's an IndividualObject. So the muffler is not an instance of FredsCar; it's a part of Fred's car.

IndividualObjects are important, but so are Collections. The trouble comes because some real-world things may exhibit properties that seem to make them both sorts of things. The solution for these things is to have two separate units for the two aspects.

For example, FredsCar (an IndividualObject) and FredsCarPart (a Collection). The *parts* of the former are precisely the *instances* of the latter. The setOfParts of FredsCar is FredsCarPart; the setOfPartsOf of FredsCarPart is FredsCar.

One final example: these two separate units do exist in the KB: AmericanPublic (an IndividualObject) and AmericanPerson (a Collection). The setOfParts of AmericanPublic is AmericanPerson; and setOfPartsOf of AmericanPerson is AmericanPublic.

5.1.7. Intangible versus TangibleObject versus CompositeTangible&IntangibleObject.

Every unit in Cyc is an instance of *exactly one* of those three sets. Let's see what they're all about.

Intangible — This is any Thing that has no mass (or, more precisely, no mass-energy). Intangibles cannot be "weighed," even in principle. Some examples are:

- Person (the set of all people; you can never put a *set* on a scale)

- TheNumber42 (it's hard to weigh these types of individuals, too)

- TheEarthMoonSunTriangle (we may measure, but never *weigh*, a triangle)

- TheCycProgram (see anecdote below)

- The1988TexasDrunkDrivingLaw (the weight of law notwithstanding)

- Plus (mathematical functions and other procedures are massless)

- DiningInARestaurant (this is the general process; it is a collection)

- DougEatingDinnerAtChezFredOn9/5/88 (an instance of that last set)

- Guha'sMind (he may have a brain, but his mind clearly has zero mass)

(A government official once asked what the weight was of a piece of software, and wouldn't take zero for an answer. As he said, "Everything has *some* weight!" He finally went away happy with the answer "One picogram.")

TangibleObject — Any thing that does have mass-energy and has no intangible aspects. Intangibles have no tangible aspect; conversely, Tangibles have no intangible aspect. A hydrogen atom floating in space is a good example of a pure TangibleObject; so is a person's body.

We can't conceive of a collection having mass, so every TangibleObject must also be an IndividualObject. That's why the name of this unit is not just Tangible, but rather TangibleObject (we could have called it TangibleIndividualObject). In Cyc terms, TangibleObject is a spec of IndividualObject. That is, TangibleObject.genls.IndividualObject.

(A note to philosophers: This is not to say that we are adopting the classical dualist position, any more than one does when saying that a series of flip-flop settings implements an abstract algorithm.)

A rock is a TangibleObject. It has spatial and temporal existence, and no abstract aspects of interest to a materialist. That's not to say it can't play a role in some script, of course — such as serving as the murder weapon in a stoning event.

A person also seems solid enough, but has many properties, basically oriented around mind and agenthood, that are more appropriate for intangible objects. The same goes for a country, like France. It is has mass, and yet it can issue proclamations and buy and sell things, too. We thus need a category of entities that have both tangible and intangible aspects.

So let's consider those IndividualObjects that have both tangible and intangible parts. For instance, George Bush's mind is an Intangible and his body is a TangibleObject. What about GeorgeBush "as a whole" — into which category does that unit fall? We have a special category for these composite sorts of things: CompositeTangible&IntangibleObject.

CompositeTangible&IntangibleObject — These have two important slots, physicalExtent and intangibleExtent. So for GeorgeBush we'd have:

```
GeorgeBush
    instanceOf: Person...
    allInstanceOf: CompositeTangible&IntangibleObject...
    physicalExtent: GeorgeBushsBody
    intangibleExtent: GeorgeBushsMind
    interestingness: High
```

```
GeorgeBushsBody
    instanceOf: HumanMaleBody
    allInstanceOf: TangibleObject...
    physicalExtentOf: GeorgeBush
    weightInLbs: 200
    speed: Low
    interestingness: Low

GeorgeBushsMind
    instanceOf: HumanMind
    allInstanceOf: Intangible...
    intangibleExtentOf: GeorgeBush
    speed: Moderate
    interestingness: Moderate
```

This illustrates one reason for "teasing apart" the various aspects of GeorgeBush: we might have a slot (like interestingness) that has different values for his tangible part (his body), his intangible part (his mind), and the composite that is "the whole person." This may seem like a luxury, but it is a distinction humans do easily make and therefore must represent; it is a distinction that we occasionally *need* to make (for example, think of the movies *Frankenstein*, *Freaky Friday*, *The Exorcist*, and *Big*).

In practice, the slot intangibleExtent is rarely used, because it has several more specialized, more precise versions, and one of them is usually what's intended: e.g., functionalExtent, mentalExtent, spiritualExtent.

Often, we blur the tangible/intangible/composite distinction in everyday speech. We verbally refer to Bush simply by name both when we say something about his body ("Bush weighs less than Gorbachev") or when we say something about his mind ("Bush is smarter than Gorbachev"). This is tolerable because our listeners are able to easily understand what we mean — and that, in turn, is because the speaker and the listeners share enough consensus reality knowledge to make the disambiguation task quick and sure. Weight can make sense only for Bush's body; smartness can make sense only for his mind.

Cyc, too, is (barely) able to accept and generate ambiguous statements like that; so long as it understands the difference "deep down," the rest is considered merely an interface issue.

It's worth making the distinction internally, because there will be sentences that could in principle be taken either way, as applying to his body or to his mind, such as "Bush is quicker than Gorbachev."

What other kinds of CompositeTangible&IntangibleObjects are there, besides people? Clearly, each intelligent agent has this duality, even if it's not human: FidoTheDog (its body and its mind), ShakeyTheRobot (its hardware and its software), and so on. Let's discuss a few less obvious examples of composites: MCC, France, and this book.

Why do we think of companies as CompositeTangible&IntangibleObjects? Consider MCC. It has a physical side (its building, the bodies of its employees) and an intangible side (its research output, its contractual agreements with government agencies and other companies). Its intangible side makes it an intelligent agent: it's capable of reacting to novel situations, learning from experience, communicating with other intelligent agents, and so on.

That argument applies to all types of organizations, of course, not just companies. It even extends to nations (that is, to allInstances of Country). The physical extent of a country — say France — is its land, the buildings and creatures that sit on that land, the minerals that lie underneath it, and so on. The functional extent of a country includes its government, the laws and agencies, the will of the people, the collective intelligence of the people, etc.

But the class CompositeTangible&IntangibleObject is wider still. It includes this book you're reading, which has a physical part (the physical object that you can hold in your hands and look at and use as a paperweight or as kindling) and an intangible part (the meaning or content you can hold in your mind). Other types of publications have their own idiosyncratic tangible parts (which might be film or videotape or audiotape) and intangible parts (plot, theme, dramatic device, characterization, and so on).

5.1.8. Stuff. This is a continuation of the material presented in section 4.1.6 on the unit representing Gold (an instance of Collection and a spec of Stuff and TangibleObject) as opposed to the unit representing AllTheGoldInTheUniverse (an instance of Gold and, hence, of IndividualObject and TangibleObject).

Stuff — When you cut up some stuff, you get lots of little pieces of the same stuff. The unit Stuff represents the set of all pieces of any substance; PeanutButter is a spec of Stuff. Its portions or instances are all the various individual globs of peanut butter. Each of those pieces of PeanutButter is a piece of Stuff.

Here are some other instances of SubstanceType: Wood; Water; Time; Walking; Energy. If you take a portion of water and divide it into ten smaller portions, each of those is a full-fledged portion of water. We say that Walking is a type of stuff because if you imagine dividing an hour of walking up in half, each of those two halves can be treated as a full-fledged walking event.

So things can be spatially stuff-like (for example, Water) or temporally stuff-like (for example, Walking).

Intrinsic properties can be inherited from a type of stuff to its instances. From Water, we can inherit (to all pieces of water, that is, to all instances of Water) a default value for density, physicalState, purity, color, smell, unit of measure, price per gallon, and so on. We cannot inherit *extrinsic* properties (such as precise location, mass, size, total price), because they will vary from one piece of water to another.

It is important to distinguish Stuff from IndividualObject. If you take an axe and smash Table85 (an IndividualObject) into ten pieces, none of them is likely to be a Table. But if Table85 were made of wood, and recorded as an instance of Wood (the collection of all wooden things), then after the hatcheting all ten pieces would still be instances of Wood.

Table85 is an instance of Table (which in turn is a spec of IndividualObject), and it is also an instance of Wood (which in turn is a spec of Stuff). Table85 gets intrinsic properties inherited from Wood (density, flashPoint, smell, color, hardness) and extrinsic properties inherited from Table (numberOfLegs, sellingPrice, axes of symmetry). Each of the ten smashed pieces is still Wood, hence each piece keeps all the intrinsic properties, but the pieces are not little tables, so each piece loses the extrinsic properties. Each piece of the table still has more or less the same density, flashPoint, smell, color, and hardness as did the original table; but each piece does not have four legs, nor would it sell for as much as the original table, nor is it still as symmetric. (These are all *defaults* that are preserved or lost — of course there can be exceptions!)

Similarly, Walking might inherit, to its instances, default values for unitOfMeasure, rateInMPH, howAttentiveThePerformerMustBe, and so on. Now consider the event that consisted of your walking from your house to your car this morning. If you divide up that event into ten segments, each of them is still an instance of Walking — and still gets those same default values.

5.2. Event, Process, EventType, and ProcessType

Event — This is the set of things that may have a temporal extent (startingTime, endingTime, duration). This is therefore also the set of things that relate to one another by temporal relations, such as before, after, startsDuring, contiguousAfter, and so on.

Each event has — by definition — all the various temporal attributes (startingTime, duration, before, startsDuring . . .), at least in principle; it is situated in some particular piece of time. WorldWarII is an unfortunate instance of Event (it's also an instance of the collection War, which is a spec of Event). Other examples of Event: the writing of this chapter; your reading of it; and the sound of some firecracker exploding.

Process — Suppose you ate some popcorn last night at the movies; let's say it took you about 10 minutes. Now consider the third minute of that ten-minute interval. Imagine watching a video of yourself during that minute. What were you doing? You were eating popcorn. Any "temporal slice" of a PopcornEating event is just a (smaller) PopcornEating event. We say that PopcornEating is a *Process*. If you take a temporal slice of an event where some Process is being carried out, that same process is still going on in that temporal slice.

Here is an important analogy: *Process is to Event as Stuff is to IndividualObject.*

In the case of Stuff like PeanutButter, you could take a lump of that stuff, divide it into ten smaller lumps, and each of them would be a (smaller) lump of PeanutButter. Just as there are specs of IndividualObject (like Table) that aren't specs of Stuff, so too there are specs of Event (like PlayingTwoGamesOfTennis) that aren't specs of Process. Thus the need to have ProcessType.

PlayingTennis is an instance of ProcessType, but PlayingTwoGamesOfTennis isn't. Imagine any instance of PlayingTwoGamesOfTennis; for example, FredAndBobPlayingTwoGamesOfTennisRightAfterLunchOn9/13/89. Now imagine the third minute, say, of that event. It might still be an instance of PlayingTennis, but it (all by itself) is certainly *not* an instance of PlayingTwoGamesOfTennis. Another example of a type of Event that's not an instance of ProcessType is GettingTenYearsOlder.

EventType and *ProcessType* — The collection of all types of Event is EventType. Thus, Event is an instance of EventType, and so is EatingPopcorn and PlayingTennis and PlayingTwoGamesOfTennis and GettingTenYearsOlder.

The collection of all types of Process is ProcessType. Thus, Process is an instance of ProcessType, and so is EatingPopcorn and PlayingTennis and Aging and Walking.

The basic inherited piece of knowledge that each instance of ProcessType gets is:

> *"For any one of your instances,*
> *for any portion of it,*
> *   it's still an instance of you."*

What does that mean? Consider some instance of ProcessType; say, EatingPopcorn. Various properties would be inherited to any instance of EatingPopcorn — any event in which someone ate popcorn. The inherited slots (and their values) would include

```
typeOfFoodConsumed:                (Popcorn)
rateOfConsumptionInOzsPerMinute:   (2)
```

Consider any one instance of EatingPopcorn, a particular event: for example, FredEatingBox92105OfPopcorn. This event might have occurred last Sunday at the local movie theater. Now consider any portion of this event — say the first five minutes, or the middlemost minute, or whatever — and represent it explicitly by a unit: TheFirst5MinsOfFredEatingBox92105OfPopcorn. That unit *must* also be an instance of EatingPopcorn. That's the point of the italicized fact we stated a couple paragraphs ago, the fact that got inherited to EatingPopcorn.

That "stuff-like" behavior does not carry over to instances of EventType, however. Let's pick some instance of EventType; say, EatingOneBoxOfPopcorn. The italicized fact does *not* get inherited to EatingOneBoxOfPopcorn, because it is not an instance of ProcessType (it is an instance of EventType). Some extrinsic properties are inherited to all instances of EatingOneBoxOfPopcorn, namely

```
quantityOfBoxesWorthConsumed:    1.0
durationInMinutes:               15
volumeOfStuffConsumedInOzs:      30
```

Consider an instance of EatingOneBoxOfPopcorn, say FredEatingBox92105OfPopcorn. Hey, isn't that the same unit we used in the above paragraph? Sure! No problem — its allInstanceOf includes both EatingPopcorn and EatingOneBoxOfPopcorn, plus several other things as well, such as Eating, PerformingAnAction, Process, Event, Intangible, and Thing. Now consider any portion of this event — say, the first five minutes — and suppose we represent it explicitly by a unit, the same unit we saw in the previous paragraph: TheFirst5MinsOfFredEatingBox92105OfPopcorn. That unit is *not* an instance of EatingOneBoxPopcorn. Fred eats only about a third of the box, not a whole box, during the first five minutes. That unit *is* (as we said earlier) an instance of EatingPopcorn.

That's what it means for the italicized fact to inherit to instances of ProcessType (such as Walking, or EatingPopcorn) but not to instances of EventType (such as EatingABoxOfPopcorn, or WalkingToTheStoreAndBack, or PlayingTwoGamesOfTennis).

If you faint in the middle of a WalkingToTheStoreAndBack event, you didn't really carry out the action WalkingToTheStoreAndBack. But if you faint during an episode of Walking, you really were Walking during that first few minutes (or however long it was until you fainted).

If you look along the specs (subsets) hierarchy in Cyc, you'll notice below Process a sequence of collections that alternate between a ProcessType and an EventType. For example,

Process   ← an instance of ProcessType
  \
   Event   ← an instance of EventType
    \
     Eating   ← an instance of ProcessType
      \
       EatingABoxOfPopcorn   ← an instance of EventType

This is not unlike what happens underneath (tracing specs links from) Stuff; there is an alternating sequence of SubstanceType and ObjectType collections:

Stuff   ← an instance of SubstanceType
  \
   IndividualObject   ← an instance of ObjectType
    \
     Water   ← an instance of SubstanceType
      \
       Lake   ← an instance of ObjectType

(You may find it strange that all three of these hold:

Lake is an instance of ObjectType and a spec of Water
Water is an instance of SubstanceType
Lake *isn't* an instance of SubstanceType

There is no contradiction there. Just because X is an instance of C, and Y is a spec of X, doesn't mean that Y has to be an instance of C. For example, Integer is an instance of InfiniteSet, IntegersFrom1to10 is a spec of Integer, but IntegersFrom1to10 is clearly *not* an instance of InfiniteSet.)

The basic inherited piece of knowledge that each instance of SubstanceType gets is:

"For any one of your instances,
   for any portion of it,
     it's still an instance of you."

For example, Lake is an instance of ObjectType, but not of SubstanceType; a little piece of a lake is not itself a lake. Let's examine this in more detail.

First, if we consider Lake Michigan as a big piece of water, then it is an instance of both Lake (an ObjectType) and Water (a SubstanceType). If we take some small portion of the Lake, like the bit Fred is about to swallow because his mouth is open, that thing is still a piece of Water (that's what the italicized fact says), but it's not a Lake. Lucky for Fred!

Water inherits to its instances (pieces) various intrinsic defaults, such as

color: transparent
taste: none
density: 1.0
breathability: Low
drinkability: High

Those defaults are (more or less) true of Lake Michigan, and — to the same extent — they're true of that mouthful of water that Fred is swallowing.

Lake inherits to its instances various extrinsic defaults, such as

avgSize: StadiumSized
waveHeight: Low
sportsPracticedOnIt: Boating, Swimming, Fishing
depthInMeters: 20

They're true for (that is, plausible default guesses for) Lake Michigan, but they're certainly not true of that mouthful-sized bit of the lake.

So ProcessType is to EventType as SubstanceType is to ObjectType as TangibleSubstanceType is to TangibleObjectType.

The most general instance of ProcessType is Process. All other instances of ProcessType are specs of Process; conversely, all specs of Process are instances of ProcessType. Similarly, the most general instance of EventType is Event, that of SubstanceType is Stuff, and that of ObjectType is IndividualObject.

In many ways, we could dispense with units like Event and Process and Stuff; the real "power" is in the units EventType and ProcessType and SubstanceType. For now, though, all of those units are kept around.

Each instance of ProcessType bequeaths to its instances various intrinsic properties — such as the rate at which the process takes place, the level of attentiveness required during the process, the type of performer required, the *type* of attributes that change, and so on. Each instance of EventType can bequeath to its instances various extrinsic properties — such as the expected duration, expected list of changes (that is, not just the types but the total *magnitude* of the changes) caused by the event, and so on.

EatingPopcorn might inherit some default facts to its instances, such as the rate at which the popcorn gets eaten, the body parts that the performer ought to have, etc.:

```
EatingPopcorn
   instanceOf: ProcessType
   allInstanceOf: ProcessType, EventType,
      Collection, Intangible, Thing
   genls: Eating
   allGenls: EatingPopcorn, Eating, Ingesting,
      PerformingAnAction, Process, Event,
      IndividualObject, Intangible,
      RepresentedThing, Thing
   allInstances: FredEatingBox839120fPopcorn
   ouncesConsumedPerMinute: 4
   bodyPartsRequiredOfPerformer: Teeth,
      Mouth, Throat, Stomach, Brain
   likelyCoOccurrence:
      WatchingAMovieAtAMovieTheater
   degreeOfAttentivenessRequired:
      AutoPilotLevelOfVigilance
```

EatingOneBoxOfPopcorn might inherit, to the events that form its instances, a very different series of default facts:

```
EatingOneBoxOfPopcorn
   instanceOf: EventType
   allInstanceOf: EventType, Collection,
      Intangible, Thing
   genls: EatingPopcorn
   allGenls: EatingOneBoxOfPopcorn,
      EatingPopcorn, Eating, Ingesting,
      PerformingAnAction, Process, Event,
      Thing, IndividualObject, Intangible,
      RepresentedThing
   allInstances: FredEatingBox839120fPopcorn...
   durationInMinutes: 15
   totalCostToPerformerInUS$: 2
   engendersFeeling: FeelingStuffed
```

If you consider a particular event, FredEatingBox83912OfPopcorn, it would be an instance of both EatingOneBoxOfPopcorn and EatingPopcorn and would inherit both types of default information. From EatingPopcorn, it inherits what's *going on during* the event. From EatingOneBoxOfPopcorn, it inherits information about the global "before and after" changes to the actors and the end result to the world.

```
FredEatingBox83912OfPopcorn
   instanceOf: EatingOneBoxOfPopcorn
   allInstanceOf: EatingOneBoxOfPopcorn,
      EatingPopcorn, Eating, Ingesting,
      PerformingAnAction, Process, Event,
      Thing, Intangible, RepresentedThing,
      IndividualObject
   performer: Fred
   object: BoxOfPopcorn83912
   date: 9/10/88
   ouncesConsumedPerMinute: 4
   bodyPartsRequiredOfPerformer: Teeth, Mouth,
      Throat, Stomach, Brain
   likelyCoOccurrence:
      WatchingAMovieAtAMovieTheater
   degreeOfAttentivenessRequired:
      AutoPilotLevelOfVigilance
   durationInMinutes: 15
   totalCostToPerformerInUS$: 2
   engendersFeeling: FeelingStuffed
```

Later, we'll see that Process and Event are coextensional; an instance of one of them *must be* an instance of the other. Why not just merge them together into one unit? The reasons are twofold:

1. The substance-like nature of processes (that is, of instances of ProcessType). In other words, *ProcessType is quite different from EventType, even though their respectively most general instances, namely Process and Event, are coextensional.*

    (By the way, many of those processes are so specific that they turn out to have only one instance, one event, and those singleton-processes are almost never worth defining.)

2. The fact that there are some useful slots that each Process can have (for example, subProcesses, temporalGranule, rate) and some useful slots that each Event can have (for example, startingTime, dura-

tion, contiguousBefore). Whenever some slots "start making sense" at a collection (that is, are legal slots that each instance of the collection may have), it's worth representing that collection as a separate unit.

A similar coextension occurs between Stuff and IndividualObject, though SubstanceType and ObjectType are quite different sets. The two general italicized facts, several paragraphs above, get inherited to, respectively, all instances of SubstanceType and ProcessType, but not to any instances of ObjectType or EventType.

(Many of those types of stuff are not worth defining, because they're so specific that they have only one object that's an instance of them (for instance, BertrandRussellStuff — the substance of which Bertrand Russell was composed). There really never was and (we hope) never will be any other object than BertrandRussell himself that was composed of this stuff.)

The last two "not worth defining" remarks are reminiscent of the pragmatic policy we have (as humans and as designers of Cyc) of not defining and naming most collections that are singletons. Humans go one step further, of course, and get sloppy about distinguishing (at least in casual conversation) the singleton set from its element.

One ubiquitous "passive" type of process is *SomethingExisting*. It's a fairly general instance of ProcessType; a large subset (spec) of Process. Each tangible object that exists can be said to be carrying out an instance of the SomethingExisting process. It's a kind of *process* (not just a kind of event) because it's temporally stuff-like: if Lenat was existing today, he was also existing from 3 to 4 p.m. today.

Anything that can have an *age* is, during its interval of existence, carrying out its own instance of SomethingExisting.

Each tangible object is therefore an instance of Process and (because Process and Event are coextensional) also an instance of Event. This is true not just for each TangibleObject, but also for each CompositeTangible&IntangibleObject and each Intelligence (that is, anything that is the functional extent of some composite object). All instances of those collections are space-time-intelligence events, and they are running the very general process of existing.

Here's another way to view this situation. The thing we call Table15 has been through lots of particular events in its "lifetime"; it has passed through stages like Table15BeforeItWasSold, Table15InFredsOldHouse, Table15InFredsNewHouse, Table15InFredsGarage, Table15InFredsGarageSale, Table15InJoesJunkyard, etc. Some of these events are subevents of others — for example, all of those units that mentioned "Fred" in their names are subevents of Table15WhileOwnedByFred. Here is one important point: What we *call* "Table15" is really just *the minimal super-event of all of these various Table15 . . . events during its period of existence.* It is the "smallest" event whose subevents include all of the Table15 . . . events. Its startingTime is the earliest of all of their startingTimes; its endingTime is the latest of all of their endingTimes; and so on. Table15 can thus have a startingTime, an endingTime, a duration, and so on.

But just because we use the same name to refer to all those different historic incarnations of Table15 doesn't mean that they are all the same "thing." In fact, it is essential to understand that they are (in many ways) quite distinct objects, though they are obviously related to each other. Well, how are those incarnations of Table15 related to each other? They're all *temporal subabstractions* of the same entity, Table15, just as ReaganAsAnActor, ReaganAsCaliforniaGovernor, and ReaganAsUSPresident are all temporal subabstractions of the entity RonaldReagan.

Entities are things that have no temporal superabstraction, that can (and usually do) have some temporal subabstractions. Entities usually continue to exist continuously over time, throughout their lifetime. That is frequently not true for their subabstractions; for example, consider BushWhileEating, which exists a couple hours every day.

Having separate units in Cyc to represent each "state" that Table15 passes through is a potentially explosive policy, and it leads us headlong into the frame problem. A later section deals with how Cyc copes with this. The basic answer is that:

- We bother to make those separate units only when there's some important change to the table (this controls the "explosion" in the number of units in the system)

- We explicitly state only what has changed and let a form of inheritance preserve the unchanged attributes (this "temporal projection" controls the frame problem in this case).

Similarly, Fred is viewed as a space-intelligence-time composition, an amalgam of FredAsABaby, FredAsATexasResident, FredAsALawyer, FredWhileEating, FredWhileAngry, etc. (Notice that these various events needn't be temporally disjoint from one another.)

This view, though possibly counter-intuitive, is one that we have been led to empirically, by looking at lots of cases of "what needs to get expressed." It seems to allow us to say the things we would like to say. We'll see this in detail later.

5.3. Slot — and Other Useful Sets of Slots

In section 4.2.2 we articulated four criteria for having a collection of slots exist as a separate unit in Cyc — well, three and a half criteria. For instance, we want to *avoid* having collections like AutomobileSlot, AmericanAutomobileSlot, CompactAutomobileSlot, etc., that mimic the collections of individuals that exist (Automobile, AmericanAutomobile, CompactAutomobile), unless we have some special reasons for their existence. Briefly recapping, the four reasons were:

1. The collection of slots C has a non-empty canHaveSlots slot.

2. Its definition is large and/or complex and/or slippery.

3. There are lots of other slot/value pairs on C, or SeeUnits on them.

4. It sounds natural to human beings (this is a shaky reason!)

So, based on this, what are the high-level sets of slots that exist in Cyc?

One collection that deserves to exist is *Slot* — the set of all slots. It has some crucial canHaveSlots: namely, makesSenseFor, entryIsA, entryFormat, slotConstraints, and lots more! Every unit representing a slot can and should have those slots.

One partitioning of Slot is into BookkeepingSlot and DefiningSlot.

Each *BookkeepingSlot* talks about the units on which they sit *qua* units, as data structures in the Cyc computer program. Here are some instances of BookkeepingSlot:

myCreator
myCreationTime
myLastEditor
averageSlotLength
unitNotToBeDumped?

Each *DefiningSlot* talks about the entities *represented* by the units. For example:

height
hobbies
nationalAnthem
instanceOf
iq

So the DefiningSlots, sitting on the Fred unit tell things about Fred; and the BookkeepingSlots tell things about the Fred unit.
    BookkeepingSlot is partitioned into:

- DynamicBookkeepingSlot — slots that deal with inheritance, caching, demons, the agenda, and other CycL inference mechanisms — for example, level4PutFeatures, backwardInheritancePaths, toTranslateConstraintInformation, alreadyComputedSlots.

- StaticBookkeepingSlot — these are the metaslots that do *not* encode aspects of the CycL inferencing procedures — for example, myCreator, myCreationTime, copiedFrom.

A different set of divisions of BookkeepingSlot is based on which units can legally have those slots. At present, the members of this set are:

BookkeepingSlotForAnyUnit
BookkeepingSlotForSlots
BookkeepingSlotForCollections

One spec of BookkeepingSlot that cuts across all the other partitionings is PolicySlot. These are slots that describe and define Cyc "policies." *Policies* affect what Cyc does when one user steps on another's toes, such as when one user deletes something that the other user recently entered into the KB — for example, policyMessageToOwner, policyMessageToViolator, policySubjects, policyConsequents, policyAntecedent, policyOwner.
    By the way, there are slots related to the CycL metalevel — namely the agenda — but those are not BookkeepingSlots. (For example, agendaPriority, which sits on each task, really does tell something about that agenda task conceptually, not about the unit representing that task.)
    Now let's turn from BookkeepingSlot to DefiningSlot.
    DefiningSlot is partitioned into the following three collections: IntensionalSlot, TaxonomicSlot, and ExtensionalSlot. Each of these slots meets all of our criteria for having slot categories exist. They are important, they are natural, there is some special stuff to say about each one, and their definition is slippery, to say the least.

- IntensionalSlot — slots that capture the intensional definition of a thing: for example, makesSenseFor, majorCrops, argumentType

- TaxonomicSlot — slots that interrelate families of units into hierarchies: for example, genls, specs, instances, instanceOf, parts, partOf, subAbstractionType

- ExtensionalSlot — slots that relate extrinsic properties of a thing: for example, color, lastName, closestNeighbors, physicalExtent

By the way, notice that most of the slots that make sense for slots (for example, makesSenseFor, entryIsA, entryFormat) express intensional properties of all of the different (extensional) occurrences of that slot throughout the KB. Thus, they are instances of IntensionalSlot, not ExtensionalSlot.

6. Representational Thorns, and Their Blunting

In this chapter, we describe in detail the representational problems that have appeared in Cyc. Most of these are long-standing problems from philosophy or AI. For each, we give what we believe to be a pragmatically adequate solution. (What counts as a *solution* to a representational or ontological problem is of course itself a knotty problem.) These are not 100-percent-complete solutions, but each has shown itself to be an adequate way of handling the problem. They have withstood testing by personnel both sympathetic and unsympathetic, skilled and unskilled in various disciplines. Incidentally, some of these sections may repeat a little of the material from chapter 5; however, in such cases, this chapter goes into much more detail.

6.1. What the Universe Is Made of — Stuff and Things

6.1.1. Stuff Is Coextensional with IndividualObject.
As we said earlier, individual objects are things that have parts, and stuffs are things each of whose portions are composed of the same stuff. Person is a type of individual object; so, for example, Fred has parts (Fred'sHead, Fred'sLiver, etc.), and each part is definitely *not* a miniature little person! Dirt is a type of stuff; so, for example, LumpOfDirt85 has no "parts" *per se*, but you can break it down into portions, and each portion *will* be a full-fledged instance of Dirt.

The distinctions and relations between these two categories constitute one of the classic problems in philosophy (and knowledge representation). In linguistics, the corresponding problem is that of mass nouns *versus* count nouns.

Stuff is the most general, or generic, substance. All the various instances of SubstanceType are specs of Stuff. A particular portion of a substance, such as Lump90004OfPeanutButter, would be an instance of PeanutButter and hence also an instance of Stuff.

IndividualObject is the category of all discernible, separable, distinguishable objects. So, for example, Person (the set of all people) is a spec of IndividualObject, and Fred is an instance of Person and hence also an instance of IndividualObject.

The relation between individual objects and stuff in Cyc is a strange one, namely IndividualObject.*specs*.Stuff and also IndividualObject.*genls*.Stuff! To take that one step at a time, first let's see why the first assertion was made — namely that Stuff is a spec of IndividualObject. The justification for this is as follows.

Consider a typical substance, such as peanut butter. An instance of PeanutButter is some particular physical lump of peanut butter — hence, it is also necessarily an individual object. This really means that the set of pieces of peanut butter (PeanutButter) is a subset of the class of all objects (IndividualObject). The same argument holds for any kind of substance. So all subsets of Stuff (for example, PeanutButter) are subsets of IndividualObject. Hence, Stuff is a subset (that is, spec) of IndividualObject.

But the situation is even worse. The "inclusion" goes the other way, too! Namely, IndividualObject is a spec of Stuff! The justification for this is as follows.

Fred — who's an individual object — can be thought of as being composed of "FredStuff." This is *possible* thanks to the continuity of matter over time; but is it *useful*? We rarely define one-of-a-kind sorts of stuff, like WashingtonMonumentStuff or GeorgeBushStuff, though there are some cases of this (for example, wielding any piece of the planet Krypton as a weapon; cherishing any fragment of a saint's body).

There's not much that can be usefully inherited from Stuff, so this direction of the equivalence is treated as more of an intellectual curiosity than a pragmatic part of the ontology (that is, we don't make a big deal of the fact that IndividualObject is a subset of Stuff).

In other words, it's much more useful to define various sorts of *homogeneous* stuff (like blood, concrete, and walking) than it is to define one-of-a-kind sorts of stuff. Nevertheless, theoretically, we admit that Stuff and IndividualObject are coextensional. Any instance of one is an instance of the other.

So we've put you into a situation where Fred is considered an instance of SpatialStuff (he's made out of FredStuff, or, if we mercifully choose not to define such goo, he's made out of Stuff). You will be relieved to know that, at present, only important, well-known sorts of Stuff — mostly homogeneous stuff — are defined in the system. We want to keep it that way!

6.1.2.   Separating the Collection PieceOfGold from the Stuff Gold.   In the last chapter, we explained the difference between SubstanceType and ObjectType. To reiterate:

SubstanceType is the collection of all types of stuff. The instances of this set are, for example, PeanutButter (the set of all lumps of peanut butter) and Water (the set of all pieces of water). The most general instance of SubstanceType is Stuff.

ObjectType is the collection of all types of individual objects. Some of its instances are Person (the set of all people) and WalkingToThe-StoreAndBack. Its most general instance is IndividualObject.

As we said earlier, the basic inherited piece of knowledge is:

> *For each instance S of SubstanceType,*
> *   for any one of its instances I,*
> *   for any portion P of it,*
> *   P is guaranteed to be an instance of S*

For example, consider an instance of SubstanceType — say, PeanutButter. Consider an instance of that set — say the large mass of peanut butter spread on that cracker in front of you. Consider a portion of that — say, the little piece you're about to bite off of the cracker. That little piece is guaranteed to be an instance of PeanutButter, just as the whole cracker-sized lump of the stuff was.

That's true for each stuff (for example, Water), but in general it is not true for each kind of individual object (for example, Lake). A small portion of a bucketful of water is still a portion of water; but a small piece of a lake is not still a lake. And that's an important reason for distinguishing SubstanceType from ObjectType.

Hold on a minute, you may say. What's this about PeanutButter being the set of all lumps of peanut butter? Where did that come from? We already argued that a substance, such as Gold, can't be an IndividualObject. By our partition of Thing, it must therefore be a Collection. Hmmm . . . that's a little too pat. Let's look deeper.

Is Gold then anything other than the collection PieceOfGold? We would argue that extensionally it is not — each instance of one of those two collections is an instance of the other. X can't be a lump of gold unless it is some portion of Gold. And any portion of gold is a PieceOfGold.

Well, if the two sets are coextensional, should we have them both? If we don't want to have them both, which one is most useful?

We said that the IndividualObjects with which any system must be concerned are the lumps of gold or peanut butter. But what is important about lumps of gold as a class is their common density, atomic composition, melting point, value per ounce, and so on. *Intrinsic* properties such as these are inherited from a type of stuff to its portions.

That justifies having the set Gold. What about PieceOfGold? There may be some extrinsic properties inherited to each piece of gold, such as their average weight, diameter, and so on. If so, PieceOfGold deserves to exist as a separate unit as well.

Incidentally, this leads to the conclusion that WhiteGold is a spec (subset) of Gold, in the same way that CompactCar is a spec of Car. No problems seem to arise with this way of thinking.

A final piece of evidence comes from the consideration of what happens when we specialize a substance too far. MilitaryOrdnance is a card-carrying substance — it's sold by the ton and so on. But when we look at instances of MilitaryOrdnance that have a particular shape, say Rifles, we suddenly get a class of very concrete IndividualObjects. This suggests that the relationships between substances must be the same as the relationships between object classes, namely subset and superset (specs and genls), because the two hierarchies are so intimately intertwined.

6.1.3. Defining "Intrinsic" and "Extrinsic" Properties.   So what's the difference? Why, for example, are there such clear linguistic differences in the treatment of mass nouns and count nouns?

Consider once again the example of a wooden table (Table85). It is an instance of both Table, which is an ObjectType, and Wood, which is a substanceType. By virtue of its being a Table, Table85 gets defaults for various extrinsic properties, such as its number of legs, approximate size, weight, cost, and so on. By virtue of its being a wooden object, it gets default intrinsic properties such as its flash point, density, previously-alive nature, and so on. If we take an axe and break up Table85 into ten pieces, none of the pieces has the same cost, weight, number of legs, or size as the original, but they each still have the same flash point, density, and previously-alive nature.

So if we make a table out of wood, it inherits extrinisic properties from its being a table, and intrinsic properties from its being made of wood. More generally:

If we make an object of type X out of substance Y,
*then it inherits default **extrinsic** properties from X,*
*and it inherits default **intrinsic** properties from Y.*

Instead of grappling with how to independently define intrinsic versus extrinsic, let's take the above italicized statement as the *definition* of those two terms. This is bound to raise the hackles of many people at first, but it sort of grows on you.

So intrinsic properties are *defined* as ones that get inherited to you from the type of Stuff you're made of; extrinsic properties are *defined* as ones that you inherit because of the type of IndividualObject you are an instance of. A later section talks in greater detail about the notion of temporal and spatial intrinsicness.

6.1.4. Grain Size and Mob. Every type of substance has associated with it the notion of the smallest granule, namely the building blocks that make up the smallest possible portion of that substance. For instance, with Wood, its granule is the PlantCell; for Water, it's the WaterMolecule; for Walking, it's TakingAStep; for Eating, it's the BitingChewingSwallowing sequence.

Anything smaller than the granule is not considered to be a portion of that substance. One granule, or even a few granules together, is borderline. If you take one step, are you walking? If you have three water molecules, do you have a small body of water? The smaller the number of granules, and the smaller the relative number of granules (to the number present in a "typical" portion of the stuff) the more violations there will be of the stuff's default properties.

So if we keep hacking at Table85 until the pieces are on the order of a few plant cells in size, it no longer is correct to say that each one of them is a piece of wood — and the various intrinsic properties would not inherit down to them any more.

Of course, as one moves even further down in grain size, the granules themselves get broken down into stuffs; for example, a single woody plant cell contains some cellulose. The granule size of the substance cellulose is down at the molecular level. And so on, with alternating stuff/individual units, as one continues restricting the size of the object under consideration.

The substance-like nature of a portion of a substance really comes through when one is dealing with a *Mob* of granules. We define a *mob* to be a large but indeterminate number of granules. For example, there is a mob of sand grains on Hawaiian beaches; there is a mob of hairs on Fred's head; there is a mob of water molecules in this glass of water; there is a mob of stones in that wall; a mob of townsmen in that lynching party; a mob of converts during a crusade; a mob of flowers in a field of wildflowers; a mob of hours in your life; and a mob of body segments in that worm that's crawling up your leg.

You may be able to get an approximate number, or a ballpark estimate, or a range, of the number of granules present — but usually *you don't even care* much about that level of approximation. You just know that there are enough of them to treat them like a substance, and then you do so.

Does this lead to problems? Theoretically, of course it does. When you remove a stone from a heap of stones (a mob), you have a heap of stones left. But when you get down near the grain size of the stuff (in this case, each stone is a granule), you no longer have a mob, and it becomes less and less likely that the various intrinsic defaults will continue to inherit.

6.2. Time

6.2.1. Temporal Objects (Events) and Temporal Stuff (Processes).

The relationship between IndividualObject and Stuff holds not just in the spatial domain but also in the temporal domain.

TangibleStuff: The category for things that are *spatially substance-like*. Its specs include PeanutButter, Water, and Wood.

TangibleObject: The category for things that are *spatially object-like*. Its specs include Person, Table, and Lake.

As we saw above, Tangible Object is a genl (superset) of TangibleStuff, and indeed is (at least theoretically) coextensional with it.

Event: The temporal analogue of TangibleObject.
Process: The temporal analogue of TangibleStuff.

Consider an event, like your reading this book right now. Any temporal slice of this event (say, the last ten seconds) still has the same values for properties such as energy consumption rate, reading rate, enjoyment level, etc. But properties such as the total energy consumed in reading this book, total time taken, lessons learned, etc., will have a quite different value for the whole reading event than for just the last ten seconds.

The "substance versus object" relationship seems symmetric in the spatial and temporal dimensions. However, there is an interesting breakdown of this symmetry, as follows:

> *All things that are substances in the spatial sense are also necessarily substances in the temporal sense — but not vice versa.*

This is a sweeping statement to make, but we have come to believe it is true. It stems from the fact that spatially substance-like things always seem to exist over some nonzero interval of time. That is, this is really because of one of the fundamental aspects of Nature — namely, that there are few truly abrupt changes, at least at a macro level.

To see why the "not *vice versa*" is true, consider Table85, which is sitting in my kitchen from 3 to 4 p.m. We have already seen that it is not spatially substance-like: The weight, price, etc., of the various pieces of the table are different from one another, and certainly none of the little pieces is itself a table. But it is temporally substance-like: If you imagine each of the 60 one-minute-long time-slices of the table from 3 to 4 p.m., there is very little difference among them, and each is an instance of the SomethingExisting process, as was the original hour-long event (and, for that matter, the entire twenty-year-long event of Table85 from its creation to its destruction).

We'll return to further explain and justify our general claim a little bit later.

6.2.2. SomethingExisting (an Important Spec of Process).

A surprising fraction of things in the world falls under the collection Event. We'll take a look at some of them now, and then turn more generally to the issue of how we represent time.

Two of the most important specs of Event are Process and SomethingOccurring. We've dealt with Process before; in this subsection we'll focus on an important spec of Process, namely SomethingExisting, and in a later subsection we'll turn to SomethingOccurring.

"Process" represents the most general of the collection of events that are substance-like. Each temporal slice of (any instance of) a process is an instance of the same process — for example, Walking, Talking, Eating, Reading. The first ten seconds of reading this paper is, considered separately, still an instance of Reading. Another name for Process might be TemporalStuff.

Some events have some properties called *static* properties. That is, properties having the same value for all temporal slices of the event. For example, when Fred paints a picture, the "performer" is a static property, because the same person — Fred — does the thing all the way through from start to finish. Also, in that case, the "location" might be static, if all the painting is done at the same location.

> *Any (type of) event such that all of its intrinsic properties are static, is, of necessity, a type of process.*

Why? By definition, a static property is invariant over all temporal slices of the event; so any temporal slice of this event will have exactly the same values for all of its intrinsic properties. Hence, it is a process (or, at least, a new kind of process could be defined of which this would be an instance). If someone is ice skating around in a circle, over and over again, then all of the intrinsic properties are constant (e.g., their speed, the number of revolutions per minute, the number of calories being burned per minute, etc.). This is therefore an instance of a process; if no appropriate one exists, we could always define a new one: SkatingAround&AroundInACircle. (Its granule might be SkatingAroundOnceInASingleCircle.)

The collection of these static states of objects is called SomethingInSomeState. BeingHappy is a spec of this, for example. In principle, there can be few instances of SomethingInSomeState, because almost nothing is completely static (or, for that matter, completely dynamic). Every object does have *some* static aspects, however, and it is these aspects we are interested in representing here.

One of the most interesting states is simply existing. This is represented in Cyc by the collection SomethingExisting. Everything that exists is viewed as executing that process continually during its lifetime. When we feed a log to a papermill, the log finally stops executing the process of existing. At that moment, the log ceases to exist (as a log), and some new object (some new portion of wood pulp) begins to exist.

What are the fundamental types of things that carry out the process of existing?

1. Well, TangibleObject springs to mind! "Rock80921 existed from 1 million B.C. until 1950 A.D." That is, each instance of the set of all tangible objects carries out that process, SomethingExisting.

2. Also, Fred can be said to be existing. More generally, anything that has some tangible part — for instance, any CompositeTangible&IntangibleObject, such as Fred — can be said to be existing.

3. Finally, we choose to include anything that has a functional aspect — including any instance of Intelligence — for two reasons:
   a. Each CompositeTangible&IntangibleObject will also by definition have an intangibleExtent (an instance of Intelligence) during the time interval over which it exists as a Composite
   b. We can easily *conceive of* such an intelligence living on even after the tangible portion is destroyed.

This is not an argument one way or another about the existence of immortal souls, or ghosts, or astral projection, or heaven. It's just that we can easily *imagine* such things — we can *imagine* minds "existing" without bodies — hence, there should be an appropriate, consistent way to easily *represent* such things.

Notice that we're saying that Fred is an instance of TemporalStuff. All during his lifetime, he's running the process of existing, so he is an instance of SomethingExisting, which is a spec of Process (which is the same as TemporalStuff), which is a spec of Stuff.

To recap: Because it's a genl of SomethingExisting, the set Event includes all tangible objects (such as this piece of paper, or Fred's body), some intangible objects (such as the ideas this chapter is trying to convey, or Fred's mind), and all composite tangible/intangible objects (such as this book in toto — its content and physical form) — or Fred in toto — his body and mind).

TangibleStuff (= SpatialStuff) is a spec of Stuff and of TangibleObject. TangibleObject in turn is a spec of SomethingExisting, which in turn is a spec of Process (= TemporalStuff). That's why, earlier, we made the asymmetric statement that everything that is spatially a substance is also temporally a substance.

Let us clarify this with a couple more examples.

Example 1: PieceOfPeanutButter935DuringWeek35Of1989. That's a particular individual object. Its spatial substanceness is quite obvious: the westernmost 30 percent of that lump of peanut butter shares all the *intrinsic spatial properties* of the whole lump: color, density, pricePerPound, and so on. These properties are held more or less in common among all the spatial slices of that object. Of course, the farther away from this slice the boundaries of another slice are, the more properties might have a different value (for example, those parts of PieceOfPeanutButter935DuringWeek35Of1989 that are toward the center may be less stale than parts near the outer surface).

But what does it mean to say that this object is *temporally* substance-like? All it means is that if we take a temporal slice of this thing (say the first three days of the week), this new unit — PieceOfPeanutButter935DuringTheFirst3DaysOfWeek35Of1989 — can have the same *intrinsic time-related properties* as those of the original whole piece (for example, the rate at which peanut-scented pheromones are emitted).

Example 2: Fred. Although theoretically Fred is spatially substance-like, the only (defined!) substance he's an instance of is TangibleStuff. And nothing much gets inherited from there, so for all intents and purposes we can ignore the spatial substanceness of Fred. Good thing, too.

However, Fred really is *temporally* stuff-like. Fred himself, as a temporal whole, is an Event; he has a startingTime, and (though he is not so morbid as to dwell on it) an endingTime. If we consider a temporal slice of Fred — say, FredDuring1985 — that unit will probably share most of the same *temporally intrinsic properties* as other temporal slices of Fred: first name, last name, father, mother, social security number, occupation, and so on. The closer the temporal slice — the less far away its boundaries are from the boundaries of 1985 — the more properties will be in common, or at least similar to one another. This phenomenon, of certain properties varying in certain ways over time, will be dealt with in more detail in section 6.2.4, "Temporal Projectibility."

6.2.3. What "Space-Time Regions" Are Really Worth Representing?

What is at issue here is the continuity of properties along spatial and temporal axes. We can view the universe as a large, four-dimensional continuum divided up into lots of interesting pieces. Each of the pieces will normally have some contiguous spatial extent and some continuous temporal extent, although it need not be such a "convex" region of space-time, nor even a "connected" one. Such interesting regions comprise *most* of the instances of the collection IndividualObject.

What *else* makes for an IndividualObject that's worth representing? Well, there's FredsMind, or TheIdeasInThisBook — in short, entities in "intelligence space." Most intelligences are just the functionalExtent of some CompositeTangible&IntangibleObject, which in turn has a physicalExtent in space-time. (For example, most human minds are fixed in human bodies.) So one can imagine a larger space, which we might call *space-time-intelligence space*, and it is interesting regions of *that* space that comprise, precisely, the instances of IndividualObject in Cyc.

So what makes one region of space-time (or space-time-intelligence) more interesting than another? When is an object interesting enough to warrant separating it, representing it, remembering it, and naming it?

There are two *necessary* criteria:

1. An interesting object must have a nontrivial collection of properties that are roughly constant across its temporal or spatial extent and that thus can be said to apply to the object as a whole.

2. In addition, an interesting object should not be a part of a larger object (including a larger intelligence) for which all the same properties hold.

   There are no clear-cut *sufficient* criteria, but some vague ones are listed below. (It is no accident that these conditions are very similar to those for deciding whether or not to create a new unit to explicitly represent some *collection*.)

3. There should be some processes (be they physical or mental) that operate on, or produce, this object. (This is a special case of criterion 1.)

4. Those processes that meet criterion 3 should be of interest to human beings (or to other intelligences that are of interest to human beings).

For example, some random segment of the peanut butter in a jar is not an interesting object, but as soon as it gets on my knife it bears thinking about. Now, how can Cyc be told about these fascinating details of the universe? And what do these revelations mean for our representation of facts about space telescopes and mainframes and driving a car?

6.2.4. Temporal Projectibility. [*Note:* the motivation for the concepts introduced in section 6.2.4.1 may not be clear until you have read section 6.2.4.2.]

6.2.4.1.
TEMPORALLY-
INTRINSIC?

How do we know what properties carry over to temporal/physical slices and what properties don't? For example, we have no trouble answering questions such as the following:

1. What was AbeLincoln's name when he was 12 years old?

2. When his left elbow was 12 years old, how old was his right elbow?

3. What (if anything) do you think his left elbow was called?

4. Was he always solid? What about his left elbow?

5. When he washed up, did he wash his left elbow?

6. About how tall was he when he was four?

7. He was elated when he heard he'd been reelected; about how long did that feeling of elation last?

At least approximately, we can consider this "carrying over of properties" to be just a function of the property (and of course the granule size).

Some properties carry over to temporal (but not spatial) slices:

• name — Once you get one, it sticks with you most or all of your life.

• socialSecurityNumber — Like your name, this stays with you most or all of your life.

• height — Given height at age X, we can *estimate* height at age Y.

Some properties carry over to spatial (but not temporal) slices:

- dateOfLastFullWashing — That's when your elbow was washed, too.

- owner — If X is owned by Y, then (usually) so is each portion of X.

- heightAboveSeaLevel — Given that your body is frozen in time for a moment, we can calculate this value precisely for one part in terms of another; also, the values will all be roughly equal at that moment.

Some properties carry over to both temporal and spatial slices:

- granule — A piece of water has "water molecule" as its granule; the same is true both over time and if you consider just a portion of the water.

- creator — Unlike an owner, your creator, once determined, is fixed forever. Also, usually the whole individual object has one creator.

- dateOfCreation — For example, your birthday is the same year after year, and it's the same for your elbow as for your whole body, presumably.

- age — You and your elbows are all the same age, and, given your age in, say, 1980, it's easy to figure your age in 1988.

How are these relationships represented in Cyc? Every slot may have the following two slots: temporallyIntrinsic? and spatiallyIntrinsic?. Each of them is filled with a TruthValue (T or NIL).

So temporallyIntrinsic? is True for name, socialSecurityNumber, height, granule, creator, dateOfCreation, and age. And spatiallyIntrinsic? is True for dateOfLastFullWashing, owner, heightAboveSeaLevel, creator, dateOfCreation, and age.

Unfortunately, we have been unable to develop a universal theory that enables us to mechanically, automatically compute these two slots. It's trickier than we thought at first; for example, endsBefore is temporally intrinsic but startsBefore is not! (If x endsBefore y, any temporal piece of x must also end before y. But just because x startsBefore y doesn't necessitate that each piece of x does — for example, 1988 started before the 1988Election, but some temporal pieces of 1988, such as December1988, won't satisfy that relation.)

Exercise for the reader: Disprove our claim about trickiness, develop the general rules for automatically deciding whether a slot is temporallyIntrinsic?, spatiallyIntrinsic?, both, or neither, and then let us know.

Hint: Here is one of the general rules we came up with:

Slots that originate from any of the allInstances of ProcessType are usually temporallyIntrinsic, and those that originate from TangibleSubstanceType are usually SpatiallyIntrinsic.

Let's look at an example. One of the allInstances of ProcessType is IntakeProcess. It has the following two canHaveSlots: typeOfThingTakenIn — the kind of stuff that gets inputted, and inTaker — the agent that's doing the inputting.

Now consider any instance of IntakeProcess; for example, Fred inhaling his next breath. It would be represented by a unit:

```
FredInhalingBreath83912
   typeOfThingTakenIn: Air
   inTaker: Fred
```

Any temporal slice of FredInhalingBreath83912 would have the same value for typeOfThingTakenIn and inTaker. But that's precisely what it means for a slot to be temporallyIntrinsic.

That is, those two slots — inTaker and typeOfThingTakenIn — are temporallyIntrinsic, and that knowledge should be added to Cyc. Adding it to Cyc means that the units representing typeOfThingTakenIn and inTaker should each be given a T (= True) entry on their temporallyIntrinsic? slot.

The point here is that we didn't have to add this knowledge manually, because of the general rule — the "Hint" — above. That is, "temporallyIntrinsic?: T" was *inherited* to those two slots because they makeSenseFor something that is in ProcessType.allInstances.

Here's how we represented that general rule in Cyc, using inheritance. Recall that here we use *indentation* to signify "inherits to."

```
ProcessType
   instanceOf: (Collection)
   genls: (SubstanceType)
      .

      .

      .

   allInstances:    ← For each instance X of ProcessType,
      canHaveSlots:    ← for each canHaveSlot s of X,
         temporallyIntrinsic?: (T)    ← assume that s is
                                         temporallyIntrinsic
      .

      .

      .
```

Before leaving the topic of intrinsicness, let us go a little deeper into this notion. We talked about two kinds of intrinsicness, spatial and temporal. This was basically defined as follows, *"a slot s is temporally intrinsic if for all u, for all x in u.subProcesses, x.s = u.s"*. If you replace *subProcesses* with *spatialParts,* you get the definition of spatial intrinsicness.

Isn't it possible to generate more kinds of intrinsicness by choosing other such "parts" slots? Yes! How does our representation handle this? We have a slot called intrinsicAlong, which any slot may legally possess and which is in turn filled with one (or more) slots.

So you can state that typeOfThingTakenIn is temporally intrinsic either by giving it a "temporallyIntrinsic?: T" slot/value or by giving it an "intrinsicAlong: subProcesses" slot/value.

Spatial and temporal intrinsicness are given a slightly special status because they are the most commonly occurring kinds of intrinsicness.

6.2.4.2.
TEMPORAL-
SUBABSTRACTIONS

We said earlier that the different instances of SomethinginSomeState each represent the static aspects of things (for example, BeingHappy). Unfortunately, it's the rule rather than the exception that things change in this world; for example, Fred's state of BeingHappy comes to an end. There are not many facts we can state about an object X that hold true for its entire period of existence. How do we handle this?

Consider a person, Fred, and consider one of his attributes, say, his occupation. As he goes through the different phases of his life, his occupation changes (for example, he was a plumber during the 1970s and a programmer during the 1980s). How do we represent this?

To answer that, let's step back and consider what the *Fred* unit itself represents. It represents Fred throughout his entire period of existence, his entire lifetime. Its startingTime is his birth date, its endingTime is his death date, its duration is his life span. According to the ontology in Cyc, Fred is nothing but a composition of space-intelligence-time events.

So a phase in his life (for example, Fred during the 1970s) is a slice of this composition. We represent it by a separate unit: FredInThe70s. The relationship between Fred and FredInThe70s is similar to the relationship between a loaf of bread and one slice of it. FredInThe70s is said to be a *temporal subabstraction* of Fred. In order to represent this in Cyc, we list FredInThe70s as an entry on the subAbstrac slot of Fred. Temporal subabstractions needn't be a single interval of time, nor tied to some absolute dates, as is FredInThe70s; for example, one temporal subabstraction of Fred that might be worth explicitly having in the system is FredWhileEating.

All the various incarnations of Fred form a hierarchy under the subAbstrac relation. Notice, though, that FredInThe70s and FredWhileEating intersect, yet neither one completely contains the other.

As you might expect, subAbstrac has an inverse slot, called

superAbstrac. There is also a pair of slots — allSubAbstrac and allSuperAbstrac — that represent the Kleene Star of subAbstrac and superAbstrac.

Now, what would it mean if we were to assert Fred.occupation.Plumber? That is, what are the semantics we would like to have for the occupation slot? There are two options.

1. It could mean that *some appropriate temporal subabstraction* of Fred works as a plumber. If this is what we really intend, then a better but longer name for the occupation slot would be the following: someAppropriateSubabstractionHasThisOccupation.

2. It could mean that all of Fred — from its starting time to ending time — really has this value. In this case, we'd better put the slot/value "occupation: Plumber" on FredInThe70s, not on Fred. If we asserted Fred.occupation.Plumber, it would mean that he worked as a professional plumber from the moment of his birth to the moment of his death!

Let's look at some of the pros and cons of each of these options. The first option would, at first sight, allow us to do away with units such as FredInThe70s. Instead, we could just place our assertions on the unit Fred itself. But how then do we convey that it was during the 1970s that Fred had this occupation? In that case, we cannot help creating *some* extra unit, probably the unit FredInThe70s. But watch out! In this case we can't use the same slot, occupation, on the new FredInThe70s unit, because there we *do* intend it to mean "all during the 1970s." So the second version of the slot would be needed when we wanted to indicate the precise subabstraction for which we intended the relation to hold. So option 1 leads us to have both of the Fred units *and* two kinds of occupation slots. Is it really necessary to have both these flavors of the occupation slot? Well, not really, because the former is computable from the latter (vice versa is not true). By choosing option 2 instead, we have both of the Fred units and only one type of occupation slot.

So, without too much enthusiasm, we were led to adopt the semantics corresponding to option 2, not option 1. Our lack of enthusiasm stems from the fact that in colloquial conversation, in English, people generally mean what option 1 states when they say, for example, "Eisenhower was a general and a President."

Our approach is therefore to create units corresponding to each of the different, important temporal slices of Fred's life. These temporal slices are the temporal subabstractions of Fred. Fred's temporal subabstractions might be the units FredInSchool, FredInTexas,

FredWhileAsleep, FredDuringThe1970s, FredAsAChild, FredDuringHisFirstMarriage, FredInFirstGrade, FredWhileEating, etc.

Subabstractions may in turn have further subabstractions, and so on. (For example, FredInFirstGrade is a subabstraction of FredInSchool.) One of the main motivations for using the notion of subabstractions of objects (to bundle up a set of properties about it) is a belief that there are clusterings of related properties. And those clusterings are ubiquitous and powerful. If this were not true, it would be simpler just to have a unit for each property of an object: FredBeing6FeetTall, FredOwningFido, etc.

6.2.4.2.1. ENTITIES.   There is something special about the unit Fred, compared with all those various subabstractions of Fred: Fred has no superabstractions, and all the others do. Any IndividualObject that has no superabstractions is called an *entity* and is an instance of the collection Entity.

This comes in handy when we state constraints like "every person has one mother" — Fred.mother can have more than one *entry*, so long as they're all subabstractions of the same entity. For example, the mother slot of Fred could be filled by: JaneAsLawyer, JaneAsAJudge, JaneAsARetiree.

An exhortation: we must be clear about the meaning of each slot. For example, would it be wrong to insert Jane as an entry on Fred.mother? Doing so might mean that every temporal subabstraction of Jane is Fred's mother. Was Jane, even as an infant, Fred's mother? No, she wasn't anybody's mother. So either we must broaden the meaning of "mother" (to include "some appropriate temporal sub-abstraction is, was, or will be the mother of") or else we'd better list on the mother slot of Fred only temporal subabstractions of Jane after she'd delivered Fred. This is similar to a choice we made earlier; as we did then, we opt for the latter — for having a more precise subabstraction of Jane, such as JaneAsAMother, or JaneSince1969, and so on. Each of those units has the property that they are subabstractions of Jane, and, *during their entire time interval,* Jane was Fred's mother.

Each temporal subabstraction of Fred can have its own idiosyncratic values for slots (age, occupation, weight, maritalStatus, fatherOf, and so on). This allows us to handle the changing aspects of Fred. It is also consistent with our earlier approach of conceiving people as composite tangible (body) and intangible (intelligence) entities.

There is a potential problem — or opportunity — here. FredAsAnInfant and FredAsAnOldMan are not 100-percent independent units. Lots of slots are probably *unchanged* from one to the other: gender, firstName, parents, nativeLanguage, etc. These are precisely what we earlier referred to as the temporallyIntrinsic slots. Their values on one subabstraction of Fred can be inferred by looking at their values on any other subabstraction of Fred.

Some slots *change monotonically* over time (for example, height), so we know that we can guess at Fred's height by looking at all earlier subabstractions and taking the maximum. We can even do better than that for attributes like height, where we know the general growth curve for people as a function of age. For example, if we knew Fred's height at age 1, 6, and 10, we could extrapolate pretty well to guess his height at age 11.

6.2.4.3. AT LAST: PROJECTIBILITY
How do we decide which attributes carry over from one temporal subabstraction to another and which don't? This is just a case of the frame problem. This subsection describes the solution implemented in Cyc.

We wish to use two types of information:

1. Information about the "temporal projectibility" of attributes — for example, the fact that birthDate is 100-percent invariant from one subabstraction to another. In Cyc, every slot s (that instances of SomethingExisting may have) can in turn have slots (that is, slots on the s unit) that indicate its projectibility over time. This projectibility has the following components in its definition:
   a. The time range over which this property may be projected.
   b. The certainty and confidence with which it may be projected.
   c. For numerical attributes: the growth and/or decay curve shape.

2. Information about the specific entity itself (such as Fred). This includes information about the different scripts in which the actor has taken part. If we know that Fred took part in a growth-hormone experiment at age 10, we'd be more circumspect in predicting his height at age 11. Let's take another example: the mood that Fred has. If FredAt7:42pmToday is very happy, we would normally project his happy mood as continuing for several minutes, perhaps even continuing for hours. But if FredAt7:43pmToday is undergoing a spanking, he is not likely to be so happy.

So if the actor has taken part in some script that could have changed that attribute, that fact takes precedence over the weak sorts of inheritance in the first category of information. *Symbolic justification dominates blind numeric propagation.*

In many cases, though, numeric information of type 1 is all we have; luckily, it's usually good enough to act on in the real world. When we are fortunate (or thorough) enough to have symbolic information of type 2, it is often possible to derive a "cached" value of type 1 from it.

So type 1 can be thought of as default information about type 2, in a form suitable for the task of rapidly projecting attributes.

For example, we know that most children eat, gain weight, get taller, and so on. If we were to examine JoeAsAFiveYearOld and try to guess his weight two years later, we could probably do a reasonably accurate job, even though there is no explicit script corresponding to the thousands of meals he's eaten during those two years, the various excretion and secretion events, and other events that altered his weight in the meantime. The projectibility information (the growth and weight curves for children) tell us, in a condensed, implicit fashion, that Joe would have taken part in some events that would have had a particular roughly-predictable effect on his weight.

How does temporal intrinsicness relate to the problem of projecting attributes? In a sense, the two problems are similar: in each case, we are trying to transfer properties from one temporal piece of something to another. The problems are different in that the problem of temporal intrinsicness deals with time pieces with certain well-defined properties — namely, one is contained within another.

Before carrying on, let us look more closely at the problem of projecting the values of slots that relate events, as opposed to slots that define other attributes (such as color) of objects.

If we were to say that an object X is Red, then all temporal sub-abstractions of X must be Red. However, if we were to say that FredInThe70s.wife is JillInThe70s, is it right to say that FredIn1976.wife is JillInThe70s? Not really, because these are two events with different temporal sizes. Also, the temporal constraint imposed by the relation wife is that the two events (that is, FredIn1976 and the entry on his wife slot) be cotemporal.

So in the case of relations between events, the intrinsicness/projectibility information has the implicit semantics:

> If $u.s.v1$ and the other projectibility information is satisfied,
> then $u'.s.v1'$ where u' and $v1'$ are subabstractions of u and $v1$ that sat-
> isfy the constraints placed by the slot.

So FredIn1976.wife would not automatically get JillInThe70s filled in, because the coTemporal constraint (imposed by wife) is not satisfied. If JillIn1976 didn't already exist, that subabstraction of JillInThe70s would have to be created (this can be done automatically) if we wanted to explicitly represent the unit filling the wife slot of FredIn1976.

An interesting observation here is:

> In real life, there are very few relations worth stating between two differ-
> ent objects that don't overlap at least a little bit in time.

Because of this, the most common temporal constraints placed by a slot are "same endpoints," and, more generally, "overlaps in time."

A notable exception to this is the causal relationships. In such cases, the constraint is "starts before start of" — that is, if E1 causes E2, then E1 had better not start after E2.

Before leaving the topic of temporal projectibility, let us try to play our usual game of looking for analogies between spatial and temporal attributes of things. Does it even make sense to talk about *spatial projectibility* and, if so, what does it really mean?

We believe it does make sense. For example, we could talk about the spatial projectibility of the field strength of an electromagnetic field. Or the spatial projectibility of the temperature around a flame. Or the spatial projectibility of house rental rates around Palo Alto. So this concept may play an important role in lots of common-sense reasoning.

Principles similar to those usable in temporal projectibility apply here in the spatial domain as well. But the analogy is not perfect: For example, in the temporal domain we have the notion of a script occurring, whose resultant event changes some attribute of an object so that later temporal subabstractions have the changed value. That notion has only a rather fuzzy spatial analog: namely, that there be some spatial object (unfortunately, this might just be a piece of empty space) connecting the two points in space between which we are trying to project the attributes. (Of course, the absence of an aether was given up by physicists only in this century, and even then only reluctantly.) This is one of the topics for future research.

6.2.4.4.
INTERVAL-BASED
QUANTITY SLOTS

Next, we'll consider further the semantics of slots, such as weight, height, etc., that make sense for different instances of #%SomethingExisting. We'll begin by taking a look at a couple of examples:

Example 1: Suppose we have a unit FredsBodyIn1989, which is a subabstraction of Fred's body representing a duration of one year. We wish to specify the weight slot for FredsBodyIn1989. Now here's the problem: on the one hand, weight is a temporally intrinsic slot, so whatever value we fill in must hold for all portions of that year. But on the other hand, Fred kept eating and excreting during 1989, so his weight varied during this subabstraction. So we really can't in good faith fill in FredsBodyIn1989.weight with any one number.

There are a couple of options available. The first one is to create a qualitative version of this slot, say qualitativeWeight, and specify a value for FredsBodyIn1989.qualitativeWeight. This would be semantically okay because we could argue that his qualitative weight must have remained the same. However, this is not a desirable option for a few reasons. Not only would we end up with twice as many slots, we would also have to create an unreasonably large number of qualitative values. The next option is to write a constraint specifying the limits on his weight for all the subabstractions of this Fred during 1988. This is not desirable from a computational standpoint.

Example 2: Even if we were to consider a temporal subabstraction that has a zero duration, it is not possible to specify Fred's body's weight exactly, but rather only to some limited accuracy.

Examples 1 and 2 are not as unrelated as they may initially seem. They are both related to the inherent limitations on what can be said about something with a temporal extent, with the limitation increasing as the temporal extent increases.

Because we can't really specify a weight, try as hard as we may, let us try to redefine the semantics of slots such as weight. An interpretation that is often used for such numerical valued attributes is that any representation of these is a representation of an *interval* within which the "actual" value of the attribute may be said to lie.

This seems to be a convenient interpretation. The category of slots for which this interpretation holds is called, in Cyc, #%IntervalBasedQuantitySlot. When we say that FredsBodyIn1989.weight is in some interval, this is true for all the subabstractions of this subabstraction of Fred's body. So our original problems can be solved using this scheme.

Let us suppose that for some large set of units we use the same interval to talk about some attribute of these units (for example, the calendar year 1989). In this case it seems reasonable to create a unit that represents this interval. This named time interval can also be viewed in a sense as a qualitative value.

This raises another interesting question — namely, should our intervals be bounded in both directions? There is no *a priori* reason for doing so. In practice, we also use intervals such as GreaterThanZero, LessThanZero, etc.

This raises the next question, namely, what are the semantics of functions such as plus ($+$), minus ($-$), with this mixture of qualitative and quantitative values? The answer is that these are now generic functions; that is, the precise calculus used to combine these numbers is dependent on the types of arguments.

Another problem that crops up when talking about attributes such as length is that of units of measure (meters versus yards, for example). There are three approaches to dealing with this.

1. Have only one unit of each type (for example, adopt the cgs system and live with it, even if there are a lot of centimeters between New York and Tokyo). This is an extreme pain, at least if we don't convert it when talking to human users.

2. Have many slots like lengthInFeet, lengthInMeters, lengthInMiles. Apart from the utter ugliness of this solution, it presents many consistency problems and gets computationally bad very soon.

3. Unlike the previous two approaches, which attempted to specify the units of measure implicitly, this method allows them to be specified explicitly as a number/unit-of-measure pair. *Implicit* units of measure had the advantage that the entryIsA of these slots could be stated simply as Number. Although this seemed convenient, it is actually bad because such a scheme does not make the required distinctions in the ranges of slots, such as length and volume. The entryIsA of slots such as length, volume, etc., is now, respectively, a set of attributes such as Distance, Volume, etc. Attributes such as #%Volume are collections, with their instances being the volumes of different objects. Each Distance, or each Volume, can have both a numeric magnitude and an explicit units-of-measure. Of course, the units-of-measure that can be used to specify an entry for a quantity slot will depend on the units in which that quantity is measured.

Interval-based quantity slots are extremely important, so let's take a closer look at them. To recap, some slots, such as *length, temperature, weight,* and *duration,* measure quantities. Such measurements usually specify not just a single "point" value, but rather an *interval* within which the "real" value is expected to lie. Let's now discuss some issues about representing and reasoning with such interval-based quantity slots.

Consider representing the length of a table. Suppose someone tells you that the table's length is 10. Two issues crop up immediately:

(a) The *precision* of the value. Since we cannot really give the exact length of the table, we would like to specify an interval within which we believe the actual length of the table lies, e.g., "10 plus or minus .05".

(b) The *unit of measurement* being used. We would like to use any of the available units of measure for talking about the length. We want one *length* slot, one *width* slot, one *height* slot, etc., and we don't mind creating a single slot for each *type* of unit of measure (*Feet, Meters, Inches,* etc.). But we would like to avoid creating a new slot for the Cartesian product of all those — that is, avoid having to create hundreds of different slots like lengthInMeters, lengthInFeet, widthInMeters, widthInFeet, heightInMeters, heightInFeet, etc.

To solve both these problems, we allow each entry on a slot like length, weight, duration, and temperature, to be a list:

```
(<Unit of measure> <number> ·
  <range-arguments>)
```

For example, Table83.length might contain the following entry:
(#%Feet 10 : + .05 : − .05)

The "dot" means that there can be 0, 1, 2, or more range-arguments;
they are optional and there can be any number of them. Today, the
only legal range arguments come in pairs: : + followed by a number,
: − followed by a number, and :dist followed by a unit representing a
probability distribution. [The idea is that most of the time, you have a
rough +/− idea of the accuracy of a measurement; sometimes you
have separate + and − error-ranges; and sometimes, less often, you
know a more complicated distribution.]

Entries of this form are called *quantity space terms,* abbreviated QST.

Let's take a closer look at the length slot of the unit Table83. The
#%entryIsA of #%length is #%Distance. Going to the
unit #%Distance, we see it has the slot #%measuredIn, whose entries
are #%Feet, #%Meters, #%Inches, and so on. The <Unit of mea-
sure> must be an instance of UnitMeasure.

Alternatively, we may elect to give the interval a name. Suppose we decide it's worth creating a unit to represent (#%Feet 10 : + .05 : − .05), and
we call that #%TheLengthOfTable83. *That unit is also a legal QST.* In this
case it would have the four slots:

```
#%TheLengthOfTable83
    #%meanQuantValue: (10)
    #%maxQuantValue: (10.05)
    #%minQuantValue: (9.95)
    #%unitOfMeasure: (#%Feet)
```

and Table83.length would have #%TheLengthOfTable83 as a
full-fledged entry, instead of having the list (#%Feet 10 : + .05 :- .05)
as an entry. We could either say

```
#%Table83
    #%length: ((#%Feet 10 :+ .05 :− .05))
```

or

```
#%Table83
    #%length: (#%TheLengthOfTable83)
```

Let us next take a look at some of the slots to be used to describe the
different units of measure. There are collections such as
#%MKSUnitOfMeasure, #%FPSUnitOfMeasure, etc., that denote the
standard systems of units of measure. We also have collections such as
#%UnitOfCurrent, #%UnitOfDistance, etc.

So, e.g., #%Centimeter is an instance of both #%UnitOfDistance and #%CGSUnitOfMeasure. It is also an instance of #%DerivedUnitOfMeasure (as opposed to a #%SimpleUnitOfMeasure) since it is derived from #%Meter. (Namely, by multiplying the length in meters by .01).

```
#%Centimeter
    #%instanceOf: (#%UnitOfDistance
                   #%DerivedUnitOfMeasure
                   #%CGSUnitOfMeasure)
    #%measureOfQuantity: (#%Distance)
    #%basicUnitOfReference: (#%Meter)
    #%unitMultiplicationFactor: (.01)
```

This simple "scaling" scheme works for about 95% of the unit conversions (from one unit of measure for a quantity to another unit of measure; from inches to centimeters to light-years to angstroms). For most of the rest of the conversions, it suffices to do a scaling plus an "offset." Consider how temperature in degrees Fahrenheit is calculated from temperature in degrees Centigrade: multiply by 9/5 and add 32. In Cyc, we represent this:

```
#%DegreeFahrenheit
    #%instanceOf: (#%UnitOfTemperature
                   #%DerivedUnitOfMeasure
                   #%FPSUnitOfMeasure)
    #%measureOfQuantity: (#%Temperature)
    #%basicUnitOfReference: (#%DegreeCentigrade)
    #%unitMultiplicationFactor: ((/ 5 9))
    #%unitOffsetFactor: (32)
    #%unitConversions: ((#%DegreeCentigrade
        (#%Plus 32 (#%Times entry 9/5)))
```

In this case, the referent (#%DegreeCentigrade) and conversion formula are synthesized by Cyc, from the entries given on the other slots. Similarly, #%DegreeCentigrade might point to #%DegreeKelvin as its basicUnitOfReference, in which case it would need no unitMultiplicationFactor, but would have a nonzero unitOffsetFactor.

In general, if there is a more complex conversion algorithm than just m•x + b, you can manually place that more complex formula on the #%unitConversions slot. For instance, if one wanted to define a new unit of temperature which was the natural log of degrees Kelvin, one would create a unit for it and give it a #%unitConversions slot with one entry, namely the list (#%DegreeKelvin (#%NaturalLog entry)).

[Notice the use of the special variable "entry", in the entries on this slot.]

Consider the unit of measure "watt." We would like to say that this is obtained in some fashion from the units gram, centimeter, and second. This is done using the slot obtainedFromUnits. We use the slot unitExpansions to *define* a watt. This slot will contain the entry (((#%Gram 1)(#%Centimeter 2)(#%Second -1)) 1). This implies that 1 watt = 1 gram × 1 Centimeter × 1 Centimeter × 1 / 1 Second. (The last 1 is a constant multiplication factor to account for possible scalings, e.g., to define horsepower in terms of gram, centimeter, and second.) There may be many unit expansions for a given unit.

```
#%Watt
   #%obtainedFromUnits: (#%Gram #%Second
      #%Centimeter)
   #%unitExpansions: ((((#%Gram 1)
      (#%Centimeter 2)(#%Second -1)) 1))
```

How do we express the relationship between the slot #%length and the measurable quantity #%Distance? We assert

```
#%length.#%measuresAttribute.#%Distance.
```

Notice that #%measuresAttribute is a specSlot of #%entryIsA.

Before we consider the manipulation of these terms, let us consider the significance of this representation. There are two orthogonal issues: One is the flexibility this provides in choosing and using units of measure. There's nothing particularly startling about this, but it is a necessary ability. The second issue is more interesting: using intervals to talk about quantity spaces. The advantages of this (apart from trying to be "honest" while talking about things such as lengths, etc.) fall into two main categories:

(i) We have not imposed any restriction on the properties of our intervals other than the fact that they must be convex (e.g., it's okay if they tend to infinity; it's okay if they are of varying sizes; etc.). This allows us to state information across a wide range of granularities. And this should make it easier to get a better mix of qualitative and quantitative representation.

(ii) We would like to inherit defaults for the weight of walruses, the height of houses, the cost of cats, etc., but given the variation in such things it is difficult to specify a meaningful single numeric average. However, we can easily specify default intervals and more detailed distributions (e.g., sharply bi- or multimodal ones, such as those involving subjective judgments about religion, sex, politics; or those that vary as a well-understood function of other variables, such as the size and weight of lions as a function of their age).

Now let us consider the manipulation of these QST terms. The legal operations allowed on these terms (as of now) are: #%Times, #%Difference #%Plus #%Quotient #%GreaterThan #%LessThan, etc.

Three interesting issues are:

Issue 1 — dealing with named intervals —

(a) It is possible that the intervals tend to ∞ or $-\infty$. The standard case of this occurs when we split up the quantity space into three parts: less than zero, approximately 0, and greater than zero.

(b) It is also possible that the intervals are bounded. If the intervals have mean, max, min, etc., then we simply convert these named intervals to the unnamed syntax and then proceed. In some cases (e.g., when talking about Hardness or Wetness) it is very hard to specify numbers for these slots. However, we might still want to define operations such as GreaterThan, Plus, etc., for these quantities; that is, we would want GreaterThan, Plus, and the other functions to behave as polymorphic functions: based on the types of the arguments, a different procedure is adopted. This is done as follows.

(i) For GreaterThan and LessThan, the slot *allFollowingQualitativeState* and its inverse are used.

(ii) How do we "extend" functions such as Plus and Quotient, so that they can operate on QSTs? On the *collection* for the quantity space (e.g., Wetness, RelativeHardness, Temperature, etc.) we place the slot *#%quantityRelationDefinition*. This contains a set of entries of the form (<Function> <function-definition>). <Function> would be #%Plus (or Quotient, etc.) and <function-definition> has the following syntax: (((arg1 arg2) result1) (arg1 arg3) result2) . . .). For example, if you want to "add" the wetness of a damp object to the wetness of a moist object, you end up with a damp object. So we could define the operation Plus on Wetness by placing the following entry on Wetness.quantityRelationDefinition:

```
(#%Plus
   (((#%SoppingWet #%VeryDry) #%SoppingWet)
   ((#%Damp #%Moist) #%Damp) . . . ))
```

Issue 2 — unit-of-measure coercions —

When quantities in different units of measure get added, multiplied, or otherwise combined, the appropriate coercions should take place. (For example, in order to add 10 feet to 3 meters, we have to convert one to the other unit of measure.) At that time, and to the extent detected by the system, more complex units (such as kg-meters/sec-sec) should be replaced with simpler ones (such as newtons).

Issue 3 — the size of intervals —

What happens to the ranges (the $:+$ and $:-$ bounds) and the distributions, when we add, subtract, multiply, etc., these QSTs? This depends a lot on how we interpret our intervals. Suppose (we believe that) the likelihood of the quantity having a certain value is defined by a uniform probability distribution over the interval. In this case, manipulating these intervals will very soon give us such large intervals that these become quite meaningless. On the other hand, we could make use of the more specific distribution information and actually add, multiply, etc. these intervals. However this could get very computationally expensive. Luckily, if there are a small number of distributions that actually occur, we could store parameterized solutions and use these cached solutions. The distributions, in turn, are often gotten by default, inherited based on the source of measurement, the type of quantity being measured, and so on. [The implementation of this last, important technique — cliched combining of inherited distributions — has not yet been accomplished.]

6.2.5. SomethingOccurring, Changes, and Scripts.

Having briefly discussed the representation of the static aspects of things, we now turn to representing their dynamically changing aspects. For instance, how would we represent in Cyc the fact that Fred is losing hair at the rate of five hairs per day? (We will get around to answering this particular question by the end of this section.)

When some entity X undergoes some sequence of changes, we have different subabstractions of X, representing X in each of the states it has been through. The obvious question is: how do we represent *in more detail* the way that these changes are brought about?

The answer is: Scripts. This of course builds on work by Roger Schank and friends (which is why we've chosen to call these units scripts), and on even earlier work on Schemata, but we've added many additional slots and wrinkles and interrelationships.

Each script in Cyc is a bundle of information about something happening: actors, before/after states, explicit changes, relations to other scripts, goals achieved, enabled, thwarted, and so on.

We don't have the unit "Script" in Cyc; instead, we call the set of such things SomethingOccurring. Let's see where this fits in the Cyc ontology. Event has, as its only spec, Process — with which it is co-extensional. Process in turn is partitioned into

SomethingOccurring (the set of all scripts) and
SomethingInSomeState (an important spec of this is
    SomethingExisting)
Interval (a pure "piece of time," such as TheYear1988)

Two classes of scripts occupy almost all of the time of the Cyc builders, Cyc itself, current Cyc users, and (we expect) long-term users of the system. These form a partition of SomethingOccurring:

- Tangible objects being subjected to physical (including chemical) forces

- Intelligent agents (including animals and organizations) making decisions

Various types of constraints are also present in each script:

- *Typing* of the actors (for example, Drinking must have an Animal as its performer and a liquid as its object)

- *Intra*actor constraints (those that involve a single actor at a time; for example, that the performer is usually Thirsty before the script takes place)

- *Inter*actor constraints that must be — or usually are — true (for example, the performer and object must be in contact during the course of the action)

Each script also contains a list of the subprocesses that come together to make up the overall composite "action," plus a set of constraints on those subprocesses and an explicit statement of how these subprocess parts work together to carry out the global script action.

That last item is very important: usually there is a separate unit that represents the *structure* whose "parts" are the subprocesses and whose interpart relations specify how the subprocesses fit together with each other into an integrated whole.

For instance, in the case of the process DrivingAnAutomobile, the subprocesses are: entering the car, starting it, steering, working the gas and brake pedals, observing the road, turning, parking, signaling, checking the gauges and other instruments, and so on. The *structure* that explains how these fit together is itself a separate unit in Cyc, DrivingAnAutomobile-Structure. Each of the subprocesses can be a full-fledged script, with subprocesses (and, hence, structure) of its own.

This is what allows Cyc to take a "gray-box approach" to processes. That is, 99 percent of the time, it can treat processes as black boxes, ignoring the subprocesses and subprocess structure. But when necessary, that deeper level is there to be used.

When might it be necessary? One case is: You're *planning* to drive to the airport to pick up your would-be employer, and your whole life may be different if you're late. Hence, you may spend some time the day before checking out the car and the route you're going to take.

Another case is: You're actually driving to work, and the car begins to make funny noises and lose power. At that time, you'll begin to think about the fact that the car has an engine, and a fuel system, and a cooling system, ...

Another case: You're driving to work and you hear on the radio that the road up ahead is blocked by an accident. At that time, you'll probably "dynamically re-plan" your route, rather than continuing to rely on the "cached" one you use every day.

We call the category of scripts in Cyc SomethingOccurring; we could also have called it Script. Scripts are the basic units that allow us to talk about *the change itself* as opposed to "an entity being in some static state."

Let us briefly look now at the Cyc model of *changes* and how they take place. In order for Cyc to be able to represent and intelligently reason about changes, it needs to distinguish the agent that causes the change from the change itself.

So there are the two basic conceptual entities involved in talking about the dynamic aspects of things:

- *Changes*: These are instances of ChangeConstraint. That is, the CycL constraint language is also adequate to serve as a "change language."

- *Things that cause these changes*: Instances of SomethingOccurring (= the set of all scripts). That is, each particular change is caused by some specific event.

Let's look at an example. Consider the statement "Fred became richer." The information in this sentence tells only of the change that Fred underwent. This information could reside on a unit, say Change45. Neither this unit — nor the sentence "Fred became richer" — tells anything about *how* this change came about.

```
Change45
    english: ("This represents a change for the
        better in Fred's wealth")
    instanceOf: (ChangeConstraint)
    allInstanceOf: (ChangeConstraint,
        ConstraintOnASlot, Intangible,
```

```
          RepresentedThing, Constraint Relationship,
          IntangibleObject, Thing,
          SlotOrConstraintOnASlot, IndividualObject)
      eventCausingChange: ()      ← unknown, unspecified for now.
      slotsChanged: (wealthiness)
      slotChangeConstraints: ((IncreaseChange
          Fred001 wealthiness))
```

Notice that the eventCausingChange slot on Change45 is blank. That's what it means for Cyc "not to know how the change came about."

Notice the use of IncreaseChange. This is what we call in Cyc a *change predicate*. As you might expect, in the current Cyc KB, the unit #%IncreaseChange is an instance of the unit #%ChangePredicate. Change predicates will be covered in more detail later, in section 6.6.1.

Notice that the slotChangeConstraints mention a temporal sub-abstraction of Fred (Fred001) rather than "all" of Fred. If we just put *Fred* there, it would mean that Fred's wealth was increasing all during his lifetime. That *might* be what "the speaker" meant, but it's more likely that "Fred became richer" really applies only to Fred in the state we just "left" him, a state that is set by the context of the previous sentence, or by default to "a time that is slightly before the sentence was spoken." (Of course, the speaker *might* have meant that Fred kept getting richer all during his lifetime, and in that case, the slotChangeConstraints slot would contain the entry "(IncreaseChange Fred wealthiness)."

Suppose we find out that the actual means by which Fred became richer was by robbing a bank. How do we represent this? We create a unit representing this bank robbery event; let's call it Robbery99.

One of Robbery99's actors is Fred. More precisely, it is some temporal subabstraction of Fred. It's probably a significant enough event in Fred's life to make it worth creating a whole new unit to represent the subabstraction of Fred that committed the crime.

Robbery99 would be a script; that is, an instance of SomethingOccurring. In its resultantChanges slot would be a pointer to the Change45 unit. Change45 would then contain Robbery99 in its eventCausingChange slot.

```
  Robbery99
      actors: (Fred001)
      instanceOf: (Robbery)
      allInstanceOf: (Robbery, InterpersonalCrime,
                  Crime, SomethingOccurring, Thing,
```

```
          RepresentedThing, Event, IndividualObject)
     resultantChanges: (Change45)
```

Incidentally, if we had separate explicit subabstractions of Fred just before and just after the robbery, we would not *need* to explicitly have a unit to represent the change because the same information could be obtained from these subabstractions.

So, to summarize:

- A *change* unit presents a "black-boxed" perspective of the change of state in an actor, from the actor's point of view;

- A *script* unit describes the more detailed mechanism that's going on — the various causal effects (which are, recursively, described by scripts and changes!) involved in bringing about that change of state.

And this recursion "bottoms out" when we don't know the next deeper level of causation; at that point, Cyc has a change unit with no entry in its eventCausingChange slot.

One could ask: "Why do we need these (non-bottomed-out) change units at all, when they're just the outer husks of the script units?" It is true that, in most cases, all the information that is in these units could be obtained from the script that caused them. But here are five reasons why it's still useful to have the bare-bones change units also there in the KB:

1. They are a faster, simpler, way of reasoning than "from scripts," and they are often perfectly adequate.

2. They are natural — that is, they are probably roughly the level at which we humans usually do reason. We typically drop to a deeper, causal level of reasoning only when something goes wrong. Normally, we think of "driving to the office" as a black box; if there's a detour, or our car keeps stalling, then we begin to delve deeper into the "why" behind the route we take and the speed we travel and the linkages between the dashboard and the engine.

3. Eventually, our knowledge "bottoms out" in change units. That is, you can't keep on forever explaining the cause of each subprocess of each subprocess of each subprocess . . . . So, pragmatically, any finite-sized KB *must* bottom out in change units for which the underlying causal mechanism is uncertain, beneath our level of com-

prehension, beneath our level of interest, truly unknown, or (equivalently) is just a "primitive" physical force like gravity.

4. Change units are good for matching (for example, analogizing, re-pairing, etc.). They make it easy to find disparate scripts that produce similar effects. Often, you want to find a way to accomplish some change, so this is an important way of "indexing" to find relevant candidate scripts.

5. The change units are actor-oriented. They make it easy to talk about some process from the point of view of an actor in the process. Often, the actors care mostly (perhaps solely) about the changes that will be wrought to them. It makes it easy to put together a picture of the robbery from the point of view of just one actor — say, the bank teller or the robber — and answer questions about what they knew at various stages, what emotions they were feeling at various stages, etc.

To reiterate: Unlike a change unit, a script unit contains the following information:

- The actors in this script

- The constraints the actors must satisfy for that process to occur

- The different subevents that make up the script

- The causal relationships between these subevents

- The changes that take place because of this script (these are pointers to change units)

The concept of scripts is very general and subsumes concepts such as physical interaction (for example, ElasticColliding), performing mathematical functions (for example, Cosining), agents performing an action (for example, GivingAConcert), and so on.

Let us take a closer look at the different types of change-related information that we would like to state. This information falls into three basic categories:

1. Difference changes — These are changes in which the final value of the slot is known only in relation to the initial value. So, in the previous example, if we knew that Fred became richer, or became richer by 10,000 dollars, this would be an instance of a difference

change. One special kind of difference change is "remaining constant."

2. Transfer changes — Changes in which some entry on a slot value is replaced by another. If Fred went from being an instance of PillarOfTheCommunity to an instance of WantedCriminal, this would be a replacement change.

3. Final state changes — Changes that specify only that some entry v1 got added on to some u.s slot value because of the change. So, if we did not know whether Fred was already a WantedCriminal, but we wanted to assert that he was definitely one after the robbery, this would be an instance of a final state change.

In a later section (6.6.1), we shall go into the details of how these changes are represented. But we now know enough to answer the question we raised at the start of this section: How do we represent the fact that Fred is losing hair at the rate of five hairs per day?

This is nothing more than a change that is occurring, in which Fred is the actor undergoing the change. So we'd have a change unit representing this, and its eventCausingChange slot would point to a script unit that described in more mechanistic detail the balding process Fred was undergoing.

```
Change853
    english: ("This represents a hairy change
        for the worse for Fred")
    instanceOf: (ChangeConstraint)
    allInstanceOf: (ChangeConstraint, Intangible
        ConstraintOnASlot, IntangibleObject,
        RepresentedThing, Constraint, Relationship,
        SlotOrConstraintOnASlot, IndividualObject
        Thing)
    eventCausingChange: (FredBaldingEvent002)
    actorUndergoingChange: (FredInHisLateFifties)
    slotsChanged: (numberOfHairsOnHead)
    slotChangeConstraints:
        ((QuantitativeRateDecreaseChange Fred001
        numberOfHairsOnHead 5 Day))

FredBaldingEvent002
    instanceOf: (Balding)
    allInstanceOf: (Balding, SomethingOccurring...)
    actors: (FredInHisFifties)
    resultantChanges: (Change853)
```

Notice that we use the change predicate QuantitativeRateDecreaseChange, because the change is a decrease and we know the absolute rate of change.

The statement about the rate of hair loss isn't true for Fred from birth to death, but rather for some appropriate temporal subabstraction of Fred, for example, FredInHisFifties or FredIn1988 — whatever the speaker was trying to express. We might choose to make a separate subabstraction of Fred like FredWhileBalding, but that seems unlikely to be useful. Let's say that we want to express that *Fred in his late fifties* is losing hairs at the rate of five per day. The above units do that.

The very same balding event — FredBaldingEvent002 — may apply all during Fred's fifties, even though there may be different change units that specify various different *rates* of balding during this decade. For example, the Change853.actorUndergoingChange contains just FredInHis*Late*Fifties, which is a temporal subabstraction of (and only about a third of) FredInHisFifties. Notice that FredBaldingEvent002.actors contains the entire FredInHisFifties. FredInHisFifties is itself a decade-sized temporal subabstraction of FredAsAnAdult, which in turn is a large temporal subabstraction of Fred.

If we created FredInHisLateFifties and we created a slot called dailyBaldingRate, that slot of that unit could have the entry 5. So the subabstraction mechanism can be used to freeze the subject in time, at least enough for us to pretend that rate of balding is a static attribute.

We hope it's now clear to the reader why it would be wrong (or at least confusing) to simply place "dailyBaldingRate: 5" on the Fred unit, rather than on the proper temporal subabstraction of Fred. However, we don't *have* to have an awful slot like dailyBaldingRate; we can just use the change units as described above.

Just as the event FredBaldingEvent002 pointed to a temporal superabstraction of FredInHisLateFifties, it could *in principle* have pointed to the top-level entity, Fred. Why then do we need the notion of temporal subabstractions? That is, couldn't we just state the changes that took place to some entity, and calculate (as we need them) which ones were happening to Fred during, say, the summer of 1988? The answer is theoretically yes, but pragmatically you want a place to store the commonly-computed values, so you're led back to having something like FredAsAnAdult, FredAsAnOldMan, etc., anyway.

In general, we can view the set of changes to some attribute of an entity, and the set of values of that attribute for the different subabstractions, as duals of each other. If the occupation slot of Fred changes, then Fred has changed jobs, and (if we wanted to) we could define a new subabstraction of Fred. Similarly, if someone goes to the trouble to define a new subabstraction of Fred, then presumably *some* slot(s) of Fred have changed their values.

Such a view is important, because there is almost no entity in the world that is completely static and no entity that is so volatile that it undergoes changes without having some stable aspects. Even the StockMarket has many stable attributes and only a few, albeit important, volatile attributes.

In an earlier section, we discussed the temporal semantics of relations that apply to events. We considered the option of using semantics of the form "an appropriate subabstraction of u . . ." and decided not to use it. In the case of scripts, however, we seem to be profiting (safely) by using these semantics.

Consider Fred's getting a haircut. We would have a unit representing GettingAHaircut, and, if we desired it, a more specialized script like FredGettingAHaircut (maybe Fred always squirms a lot and screams at the end). In any case, imagine an instance of that script, an event in which Fred got his hair cut last September 3, the day before he started kindergarten. This unit — Fred'sHaircutOn3Sept87 — has a precise date and time on its startingTime slot, a precise date and time on its endingTime slot, and so on. Now the interesting question is: who is the *actor* in the event? That is, what is the entry on that event's recipientOfService slot? (recipientOfService is a specSlot of actors.)

Is it Fred? Fred before the haircut? Fred during the haircut? The answer is that the actor slots — the slots such as actors and recipientOfService that point to the actors in the scripts — *do* have the semantics of being filled by "an appropriate subabstraction of the actor."

"Appropriate" means that the subabstraction must satisfy various constraints. For example, the recipientOfService must be a subabstraction of Fred that includes all the moments in time during which the action is taking place. In addition, we have three other slots that point to the precise subabstractions of the actors in their before, during, and after states.

An implementation issue related to scripts is: When do we assert that the effects of a script have taken place? For example, if we were told that FredAsAnAdult was the actor in Robbery99, should we immediately go and create the appropriate subabstractions of FredAsAnAdult corresponding to him before and after the robbery? Doing so has the potential for creating an enormous number of subabstractions that might not be very useful for anything else, ever. For example, suppose someone asserts that Britain exported potatoes during some unspecified time period (less than a full year) in 1987, and we decide to create a unit representing that Exporting event. Should we immediately create two new subabstractions of Britain — BritainJustBeforeExportingPotatoesIn1987 and BritainJustAfterExportingPotatoesIn1987?

Generally, the answer is No. But in two kinds of situations, this kind of instantiation *should* actually take place:

- During a simulation. After the simulation is over, once the "answer" is obtained, the myriad of ephemeral units may be safely forgotten.

- During projection. Suppose Cyc is trying to find the values of some u.s by projecting s values from previous temporal subabstractions of u. As mentioned earlier, in doing temporal projection we take into account the different scripts that u has taken part in, to check to see if these would have changed the value of its s slot. To do this properly, Cyc must actually instantiate the effects of each such script F1, F2 . . . — that is, it creates the units representing "u just after F1," "u just after F2," etc.

6.2.6.   Pieces of Time.

6.2.6.1.   EACH EVENT IS FUSED WITH ITS timeInterval

In the above sections, we've referred vaguely to the "intervals" of time over which assertions were true, or within which events coincided. In everyday reasoning, we must be able to represent various sorts of "pieces of time" (the point in time at 3 p.m., the solid interval from 3 to 4 p.m., all the times in your adult life that you've been eating . . .) and we must be able to represent the various common, important relationships that occur between pieces of time (one piece of time endsBefore another, or is contiguousAfter, coTerminalWith, etc.). This section describes how we do that in Cyc. In a later section, we'll see how an analogous representation may be used to represent "pieces of space" and important spatial relations.

In the ontology of Cyc, the only things that may have any temporal aspects (for example, startingTime, duration, endsBefore) are members of the collection called Event. Each instance of Event represents something happening in the world (possibly a hypothetical world): Nixon's being elected President, the passing of the year 1988, etc. Events may be discontinuous; for example, if Fred read WarAndPeace a few pages at a time over a period of a year, FredReadingWar&Peace is a single event composed of several temporally-disconnected subevents.

Each event "takes place over" some such interval of time. Originally, we represented those intervals separately from the events; we had a collection called TimeInterval, whose instances were pieces of time; only TimeIntervals could legally have temporal aspects; events could merely point to the timeInterval over which they occurred, by using the slot timeInterval.

This led to a lot of wastefulness: for example, the unit representing "the time interval that the Knights Hospitaliers controlled Malta" is not really usable for any other purpose than to serve as the timeInterval for the event KnightsHospitaliersControllingMalta.

So, at first with trepidation, later with more assurance, we began merging the events and their time intervals. Finally, we took the plunge and fused the two categories, so that KnightsHospitaliersControllingMalta represents both the event and its time interval, and *it* can have a startingTime slot, an endsBefore slot, and all the other temporal slots.

Similarly, we don't have a separate unit for Napoleon and for TheIntervalOfTimeNapoleonLived. Rather, we allow the Napoleon unit to have a startingTime, endingTime, duration, startsDuring, endsBeforeEndingOf, and the dozens of other temporal slots we'll describe below.

6.2.6.2. EASILY CONCEPTUALIZED TIME INTERVALS

In Cyc, what kinds of intervals can be represented — what sorts of "pieces of time"? It would seem that we want all of the following:

- Points ("3 p.m. today")

- Solid intervals ("3 to 4 p.m. today")

- The union of any two intervals ("noon to three on Saturday and Sunday")

- The intersection of any two intervals ("some Monday in July")

- The difference of any two intervals ("all the time Fred spent at the office today other than when he was at lunch")

- Repeated intervals ("the innings in this baseball game" or "all the time you've ever spent driving to work")

- Relative fractions of intervals ("the first third of 1990")

- Defined pieces of time (we can refer to them by name in defining new ones; for example, "1990" is the name of a one-year-long piece of time)

But there's a problem. If we allow unbounded application of those few innocuous-sounding "wants" — infinite unions and intersections and differences — it is possible to come up with truly horrible pieces of time, such as "the irrational moments from 3 to 4 p.m. today" or "the Cantor set of moments from 3 to 4 p.m. today."

We handle this in Cyc by permitting only *easily conceptualized* time intervals (ECTIs). An *ECTI* is a single application of one of the eight rules listed above.

Here's an example of *six* simultaneous applications of some of the eight rules above: "All the time that Fred was at work during 1980, except when he was eating, using the restroom, or walking to/from his office, plus the time he was driving to work or talking about it to his kids."

Above seven simultaneous applications, hang it up; you have to give some of those things a name (that is, use the last rule in the list above). Once you do that, you can use that named piece of time as a building block, and you can build more esoteric intervals in terms of it. We hope that every piece of time that someone bothers to name in Cyc is a meaningful concept.

There's no magic here, merely pragmatism. Listen to the sentences you utter or hear, or the thoughts you think to yourself, and notice the pieces of time that you reason about; we think you'll find, as we did, that they're all ECTIs.

Notice that our representation combines the following notions of what "a piece of time" is — two notions that are obvious, natural, popular, and (individually) inadequate:

- A piece of time is a solid interval of the Real time continuum

- A piece of time is any set of points on that continuum

The next two sections cover the various temporal relations that derive from each of these two models of a piece of time.

<table>
<tr><td>

6.2.6.3.

INTERVAL-BASED RELATIONS AMONG TWO OR MORE PIECES OF TIME

</td><td>

Well, so much for representing various pieces of time. What about *relating* one such "event" to another — as in "1990 *is right before* 1991" or "The Battle of Gettysburg *took place during* the Civil War"?

Earlier, we talked about one important temporal relation: subabstraction. This is the relation that holds between FredAsAnAdult and FredInHisLateThirties. Some others are pretty obvious: before and after, for example. We mentioned a couple more in the previous paragraph (is RightBefore; tookPlaceDuring). There are many more of these — 51 of them at last count. We'll take a closer look at some of them below.

The absolute simplest temporal relations are those that can occur between a pair of points in time: before, after, simultaneousWith. That's the full set of possibilities. Now let's turn to how to relate pieces of time that are more complex than just a pair of points.

Try #1: In order to state the relationship between two *sets* of time points — two events E1 and E2 — just state the relations between pairs of points in the two sets and give the locations/ordering of these points in the sets themselves. Unfortunately, because the number of

</td></tr>
</table>

points is large, this could be a complex task. For example, the time from "3 to 4 p.m." contains an infinite number of distinguishable points! (Okay, if you believe in quantum mechanics, there's only a finite number, but it's still a big, big, big number.)

Try #2: Let's introduce a simplification. In order to relate events E1 and E2, just state the relations between pairs of "interesting points" in the two events. Well, maybe something like that could work, but how do we know which points are interesting? The answer is empirical: Face it, most points in an interval just aren't interesting. The *starting* and *ending* points of the sets are usually the most interesting points. More generally, the interesting points are those whose location within the set we have bothered to define.

Naturally, this is a *useful* fact only if the defining was done *independent* of the task of relating E1 to E2. That's one good thing about starting and ending points. Somewhat surprisingly, for most events that we've dealt with so far, *their only interesting points are their starting and ending points.* So we created dozens of relations that are compositions of the three primitive relations applied to the starting and ending points of two events. Some of these are: startsBeforeStartingOf, contiguousBefore (that is, "meets"), endsDuring, startsDuring, etc.

Here's a fuller list:

```
repeatedInEvents hasOccuringDuring
occursDuring partOfUnionOf hasStartingDuring
hasEndingDuring simplifiedEventIn notBefore
eventsWhoseBoundsIntersectMine
startsAfterStartingOf simplifiedEvents
setUnionOf notAfter startsAfterEndingOf
setIntersectsWithPositiveMeasureWith
setDisjointWithEvents follows
noOfRepetitions-Event nextEventOccurrence
repetetionInstanceOf repetitionInstances
finitelyRepeated? noOfSubIntervals
previousEventOccurrence eventIndex
noOfRepetitions-Structure snapShotOf
coincidentSnapShots snapshotTime preceding
eventContains eventContainedIn
endsBeforeStartingof superEvents subEvents
intervalsWhoseBoundsIntersectMine
startsBeforeStartingOf contiguousBefore
contiguousAfter overlapsEnd endsDuring
startsDuring coterminal cooriginating
overlapsStart sameEndPoints before
simultaneousWith after
```

Here are more detailed definitions of a couple of them, in terms of simpler ones. This list was generated by asking Cyc to do so — that is, by getting the #%relnExpansion slot of allInstances of #%TemporalRelation. Each expansion is in terms of the two events E1 and E2. There is no relnExpansion for the three primitive relations: before, after, and simultaneousWith.

```
#%occursDuring.#%relnExpansion
((#%before (#%startingTime E2)
           (#%startingTime E1))
 (#%after (#%endingTime E2)
          (#%endingTime E1)))

#%preceding.#%relnExpansion
((#%simultaneousWith (#%startingTime E2)
                     (#%endingTime E1))
```

6.2.6.4.

SET-BASED RELATIONS AMONG TWO OR MORE PIECES OF TIME

So, for the case of the relations mentioned in the section above, the set-based abstraction degenerates into an interval abstraction. However, there is a class of important temporal relations that are not easily expressible through the use of these interesting points. These are relations for which we need to fully exploit the set-based nature of these events. An example: "Mondays are *temporallyDisjointWith* Wednesdays." Another example: "My happy times always seem to be *during2* the time we spend together."

In English, we say "E1 was during E2" to mean two separate things:

- E1 started after E2 started, and E1 ended before E2 ended (during1);

  or

- each instant in E1 is also an instant in E2 (during2).

If February began and ended on a Monday in 1845, then the event E1 = "Wednesdays during February, 1845" would be during1 the event E2 = "Mondays during February, 1845." Because E1 and E2 are disjoint, however, E1 would hardly be during2 E2. During1 is an *interval*-based temporal relation, and is one of the dozens we defined purely in terms of starting and ending points. During2 can't be expressed in terms of any particular *special* points in E1 and E2; what we need to say is *"for all* points x in E1, x is also in E2." But that's just the definition of subset — which leads us to the following.

In order to be able to state "during2" and "temporallyDisjointWith" and other such relations, we fall back to the "set of points" abstraction and use a bunch of elementary set-theory predicates for representing notions such as containment and disjointness.

These fundamental set-theory predicates can be composed to form new relations, but surprisingly few of them have turned out to have very broad usefulness.

Any given pairs of events E1 and E2 may have both of these kinds of relations (interval-based and set-based), because in effect we have a dual abstraction of events. Of course, relations based on one abstraction could imply relations based on the other abstraction: if E1 endsBefore TheStartingOf E2, the two events are also necessarily setDisjointWith each other.

Here are five slots that do indeed have a #%setRelnExpansion. We listed them in the previous section when we listed the full set of TemporalRelations. All five have a set-based #%setRelnExpansion. The first three have no interval-based #%relnExpansion, but the last two do. In fact, the last two are only partially expressible in set-theoretic terms — that is, without talking about starting and ending points of E1, E2.

#%setUnionOf
#%setIntersectsWith
#%setDisjointWithEvents
#%endsBeforeStartingof
#%startsAfterEndingOf

Their #%setRelnExpansions are

#%setUnionOf: ((#%SetUnion E1 E2))
#%setIntersectsWith: ((#%SetIntersection E1 E2))
#%setDisjointWithEvents: ((#%SetDisjoint E1 E2))
#%endsBeforeStartingof: ((#%SetDisjoint E1 E2))
#%startsAfterEndingOf: ((#%SetDisjoint E1 E2))

6.2.6.5. OTHER WAYS OF DESCRIBING PIECES OF TIME

In addition to describing a time interval by relating it to other intervals, a number of other attributes may be used to describe it. Recall that a time interval is, in Cyc, fused with the notion of the temporal aspects of an event. Here, then, are some of the other temporal attributes that an event unit can have:

- Openness versus closedness of an event: Consider any piece of time as a subset of *R1* — the real number line. (Actually, in Cyc, the Time Axis is the half-infinite *ray* that begins at $x = 0$, which corresponds to the Big Bang.) Then the standard mathematical definition of openness and closedness applies to that set of points. If the closure of E1 equals E1, then E1 is a closed event. If the closure of E1 minus the boundary of E1 equals E1, then E1 is an open event. Events can also be neither open nor closed; for example, they can be half-open or something more complicated than that. Safety advisory: Be prepared to grab for the "extreme finiteness" guarantee of ECTIs at any moment, if you feel yourself slipping toward some counter-intuitive infinite set of disconnected points.

- Discontinuousness of an event: This attribute is used to denote whether the set of points can be abstracted as a convex set. Namely, is there any point in time that is after the startingTime of E1, before the endingTime of E1, but yet not in E1? Again, the "extreme finiteness" guarantees that there won't be many discontinuities in the event.

- Measure and duration of an event: We mentioned these attributes briefly earlier. They are two of the most common attributes used to denote the size of the event. The *duration* is simply the time difference between the starting and ending time. The *measure* is the total real time during which the event was "really happening." Thus the *duration* of "FredWorking9to5ThisWeek" might be 1 week, but its *measure* might be just 40 hours. Notice that if E1 is not discontinuous, its duration and measure will be the same. Also notice that, thanks to "extreme finiteness," we can get the measure of an event by just adding up the durations of all its separate component pieces (the duration and measure of a point are both zero).

6.2.6.6.
REPEATED EVENTS

We haven't said much about the concept of a repeated event. The two most useful classifications of repeated events are based on the two characteristics:

- The regularity of repetition

- The finiteness of the repetition

Thus, RepeatedEvent has two partitions in Cyc. (As we discussed much earlier, a *partition* of a collection C is a set of subsets of C such that each pair of the subsets is disjoint and the union of the subsets covers all of C.)

One partition of RepeatedEvent is into FinitelyRepeatedEvent and InfinitelyRepeatedEvent; the former breaks down based on whether you know how many repetitions there are; the first of *those* in turn breaks down based on how many repetitions there are.

The other partition of RepeatedEvent is into RegularRepeatedEvent and IrregularRepeatedEvent. Instances of the former can have some special slots like periodOfRepetition.

In all cases, the idea is to describe separately two parts of the repeated event: the inner event (the thing that's being repeated) and the nature of the repetition (how often, how regular, etc.).

An interesting issue comes up in the case of a repeated event whose subevents always form a never-ending (sort of) cycle; for example, a-b-c-d-a-b-c-d-a-b-c-d . . . . The issue is: How do we decide what the granule should be; should it be a-b-c-d, or b-c-d-a, or c-d-a-b, or d-a-b-c? Let's look at a few examples:

- Breathing, where the a-b-c-d cycle is "inhale, wait a little bit, exhale, wait a bit"

- A car engine running, where the cycle is "intake, compression, ignition, exhaust"

- Hunt-and-peck typing, where the cycle is "decide what letter you want to type next, position your finger over that key, push the key down, let it up"

(Naturally, this section applies to cycles with any number of repeated subevents, not just those with four repeated subevents!)

Why does it seem natural and intuitive for us to start the description of the Breathing cycle with "inhale", the car engine with "intake," the typing with "decide"? Theoretically, we could have started at any point in the cycle. But all the people we surveyed broke the cycles at these same points. Why? We believe there is a modest body of heuristics at work here. Four of these heuristics are:

- If subevent x directly causes/enables subevent y, then x should precede y in the listing of a cycle's subevents.

- If something is being inputted and transformed and outputted, then its "life cycle" is a natural model for the cycle.

- If subevent x is "idling" or "waiting" or "doing nothing," then it should not be the start (first listed subevent) of the cycle.

- If two adjacent subevents x and y are both relatively brief, compared to the subevents that come earlier/later than they do, then x and y should not be separated (that is, y should not be chosen to be the "first" subevent in the ordering of subevents in a cycle).

These heuristics explain the cases above. We can also apply them to, for example, WhaleBreathing. Unlike humans, when whales inhale, they hold their breath a long time. Yes, a very long time. They're still holding their breath. Okay, now they exhale, and then almost immediately they inhale again.

Our first two heuristics above would favor splitting the whale breathing cycle as inhale-wait-exhale-short wait, just as they favor starting out HumanBreathing with the inhale subevent. The third heuristic reinforces not starting with the "wait" subevent. But the fourth heuristic says that in the case of WhaleBreathing, it might make sense to start with the "exhale" step, because it's short and it's followed by the short wait and the short "inhale" step. The interesting thing here is that humans are indeed divided on this issue if you ask them for the subevents in whale breathing. In *Moby Dick,* for example, Ahab and the other whalers clearly think of the cycle as beginning with the exhale (spouting) subevent. They gear up to act frantically *during* the all-too-brief exhale-inhale subevents that punctuate the long periods of submergence.

A final interesting note about RepeatedEvent. Often, the apparent named "granule" is not the true full-cycle granule, but rather only a subset of the subevents in a cycle. In the case of HumanBreathing, the granule appears to be "TakingASingleBreath&LettingItOut," but that involves inhaling, waiting briefly, and exhaling. The waiting step between exhaling and inhaling just doesn't figure here. The true cycle has four steps, not three. Or, employing the "common" pseudo-granule, it could be conceived of as an alternating sequence of just two steps: TakingASingleBreath&LettingItOut alternating with WaitingAWhile.

It is common for the final "pausing" step to be omitted from the commonly-thought-of and named "granule." For example, if you ask people to describe their entire daily routines, their descriptions typically start with "getting up in the morning" and end with "going to sleep," thereby omitting the long sleep ("waiting") period itself.

6.3. Causality and Related Issues

6.3.1. Causality. Causal relations can exist in Cyc between Events (later we extend this). There are different kinds of causal relationships, and *much of the power comes from teasing apart the various dimensions and contents of causality-space.*

At the most primitive level, when we say "E1 causes E2" in Cyc, we mean two things:

- We mean that E1 temporally preceded E2. This gets a little tricky in cases where E1 isn't finished before E2 starts, but basically all we insist on is that E1 *startsBefore* E2.

- We mean that there is some sort of mechanism (possibly unknown) behind the causation. In philosophy, that mechanism is termed the "implication" of E2 by E1.

There are some good reasons for delving into those mechanisms, at least a little bit. Yet the overwhelming pragmatic *use* of "E1 causes E2" is simply the following:

When faced with an event similar to E1,
predict that some event similar to E2 will follow.

That's about it. Less often — and with much less certainty — we use the "E1 causes E2" assertion *abductively*. That is,

When something like E2 occurs,
suspect that something like E1 preceded it.

Even that tiny bit of structure — dividing causation into "temporal precedence" and "mechanistic implication" — is enough to give us several useful classifications of the various causal relations.

One of those classifications is based on the temporal relation involved. The two fundamental classes of temporal relations (interval- versus set-based) induces a partitioning of causal relations into two classes. The following examples illustrate what is meant by this.

Consider the relationship between these two events:

E1 = an explosion taking place
E2 = a car getting damaged because of it

All that we know or care about here, temporally, is that the explosion began before the damage to the car began — the starting point of E1 was before the starting point of E2. In Cyc terms, E1 startsBefore E2. This temporal relationship is based on an *interval*-abstraction of time.

On the other hand, take a relationship such as mutuallySustaining.

E1 = poverty in America during the 1970s
E2 = illiteracy in America during the 1970s

In English we might say "poverty and illiteracy were mutually sustaining problems plaguing America all during the 1970s." What's meant here is that each bit of E1 (partially) causes a *slightly later* bit of E2, and each bit of E2 (partially) causes a *slightly later* bit of E1. So the temporal relation implied by this is clearly one based on E1 and E2 as full-fledged sets of points; we can't represent this just in terms of the starting and ending times of E1 and E2 (indeed, E1 and E2 are coTemporal). So this temporal relationship is based on a *set*-abstraction of time.

Another example of this is "leadsToEachTime", as in: "Whenever JFK ate a big meal, it made him drowsy." JFKEating and JFKBeingDrowsy are two compound events. Each of them is composed of tens of thousands of separate solid intervals unioned together. Just knowing the startingTime and endingTime of the two compound events does not even begin to convey the temporal relationship implied in the sentence; both JFKEating and JFKBeingDrowsy probably started the day he was born and ended the day he died, so just knowing the two startingTimes and endingTimes is of no help at all.

At the moment, a number of slots in Cyc correspond to different kinds of causality. The *way* to represent it has been worked out and tested with examples like those above. Still, someone has to "really do it" for a large number of complex cases.

6.3.2. Intentionality.

We — and Cyc — distinguish between the concepts of intentionality and causality. When we cause things in the world, sometimes we mean to cause them, and sometimes we don't. When a nonsentient entity causes something (for example, the primordial sun forming the solar system), it is of course always unintentional.

(If you disagree with this — if you ascribe intentions to inanimate objects — you do not share our consensus reality. In which case, you can change your view of the world, convince us to change ours, build your own version of Cyc, just go away, or enter your minority opinion as a *Belief* in Cyc, which we'll discuss soon.)

What does it mean for an action to be *intentional*? It means that the performer was an Agent who had the Intention of doing E1, and then did it. That is, before the agent carried out E1, he had some Expectation (a belief about the future) in which carrying out event E1 would lead to some desired state of being for the agent. That might be an absolute desirable state (a Goal), or, much more likely, just a desired Change (an improved state of being, still heading toward some Goal). Often, E1 will then be one of the scripts (that is, E1 will be an instance of SomethingOccurring) to which the Change unit points as being relevant for achieving that change.

That's what *rationality* is all about: having and using knowledge to achieve goals. That is, identifying some unsatisfied goals and using them to select actions that — you hope — will help satisfy those goals without creating worse problems for you in the process. That process is akin to means-ends analysis, or, more generally, best-first search. Carrying out this process successfully requires lots of knowledge, which is where Cyc comes in.

An agent's having an Intention may therefore be one of the causes for event E1, which then causes E2. Often, in English, we'd loosely say that the agent also caused E2. For example: "High death tolls on the highways caused today's cars to have seat belts." We even say that now in law: an accidental murder during the commission of a felony counts as premeditated murder. Internally, however, Cyc must carefully distinguish true intention from unintentional causality.

Why? That is, why attempt to distinguish clearly between intentionality and "raw" causality? Let's look at an example. Say Fred is building a fence around his house. From the perspective of one of his neighbors, the intention behind this could be that Fred is trying to act unfriendly. From the perspective of Fred himself, this could be to ensure his privacy from the prying eyes of his neighbors. In any case, these are clearly *intentions* we're talking about here. Now consider a neighborhood dog that Fred isn't even aware of. Suddenly, that dog can't get into Fred's yard any more. Did Fred *cause* that by building the fence? Sure. Did Fred *intend* that? Surely not. So *intentionality* and *causality* are not the same thing. *Causality* is fundamental, whereas *intentionality* is very much related to the perspective chosen.

Caution: Our *description* of causal relations is probably somewhat influenced by *our* intention of describing it! For example, we often view a car from a functional perspective; we see the relationship between the steering-wheel and the changes in the car's direction purely from the perspective of the way humans have designed it to work. "What caused the car to jerk to the left? Jerking the steering-wheel to the left." The true chain of *cause and effect* here may be quite long and convoluted, involving umpteen gears and rods and sensors and power steering fluid pumps. But the functional, *intentional* path from steering wheel to tires is very short in our minds.

Most of the manufactured things that surround us have a clear intended use. We see them through the heavily filtered lenses of that designated function. This is the consensus reality point of view, not just for automobiles, but for a large portion of human-designed objects. It is a good perspective most of the time; given that humans must ignore some 99 percent of what's going on around us, it lets us ignore the right 99 percent. Most of the time [Norman, 1988]. It may *not* be so great if you need to brainstorm [Adams, 1986], or worry about how something might fail, or debug it if it does fail. Cyc treats "the intended use of X" as the default point of view for the functional extent of X, just as we do, but both we and Cyc can rise above it (well, actually delve down below it) when necessary.

6.4. Intelligent Beings

How does Cyc represent people, countries, and other intelligent beings? Interestingly enough, Fred isn't just a lump of meat (a TangibleObject), and he isn't just an intangible Intelligence, so what is he? He's an amalgam of the two, a composite. Thus, we have (as described in an earlier section) a third type of entity besides tangible objects and intangibles, namely CompositeTangible&IntangibleObject. Its instances have both a physical, substantial aspect (physicalExtent) and a mental or message-content aspect (functionalExtent).

Let us take a closer look at CompositeTangible&IntangibleObject. Its instances are considered composite in the sense that their nature, their criterial essence if you will, involves a combination of tangible and intangible attributes. Their physical component is the means by which they directly interact with the world. Their intangible component usually involves some kind of symbol manipulation and communicating. If it's sufficiently sophisticated and dynamic and flexible, we refer to the entity as *intelligent*, and the intangible component is termed an Intelligence (a mind or will or spirit). In the case of simpler composites, such as a book, we may regard its intangible component as the entity's content or message or function (as opposed to form).

6.4.1. Signal, Animal, Agent. Let us take a brief look at some of the main collections that currently come under (are subsets of) CompositeTangible&IntangibleObject.

- Signal — Each member of this collection will have some (relatively) simple and stylized physical aspect (such as the electromagnetic waves of a television signal or the pages of a book). That physical form is little more than a wrapper or container used to contain and convey some bits of information (the intangible component).

- Animal — All animals are presumed to have a tangible component that is their physical body and an intangible component that is their "mind." We are not supposing that all animals are intelligent, of course.

    An important distinction: The standard biological taxonomy of animals (into phyla, order, class, genus, species, etc.) is not the same as, nor even strongly reflected in, this part of the hierarchy! Linnaean taxonomy is based on physical structure and evolution, not on function, so the Linnaean classification of animals comes under the collection of the physical bodies of animals, the Cyc unit called Animal-Physical. By contrast, the classification of animals under Animal is based on homology (combinations of form and function) and includes things such as the quality of the animal's perceptual and sensory system, speed and type of reflexes, hormonal and immune system mechanisms, etc. Similarly, there could be in Cyc, under Animal-Mental, a third classification of animals based purely on their mental traits: their level of intelligence, temperament, personality, attention span, seriousness versus playfulness, ethics, and other "mental" attributes.

- Agent — This subset of CompositeTangible&IntangibleObject includes those things that are capable of conscious (or at least apparently deliberate) decision-making, controlling other things, and playing an active role in scripts. Besides most macroscopic animals, we'd also include computers, corporations, clubs, countries, and so on. Purely passive CompositeTangible&IntangibleObjects, such as books, would just barely *not* fall into this category. Computer-based interactive novels are teetering on the edge and . . . yes, the best of them just made it into the Agent category.

   The further classification of Agent in Cyc is primarily based on whether the agent is intelligent or not, and on whether it is a *single* IndividualObject (such as a person or a computer) or a *collective* system (such as an angry mob, a beehive, a country, or a computer network).

6.4.2. Countries as CompositeTangible&IntangibleObjects.   While we are on the topic of countries, it is worthwhile taking a look at the basic ontology of those sorts of things. Countries, states, cities, and so on, have a physicalExtent, which is the geographical region where they are, the actual dirt they sit on, the air above and the minerals (and geothermal energy) below, the buildings, roads, inhabitants' bodies, etc. They also have a functionalExtent, which is their political component: their government, the community of inhabitants' minds, the daily operating of the businesses and schools, etc.

   Consider EgyptIn1986. Its physical extent might be represented by a unit called PhysicalEgyptIn1986, though it's likely to be a larger temporal subabstraction, because its 1986 borders, geology, ethnic mixture, etc., are substantially the same as they were immediately after its war with Israel several years earlier. Its mental extent might be represented by a unit called PoliticalEgyptIn1986 (or, to be less biased, FunctionalEgyptIn1986).

   A similar triple of units could exist for each city in Egypt, each Egyptian resident, etc. The set of all Egyptian people might be represented by a unit called EgyptianPerson, and we could also have, if we wanted to, EgyptianPersonIn1986. (Presumably that unit would exist only if we had something special to say about it.)

   This raises an important point. EgyptianPersonIn1986 is not a temporal subabstraction of EgyptianPerson! At first we were tempted to call it that. However, this would not really make sense, because the set of Egyptian people is not an Event but a *collection of the events* consisting of all those people each living their lives.

Well, surely something *like* subabstraction is going on here! Yes, it is: Consider AbdulIn1986 (sorry, Fred doesn't sound Egyptian enough). It is a temporal subabstraction of Abdul. AbdulIn1986 is a member of EgyptianPeopleIn1986, and a member of EgyptianPerson.

So the relationship that holds between TheSetXIn1986 and TheSetX is that each *member* of the former is a temporal subabstraction of a *member* of the latter. We represent this in Cyc by recording that TheSetXIn1986 is a subAbstraction*Type* of X. We'll talk more about the ... *Type* units and slots a little later on.

But recall that all people are also processes; that is, they're carrying out the (rather autonomic) process of SomethingExisting. That leads to an interesting relation between these two slots: genls and superAbstractionType.

What we're going to show is that, for a set X, because XIn1986 is a subAbstraction*Type* of X, it necessarily follows that XIn1986 is a sub*set* of X. Why? Let's pick on AbdulIn1986 again, to stand as a typical member of XIn1986. What we have to show is that he's also an element of X. That is, we have to show that he's an instance of EgyptianPerson.

Because AbdulIn1986 is a Person, he's also a Process, so he's (at least temporally!) substance-like. AbdulIn1986 is a temporal "piece of" Ab-

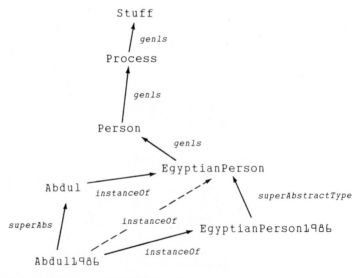

Figure 6–1: Diagram of Abdul1986

dul, who is also temporally substance-like. What type of Stuff is Abdul an instance of, exactly? Why, the X type of stuff!
(X = EgyptianPerson.) So each of Abdul's temporal subabstractions, including AbdulIn1986, must (because of temporal stufflikeness) also be a member of X. See Figure 6-1.

The final result is that the slot superAbstractionType is a specSlot (specialized form) of genls. So as soon as we say that, for example, HumanChild is a subAbstractionType of Person, we can conclude that HumanChild is also a spec of Person.

6.4.3. Should We Bother Splitting Up CompositeTangible&IntangibleObjects?   Another question that crops up while discussing the representation of composite tangible and intangible entities, such as people, is this: Is splitting up a person into a physical part and a mental part carrying things too far under the guise of precision? Wouldn't everything still be clear if we had a single unit that represented all the aspects of the person or city or whatever?

The answer to this is provided by a simple counterexample: consider The Frankenstein Monster. What's his age? His physical body has one age, his mind has another, and the amalgam of the two has a third value for age. That's a bit extreme, we admit, but the point is that you have no problem conceptualizing those three separate things, each with their own age. Another example where this kind of distinction between the physical and functional extents seems to stand out is France during World War II, or any government in exile. Many other slots (for example, interestingness) also make sense for tangible, intangible, and composite entities.

However, there is a valid point in the objection that, because human beings are so used to ambiguity (for example, in language), they can be confused or daunted by the extreme preciseness of the Cyc knowledge representation. However, we believe that this is more of an *interface* problem than a *representation* problem.

There ought to be (and we are working toward) a natural language interface that does two things: (a) resolves ambiguity in user-supplied utterances, and (b) adds color, discourse variation, ellipsis, anaphora — and ambiguity — to utterances Cyc wishes to make to the user. (This NLP project is being done in collaboration with Elaine Rich, Jim Barnett, and other AI and Human Interface researchers at MCC.)

So, for now, we will staunchly maintain our tripartite internal representation of all intelligent agents: countries (Egypt, PhysicalEgypt, PoliticalEgypt), people (Fred, FredsBody, FredsMind), organizations such as the Boy Scouts and the PLO, companies, clubs, foundations, boards of directors, and, right at the fringe of agenthood, today's more sophisticated distributed man-machine networks (such as AI-LIST) and computer programs (such as Cyc, of course — just ask it!).

6.4.4. Computers as Agents.

Earlier, we mentioned that people exhibit an individual intelligence, whereas organizations exhibit a collective intelligence (hive mind), and this distinction is present in the Cyc ontology. But consider the following interesting category of composite entities: Computer (the set of computers running various programs).

Each computer has a physical extent (the hardware) and a functional extent (the software, or rather, the knowledge in the software). However, whether these are individual or collective intelligences is an open question. A distributed system seems collective, and a standalone workstation seems individual, but. . . . . Readers of Minsky's *Society of Mind* [1985] might find it easy to view a *person* as a collective intelligence, after all.

Caveat

The remainder of 6.4 contains some very early thoughts on these subjects and a lot of work needs to be done before anything can come of it.

6.4.5. Further Thoughts on Agenthood, Agreements, Voluntary Action, Etc.

We have already discussed the standard elements of our ontology (agents, events, etc.). In addition, we also recognize *propositions* as first-class objects in our ontology (though this does not mean we want to create units for each of them).

Given an agent A and a proposition P, the agent can have an *attitude* toward P. What sort of "propositional attitude" can A have about P? A might hope that P comes true, be afraid of P, believe that P already is true, and so on. In other words, the possible propositional attitudes include goals, beliefs, dreads, etc.

An agent A is related to various events by various *actor relations*. For instance, it could be related to an event by the slot #%murdererIn, or the more general slot #%performerIn, which makeSenseFor Agent and whose entryIsA Event. An example of such a relationship would be LHOswald.murdererIn.AssassinatingOfJFK.

So one special subset of the events to which A is related is the set of activities that A *performs*. By this we mean something like intentionally did something; that is, the Earth does not *perform* rotation; a person does not *perform* slipping on a banana peel, although perhaps some slapstick comedians do. Perhaps a better name for the relationship would be intentionallyPerforms or purposelyPerforms.

We could take this relationship as given, as primitive, but it would be much more powerful if we could actually *define* what it means for A to purposely perform E. A rough cut at the definition is something like the following:

> *Agent A purposely performs event E if and only if there is some proposition P which has the following properties.*
> *(a) P is on the goals list of the agent*
> *(b) A believes that performing E will "cause" P to be true (later)*
> *(c) A is criterial to E taking place. Without A, E couldn't occur.*

(It might be safest to refer to the variety of causation described in (b) as cause-1 and talk about it later.)

It is to be noted that these are merely defaults, and it is quite easy to come up with instances where these are not really true. In general, however, it seems useful to use these defaults.

Notice that (a) and (b) alone constitute "motive" or purpose:

$$purpose(A, E, P) => goals(A, P) \land believes(A, cause\text{-}1(E, P))$$

The next notion to consider is the reaction, of an agent A, to P going from his *goals* to his *beliefs*. That is, P is not merely desirable, it now is a wish come true (as far as A believes!).

There are two issues here. The first one is that of representing the change (in his attitude toward P itself), and the second one is that of representing his reaction to the change.

The ontology of changes was explained in brief earlier. This is a slight extension of that. First, no unit corresponding to the change needs to be created. Next, we can talk about changes in the value of (u s). We get the following ways of talking about changes:

- change-1 (s subabs-1 subabs-2) → this is a function whose range is the "concept of the change" in the value of the slot s between the subabstractions.

- change-2 (s v1 subabs-1 subabs-2) → again, this is a function whose range is the concept of the change in v1 occurring or not occurring on the slot s between these two subabs.

- change-3 (P event-1 event-2) → this is a rather general predicate that says that the truth value of P has changed from event-1 to event-2 (which may be intervals or subabstractions or whatever)

[Note that this categorization of changes is orthogonal to the one mentioned previously. In practice we use a combination of the two.]

If A.goals.P, and then A.believes.P, we would expect A to be "happy" or "satisfied" about the change, and about the final state. We can express this as:

> IF (not (believes A1 P)) ∧
>   (goals A1 P) ∧
>   (believes A2 P) ∧
>   (laterSubAbs(A1 A2)
> THEN satisfied(A2 P)

The next notion we need is a flavor of causation that says that a proposition being true is the *ramification* of an event. To express the notion that P is true as a ramification of E, we state a default rule that says that P is true because some property is true about E. We'll call this flavor of causation "Causes-1". So this defines causes-1(E s v1 P).

In addition, we want to say that if there has been a change, there has to be some cause for this (that can account for this). This is what differentiates causes-1 from material implication. So we get

```
change3(P e1 e2) ⇒
   (ThereExists y, s, v1 such that
     (can-cause y P) ∧
     (causes-1 y s v1 P) ∧
     (after y e1)∧(startsBeforeStartOf y e2))
```

A couple of notes about this. First, this is only a default rule, because even if the property did not hold for the event, it is possible that P would be true. For example, I might state: "Because I went to the shop," I got delayed. However, maybe I would have gotten delayed even if I had not gone to the shop.

Second, we think there is something missing from the ontology, because there is no easy way to say that an event did not occur. Consider the following. I tell you that I saw Fred at the shop. Let us call this event-1. Let us suppose this is indicated by placing some slot on event-1. Next, I tell you that I really did not see Fred, but saw Jim. Would you say that event-1 did not occur? What if I changed other slots on event-1 so that it now said that I went to see a movie. Surely event-1 as we knew it earlier did not occur. However the unit event-1 still exists and so event-1 must have occurred.

This is actually a deep problem related to the denotation of a symbol. We won't go into this further, but this should indicate the reason why we formalized my statement as "some property is true of the event." However, in the rest of the book, we shall use the notion of an event occurring or not occurring, in the hope that we shall find an adequate definition of this notion.

If the event is an action/activity, we can treat this as an "atomic" entity and consider it as equal to the conjunction of some "defining" conditions for the activity, such as its type and performer. Anyway, assuming we understand what it means for an event to have occurred, we use the term *occurs(event)*. (Later we shall attempt to define the notion of *occurs*.) The main motivation for doing this is to avoid having to use stupid-sounding sentences such as causes-1(event-1 s v1 P), instead of being able to use more simple notions such as causes-1(event-1 P). In practice, one should be able to replace occurs(event) with some more complex proposition. So rather than saying that an event did not occur, we say that the proposition is false.

We now come to the reason why we wanted to introduce the notion of causes-1. The basic intuition we want to state is that if an agent is responsible for causing something that fulfills a desire of another agent, the other agent feels obligated toward, and often rewards, the first one.

To be a bit more precise, if an agent A performs an activity E and E.causes-1.P, and A is responsible for E, and P is on the goals list of A', and a later subabstraction of A' believes that P is true, then that later subabstraction rewards A with something (call it X for now). We can write this (skipping the beliefs part for now) as:

IF performs(A, E)∧
  causes-1(E, P)∧
  responsible(A, Occurs(E))∧
  laterSubabs(A A1)∧
  happy(A' P)∧...
THEN (ThereExists X Reward rewards(A' A1 X))

(The reader should interpret "responsible(A, Occurs(E))" as meaning that A is responsible for E's occurring.)

Again, this is just a default rule, because A' might be ungrateful. It must be noted that this notion is not really about people being grateful. It is the first step in making precise the notion of social (and other) contracts, etc. We shall see soon how various constraints get imposed on X. Also it is quite likely that we don't really want this rule in the KB, but instead we want five or six more specialized versions of this.

In general, if an action E causes P to be true, and if A is responsible for E's occurring, then we shall assume that A is also responsible for P. This corresponds to the intuitive notion that an agent is responsible for the results of the actions for which he is responsible. (We might or might not want to add another default that says that an agent is responsible for the actions he performs.)

responsible(A Occurs(E)) $\land$ *causes-1(E P)* $\leftrightarrow$ *responsible(A P)*

Note the two-way implication. This basically says that for an agent to be held responsible for something, he must have done something that caused that thing.

Also the converse holds for ($\neg$ P); that is, we have some notion of punishment, or at least of crimes of omission.

A note on this relation "responsible." This is a function from agents to propositions. The time period associated with these propositions could be before or after that associated with the agent. So the same relation is to be used for both saying that Mary (yesterday) is responsible for the credenza's being here today and for saying that Mary (tomorrow) is responsible for the credenza's being here today. What if the credenza had not made it here? That does not really affect the truth of the statement of responsibility, because *saying responsible(A P) only indicates the relation between A and P, and does not say that P is true or false.*

The next notion we consider is that of an *agreement*. An agreement is something that includes the following in its definition:

- A set of propositions $\{P_i\}$; these are the clauses, the various things that are being agreed.

- A set of *n* agents $\{A_i\}$ who have "entered into the agreement." As a default, all these agents can be assumed to believe $\{P_i\}$ to be true.

- The agreement assigns a set (a subset of $\{P_i\}$) of responsibilities to each agent. Notice that a particular P_i might get assigned as the responsibility of several agents, not just one. We also have the default rule that if A_j gets assigned P_k, then P_k makes it onto A_j.goals. The most common and important special case of Aj getting assigned P_k is where P_k is nothing but the requirement that A play a particular role in some event.

- Each agent engages in a set of transactions with the other agents. The terms of the transaction are defined by the agreement. We shall return to this later, when we talk about transactions.

- Associated with the responsibilities are a set of rewards. Note that this is in addition to the transactions. As we shall see later, transactions are rather rigid in their perspective, whereas the notion of reward is far more flexible and perhaps ubiquitous.

- In addition to the rewards, etc., for actions performed, there may also be punishments for certain actions (certain actions may even be forbidden).

- Agreements can have certain agents specified as enforcers, and certain agreed-upon enforcement rules (and compiled scenarios.)

We shall say this as follows:

states(agreement-1, P)/\ agrees(A, agreement-1) → believes(A, P)

assigns-responsibility(agreement-1, P, A)/\ agrees(A, agreement-1)
  → responsible(A, P)

forbids(agreement-1, E, punishment-1)/\ agrees(A, agreement-1)/
  performs(A, E)/\ enforcer(agreement-1, A1)
  → punishes(A1, A, punishment-1)

This default needs to be worked out a bit. It does not make enough of a distinction between rewards/punishments and the effect of violating the terms of a transaction as laid down by the agreement. We shall come to this again after dealing with transactions.

Related to the notion of an agreement forbidding an action is the concept of a right or a privilege. There are two versions of the notion of a *right*. The first one states that at some given moment *there is no agreement that forbids* an agent from performing some action E. This is not a very interesting concept. The tougher thing is to talk about "inalienable rights" or rights that are *guaranteed*. If we consider a right as some kind of "being allowed to perform an action" we get the following definition of right.

hasRight(A, E) → not(ThereExists x y instanceOf(x Agreement)/
  agrees(A, x)/\ forbids(x E y))

In most cases, we will have to use some intensional variety of hasRight, such as hasRightType.

There seems to be an intuitive classification of agreements into "formal" or "informal" ones. This notion seems closely tied to the identity of the enforcer for an agreement. There is a common agent called "the law" that has an agreement with a set of agents called "legal entities." One of the terms of this agreement (that is, the law) is something like the contract law, which basically says that it (that is, the executive) can be the enforcer for the agreements that fall into this category of formal agreements. Note that this says only that the law *can* be the enforcer. It is possible that some other agent will (try to) enforce the agreement — for example, a collection agency — and only when it fails will the law interfere. We can state this as:

instanceOf(agreement-1 FormalAgreement)/
agent-of-agreement(A1, agreement-1) /\ forbids(agreement-1 E
    punishment-1)/
agrees(A, agreement-1)/\ performs(A, E)/

(not (can-perform, A1, punishment-1))
$\rightarrow$ *punishes(Law, A, punishment-1)*

This makes use of the slot agent-of-agreement. Many agreements define an agent, this agent usually being some kind of institution. If that institution cannot enforce the agreement, the law acts as the enforcer for this agreement.

Often, though an agreement does not explicitly state that some action is forbidden, it is argued that the agreement *implies* that the action is forbidden. This is a rather special kind of implication, though. It often can be logically inferred that certain actions are forbidden; but the law seems to use some kind of *limited rationality,* and only those actions that are relatively "directly" forbidden seem to be considered to be forbidden.

It's difficult — but vital — to capture this notion. It may be because of this that agents seem to take part in a lot of *informal agreements*; that is, the range of possible actions in a situation is wide enough to make an explicit listing of all the actions infeasible, and attempts to develop a generalization of these actions seem to include too many other allowable actions. We are still left with the task of formalizing these "informal" agreements. The reason we think we can do it is that law seems to be a monotonically reasoning agent. That is, if one law implies X and another implies not X, there is no mechanism for handling this contradiction; it is too hard to avoid this at legislating-time, and part of the judiciary job seems to be that of handling this.

So the basic plan for handling informal agreements is to have general rules that might forbid certain actions that are indeed allowed, and to have in addition other rules that imply that the rules defining actions that are allowed should override the general rules.

The next notion we have to deal with is that of the *resources* an agent poses/controls. Because the notions of resources and transactions are defined using each other, we first give an informal description of a resource and then deal with transactions and give more precise descriptions of each of these concepts.

Agents have resources. A *resource* is anything that can be a tender in some transaction. This is a rather restrictive notion of a resource. If you don't like it, replace the term *resource* with "possession."

A *transaction* could be thought of as a change in control of some tender. Combinations of transactions form *exchanges*. Exchanges impose restrictions on the value of the tenders exchanged, etc.

This brings us to the notion of the *value of something*. Things have values only with respect to agents measuring them in terms of utility. For now, let's not consider these as marginal utilities. In addition, things also may have a value in some context-independent sense (say, in terms of some currency).

Two important kinds of "fair" transactions are those in which the values of the tenders exchanged have equal values in an absolute sense and another in which each agent perceives itself as getting into a "better" state as a result of the transaction.

Actually drawing the line between the two seems rather hard. If the transaction results in P1 and P2 being true, we can assume that one of the agents had P1 on his goals and the other had P2 on his goals. These actually form the *purpose* for their performing the transaction.

This is extremely weak, however, and it is important to be careful with this concept.

An *activity* is more general than a transaction and can involve one or more agents. (Notice that transactions generally require at least two separate agents, though sometimes you're transacting with another aspect of yourself, or with yourself at a later time, etc.) Carrying out an activity usually involves the conversion of a resource from one form into another. *Resources* include things such as information, effort, time, space, energy, mass, etc.

Let us now try to make more precise the notions discussed in the earlier paragraph. First, we want to say that in a transaction T1, there are agents A1 and A2 and there is some resource R such that there is a change in the relationship (Q) between R and A2 after T1. Note that we can't just say A2 *owns* R, because our notion of transaction includes concepts such as services, etc. We can state this as

$$
\begin{aligned}
&resourceTransfered(T1, R) \wedge \\
&\quad instanceOf(T1, C) \wedge \\
&\quad fromAgent(T1, A1) \wedge \\
&\quad toAgent(T1, A2) \wedge \\
&\quad transferType(T, Q) \\
&\rightarrow Q(A2, R)
\end{aligned}
$$

Note that this is not a single rule but a schema or an inference template, and the descriptions of the different transaction types will define the instances of this inference template. Also note that this is not really complete, because we will want to include more clauses about the relation between A1 and R, etc. This notion of a transaction, although it seems superficially similar to a Schankian primitive TRANSfer, is not really so similar to that notion, because Cyc has many different types of transactions that add additional constraints on A1, A2, R, etc.

Next, we want to talk about *exchanges* and say that in an exchange the values of the objects involved in the transactions are the same. Assume that the two major types of exchanges are called Exchange-1 and Exchange-2 and the corresponding notions of values are called value-1 and value-2. So we get the main constraints that define the two kinds of exchanges:

> *instanceOf(e1 Exchange-1)/*
> *participant(e1 A1)/*
> *participant(e1 A2)/*
> *receives(e1 A1 X)/*
> *receives(e1 A2 Y)*
> → *(equal (value-1 X A1) (value-1 Y A2))*

> *instanceOf(e1 Exchange-2)/*
> *participant(e1 A1)/*
> *participant(e1 A2)/*
> *objectInvolved(e1 X)/*
> *objectInvolved(e1 Y)*
> → *(equal (value-2 X) (value-2 Y))*

Next we want to say that if an agent performs a transaction, he usually has a *purpose* for doing so. This is quite trivial to say (however, *using* this concept could be more complex):

> *participant(e1 A) → (ThereExists p Purpose purpose(e1 A p))*

An important category of goals an agent has (usually) is the desire to possess resources. This is trivial to state if we just wanted to state each of these things individually (that is, people want to have money, fame, etc.).

Instead, to make things simpler, we introduce the notion of a *goal set*. A goal set is similar to a set of shared beliefs and ideologies, which would be a belief set. We can have goal sets corresponding to type-A persons, type-B persons, governments, etc. So we get

> *instanceOf(goal-set1 Goal-set)/*
> *defines-goal(goal-set1, P)/*
> *shares-goal(goal-set1 A1)*
> → *goals(A1 P)*

The next thing we want to say is that *agents use the resources that are available to them to achieve their goals* (arguably, this is one of the hallmarks of rationality). We first tried to say this as

> *goals(A, P)/\ can-cause-1(E, P) → performs(A, E)*

This is clearly insufficient, however, because it does not include any notion of choice among the possible actions an agent could perform. There are two issues here. First, we could argue that P should really be the "overall" goal, and agents deterministically choose those actions that optimize the overall goal. This is not really right, because even intermediate goals can be on our goal list. Also, we would like to be more symbolic (by this we don't mean just writing formulae, but something better than postulating optimizing functions, etc.) than decision theoretic.

Before we can do that we need to address the notion of *preferences*. When we are dealing with defaults, we can say that even though P1 and P2 have the strength T (by default, they are true), we can say that one is *more likely than* the other. This basically means that if we had to choose between an extension in which P1 was true and another in which P2 was true, we would choose the more likely one.

We need a corresponding notion in the context of goals — namely, that of preferences. So if P1 and P2 are goals of A, we can say prefers(A P1 P2), which means that though both of them may be on A's goals, in case of a conflict A would prefer P1. This lets us modify the earlier statement to

goals(A, P)$\wedge$
can-cause-1(E, P)$\wedge$
(not (ThereExists x prefers A (Performs(A, x) Performs(A, E))))
$\rightarrow$ *performs(A, E)*

This is still not sufficient, because it does not even mention the ability of the agent to perform the action. So we need the notion of canPerform. This will have to be defined in terms of things that include "the activities require certain resources" and "the agent must have an appropriate form of control over the resource," etc. We are still working on this.

Note that this is not intended to be some kind of panacea for all problems. We still have two major tasks: (a) determining the preferences of agents and (b) efficiently searching for the E used earlier.

The next topic is an interesting one. We said earlier that information, too, is a form of resource. It is one of the important classes of resource agents try to possess. The decisions agents make (possibly after running the previous rule) could be thought of as information, and such decisions constitute a very special kind of resource. So agents must expend resources in deciding which activities to engage in. Note that this recursion dies quickly, because the base case (where there is just one option open) occurs quickly.

Next, we need to deal with the notion of *voluntary v/s involuntary*. This is a real morass. Of course, it is closely related to notions of free will, etc. One seemingly promising approach is to define the voluntary actions of an agent as those for which there is a purpose. This does not work all the time, because if someone holds a gun to my head and asks me to perform a hundred sit-ups, my performance surely is not voluntary, but I do have a purpose (namely to remain alive).

Another approach is a little more specific about the type of the purpose, insisting that the purpose not be an avoidance goal (dread). This also does not work out, because it makes things too dependent on subtle interpretation changes. For example, I pay my taxes voluntarily, but I do it so that I don't go to jail (that is, to avoid a dread). Based on whether we have a predicate called "outOfJail" or "inJail," this becomes voluntary or involuntary! We surely don't want such a dependence on the specific predicates chosen (at least not until we have a better idea of the exact dependence between the vocabulary of an agent and the unsound inference process).

The fundamental notion seems to be related to whether an agent performs an action because of events whose occurrence is taken for granted. In a sense, almost all of our actions are in some way affected by certain things not under our control, and we almost always have to take precautions, "close loops," etc.; because of this, some aspect of everything we do is in a sense "not under our control." Yet the concept of involuntary actions involves drawing a thin line somewhere.

Let us now return to the question of what it means for an event to have occurred. There are two possible approaches:

- One thing we can do is to make events "structurally strong," like physical objects; that is, they retain their identity even when a considerable number of their attributes change.

Now this is what happens in Cyc: actually physical objects too are very delicate — that is, when some attribute changes, we need to create new subAbstractions. However, the notion of *identity* is obtained by placing these subabstractions in a special relation (with an entity, etc.). It might be possible to invent some equivalent of entityhood for other kinds of events (such as sleeping, playing, etc.). One candidate for this seems to be the notion of *problem-solving context*. So from some problem-solving perspective, we could make a number of changes to some event and retain its identity, whereas from another perspective the event would have changed its identity.

We might need to bother about the notion of an event's "occurring" or not occurring. The main issue that brought this up was the notion of causes. Because we want to say that an event might cause a proposition to be true, we need a notion of an event's occurring or not occurring.

- Another thing we can do is to redefine the notion of cause and make its domain and range be propositions. So we can say cause(P1 P2); that is, P1 causes P2 to be true. This is just a subset of the standard notion of implication (possibly an important subset). We might extend this a bit and make the domain be sets of propositions. So we can have

cause({Pa Pb Pc . . . }, P2).

If we are prepared to look at the structure of these causing P's, if a number of them have the same temporal locations, we can give a name for that set of P's, thereby resulting in an event.

So in practice we replace occurs(event) in our axioms with some proposition so that rather than saying that the event occurred we say that the proposition is false. E.g., instead Of occurs (JoeGoingToMovie) we say allinstanceof(JoeGoingToMovie, GoingToMovie) performedBy (JoeGoingToMovie Joe).

6.4.6. Institutions (and Further Thoughts on Scripts, Goals, Etc.).   The specification of an institution includes the items discussed in the following sections.

6.4.6.1. THE SET OF AGENTS WHO FORM THE INSTITUTION

One element of an *institution* is the set of agents forming the institution. An interesting issue arises about those participating in institutions: Is their participation voluntary or involuntary? There seem to be a few institutions of which we are a part involuntarily. These include society, family, prison, etc. Most of these seem to be institutions we are a part of because of our birth.

For now we won't make any real distinction between these two classes. Instead we can have a predicate such as #%PartOfInstDueTo. That is, we have
#%PartOfInstDueTo (<agent> <inst> <action-type>).

So, for institutions such as family, society, etc., we have as a default the action-type being #%BeingBorn.

Another interesting issue is why these agents take part in these institutions. As a first try, we could state this easily using sentences of the form Purpose (<agent> <act of participating in inst> P), where P is a proposition that the agent wishes to see become true because of his participation in the event. However, we note two things: First, we don't want all these assertions corresponding to the actors participating in the event. Second, in general, agents are part of institutions for a number of reasons. We would like a more compact representation than having to list out all the propositions one by one. So we have the *ternary* predicate PurposeOfParticipation(<agent> <inst> <goal-set>), as follows:

PurposeOfParticipation (agent-1, inst-1, goal-set-1) $\wedge$
defines-goal(goal-set-1, P)
$\rightarrow$ *(ThereExists x*
instanceOf(x ParticipationInInstitution) $\wedge$
performer(x agent-1) $\wedge$
institutionInvolved(x inst-1) $\wedge$
purpose(agent-1, x, P))

We might want to put part of the ThereExists on the LHS (left-hand side) so that PurposeOfParticipation would not immediately imply that the agent was participating in the institution. In that case, it would imply that if it were known that he *was* participating, P would be his purpose. But this formulation seems more correct.

After dealing with the other basic notions related to institutions, we shall take a look at some of the important categorizations of institutions based on the purpose of the agents that participate in it.

6.4.6.2.
AGREEMENTS
RELATED TO
INSTITUTIONS

An agent usually takes part in a number of agreements. Two important classes of agreements include:

- The agreements between the agents that participate in the institution. These fall into two basic categories:

  - Formal agreements (these are the ones that the agents sign, etc.)

  - Informal agreements

- The agreements between the agent and other agents (usually also institutional). Important categories of this include:

  - The agreement the institution has with some governing entity, such as the government of a country. The presence of such an agreement is the criterial condition for the institution being recognized as a legal entity. An agent being a legal entity seems to indicate that it takes part in the agreement that defines the law. Also, the law might act as an enforcer for the other agreements the agent makes.

  - The agreement that the institution has with the amorphous institution called society. These are agreements that usually don't have any enforcers and that are also pretty fuzzily defined, in the sense that it is highly likely that many of the default rules that apply to agreements will fail for these sorts of agreements.

Another form of agreement associated with every institution is a "defining agreement," which defines the purpose of the existence of the institution. This agreement usually does the following:

- Defines the activities of the institution

- Defines its goals (and possibly its beliefs)

- Assigns responsibilities to various participating agents

- Handles some details specific to the type of institution

We can create spec-slots of the slot "states" — as in, states(agreement-1 P) — for each of these types of P. These may map to sets of propositions rather than just to single propositions.

We want to say that if an agent is a part of an institution, he subscribes to the defining agreement of the institution. We can state this as

```
agent-of-agreement(inst-1 agreement-1)∧
participates(agent-1 inst-1)
→ agrees(agent-1 agreement-1)
```

6.4.6.3.

TRANSACTIONS AND ACTIVITIES RELATED TO THE INSTITUTION

We need to split up the different agents who constitute the institution into a bunch of classes. There may or may not be collections dealing with these classes. The agents in each of these classes perform a similar kind of activity in relation to this institution. We can map these different classes into slots. So an initial way of saying this is:

```
role-played(inst role-slot activity-type)
```

If an agent A takes part in an institution inst in the role role-1, we could say role-1(inst A). Alternately, we can have the roles be non-slots and say this as

```
plays-role(inst A role-type) and
role-played(inst role-type activity-type)
```

There are a couple of small complications with this:

1. The actual role the agent plays in this activity-type might be ambiguous. For example, we could have an activity such as trading (that has actors buyer and seller) and a trading institution T1 with two types of actors, role-1 and role-2. Now it isn't clear whether the

agents filling role-1 play the role of buyer or seller. There are two ways out of this:

a. Make the activities specialized enough so that each of them has an unambiguous "performer." Then the implicit role attached to a class of agents and the activity is the actor slot *performer.* So rather than having just an activity called Trading, we have Buying and Selling. Although this might be all right for this example, in other cases it might lead to pathological activities.

b. Add another argument to the predicate role-played that specifies the actor slot that the agent occupies. So we have

```
role-played (inst, role-type,
                 activity-type, actor-type).
```

This, too, seems kind of messy, but there doesn't seem to be any way out of it. Possibly we could create a unit for this (and replace the inst with inst-type). In practice, we might want to use all three options. The advantage of creating an additional unit would be that we might have a whole bunch of additional things to say (for example, that this agent-type performs this kind of task only occasionally, and so on). So for now, this is the scheme in the system.

2. Suppose role-played(inst role-type activity-type actor-type). What does this really mean? A simplistic interpretation would be that given an agent A belonging to role-type who participates in inst, there exists an event of type activity-type in which the agent plays the role actor-type.

This is obviously just too simplistic, and we can say something much stronger. The answer to this problem (that is, what does it mean to say something like "A does job J at institution I"?) is closely related to the problem of defining what it means for something to be some kind of institution (say, a university). The question is not one of deciding whether something is a university but of deciding what we can conclude about it by virtue of its being that type of institution. This is closely related to an item above: the activities the institution as a whole engages in. This is dealt with now.

6.4.6.4. THE RESOURCES THE INSTITUTION HANDLES

Two main issues are involved in considering the resources the institution handles: the resources generated and the resources that are traded.

6.4.6.4.1. DYNAMIC VERSUS STATIC ASPECTS OF A SYSTEM.   In describing the structure and activities of a system, we could consider the existence of that system as a script, its parts as the actors, and the activities as subevents. There is really no distinction between this unit "the thing existing" and the unit "this thing," because the latter is just the former. The only difference might be one of calling the parts different things. These two positions correspond to a basic dualism, namely the option of viewing things as being essentially static or essentially dynamic.

For a number of things, X, when these things are in certain states, they must perform certain activities in order for them to remain in their current state. So for example, for a person to remain a person, he must perform certain physiological activities: Breathing, HeartBeating, etc. For a university to be a functioning university, it has to do certain things: run classes, etc. For a refrigerator to be working, it has to be doing something, too.

So for X to remain in some state (which could be the state of existing), it has to perform certain actions. This is a rather Aristotelian point of view — namely, that for things to maintain their status quo, they have to be doing something — but it might still be useful for some areas.

Given that X has to be performing some action E to remain "an X in state S," it seems tempting to merge the units corresponding to X and E.

This would be bad, however, because what is really happening is that the thing has some static aspects and some dynamic aspects, and these two things together define that object. This gets back to the fundamental notion of X being nothing more than some named space-time chunk.

We find some aspects of this thing X interesting, and we give it an identity. Nothing says that these things have to be purely static or purely dynamic.

It would be nice to make a clear distinction between these dynamic and static aspects. We have to be careful, because this distinction between static and dynamic aspects is something introduced by the representation. For example, let us considering a ball rolling at some velocity v. We could consider its position as a dynamically varying quantity and consider this its dynamic aspect. On the other hand, we could also use the notion of velocity (which remains constant) and consider that its static aspect. So if the dynamic aspects of the thing are fairly continuous over the time period we are considering, the question of whether it is a dynamic or a static thing is merely an artifact of the representation.

In general, it seems that purely for efficiency reasons (both computational and storage) it is nicer to store the static aspects of things, especially if these hold good for some extended period of time. (This does not solve all problems, because we might still have to generate values for the other kind of properties, such as position — but let us come to those later.)

There exists a class of things such that their identity is defined to some large extent by their dynamic aspect (it might be appropriate to use indexicals to refer to the dynamic part!).

Even for these things it might be useful to center the representation around a static model. The representation of the dynamic aspects then is a set of temporally quantified (that is, over the subabstractions of the object itself or of its parts) statements about the thing. To make the representation easier, we need to have some "templates" for writing these sentences (that is, so that writing them becomes easier). Also, so that temporal quantification really makes sense, we need to have some clear idea of what it means to be quantified over the period of existence of something — that is, we need some notion of the flow of time. (The simplest kind of template is one that says that the property is temporally intrinsic. Something can be temporallyIntrinsic and also be associated with other templates.)

We saw how the identity of an object (i.e. what it is) depends on the dynamic aspects of the thing. We can extend this notion to say that the state an object is in depends on the dynamic aspects of the thing. In addition to these dynamic aspects, there are certain static aspects that go to define the object. After all, if everything about an object is constantly changing, it is hard to think of it as an object. However, this division between what is a static aspect and what is a dynamic aspect is not a clear one. Often it is possible to represent what seems to be a dynamic aspect of an object as a fact about the static aspect of the object. This is similar to the issue of rich vs. poor objects dealt with in section 3.2.3, in discussing predicate of arity greater than two.

In principle, we could create a unit for the composite event, but reasoning with it could be tough. Also, saying that all people eat at least once a day could get expensive if we are going to need a unit saying that for each person.

The solution is to have something similar to change and structure units that individuals may share, units that state this kind of information. We think this is really different from the standard notion of a structure, because this information is strictly temporally quantified.

If there isn't much to be said about the events, we could use the set of slots (such as performsDaily, etc.) mentioned below. This is required only if we want to say that Jim had lunch with Bob every day.

**6.4.6.4.2.
APPLYING THAT TO
INSTITUTIONS**

So in the context of institutions we come up with the following:

1. There are some agents associated with the institution. These agents get classified into some number of classes such that we can say the following about each of them:

a. Why they are participating in the institution (use *goal-sets*).
b. The activities they perform — One of the messy issues is that of the time spent on each of these activities, that is, the frequency. This can be handled by having a bunch of slots like performsDaily, performsHourly, etc., and having a ternary version of this to take care of odd frequencies. It is important to note that these slots (such as #%performsDaily) sit on the individual agents. Of course, we could also have collection-level versions of these.
c. Other sundry stuff. Corresponding to each of these classes we could have slots (partSlots or actorSlots). Each of these properties could then be directly inherited, or we could create a unit corresponding to each inst-type.worker-type (these might possibly be shared across inst-types) and inherit instancehood into these collections. (They'd *better* be transferable, or people could never go from one kind of industry to another.) These are a little more complicated than simple activities; they are really exchanges. However, the unit of things exchanged may not really correspond to the unit of the activity. For now, we get away with just two slots that talk about the money exchanged (one for each direction). These two slots correspond to the salary/tuition, in the case of a university.

2. The agent itself has certain activities that define its status — These are described in exactly the same way as the activities of its constituent agents. Again, these may be simple activities or transactions or agents.

3. The agreement that binds the participant agents together — The issue is basically how do we describe agreements. At the simplest level, all we have to do is to make a list of the propositions in which all of the agents believe. However, we might need to quantify these propositions over the agents, etc. The subtle point is that we have to be careful when we assert a quantified proposition as the thing agreed in the agreement, because we could mean that the instantiations of this proposition are what the agents believe in, or we could mean that the agents agree on the quantified formula. This distinction can be made easily by having another slot that holds pairs of symbols and the domain of quantification; we then can use these variables in the proposition if we don't mean that the set of agents believes in the quantified formula. *Usually, the agreement is on the quantified formula.*

So we have a unit for the agreement and a slot that holds these propositions. The next question is that of deciding what standard agreements and standard propositions constitute agreements. The propositions that are involved in most agreements related to institutions seem to fall into the following classes:

a. What the agents are responsible for (that is, the things they have to ensure get done)

b. What actions they are responsible for performing. Items (a) and (b) are very different. In general, (b) is quite simple — it is usually those actions defined by number 1 above. Item (a), however, usually pertains to the goals of the institution as a whole. This can get hairy, but for now, we can further divide (a) into two items and handle each naively: (a1) responsibility for some of the top-level goals of the institution, and (a2) responsibility for some of the purposes of some of the activities of the institution.

4. The goals of the institution — now we come to the description of *goal-sets*. This is one of those (few) cases in which a large fraction of the problem might be solved by recognizing a few important categories and dealing with each separately. Some of the important types of goals are

a. Persistence goals, including some self goals (things like desiring to keep existing), which can be written as (ForAll x (u allLaterSubabstractions) (P x)); and goals pertaining to other things. The basic idea is that the state of the world is defined independent of previous states. (It's interesting that goals are often *not* defined in terms of future states.)

b. Change goals, including self goals (like wishing to become richer) and goals pertaining to other things. The basic idea here is that these goals are defined with regard to previous states of the agent. Such goals have the form

```
(ForAll x (u allLaterSubabstractions)

    (ForAll y (x FormerSubabs) (Q (P x) (P y)))
```

To be more specific, we could write (Q (P x) (P y)) as

```
    (Greater (value u (P x)) (value u (P y)).
```

Agents rarely seem to account for possible changes in their values in their goals.

A similar treatment can be given to change goals about other things.

We can have a slightly specialized syntax for persistence- and change-goals. The basic idea is that we need to state only P or (Q (P x) (P y)).

To reiterate: The ideas mentioned in sections 6.4.5 and 6.4.6 are extremely preliminary and are here merely to indicate some of the things we are working on currently.

6.5. Coping with Uncertainty

6.5.1. Contradictions. One of the questions often raised in the area of common-sense reasoning is: "How can machines cope and reason with contradictory information?" Clearly this is something humans seem to do all the time. Which piece of information should one use when there's a conflict? If one's inference scheme is *complete*, how does one survive?

This section will discuss how we got Cyc to represent and reason with (what at least seems to be) contradictory information. To begin with, we took a closer look at what it means for information to be contradictory. What we found were several rather distinct phenomena that get clumped together under the English word *contradictory*. By teasing apart these phenomena, we were able to "divide and conquer" them, to come up with a way of handling each one. The phenomena are:

1. Agents (possibly non-intersecting subAbstractions of the same agent) hold truly contradictory beliefs about some particular thing. For example, Fred believes that his birthday is June 18, but his mother believes it's June 17. Or: suppose that in 1980 Fred learned the truth; so FredBefore1980 believes his birthday is June 18, but FredSince1980 believes it to be June 17. This is dealt with under the section on Beliefs, below.

2. The same subAbstraction of some entity (for example, Dr. Jones at 4 p.m. today) believes and uses two pieces of information that contradict each other. For example, consider a high school student's belief about objects moving. He knows his physical laws and believes that an object in motion will keep on moving. However, when he pushes a coin across a drugstore counter, he does so believing that it will stop soon. These two beliefs are (apparently) contradictory. The question is, when does he use which piece of information? The first will get him an "A" on his physics test, the second will get him by in the rest of his life. In real life, not so long ago, physicists could propose and do productive experiments if they assumed *either* a wave *or* a particle model of light, even though they knew full well that the two were (apparently) contradictory. There are two solutions to representing and coping with this kind of contradictory information:

a. Resolve the contradiction by fitting both pieces of information into a more general model or theory of what is happening. For example, the high school student might learn about friction next semester; the physicists learned about quantum mechanics. Then, once they understand the general case, they may still keep their particular superficially contradictory simplifications around and use them as efficient heuristics in cases where they're likely to work out well. Professional physicists still view time as infinitely divisible in daily life; they still view solid objects as having a definite position when they reach for a glass; they know that they're just a seething mass of elementary particles, but they do not think about that while driving (we hope); etc. So the two problems with this solution are that it may be difficult to get that general model, and, even if you have it, it may be computationally inefficient to use it to reason from first principles all the time.

b. Believe that 2.a. could in principle be done, but it's too expensive or difficult to do right now, so just don't worry about it. Instead, just try to delineate more clearly the situations in which X leads to good outcomes, and situations in which $\neg$X leads to good outcomes. For instance, sometimes we forget something and our spouses get annoyed; other times, they don't. Contradiction? Perhaps, superficially, but it's not one that incapacitates us; we just go on building up and refining rules of thumb for predicting which sorts of things will and won't annoy them. Or consider: we see a stage magician do some terrific tricks and can't figure out how they're done. We may *never* know how they're done — we may even realize that we're never going to find out — but so what? It doesn't crumble our world model; we still believe that we could in principle find out how they were accomplished, and that, if we did, we'd find that no physical laws were violated.

Human beings have plenty of practice at doing 2.b. You might say that people just naturally assume that what we represent (and know ourselves) is almost never the real world itself but some very incomplete, imperfect model of it. We implicitly understand that we can have multiple models that are all useful, all internally consistent, and yet those models be pairwise mutually inconsistent. Only if we find a contradiction "within one single model" do we begin to worry about it, or if we accidentally chose the "wrong model" to tackle the problem with.

A quick example of different models. Imagine going to a circus and seeing Fred shot out of a cannon. One model treats Fred as a point mass; this model is useful for deciding, for example, what his trajectory will be and where to place the net to catch him. Another model treats Fred as an intelligent creature undergoing a severe mental trauma; this model is useful for impressing the audience. Ditto a model for his body suffering from a powerful explosion. Finally, there is the "insiders'" model of what's going on, which is that a firecracker is exploded just as a catapult, cleverly disguised to resemble a cannon, smoothly accelerates Fred on his way.

Perhaps all this verbage just shifts the question from "when does one use which piece of information" to "when does one use which model?" Fortunately, the latter question at least seems to be more tractable. Basically, we have to decide how we are going to characterize a *model.*

A model should contain information that defines the contexts in which that model may reliably be used, and the contexts in which it may heuristically be used. This information includes things like:

- A statement of the approximations used

- The goal of the task for which this model is being used, records of past successes and failures for this model, etc.

These become the various slots that each Model in Cyc can have.

The current state of Cyc has all this in an embryonic form. We have defined many of those ModelSlots, but there are many yet to define; we have created units for many models, but there are hundreds of common models we use in everyday life for which we haven't yet created and fleshed out units in Cyc. Gradually, as they are created, we can sweep through the inference-drawing pieces of knowledge in the KB (the rules' premises, the default inheritances, etc.), explicitly marking the models on which they rely. That way, many of, for example, the rules' premises, would be replaced by simple pointers to models, which in turn would point to situations in which they would be appropriate.

6.5.2. Multiple Models. In this section, we treat several representational issues associated with the problem of Cyc having *multiple abstractions* of the same object.

First, a quick review of terminology used in this section:

- *Object*: any space-time-intelligence region; includes all systems

- *System*: any individual, static or dynamic, that has interrelated parts (for example, Fred, or a particular FallingOffACliff event)

Each system is composed of *parts* and a set of *relations* that hold between its parts. If we change some of those relations, we are in effect defining a new and different system. This is quite obvious in practice, while running Cyc, because the relations are stated explicitly as constraints of different sorts.

As we saw above, in the case of shooting Fred out of a cannon, often we want to have different "aspects" of a single object (for example, FredAsProjectile, FredAsSentientAnimal, FredAsEntertainer, FredAsMostlyWaterFilledBag). These are what we call multiple *models* of Fred.

These models are *different from temporal subabstractions* of Fred. For instance, all of them might be models of Fred during the very same two-minute period of time. In fact, they might all be models of Fred001, which is a two-minute-long temporal subabstraction of Fred, so we could better name them Fred001AsProjectile, Fred001AsSentientAnimal, Fred001AsEntertainer, Fred001AsMostlyWaterFilledBag.

These models are also *different from the parts* of Fred. The parts of Fred, or of Fred001, include his hands and bones and mind, and each of them is a different object than Fred (or Fred001). But the various models really aren't different objects; they're all still a view of Fred (or Fred001).

By the way, the same points apply to multiple models of a dynamic object — an event such as Bobby riding his bike and delivering newspapers yesterday afternoon (let's call that Event305). There, the *different temporal subabstractions* would be time-slices of that bike-riding event; the *different parts* would be the subprocesses, such as getting on the bike, steering, folding papers, hurling them, braking, getting off the bike, honking the horn, etc.; and the *different models* would be Event305AsBusinessEvent, Event305AsAPhysicalExerciseEvent, Event305AsTravelEvent, and so on.

6.5.2.1. WHEN TO EMPLOY MULTIPLE MODELS

So: When should we do this — when should we go to the trouble to use several different units to represent the multiple models of (various "aspects" of) an object? Here is a non-exhaustive list of cases in which it's cost-effective to do so:

Case 1: It is cost-effective to use different units to represent different aspects of an object when those different aspects really form different "parts" of the object, such as a person's body and mind, and when there are some slots that apply to several parts (and maybe to the composite object), for example, interestingness, rateOfDevelopment, overallQuality. If *no* slots were legal for both FredsBody and FredsMind, we could argue in favor of merging both of those aspects of Fred together, subtly altering the semantics of "age of Fred" to mean "age of the physical extent of Fred," and altering "iq of Fred" to mean "iq of the mental extent of Fred." By the way, because both FredsBody and FredsMind are events, they can have any of the temporal attributes, such as startingTime, endingTime, etc. So we can talk about people's brains dying even though their bodies lived on for days; or we can imagine someone's mind continuing on beyond physical death (for example, a ghost). In such cases, there is a need to *be able to* have different units representing these aspects.

This also suggests a situation in which *not* to split off a new model. Consider the following bad "split-off": MyTapeRecorderAsAPhysObj and MyTapeRecorderAsAnElectronicDevice. More or less any (non-bookkeeping) slot that is present on both of these units *will have the same value on both of them*. For example, cost, location, temperature, heatGenerated, and so on, all will be the same. In such a situation, the ontological engineer should refrain from having both of those units in the system.

One of the *fallacious* arguments in favor of separating the two MyTapeRecorderAs . . .   units is that, in the context of any reasoning being done with this object, we will refer to only one of these "aspects" of the object. However, ignoring the extra information (about the other aspect) is a job for the metalevel; it is strictly an inference issue and not a representational one. This means that the relations pertaining to each aspect refer only to the appropriate attributes of the objects, and we are not interested in the attributes not mentioned by the relations we are trying to use.

One *valid* argument in favor of separating the two MyTapeRecorderAs . . .   units would be if we were to come up with particular slots that wanted to have different values on each unit. For example, interestingness; if the tape recorder were made out of a mixture of rocks and plants and seawater, it might be an ordinary sort of physical object, but it would be an unusual electronic device. (We have a battery that is interesting in this manner, as it's made out of oranges.) Notice that this is a pragmatic argument, though, one that is handled on a case-by-case basis, rather than by some sweeping dictum.

It is important to exercise care in deciding whether a slot that justifies the separation really exists. Consider the slot *controls*. In English, we can say things like "Fred's mind is controlled by Jane but his body is still controlled by Fred." So it's tempting to use this as an argument for splitting FredsMind and FredsBody as separate models of Fred. However, it is preferable to have two (actually a whole array of) slots that are more precise, because what is meant by "control" in the two cases is quite different — English just happens to use the same vague word for these two different (though metaphorically related) concepts.

Case 2: Another situation in which it is cost-effective to use different units to represent different aspects of an object is when vastly different views are held about the same object by (large populations of) different agents.

For instance, botanists view flowers as the reproducing organs of a plant, consisting of parts, such as an androceium. This is quite different from the consensus reality view, which treats a flower as a nicely scented, visually pleasing circular arrangement of petals at the top of a green stem, and little more.

Now it is quite possible (as it is in this case) that these two views are not mutually consistent. This makes it important to use the right model of a flower in the context of solving some particular problem (for example, trying to guess why Fred gave flowers to Jane on her birthday).

The example we've given here is actually pretty generic: there is often a consensus view and a radically different expert view, and often the transition from one to another is not monotonic. This also seems to indicate that multiple models of objects needed for this reason are required mostly in domains where the objects are involved in social actions of different sorts. This ability to maintain the consensus view and the expert view of an object could prove crucial in being able to integrate different expert systems into Cyc.

Case 2 is actually related to Beliefs (see the next subsection), but what's at issue here is not a clean "minor difference of opinion" but a whole radical shift. That is, it's not just two people disagreeing about a precise entry or two in some slots s_1, s_2, . . . of some unit u. The disagreement here is much deeper; it's a disagreement over *which slots* s_i are the right "questions to ask" about u, or even which units u ought to exist! The following differences stand out when multiple beliefs are compared with multiple models:

- It is possible for an agent to hold and use more than one of these multiple *models*. For example, if our botanist were to present a flower to her boyfriend, it is likely that she would still use the consensus model of the flower in deciding which flower to buy him. It is rarer and less "rational" for an agent to hold and use contradictory *beliefs*.

- The model to be used is almost always dictated completely by the context/problem we are attempting to solve rather than by the beliefs held by the actors. Again, the botanist, even though she knows a much more accurate view of the flower, still uses the consensus view because of the *context* in which she is using this information.

Case 3: Another case in which multiple models of objects/systems are needed is when there are different theories of the same system. This is especially important if those theories are mutually incompatible, but each is good for predicting the value of some attribute of the system.

These theories/models of the system could be capable of yielding different results for the same problem, and the issue may be further complicated by the agent's not being able to verify which result is actually correct.

Such alternate conflicting models of systems (including people) exist often in fields such as politics, sociology, and economics. A typical example is the difference between Lenin's view of an ideal economic system (the state knows what is best for each individual) and the capitalistic model (the individual knows what is best for him). The conclusions reached by the two doctrines are quite different, time after time, case after case. Each is sometimes wrong.

It is important for Cyc to be able to represent both of these as alternate views of an economic system, for two reasons:

• Even if Cyc "believes" in one of these views, there are many people whose actions can't be fathomed unless Cyc understands that they believe the other view.

• As shown by the state of the real world, there is no single accurate simple economic model that can be relied upon in all contexts. Usually, by using the context (that is, the script involved) and the value of the specific slot value we are trying to find, we should be able to find the right model to use. The specific way in which Cyc records this information is presented toward the end of this chapter.

Another interesting class of objects in which multiple views are required seems to be in scientific fields. Consider physics at the turn of this century, while the controversy raged over the particle nature versus the wave nature of light. The difference is that in this case, rather than these beliefs being held by different people, the controversy raged within the heads of individuals as well. Such contradictory theories also exist in some other technical areas, today — for example, in the fatigue design of mechanical elements.

Case 4: Multiple models of objects/systems may also be required when the system involved is very complex, but by making the right assumptions it is possible to solve specific problems pertaining to the system without expending too many resources. (Note: Although it is possible to make true statements about a complex system, in general it is almost impossible to give a complete description of it.)

This case is perhaps "the standard case," in which we choose a representation appropriate to the problem and thereby simplify the problem. Expert systems owe a lot of their success to this principle. They constrain their focus of attention and develop a customized representation.

6.5.2.2. MAKING THE RIGHT ASSUMPTIONS ABOUT MULTIPLE MODELS

Successfully juggling multiple models of a system hinges on "making the right assumptions," as we mentioned earlier. These assumptions fall into three broad categories:

Assumption Category 1: Assume a particular fixed level of granularity, or at least a graduated sequence of ever-more-precise slots (with the same values being placed in those more-specific slots as used to exist in the vague slots).

For example, we might say that the hand is related to the torso through the slot connectedTo. This may be sufficient if all we wanted to find out was if Fred's hand would move when we moved his torso. At another level of granularity, we could relate the hand and the torso using the relation connectedThroughBall&SocketJoint. This finer granularity could be required to figure out whether or not Fred could scratch some region of his back.

These are not incompatible representations of the same relation. We don't think there are many cases of nonmonotonicity in the change in the granularity of the representation. Hence, we expect that in general one may use the same unit for representations of varying granularity.

Assumption Category 2: Assume a graduated sequence of units having the same slots but with ever-more-precise values in those slots.

There is often a nesting of approximate representations, each of them a slight elaboration on the previous one. For example, your usual model of a car might not contain the small bulb that lights up when you open the glove compartment. But now that I've reminded you of it, you can smoothly (monotonically) move to a slightly elaborated car model in which the bulb is there.

The first kind of approximation was in the choice of slots (connectedTo → connectedThroughBall&SocketJoint), and the second kind is in the choice of which entries from a single slot's value can be safely omitted and ignored.

Assumption Category 3: Certain idealizations can be made.

In our day-to-day life, we usually treat walls as totally rigid and more or less soundproof. When we walk into a new room, we might well lean against the wall without worrying about whether it will collapse. However, there are cases, such as when we want to tear the walls down, when such an approximation is not made. In that case, some particular finite value is chosen and used for a wall's rigidity.

There is a potential argument that we need not make an assumption that the wall was absolutely rigid (in daily life) but instead could always use the actual value for the wall's rigidity, and use the usual mechanics equations to come up with almost the same answer. However, there are two basic problems with this approach. The first problem is that the computation involved in this more detailed inference is likely to be too expensive, and the second problem is that we don't know that rigidity number. We lean against our office walls safely every day without ever knowing the numeric figure for their rigidity, or even the formulae involved in calculating their behavior when leaned against. Even inheritance won't help here, because we don't even know the typical rigidity of late-twentieth-century American walls, or of any walls for that matter. But we continue to lean against them.

So we have two representations, one in which something is applying a force on an absolutely rigid barrier, and one in which something is applying a force on a finitely rigid barrier. They are instances of two different kinds of scripts, even though both of them are representations of similar events, and even though the expected outcomes of both events are determined by the same set of rules of Newtonian physics.

There is a distinct difference between (a) ignoring the finite rigidity of the wall all along, and (b) taking into account the rigidity of the wall and coming up with an answer that says it's so rigid we can ignore the effects of its movement. The two representations of the class of events corresponding to objects exerting a force on a barrier — one that approximates the barrier to be an infinitely rigid one and one that does not make this assumption — are mutually irreconcilable. Hence, we need to distinguish between the two. We could argue that we do not need a separate unit for Wall001 as a 100-percent rigid object but instead can just use a set of rules to predict the outcome that would ignore the rigidity (or rather would assume that the rigidity was ∞).

What does this mean in the context of Cyc? All this means is that we do have two different scripts, one in which some object is leaning on some barrier with a finite rigidity and another in which the barrier is perfectly rigid. Of course the latter could be a specScript of the former.

This kind of approximation is useful in reasoning about very complex systems where the complexity of the relations between the different attributes of the system poses two kinds of problems:

• The computation becomes very expensive

• There is a lack of information (even default values with any useful level of reliability are rare)

In such cases, for the sake of computational efficiency, simplified descriptions/theories of the system that ignore some of the interactions between the objects are useful. Often, they ignore some of the more minor objects completely. We think this happens often in everyday reasoning. (Note again that we are not talking about inheritance here; that mechanism is an *alternative* way of coping with these same sorts of complex situations.)

Let's take another example. Consider a doctor asking a patient some questions. Now, by the very fact that the doctor asks these questions, he could be forcing the patient to think about the answers, and that might cause the patient to change the answers, and so on. In addition, factors such as the tone of the doctor, or whether he worded the question positively or negatively, could also affect the answers. Often, these are ignored by the doctor without too much harm. However, many standard hospital intake forms contain redundant questions worded so as to detect "overly agreeable" patients.

6.5.2.3. REPRESENTING DIFFERENT ABSTRACTIONS

Let us take a look at some of the issues involved in *representing* different abstractions that make different approximations, and some of the issues involved in *reasoning* with those different abstractions. Two of the issues we have to resolve are: how the different models are inter-related, and how we select the right one in any given situation.

First, let's consider how different models are related.

The relation between the different representations of these objects is through the slot moreDetailedModel and its inverse, lessDetailedModel. Because models can be made more/less detailed along any of several different dimensions, there is a partial ordering among the different approximations. Each model contains a list of the slots regarding which approximations have been made. The most detailed model has no special significance other than that it represents the most precise knowledge about that system.

Does that mean that the most detailed model is "the real object"? No, the real object is in the world and not in the machine. Well, what we really meant to ask was "Is the unit representing X the same as the unit representing the most detailed model of X?" The answer to this question is: No, *all* the units for the multiple models of X represent the real object X. Which model you should use depends on your purpose.

Note that for certain purposes even the most detailed model the agent has may be insufficient for the task. A simple example is the task of trying to predict who is going to win the next presidential election in the U.S. or the last presidential election in Mexico.

In a way this might be going against the basic idea of intention-independent representation. However, if we are going to have a clustering of cliché models, each of which is useful for some class of tasks, the representation could still be considered to be relatively intention-independent.

Next, let's consider how we decide which model of a system to use for a given purpose. This is a big question. Its solution for the general case is quite intractable. So what we shall try to do here is suggest a couple of heuristics for the task and discuss how to represent more information regarding "which model to use when."

Before we can address this question, we need some idea of what a *purpose* is. A purpose is represented as a statement of a problem that Cyc needs (wants, intends, is trying) to solve. The primitives out of which a *problem statement* (a purpose) may be built include:

- Finding some field of some slot of some unit (A "field" includes: items believed to form the value; items believed not to be in the value; symbolic justification for those entries; things that depend on this value; and so on. See chapter 3, "The CycL Representation Language.")

- Resolving some constraint (combining it with other pieces of knowledge, especially other constraints)

- Computing the plausibility of some statement (setting up new units, each of which has "epistemologicalStatus: HypotheticalStatus", and each of which represents the statement; then testing constraints, looking for precedents in the KB, comparing each part of the statement against empirically gathered frequency data, making a *partially*-closed world assumption, and so on)

- And similar activities

Now let's return to our question, namely, how we decide which model of a system to use for a given purpose. For starters, let us take the simple case of finding the value of some slot of some object or system. (It is likely that this is the operation that will be done most frequently.)

Recall Event305, which was Bobby riding his bike and delivering newspapers one afternoon. Suppose we want to ask Cyc how successful that event was. How should that be stated to Cyc?

Obviously the problem description has to include a reference to the system under consideration, namely Event305; it must refer to the slot desired, namely degreeOfSuccess; and it must indicate that what's wanted is the value field of that slot.

If a human being wants this datum, he might view the Event305 unit, examine the display for its degreeOfSuccess slot, and click in a way that means "get me the value of this slot of this unit."

If a program wants this piece of information, it might generate a call on the appropriate CycL function:

(get4 #%Event305 #%degreeOfSuccess).

But is this the end of the story? No, it's just getting interesting.

Recall that the unit Event305 has several *different models*:

- Event305AsBusinessEvent

- Event305AsAPhysicalExerciseEvent

- Event305AsTravelEvent

- Event305AsANeighborhoodEvent

- And so on.

Which model should Cyc use? Some of these models would say the event was a success and some would say it was a failure. For example, maybe it does help Bobby stay physically fit, but it doesn't really earn him much money. So Event305AsAPhysicalExerciseEvent would have "degreeOfSuccess: High" and Event305AsBusinessEvent would have "degreeOfSuccess: Low". Even among those models that respond the same way, some of them might make — or spurn — assumptions that make the computation unnecessarily expensive. So the choice of models is important. *The model you choose determines what answer you get back, and how quickly you get it.*

The simplest answer is for users (be they humans or programs) to specify explicitly what model they're interested in at the time they pose the problem; for example, by referring to a particular Event305AsA . . . unit, rather than to Event305.

Much more useful and interesting would be for Cyc to actively participate and cooperate with the user when possible, helping to select the right model. This might include noticing when different models would give different answers, and which answers are more common or likely in this case. Cyc can currently do a rudimentary version of this.

A simple example: Cyc can safely eliminate from consideration any orthogonal models, those which do not refer to the degreeOfSuccess slot at all. For example, consider Event305AsANeighborhoodEvent; yes, it occurs in the neighborhood, but one can hardly talk about success or failure.

The choice of the right model consists of three steps:

1. Decide what the models of an object are.

2. Arrange them in some sort of order of preference.

3. Pick the most preferred one that is "legal" or "acceptable" in terms of the level of detail of the results it can give.

Naturally this script doesn't have to be followed precisely, step by step.

Let's look into each step in more detail.

Step 1: Deciding what the models of an object X are.

This is done by accessing the #%hasModelsThatAreInstancesOf slot of the EventTypes of which X is an instance. In the case of Event305, it's an instance of PaperboyDeliveringNewspapers. That unit, in turn, has the following entries on its hasModelsThatAreInstancesOf slot:

PaperboyDeliveringNewspapersAsBusinessEvent
PaperboyDeliveringNewspapersAsAPhysicalExerciseEvent
PaperboyDeliveringNewspapersAsTravelEvent
PaperboyDeliveringNewspapersAsANeighborhoodEvent

By instantiating them for Event305, the system can automatically produce the various models of Event305.

Step 2: Deciding which is the most preferred model.

How are we going to represent the preferability of the different models? This is determined largely by the slot whose value we are trying to find. Assuming we know this information for the current case, we could represent it as a list on the SeeUnit of the degreeOfSuccess slot of the unit Event305. Alternatively, on each model, we could have a slot that asks us to use that model for the purposes of computing the value of certain slots.

In the absence of this information, Cyc can use a set of heuristics for making a rough guess at it. For example: Cyc would prefer to use a model in which the slot we are trying to compute (degreeOfSuccess) is at least somewhat constrained; certainly this would make computing its value easier. Ideally, Cyc would choose a model in which degreeOfSuccess is constrained *enough* that Cyc can determine a value for it. Also, Cyc might need the values for certain other slots, and should therefore prefer a model in which the values of those slots are known.

Step 3. Verify the "legality" or the "acceptability" of the preferred model M in terms of the accuracy of the results.

While deciding whether M is okay to use, Cyc should *theoretically* use the most detailed model of the system available. It is also possible that we have default models to use for this purpose. If the approximations made by the hierarchy of models were monotonic, we could use any model that is more detailed than M for the purpose of estimating the acceptability of M. The more detailed a model we choose, the more accurate that estimate will be.

In general, M is reasonable if the answer that is going to be obtained using it is sufficiently close to that which would have been obtained using the most detailed model. However, this is obviously a computationally useless means of identifying the right model to use. So let's cut the theoretical discussion and get down to specifics. How does Cyc really determine whether M is a justifiable approximation of the object for the given purpose?

In practice, in addition to a pointer to the model under consideration from the more detailed model, we also have a predicate for determining the acceptability of the model. The question is, to which model of the object or system do we apply this predicate? (Exercise for the reader: Find a good answer to this question and let us know. In the absence of a good general answer at this time, we move on to the following.)

In the absence of such a predicate, Cyc tries to use heuristics for identifying the right model. An example of such a heuristic is: "When trying to determine the value of u.s, we are not interested in models whose primary approximations deal with s." Other information we could use for this purpose could be in the form of partial determination factors [Russell, 1988] between the slot we are trying to determine and the primary approximations of the model.

A related issue is the distinction between approximate models of systems that are instances of classes that are pure idealizations (such as point mass models of tangible objects) and those that are instances of classes that are not idealizations (such as approximating a human as a finite state machine). We are not yet sure what the implications of this distinction are, except that in the latter case it does not make sense to place the slot that lists the approximations involved in that model. However, this is handled easily using SeeUnits on individual entries (that is, what we now call SlotEntryDetails) in CycL.

The way a problem is stated can influence the choice of the model used to solve the problem. Is there any specific model that is always used to refer to objects? The model used is based largely on the type of object. Let's examine a couple of examples of this.

If a human user wanted to get the value of some attribute of FredsBody, they might "sloppily" call (Get4 Fred height). That is, they would be referring to the composite Fred rather than to its physicalExtent, FredsBody. People do that all the time, because other people are able to "decode" the lexical sloppiness.

However, if we were watching a baseball game, and we wanted to refer to some part of the field, we might be better off using a visual model and pointing to the appropriate part of the field. Even in a national pastime sport, there just aren't lexical names for all the parts of the baseball field, let alone all the paths that the ball might take. Sure, we can listen to a ball game on radio, but it's not the same as seeing it.

6.5.2.4. TYPES OF MULTIPLE REPRESENTATIONS

Let us give examples of some of these types of multiple representations and take a closer look at the details.

6.5.2.4.1. CONSENSUS VIEW VERSUS EXPERT VIEW.   Recall the example of the consensus view of a flower versus a botanist's view — an example we introduced earlier.

We have a unit for each of these two points of view, FlowerAsBotanicalObject (which would have "epistemologicalStatus: ExpertView") and FlowerAsAttractiveThing (which would have "epistemologicalStatus: ConsensusView").

Both FlowerAsBotanicalObject and FlowerAsAttractiveThing point to each other through the slot contradictoryModelTypes.

The following question arises: Is there some Flower unit that is independent of both of these units and that represents the "real" concept of the set of all flowers? The answer is no. They both are representations of the set of all flowers. It does not really make sense to talk about "the real Flower unit," even if there is a unit named #%Flower in the system, which is pointed to by both of their hasModelsThatAreInstancesOf slots. In that case, all three units are coextensional and represent the set of all flowers.

The consensus view of a flower could be a spec of something like #%BeautifulNaturalObject. The expert view is an instance of #%BotanicalOrgan. Even if we had the concept #%Flower, we could say little about that other than to just list the various views (models) of it!

Take the problem of deciding what flower to give someone. Let's consider how, in this situation, we decide which view to use. There are two ways in which this could be done. The script #%GivingAGift has the entry for its actor slot as a #%ConsensusViewOfAnObject. Suppose we create, for this particular situation, an instance of #%GivingAGift — say, we create the event #%GivingAGift001. That unit has the slot #%hasModelsThatAreInstancesOf with the entries (#%FlowerAsBotanicalObject #%#%FlowerAsAttractiveThing . . .). Because only FlowerAsAttractiveThing is a spec of #%ConsensusViewOfAnObject, we choose this model. (Alternatively, we could use a constraint unit on the #%gift slot, constraining that its #%preferredModel usually have "epistemologicalStatus: ConsensusView".)

6.5.2.4.2. ALTERNATE THEORIES.   When there are different theories for the same system, which model of the system we use depends on the problem we are trying to solve (and less on the context in which we are trying to solve it).

Let us assume we have three representations of an economic system

(EcoI, EcoII, and EcoIII). We are now given a particular economic system E, and asked to find the value of some particular slot, s1. Suppose s1 has a slot that says that the best model to use for computing it is EcoII. However, we still have to find out whether it makes sense to use this model. In order to fit our given system E to EcoII, we have to ensure that E satisfies the defining condition for EcoII — that is, it must satisfy the *defn* of EcoII.

Unfortunately, unlike the case of approximations, there is no perfect ordering of less- and more-accurate models. In fact, if we assumed EcoII was okay and applied its defn, we might find that EcoII is acceptable; however, if we had assumed EcoI and tried to apply the defn of EcoII, we might have failed. That is, often these theories (in addition to being conflicting) make assumptions that circularly make themselves legal. In order to test out whether EcoII is legal we have to assume that our object may indeed be an instance of EcoII and then check to see if the defn is satisfied.

A similar example of this sort of circularity occurs when someone is trying to figure out what a circuit does. He can get any of several answers, each of which is internally consistent, simply depending on where in the circuit he begins tracing.

Another similar example of this sort of circularity is in the verifying of what OR means in Lisp. Suppose this is the defn of OR:

```
(OR
   (evaluate the args left to right until one
      of them is true)
   (evaluate the args right to left until one
      of them is true))
```

If you already believe that OR's args get evaluated right to left, you read through this definition and nod your head; you do the same if you already believe that args get evaluated left to right.

6.5.2.4.3. APPROXIMATIONS. Consider the Diagnosing script. Let us take a closer look at the subevent called Interviewing, which represents the act of doing intake interviews with patients when they first come in for treatment.

The Interviewing script consists of a number of simple AskingAQuestion subevents. There are several models of this script. The most detailed model includes information about the effect it will have if we ask a patient this question (that is, how will it alter the answer he gives?). For instance, if the doctor asks "Are you going to make out your last will and testament soon?," the patient might decide at that moment, based on that question, that he'd better do it soon! At a more mundane level, if the doctor says "Has your neck been a little stiff lately?," the quasi-hypochondriac patient might at that moment convince himself that, yes, his neck has been a little stiff lately.

There are less detailed models of the script that totally ignore any impact that the questions might have on the answers that are given.

So on AskingAQuestion, the unit corresponding to the act of asking of a single question, we have a slot called answerGiven. There is a constraint (a SeeUnit — let's call it Z) on this slot of this unit. Z.preferredModels contains as *its* entry SimpleAskingAQuestion. Cyc goes to SimpleAskingAQuestion.intraActorConstraints, and finds various constraints that say:

- The interviewee (that's the inContextVersion of the object of the questioning process) should not be Paranoid (Hypochondriac is a particular brand of Paranoid, where the conspiring enemy is NatureQuaDiseaseQueen)

- The question should not be semantically linked to high-trauma dreads like death, paralysis, blindness, castration, being fired, going to Hell, etc. Actually, this list is not built in to the constraint; it accesses the *dreads* slot of the interviewee, and most of those dreads will inherit down to the interviewee from the particular phobias they hold from being a person, or even just from being an animal.

If all these constraints are met, then SimpleAskingAQuestion can (probably!) be done safely — that is, the asker can ignore the impact of the question on the listener and how that impact might affect the listener's answer.

If all these constraints are not met, the questioner will have to (a) knowingly live dangerously, (b) try to post-facto factor the impact out of the interviewee's response, or (c) run a more sophisticated AskingAQuestion script, one that would rephrase the question so as not to alarm the patient or ask several redundant forms of the question to increase the accuracy.

The slot preferredModels, which could be present on, e.g., AskingAQuestion, also gives Cyc some guidance by directing the search for a good model and, in some cases, limiting the set of models to consider. So if our patient passes this test, we use that preferred model and just ask him the question straight out.

6.5.3. Beliefs. Anything any agent "knows" can either be true or can be just "a belief" held by that agent. Of course this belief may be *supported* by some direct physical observations or by other agents holding similar beliefs.

Neither of these "supports" is bad, of course, but neither is foolproof: *Direct observations* make it hard to accept counterintuitive findings, such as the earth being round, or time and space being quantized. *Cobelieving communities* make it easy to propagate rumors, prejudice, and superstition.

If "we" believe something, it is part of Lenat, Guha, *et al.*'s consensus reality knowledge, and it gets put into Cyc with no separate "belief tag." Or, equivalently: Cyc believes it. The default "model" for entries with no belief tags is TheWorldAsCycBelievesItToBe, which really means TheWorldAsTheBuildersOfCycBelieveItToBe. Very little of what we're entering "untagged" is questionable; mostly it's facts like "people have two arms and two legs," or Americana like "you're not likely to get a speeding ticket in mid- or late-twentieth-century America if you're driving less than 5 m.p.h. over the speed limit."

Alas, not everyone agrees on everything. (Is Death preferable to Dishonor? Is Prolog preferable to Lisp? etc.) So we must represent minority opinions: Beliefs.

Also, various people find out things at different times. So even after some major event occurs (for example, John Kennedy's assassination), for a while some people are unaware of it while others are aware of it; hence, they believe different things. Because people learn lots of things (and forget things) all the time, their beliefs at one moment are likely to differ from their beliefs a minute earlier, a year earlier, etc.

Also, humans employ many different models while reasoning (see the previous section), and they rarely use the most general first-principle models that "really" describe reality. So we're often coming up with conclusions that are certainly wrong, at best approximately correct, and that even in that case may diverge somewhat from other agents' conclusions (because they have different models, different heuristics for selecting models, different special case memories to analogize to, etc.).

For all those reasons, Cyc needs to represent explicitly (and if possible cheaply) the situation in which different agents hold different beliefs, and it needs to be able to draw legitimate (plausible) inferences based on this information.

As with Temporal reasoning, we have found a simple and (we think) adequate way to do this. Here are some of the global constraints that help characterize the way that Cyc handles beliefs:

• Only instances of the collection Agent are allowed to hold beliefs.

- Beliefs may be held about any fact, be it a "ground level" one or a "belief" or a "rule." So Sam can hold beliefs about whether or not Fred is an American, and also about whether or not Americans typically (by default) own a car.

- If someone believes X, then he believes that he believes it, and he believes that he believes that he believes it, etc., *unless otherwise known.*

Let us take an example of a belief we would like to represent, "Fred believes that Jim is a good pianist." For interestingness, let us assume that Jim has never even seen a piano. In order to represent Fred's belief, let us go back to one of the statements made in the section on dealing with contradictory information: namely, we never have anything more than a *model* of some system in our representation.

We just told you that Jim has never seen a piano. The question is who believes that he's never seen a piano? That is, what model does this correspond to? We could place the fact baldly into the Cyc knowledge base, with no special tag as to who believes it: just insert Piano in the hasntEverSeenA slot of Jim. In that case, *Cyc* is supposed to believe it. That is, the model that the fact points to is TheWorldAsCycBelievesItToBe (implicitly). An interesting side point is whether the collection Thing represents everything Cyc explicitly believes in. We shall leave that point aside.

Note that TheWorldAsCycBelievesItToBe is usually — but not always — in agreement with the Late20thCenturyAmericanConsensusRealityModel. According to the latter, if you put a person down in a coal mine, that person's measured weight doesn't change; you can really shoot someone explosively out of a real cannon; computers can't be creative; if there were a full-out nuclear war, a remnant of humanity would still survive here and there and eventually repopulate the planet; million≈billion≈trillion; etc.

In cases like that, Cyc might "know better." So what? Well, a lot of Cyc's energy will be spent on figuring out actions involving people — guessing at what people did, or would do, in some situation. It would be downright wrong for Cyc to think that everyone knows exactly what it knows. PrehistoricCavemen had very different beliefs and skills from Late20thCenturyAmericans, whose models of the world are in turn different from TheWorldAsCycBelievesItToBe. Cyc must model the actors involved in an action when trying to disambiguate their words and deeds; less charitably, it must sink to their level, be they cavemen, connectionists, Californians, or canines.

Let's get back to Jim never having seen a Piano. This is true not in the real world but in some hypothetical world that we have just created for you, for the purpose of illustrating some details about Cyc. So how should we represent this? And how should we represent Fred's mistaken belief (in that world) about Jim being able to play the piano?

There are two very different "schemes." We adopted the first one for a while but have recently switched to the second. We include details of both schemes for the interested reader. If you prefer, you may proceed immediately to section 6.5.3.2.

6.5.3.1.
SCHEME 1 —
A SCHEME WE
NO LONGER USE

In this scheme, which has since been abandoned in favor of the second scheme, to represent this example's premise — that Jim has never seen a piano — we would create a separate unit for the context of this example. This unit would be a model that is an "offspring" of TheWorldAsCycBelievesItToBe, containing just one extra fact for now — namely, that Jim.hasNeverSeenA.Piano. We might call that TheWorldOfExample6.5.3, for instance. It would have an epistemologicalStatus: HypotheticalStatus. All of the following takes place "in that world." For simplicity, we won't bring this point up again, but will talk as if Jim really exists and really never has seen a piano.

One way to represent Fred's mistaken belief — namely, that Jim can play the piano — would be to set up a new, alternate model of Jim. This would be a whole new unit: JimAsBelievedByFredInJune1988. It would have its own set of attributes, most of which come right over from Jim (or, if we have it, from JimInJune1988). This alternate model would have at least one discrepancy: its musicalInstrumentsPlayed slot would include the entry "Piano."

Another difference is that the alternate model's epistemologicalStatus would be Belief, and it would have a believedBy slot filled with Fred (or perhaps with FredInJune1988 or some similar temporal subabstraction of Fred). Notice that if someone later adds a rule that says that all piano players inherit medicalProblems EarlyArthritis, then JimAsBelievedByFredInJune1988 *would* inherit that value, but Jim wouldn't. The two "Jim units" would point to each other, of course, but through a slot-pair like beliefsAboutMe and beliefAbout.

This scheme works fine for representing what Fred thought, in June, 1988, about the way Jim was in 1970. A unit called JimIn1970 would be created, if it didn't already exist, and it would contain a startingTime of 1/1/70 and an endingTime of 12/31/70. On it would be whatever special information existed about Jim back then, as believed by Cyc — probably just inherited from the appropriate existing subabstractions of Jim. We would also have to create a new unit called, for example,

JimIn1970AsBelievedByFredInJune1988. The latter's beliefAbout slot would point to JimIn1970. (Inversely, the unit JimIn1970 would have a beliefsAboutMe slot filled with JimIn1970AsBelievedByFredInJune1988.) JimIn1970AsBelievedByFredInJune1988 would have an epistemologicalStatus slot containing Belief, and a believedBy slot containing FredInJune1988.

The scheme also works fine for representing deeply nested beliefs, such as: "Sam in 1988 thought that Fred in 1975 thought that Jim in 1974 could play the Violin." Let's suppose that Fred didn't really think that, of course; otherwise, it's trivial! To represent this in Cyc, we'd set up a new unit: JimIn1974AsBelievedByFredIn1975AsBelievedBySamIn1988. It would be an instance of Belief, its believedBy slot would be filled with FredIn1975AsBelievedBySamIn1988, its startingTime would be 1/1/74, etc. The unit FredIn1975AsBelievedBySamIn1988 would also be a Belief, its believedBy would be SamIn1988, its startingTime would be 1/1/75, etc. The unit SamIn1988 would be a (true consensus-reality) temporal subabstraction of Sam, its startingTime would be 1/1/88, its beliefsAboutMe slot would point to FredIn1975AsBelievedBySamIn1988, etc.

There is no special logic of beliefs in Scheme 1. That is, the units FredIn1975AsBelievedBySamIn1988 and JimIn1974AsBelievedByFredIn1975AsBelievedBySamIn1988 are treated no differently than any other agents in the system. If you ask for a list of people who play the violin, Cyc will include JimIn1974AsBelievedByFredIn1975AsBelievedBySamIn1988. This is not a bug; if you instead asked for a list of "real" people who play the violin (that is, whose epistemological status is as real as anything in TheWorldAsCycBelievesItToBe) then that "false image of Jim" unit wouldn't appear in the answer. This is important when, for example, you are asking a yes/no question like "Does anyone play the violin?"

So there does need to be a set of *discourse heuristics* for when utterances have implicit "really" or "now" or "ever" or "still alive" or other such qualifiers in them.

This should not be too dismaying; consider the following dialogue with someone on the street:

Q: Can you give me the name of a famous vampire? A: Dracula.
Q: Dracula was a vampire? A: Yes, I just said that.
Q: Are vampires real? A: No, of course not.
Q: Did Dracula ever really exist? A: Yes, now we know he did.
Q: Dracula was a vampire? A: No, just an evil ruler.

Although it's superficially contradictory, it's easy enough to sort out the various referents and turn this into a consistent corpus, using discourse heuristics and a precise representation language like CycL.

One important and interesting class of beliefs is what we term an *IncrementalBelief*. This corresponds to beliefs held by agents that are guaranteed to be nothing but some *specific additions* to the consensus belief in Cyc. In this case, as the JimIn1988 unit changes, we would be justified in transferring any change to the JimIn1988AsIncrementallyBelievedByFred unit. Of course, each IncrementalBelief must record what its incremental changes are, so that, if the unit they're a beliefAbout changes *those* things, the IncrementalBelief can reduce its status to a mere Belief. IncrementalBelief provides an efficient way to reason about slightly hypothetical worlds (Now you can choose HypotheticalLight or original HypotheticalClassic.)

One final point, related to efficiency. Consider "Fred believes that all Russian persons are Red." We really don't want to go ahead and create a different belief unit for every Russian person in the system, and give them a colorOfObject slot with value RedColor. Not only would it be vastly inefficient to do so, it would probably be wrong, because Cyc is unlikely to know who exactly Fred thinks is a Russian. (Even if there is a unit like RussianPersonAccordingToFred already present in the knowledge base, it probably has only a few individuals listed.) Moreover, what Fred believes is not "a is Red and b is Red . . . ," but rather that "for all x, if x is a Russian person then x is Red."

Suppose we want to represent Fred talking to a person, Ivan, who he learns is a Russian. All along, he's really talking not to Ivan (as believed by Cyc), but rather to IvanAsBelievedByFred; but most of the time we don't need to create that Belief unit, and we don't. At the moment he discovers that Ivan is Russian, we still don't force Cyc to create IvanAsBelievedByFred. However, whenever anyone (or any part of Cyc) asks Cyc for what Fred thinks about Ivan's color, then Cyc will automatically create IvanAsBelievedByFred, and give it a colorOfObject slot with value RedColor. So that's the efficiency issue: creating Belief units only when they're genuinely needed.

Naturally, you interact with the world — and its parts — as you believe them to be. So despite the efficiency policy we just mentioned, the potential for an explosion of Belief units is still looming. We are currently working on characterizing some of the more stereotypical deviations from TheWorldAsCycBelievesItToBe, hoping to capture in a single unit a large class of misinformation that otherwise would have to be represented on many separate Agents. For example, consider: "People often underestimate the intelligence of anyone speaking their language as a second language." It would be advisable to avoid creating 10^9 x 10^9 units just to represent that simple statement.

The above scheme has been abandoned in favor of the following one.

6.5.3.2.
SCHEME 2: USING
A BELIEF LOGIC

In the following discussion, we use the notation (Believes X Fact001) to state that X believes Fact001. In practice, statements of this form are encoded in the data structure for a slot on a given unit — that is, we do not have an explicit unit for IvanAsBelievedByFred, say. Rather, a "field" on each slot of Ivan allows us to record unusual beliefs by someone (such as Fred) about that attribute of Ivan. By the way, when we use the term *fact* here, we mean any piece of knowledge in the Cyc KB, which of course can contain heuristics, uncertain information, etc.

Imagine all the facts in the Cyc KB to be organized into several KBs that are each tied to the Agent who believes that set of facts. Let us denote the set of facts an agent A believes in as KB(A). So the set of facts Cyc believes in is KB(Cyc). This is the model we earlier termed "TheWorldAsCycBelievesItToBe."

More generally, let's denote the set of facts that A believes that B believes that C believes that . . . as KB(A,B,C . . .)

An important class of the facts in KB(Cyc) is the class of beliefs Cyc has regarding the beliefs of other agents. For example, consider the set of beliefs that Cyc has regarding Fred's beliefs about the world — that is, KB(Cyc,Fred). The subset of this that is the set of beliefs that Cyc has regarding Fred's beliefs about Joe's beliefs about the world is denoted KB(Cyc,Fred,Joe).

Below, we see that F3 is an instance of KB(Joe); F5 is an instance of KB(Cyc); F2 is an instance of KB(Fred,Joe); F4 is an instance of KB(Cyc,Fred), and F1 is an instance of KB(Cyc,Fred,Joe).

F1: (Believes Cyc (Believes Fred (Believes Joe (instanceOf Ivan Martian))))
F2: (Believes Fred (Believes Joe(instanceOf Ivan Martian)))
F3: (Believes Joe (instanceOf Ivan Martian))
F4: (Believes Cyc (Believes Fred (instanceOf Ivan Martian)))
F5: (Believes Cyc (instanceOf Ivan Martian))

An agent is said to be *capable of complete introspection* if the following relation holds: Believes(A F) → Believes(A (Believes A F)) All agents are assumed to be capable of complete introspection unless otherwise specified. This was global assumption 3 in section 6.5.2.2.

There could be any number of different KBs attributed to an agent by other agents. Thus, KB(Cyc,Joe), KB(Cyc,Fred,Joe), and KB(Cyc,Bill,Joe) all contain different sets of things that Cyc believes "someone" believes about Joe.

Each KB can be considered to contain two kinds of facts: facts about the world and beliefs about the beliefs of other agents.

We can define the following two predicates for each KB: super-KB and sub-KB. So KB(Cyc,Fred) has, as its super-KB, KB(Cyc), and as its sub-KB,KB(Cyc,Fred, Bill). (Notice that this is not the same as genls/specs at all.) The agent in any KB is assumed to be aware only of the facts in itself and in its sub-KBs. When it's time to make a guess or answer a question, etc., Cyc acts as though KB(Cyc, Fred) were a relevant subset of KB(Fred). From now on, we may as well shorten KB(Cyc,Fred) to simply KB(Fred), because all KBs include KB(Cyc) in their all-super-KBs. This won't lead to any ambiguity — if you want, just stick the extra "Cyc" as the leading argument in all the following KB(. . .) expressions.

Let us now take a brief look at the inference with beliefs.

At any point, the inferencing that's going on is "with respect to the facts in some particular KB." Consider any inference mechanism provided by CycL (for example, inheritance, inverse slots, constraint checking, etc.). The mechanism can "run" if it triggers off a set of facts *entirely within KB(A)*, for some Agent A. In that case, its "conclusion" (inherited entry, inverse slot entry, constraint violation, etc.) would also be added to KB(A).

So if KB(A) includes "Iran is a customer of the U.S.A.," then the inverse link ("U.S.A. is a seller to Iran") would be added to KB(A). Assume KB(A) also contains "Iran and the U.S.A. are enemies."

If KB(A) includes the constraint "No one has an enemy as a customer," there is a constraint violation and an error message might get generated.

But suppose that constraint occurred in KB(B), but not in KB(A); then there would be no contradiction from A's point of view. If KB(B) lacked "Iran and the U.S.A. are enemies," there would be no contradiction in KB(B), either.

Of course, if A and B then got together and chatted for a while, they might each be quite disturbed by the implications of that conversation. Note that this chat has to occur in some KB(G) that not a sub-KB for either KB(A) or KB(B).

Suppose that Cyc has just been informed about the existence of Fred — he has a brand new unit, and all we know about him is that he's a Person (hence he's an Agent and can have beliefs about things). So far, though, assume that Cyc has been told nothing special about

Fred's beliefs — and neither have you! Now consider the following two questions:

Does Fred believe that the earth is round?
Does Fred believe that Doug's social security number is 234–026–5519?

Let's say both these facts are true, and Cyc knows them both. Still, the intuitively correct answers to the two questions are Yes and No. Let us examine how we get Cyc to produce that behavior.

In order to find the answer to these questions, we could go through the standard inference schemes (that is, the ones Cyc would have gone through if we had asked it if *it* knew the world was round), but this time, instead of going through them in KB(Cyc), it goes through them in KB(Cyc,Fred).

We said earlier that inference is usually confined to KBs. For proving some fact F1 in KB(Sam,Jane,Tom) we use only existing facts (including existing inference templates) in KB(Sam,Jane,Tom). However, there is an important kind of inference — *belief projection* — in which, for proving a fact in KB(X), we may do our inference drawing on facts in the super-KB of the KB(X). That innocuous statement could cause us to recursively go into the super-KB of the super-KB of KB(X), and so on. Luckily, it won't be an infinite regress; it will bottom out at KB(Cyc). So in this case, in order to determine whether F1 is true in KB(Sam,Jane,Tom) when we are using belief projection, we would operate using facts in KB(Sam,Jane,Tom), KB(Sam,Jane), KB(Sam), and KB(). (That last one is what we used to call KB(Cyc) — recall that we're omitting the initial "Cyc" argument to each KB(. . .) expression.)

But do we really want to union together all those facts? No, not really. Intuitively, we want to draw on only the outer (super-) KB — those facts that aren't contradicted in the inner (sub-) KB.

The general problem of belief projection could be stated briefly as follows. Consider KB1 with sub-KBs KBS1, KBS2. . . . Consider a fact F1 in either KB1 or one of its sub-KBs. The problem of belief projection is of deciding whether or not it is justifiable to add F1 to a KBSn that does not include F1.

An interesting subclass of the belief projection problem is as follows. Given that KB1 has a fact F1 in it, when is it reasonable to project this belief to a sub-KB of KB1? Another interesting subclass of belief projection problems involves the transfer of Beliefs from KB(A1,A2) to KB(A1,A3).

Those two examples are interesting because they seem to form a large fraction of the use of belief projection; we have seen examples of this from fields as diverse as communicating, driving, and so on.

Hence, we would like to identify some of the important factors involved in determining when such transfers may be made, and we would like to devise a simple scheme of representing and reasoning with these factors.

Let us take a closer look at how we state these *belief transfer conditions* and at some of the important factors that influence them. Some of these conclusions hold not just for these two special cases of belief projection but for other cases as well.

Let us assume we are interested in

- Adding the fact F1 from KB(A1) to KB(A1,A2)

- Adding the fact F2 from KB(A1,A2) to KB(A1,A3)

Notice that every fact is attached to some slot of some unit — let's say F1 and F2 are attached to u.s. For simplicity, let's say that F1 is a belief that u.s.v1 is true, and F2 is a belief that u.s.v2 is true. That is, each of them is a "belief" about u.s. If the believer is Cyc, the fact gets to sit in the value field of u.s; otherwise, it is relegated to sitting in the "beliefs about me" field of u.s.

Let PRED1 be the condition for adding F1 from KB(A1) to KB(A1,A2) and PRED2 be the condition for adding F2 from KB(A1,A2) to KB(A1,A3). In practice, PRED1 and PRED2 are represented by units and are entries on s.beliefAccessConditions.

PRED1 is a function of A2, u, s and v1.
PRED2 is a function of A2, A3, u, s and v1.

Even though A1 is not explicitly mentioned here, it is important; the evaluation of PRED1 and PRED2 will be done in the A1 world — that is, in KB(A1) — and the presence or absence of PRED1 and PRED2 in KB(A1) world heavily influence whether each transfer goes through there or not.

Another requirement must also be met before the transfer is permitted, but this one is not often a problem: The addition of the fact F1 should not cause any constraint C1 (which is present in KB(A1,A2)) to be violated in KB(A1,A2). This last requirement can be overridden in the following even more unusual case: P1 is known to be *preferred to* C1, and P1 holds in KB(A1,A2). This is a rare occurrence indeed, if the constraint C1 is an absolute one!

Let us take a closer look at these beliefAccessConditions and see how exactly the different arguments A2, u, s. . . . affect them. It is important to obtain a small number of these that are capable of handling most of the cases. The basic hypothesis is that though in principle there could be as many KBs as agents, *in practice only a small number of*

KBs are different in interesting ways. That is, we could consider the space of KBs to consist of sets of KBs, each of whose elements are similar.

The set of all facts in all KBs could also be thought of as being composed of sets of facts, each of which is a member of some number of KBs. So the problem of determining whether to add a fact from one KB to another can be approached in two ways:

- Approach 1: We would like to determine the likelihood that fact F1 will be present in both KB(A1) and KB(A1,A2) (or the likelihood that F1 will transfer from KB(A1,A2) to KB(A1,A3)). In general, given any fact F', we would like to determine the likelihood of its being present in any given KB.

- Approach 2: If the first approach fails, then, given two KBs, we would like to determine the likelihood of their falling into the same set of "mutually similar" KBs. That would allow Cyc to assume that the two KBs don't differ in many ways. That in turn would give it enough evidence to guess that it's likely they share any single given fact, *especially any fact for which Approach 1 fails,* because Approach 1 should catch most of the common cases.

Let's now cover three of the factors that play an important role in these conditions: The slot involved; Awareness; and the Relationship between the agents.

6.5.3.2.1. THE SLOT INVOLVED.   There seem to be two categories of slots about which something specific can be concluded:

- Concept-defining slots such as specs, inverse, genlSlots, partTypes, inheritedSlotConstraints, etc. These define the concepts and are usually shared between most agents. Even when these slots sit on individuals, their values are usually inherited from more general, widely-shared concepts.

- Individual specific information — These are slots that make sense only for individuals and that often hold idiosyncratic information. For example, socialSecurityNumber. The default for these slots is that they are *not* shared.

6.5.3.2.2. AWARENESS OF THE EXISTENCE OF OBJECTS.   One of the facts that is important in deciding whether an agent holds a belief related to a particular object X is that he must be aware of the existence of X. If it is a belief about two objects X and Y standing in some relation R to each other, the agent must be aware of the existence of both objects X and Y, and (for the belief to be a "conscious" one to the agent) the agent must be aware of the relation R.

Note: This does not mean that an agent has to be aware of the *identity* of an object in order to hold beliefs about it. For example, I believe that there are sand grains on the beach in Cozumel, even though I have never seen any of them. In this case, I have never come across these sand grains, I don't know their specific "identity," yet I believe that there are beaches in Cozumel and I believe that there are sand grains on beaches, and therefore it is reasonable for me to believe that some (unspecified) sand grains exist on the Cozumel beach. Further, it is reasonable for me to hold beliefs about those sand grains (such as: they're warm now because it's noon there). In a way, the sand grains are "existentially quantified" objects. I know about — or at least believe in — their *existence*, and that's enough "awareness" for me to hold other beliefs about them.

On the other hand, let us suppose Fred believes that all Russians are sly. This does not imply that he believes that Ivan (who lives in some small Uzbeki village that Fred has never heard of) is sly. Fred is not aware of the existence of Ivan, so it would be a mistake to say that Fred has any explicit beliefs about Ivan.

Let's revisit the issue of consensus objects versus particular objects. We said earlier that in general most agents are aware of most general concepts and unaware of most individual concepts. Fred probably knows about Person, and Running, but not about Joe, or the event in which Joe ate pizza last night.

That was clearly a "zero-th order" approximation. Fred probably doesn't know your social security number, but he probably does know his own.

Let us take a closer look at the role played by the object about which the belief is held. It has a key role in determining who probably does/ doesn't know that fact.

Case 1: The fact is about some non-individual — some category.

- General concepts such as Time, Space, Person, etc. In general most agents share beliefs about these.

- Specialized concepts such as the reproductive system of bivalves in Lake Baikal. These, and many much less specialized concepts, are usually known only to a few agents, who have some clear inference path that would lead us (and Cyc) to guess that they know the obscure fact (for example, the Agent is a Baikalogist). Except when such clear-cut exceptions can be inferred, however, the default accessibility for these is *False*.

Case 2: The fact is about some IndividualObjects.

- Individuals known to virtually every agent. For example, the sun, the instanceOf relationship, the motherOf relationship, etc. The default here is, of course, that every Agent knows these.

- Individual objects known to a large group of Agents. For example, MCC, MickeyMouse, Persia, the transitive attribute, etc. Notice that "known to" doesn't mean that the thing is real (consider MickeyMouse); rather, it just means that the Agent is aware of the existence of this concept, this unit.

- Obscure individual objects known only to those Agents who have a "need to know"; that is, for which Cyc can come up with a specific inference that says the agent would likely know about X. An example of this sort of object would be Guha's car. Almost no one knows about it, except Guha and his friends, who have a clear inference leading to their knowing about it.

This is enough to get the "first-order theory" of *awareness-projection;* much remains to be done to get a more powerful "second-order theory."

6.5.3.2.3.   RELATIONSHIP BETWEEN THE AGENTS.   The third factor that plays an important role in determining whether to add a fact from one KB to another is the relationship between the agents involved. This is related to the definition of concepts such as closelyRelatedTo, usuallyDisagreesWith, grewUpWith, etc. This kind of information is used in deciding whether to project a belief from KB(A1) to KB(A1,A2) or from KB(A1,A2) to KB(A1,A3). The inferences should be obvious.

6.5.3.3.
HEURISTICS FOR
DETERMINING THE
TRANSFER OF
BELIEFS BETWEEN
AGENTS

We've sketched out, above, a rough list of three different factors that affect the transfer of beliefs between agents. Rough though it may be, we believe that it should be possible to draw up a set of heuristics based on these factors that cover a large fraction of the cases. This set of heuristics is being worked on at present, and should be forthcoming in Cyc in the near future.

It is possible to specify the belief transfer conditions for cases that are more complex than the two special cases mentioned here — but recall that we have found those two cases to be, by far, the most common ones! But yes, we could isolate the next few simplest cases, complex though they would be, and derive the (presumably more complex) rules governing the transfer of beliefs from one KB to another in those cases.

Let's close this section on "Beliefs" by considering hypothetical reasoning as a form of reasoning about beliefs. This will bring us full circle back to our example about "Jim never having seen a piano," an assertion that is true only in the hypothetical world we wish to erect for this section of this book.

Suppose Agent A1 is doing some inferencing. We could say that A1 is engaging in *hypothetical reasoning* if it's carrying out some inference processes in a world W that is different from KB(A1). In that case, we would say that the world W is hypothetical with respect to KB(A1), or that W is hypothetical from the point of view of A1. (We need to be very clear about this, because A1 might be wrong, and W might be the "real" world!)

This is not really very different from the case where agent A1 believes something about what agent A2 might say if you asked him about Z. In this case, A2 is just A1 + a few changes — those changes are the hypotheses under which A1 is engaging in this bit of hypothetical reasoning.

This can be modeled as there being two subabstractions of the same agent A1, one of which believes in the standard KB(A1) and the other of which believes in the hypothetical KB(A1′), which is a small modification of KB(A1). The belief accessibility conditions are slightly different for the case of two subabstractions of the same agent having different belief sets; in particular, the default is that A1′ *does* know about all the myriad minutae that A1 knows about, such as A1.socialSecurityNumber (unless one of the hypotheses specifically countermands some of those facts or some of those knowings-about).

The extension of the above approach to other propositional attitudes besides "belief" has also been done in a rudimentary fashion. Some of these attitudes include dreads, goals, etc.

6.5.4. Certainty Factors (the Bottom Rung of the Food Chain)

6.5.4.1. WHERE'S OUR SELF-RESPECT?
As good doctrinaire AI researchers, our noses naturally wrinkle at any mention of numeric certainty factors. "1974 technology, and all that, you know!" It's always better to justify an entry by a list of symbolic evidence for and against it. End of discussion. Until . . .

We began to think about what it means for an entry to be sitting on a slot. Or not sitting there.

Yes, it *is* always better to justify an entry by a list of symbolic evidence for and against it. That evidence in turn is just more entries, which should similarly be symbolically justified by yet other entries . . .

This process all must bottom out *somewhere*, in entries that are just "there," with no symbolic justification. We can stop at this point, or we can go one step further and allow a numeric estimate of how sure it is that this "bottommost creature" really is (deserves to be, will turn out in hindsight to be) an entry for this slot of this unit.

6.5.4.2.

NUMERIC CF — A SCHEME WE NO LONGER USE

(*Note:* Because we no longer use numeric-valued certainty factors (CFs) in Cyc, you may wish to skip ahead to section 6.5.4.3, where we discuss non-numeric CFs. However, this section explains why we were led down the numeric path, discusses the problem we discovered with this approach, and leads up to how we overcame it by devising a five-valued logic, namely the non-numeric CFs.)

If you spurn the whole concept of a CF, what you're saying, in effect, is that all CFs are absolute — 0 percent or 100 percent (that is, just *out* or *in*, False or True).

Consider a piece of medical knowledge: "If a patient acquires a bacterial infection a few days after surgery, it's likely to be a *pseudomonas aeroginosa* infection." This is a pretty good rule of thumb; it works about two-thirds of the time. Until recently, no one knew why it was true, it just was, empirically and statistically. So it makes sense not to just have the rule sitting there in the system, but to assign it some number (such as .67) that reflects how often it gives the right answer.

By the way, physicians now know the causal mechanism at work, and the deeper symbolic explanation can be encoded: patients in the hospital have low resistance to disease; they often get flowers; and in the flower vase bottoms is the perfect culture medium for *pseudomonas aeroginosa* bacteria to grow. So the patients get flowers, the bacteria cultures grow there, and the patients can't resist the infection. Yes, deeper causal symbolic understanding *is* better than .67, isn't it? But .67 is still much better than having to make a choice between 0.00 or 1.00.

Let's just use this mechanism responsibly, and never try to "encode" information in the *n*th digit of the CFs (for example, giving one fact a CF of .901 and another of .900, because you would like the first fact to be slightly preferred over the latter. In that case, just give them both CFs of .9 and state in the KB that fact1 is preferredOver fact2).

6.5.4.2.1. (NEG)DEFAULTCF, (NEG)THRESHOLD, AND APRIORILIKELIHOOD. Now we're ready to consider what it means for an entry to sit on a slot.

For instance, consider the slot languagesSpoken, for a unit like Fred.

Suppose it currently has French and Spanish as entries. What does that *mean*?

It means that we're pretty sure that Fred speaks those two languages. How sure? Well, maybe our default certainty factor for any entry on any slot is 95 on a scale of 0–100 (that is, the entry is 95-percent likely to "really" be there; at any given moment, we'd be surprised if much more or less than 5 percent of the CF = 95 entries all over Cyc were actually incorrect).

In the case of the languagesSpoken slot, it could be that we're rarely wrong about that, so maybe the defaultCF for languagesSpoken is higher, say 98. For some slots, like psychologicalStability, we might be much less sure, say a defaultCF of 70.

If you just "place an entry" on a slot, without specifying a specific certainty factor, it's assumed that you intend that entry to have the defaultCF for that type of slot.

Of course, we might place an entry on the languagesSpoken slot of Fred with a very high CF (for example, Fred's occupation is FrenchTeacher) or with a less certain CF value (for example, I overheard Fred mutter something that sounded like French to me).

If you ask me about something that requires me to access the list of languages Fred speaks, I'm probably going to include those with a sufficiently high CF and ignore the rest. For the system as a whole, a good minimum threshold like this might be 90. For some slots, the threshold might be much higher (for example, for instanceOf, we can't tolerate a KB-wide 10-percent error) or lower (for example, for psychologicalStability, the threshold might be down around 60).

Generally, a slot's threshold is greater than 50, and its defaultCF is greater than its threshold. A good general guess (which Cyc will make) for a slot's defaultCF, given its threshold, is halfway between that threshold and 100. (That is, Cyc uses this as its default way of computing s.defaultCF, given s.threshold.)

Now suppose you ask me, "what's the chance that Fred speaks Russian?" That's an interesting question. Just because Russian isn't listed as an entry on Fred's languagesSpoken slot doesn't mean he *doesn't* speak it. Its absence just means that we don't have any special information one way or the other. Cyc could follow various schemes for estimating the likelihood of Russian "really deserving to be there":

• Look at the entryIsA of the slot. This is the collection of all legal entries for the slot. In the case of languagesSpoken, its entryIsA is Language. Divide the average number of entries on a languagesSpoken slot (among those units possibly having it) by the number of known Languages. This figure, 1.7/500 = .0034, is better than nothing.

- Tabulate the empirical likelihood of a person knowing Russian; that is, divide the number of people who speak Russian by the total number of people. This figure (450,000,000/5,000,000,000 = .09) is better than nothing.

- Do a similar calculation to that in the previous method, but only among people "similar to Fred" in important ways. That is, see which slots partially determine languagesSpoken (for example, countryOfResidence, levelOfEducation) and do your sampling only from individuals who share similar values on those slots.

- Work out the various ways that we would know about Fred speaking Russian, and see if we can symbolically conclude that he doesn't (because, if he did, we'd know about it), or (maybe!) that he does.

Each of these methods is better, and costlier, than its predecessor. Cyc seemed to be getting by satisfactorily with a simplified version of the first approach, the absolutely simplest-minded approach: look up a cached numeric value for the *a priori likelihood* (*apl*) of any given entry on this kind of slot. You don't even need to come up with a special apl for most slots; a default system-wide apl, namely 3 (that is, 3 percent), is perfectly fine.

For most (useful) slots, the *apl* will be well below the threshold. If it's not below the threshold, that means that all legal entries for the slot are assumed to be sitting there, unless noted otherwise. Very few slots have such a semantics (for example, isNotAcquaintedWith, wasNotBornOnTheSameDayAs, isUnawareOfTheExistenceOf).

The idea here is that even though most of the 500 legal entries are absent from the languagesSpoken slot of Fred, they are still there with *some* small nonzero chance. (Otherwise, we would have some new definite knowledge about which languages Fred *doesn't* know — and we don't have that knowledge either.)

So you can imagine that the languagesSpoken slot of Fred has all 500 possible entries, and each one has a numeric CF. Most of those CFs are the same small figure (perhaps 3 percent). A few have higher CFs (say French at 100, German at 95, and Spanish at 75), and a few have lower CFs (say Prakrit at 0 and Algonquin at .001).

If you ask which languages we "know" that Fred speaks, the quick answer is gotten by sweeping together those with CFs above threshold — in this case, say, above 90.

If you ask which languages we "know" that Fred doesn't speak, it would be only those below some negative threshold (generally far lower than the apl). For example, languagesSpoken.*negThreshold* is 2, which means that about 2 percent of the answers Cyc will give to that question are probably wrong. Slots that can't tolerate that high an error level — for example, instanceOf, have their negThreshold set close to, or even equal to, zero.

If we explicitly tell you that Fred doesn't speak Algonquin, then you'd record it with a still lower CF (for example, .001 percent), which might be (and is) called the defaultNegativeCF.

If we were absolutely sure that Fred spoke Tamil, it would get entered with a CF of 100; if we were absolutely sure he didn't, it would get entered with a CF of 0. Warning: the defaultCF, threshold, negDefaultCF, etc., for each slot is (and should be) carefully considered, and after it has been determined, users should almost never have to enter any entries on that type of slot with idiosyncratic CFs.

Again, although users *can* specify a precise CF value for each entry on u.s, they'll *usually* just specify one of the following:

- "It's 100-percent guaranteed to be on there" — give it a CF of 100

- "We 'know' it's on there" — defaultCF — abbreviated as "T" — often around 95

- The threshold of the slot is here, close to the defaultCF — often around 90

- "We aren't sure about it" — apl — abbreviated as "~" — often around 3

- The negThreshold of the slot is here, close to the negDefaultCF — often around 2

- "We 'know' it's not on there" — negDefaultCF — abbreviated NIL or "−" — often around 1

- "It's 100-percent guaranteed not to be on there" — give it a CF of 0

The threshold for a slot is also used to control forward inference. In general, we would like not to infer entries on slots that have a certainty very near the slot's aPrioriLikelihood. The danger is that we could waste a lot (that is, almost all!) of Cyc's time drawing inferences that are just slightly above or below the aPrioriLikelihood of the slots on which they sit. All we really care about are inferences whose conclusions have CFs that are above the threshold of the slot (or below the negThreshold of the slot; see below). The threshold is often used as the cutoff CF, so that any entry would need to have a CF greater than the threshold in order for the system to forward-propagate on it.

When would you specify, "We aren't sure about u.s.v1"? Suppose an entry v1 got inherited to u.s, but you disagreed with the reasoning that led to that inheritance. You don't want to definitively make a statement that the entry *can't* be there or *isn't* there, you just want to abstain; you want to reinstate the *apl* CF for that entry.

Let's examine a case where this might arise. First, suppose we use inheritance to infer that children of teachers usually get good grades. In Cyc, we'd say:

```
SchoolTeacher
   children
      gradeQuality: Good
```

But what about children of gym teachers? We want to reset the chance of "Good" coming up back to the same setting it would have for non-teachers' children — not higher (as for non-gym teachers) but not lower, either. We could say:

```
GymTeacher
   genls: SchoolTeacher
   children
      gradeQuality: Good #@~
```

The "#@" just means "the preceding entry has this CF," and the "~" means "whatever *apl* this slot has." So the net effect is to cancel out the inheritance statement made on SchoolTeacher. When asked whether children of gym teachers get good grades, Cyc would respond neutrally, "no special information one way or the other." Notice that this is different from saying

```
GymTeacher
   genls: SchoolTeacher
   children
      gradeQuality: Good #@NIL
```

which would mean "children of gym teachers do not get good grades." The #@NIL means "the preceding entry has CF of negDefaultCF."

In a way, these are all poor examples, because we could easily come up with some symbolic reasons for *why* we expect u.s to contain or not contain v1. For example, you could introspect on your existing world knowledge, and spin out a long, detailed symbolic story about why French citizens speak French, why we would be surprised at a French teacher who couldn't speak French, why someone who speaks French and Italian probably speaks Spanish, etc.

In all such cases, the CFs should be attached to the inheritance or classification rule (or whatever) that is concluding this entry's existence. That CF will then percolate to the symbolic reasons sitting on the various entries of the languagesSpoken slot of Fred, and Cyc will figure out how to combine them.

For those of you who must know, Cyc currently employs the following incredibly simple algorithm when combining multiple CFs.

- For each CF that is above the threshold: take the maximum

- For each CF that is below negThreshold: take the minimum

- In any other situation: take the average

Gasp! But shouldn't that first "take the max" be replaced at least by some formula like $(1 - (1 - CF1)^*(1 - CF2)^* \ldots)$? And shouldn't you worry about the independence of the reasons? And shouldn't . . . ? Wait. We intentionally have chosen a painfully simple, computationally fast combining function. If you don't like it, don't use so many CFs; fall back on reasons more!

6.5.4.2.2. THE PROBLEM WITH NUMERIC CFs. Why did we abandon the ugly but apparently well-motivated numeric CF scheme? Consider the following all-too-common scenario:

One knowledge editor enters A1 (a u.s.v1 assertion) with CF 97 and another assertion A2 with CF 96. The person doesn't really know the absolute likelihoods of A1 or A2, but (a) both are pretty likely, and (b) A1 is a little more likely than A2. For instance, A1 is the assertion that slum dwellers are poor, and A2 is the assertion that ghetto dwellers are poor.

Another knowledge editor enters A3 with CF 98 and A4 with CF 95. As before, the intent is that (a) both are pretty likely, and (b) A3 is a little more likely than A4. For instance, A3 is the assertion that American kindergarten teachers typically watch TV at least once a week, and A4 is the assertion that they read a newspaper article at least once a week.

The catch is that, with numeric CFs, these knowledge enterers have also entered additional — *unintended* and probably *false* — comparisons, such as "it's more likely that ghetto dwellers are poor than that American kindergarten teachers read a newspaper article at least once a week." And "it's more likely that American kindergarten teachers typically watch TV at least once a week, than it is that slum dwellers are poor."

The problem, therefore, is that all numbers are commensurable to one another. When knowledge enterers began assigning absolute 0–100 numbers to each u.s.v1, the intended greater-than/less-than relationships got lost in the explosion of unintended emergent ones. And the genuine absolute numeric values (for example, "93 percent of the time, this really does occur") got lost amid the sea of numbers that were being pulled out of the air just to encode the intended "more-likely-than" relationships (as between A1 and A2, above, where the knowledge enterer of course had no idea what the actual fractions were, just that A1 was a little more likely than A2).

6.5.4.3. NON-NUMERIC CF — THE SCHEME WE NOW USE	As you must already realize, we no longer have numeric CFs. So let's present and discuss the current semantics of uncertainty — and of default rules — in Cyc.

6.5.4.3.1. TRUTH VALUES.   There are three truth values:

- True

- False

- Unknown (that is, neither true nor false)

Any one of the above three truth values may denote the truth of a statement such as s(u v1) — which is another way of writing u.s.v1. Another way of looking at this is that the truth value of, say, Fred.zodiacalSign.Pisces must be True, False, or Unknown.

Actually, as we'll see below, both true and false come in two flavors, depending on whether we're absolutely certain of the assertion.

6.5.4.3.2. RULES.   Rules, such as A → B, are first-class objects in our language; that is, each rule may be represented by its own unit. Such units can have many different slots; some serve bookkeeping roles, some help to define the If- and Then-parts of the rule, some help to situate the rule in the various hierarchies that make up rule-space. Let's consider that last kind of slot, which sits on a unit representing a rule. One of the useful "rule-space hierarchies" is defined by the following slot (and its inverse): moreGeneralRules (and lessGeneralRules). Another is defined by "canPossiblyTrigger" (and its inverse, "canBeTriggeredBy"). Yet another hierarchy among the rules is induced by the slot "overrides" (and its inverse "overriddenBy") which points to other rules over which this one takes precedence.

As we've discussed before, a rule can be represented in Cyc by any of dozens of inference features (inheritance, transfersThro . . .) Each rule, though, regardless of what *syntactic* form it has, must have one of the following two flavors (we're assuming the rule is equivalent to A → B):

- Monotonic — if A is accepted as true, then B is accepted as true

- Default — if A is accepted as true, and no rule that overrides this rule contradicts what it's saying about B, then accept B as true

What does "contradicting" mean? In general, each of the following contradicts the other two:

X is true
X is false
X is unknown

The *overrides* relationship is just a slot, so it may therefore itself be inferred or computed. However, for simplicity and efficiency, we do not guarantee that Cyc will handle correctly the case where a *backward* rule concludes something about R1 overriding R2. Again, for efficiency, a closed-world assumption is made in concluding facts about the overrides relation and in looking for other rules.

Given two rules, if no explicit *overrides* relationship is specified between them, the usual closeness criteria will be applied (for example, letting the default height for men override the default height for people, even though Fred is a member of both sets).

Because rules are stated using different features, there could be some confusion about what the "unit for a rule" means. Here is what it means: it refers to *the rule at the epistemological level*. If we enter the rule in some other form (for example, as an inheritance), CycL converts it to a general constraint language expression and creates a new unit to represent the rule in that form. Only such epistemological-level sentences may have explicit overrides slots.

In most AI systems, the notion of defaults usually makes sense only for entries that have been *inferred* by some means. In Cyc, though, a large majority of all the assertions are "local defaults." These correspond to assertions that were made (a) by a human user, in a situation where he is less than 100-percent certain of that assertion, and (b) by CycL itself, as the conclusions drawn by default rules of the form True → s(u v1).

As we said earlier, both true and false come in two flavors. The two flavors of true are referred to as 100 (absolutely certain) and t (currently believed to be true, but capable of being overridden), and the two flavors of false are referred to as 0 (absolutely impossible) and - (currently believed to be false, but capable of being overridden).

The conclusions of a *default* rule can be T, -, or ~ (which is the symbol for Unknown).

The conclusions of a *monotonic* rule will have a strength of 100 or 0 if all the terms in the antecedent also have one of these strengths. Otherwise, the conclusion has a strength of T or -. That is, if we are only pretty sure that Fred has 2 sons and 2 daughters, then we are only pretty sure that he has 4 children, even though we are 100-percent sure of the "rule" that $2+2=4$. If we were 100-percent sure that he had 2 sons and 2 daughters, then we'd be 100-percent sure he had 4 children.

What exactly, then, is the difference between T and 100; how is one to interpret these conclusions? T is best interpreted as default (or non-monotonically true) and 100 is best interpreted as meaning monotonically true. That is, if u.s.v1 has a certainty factor of T, the *addition* of some other fact to the KB might cause the removal of this entry. However, if the entry is there with a CF of 100, the only thing that can cause the *removal* of this entry is the removal of some fact (for example, this fact itself!) from the KB.

From the above perspective, we can view the difference between T and 100 (or between - and 0) as just something way down at the level of the implementation. Strictly speaking, Cyc users need not make any distinction between an entry with a CF of T one with a CF of 100 (or between an entry with a CF of 0 and one with a CF of -). That is, at the implementation level, T and 100 are "merely" two flavors of the same truth-value (true), and - and 0 are also "merely" two flavors of the same truth-value (false).

The only situation in which any distinction is made between T and 100 is in dealing with incommensurable competing sources. Here, each source carries a measure of support that is indicated by one of $\{0, -, \sim, t, 100\}$.

Here is the "contention resolution" table, which is used to decide what the final CF should be, given two incommensurable sources:

	0	–	~	T	100
0	0	0	0	0	x
–	0	–	–	~	100
~	0	–	~	T	100
T	0	~	T	T	100
100	x	100	100	100	100

Here, the "x" represents a genuine monotonic contradiction that must be dynamically resolved.

In case there are three or more separate incommensurable sources, the following combination algorithm is used: combine the very highest (closest to 100) and the very lowest (closest to 0) CFs of all the sources.

So if you write a rule $A \rightarrow B$, under what circumstances will B get asserted with strength T and when will it get a CF of 100? This depends upon the CF of the rule (that is, whether it's monotonic or default) and on the CFs of the support of A (that is, the highest and the lowest source for A together yield a combined CF for A). We're assuming here that both the rule and A have CFs of either T or 100. The CF of B is determined by this table:

CF of A	CF of Rule	
	T	100
T	T	T
100	T	100

That is, the net CF of B is 100 only if both the rule is monotonic and the CF of A is 100. Otherwise, the CF of B is concluded only to be T.

There is one pair of controversial entries in the 5×5 contention table above that describes how to determine the truth value of u.s.v1 when there are conflicting rules that don't override each other. Namely, notice that - and T "combine" to give ~. This means that there is no difference between there being some unresolved contention about some fact and there being no information.

This is not only computationally easy to handle, but any other *syntactic* choice leads to wrong answers in many everyday reasoning tasks. For example, consider adjudicating an argument about something you are totally unfamiliar with — say an argument involving a hobby you know little about (for example, whether it's good or bad to use camphor to catch Luna moths). One person, on one side of the argument, raises ten weak reasons, and an opponent raises one good reason on the other side. Both parties agree that there are ten weak reasons on one side, and one good one on the other. Who do you, as judge, decide in favor of? The answer of course is that you can't tell. The arguments might combine to yield a win for the first side . . . or the second. You can't tell unless you know something about each "side" of the argument! That is, you can make a better guess than Unknown only if you have some semantic information, some *overrides* information, that we don't have in this case.

What happens when a monotonic rule concludes something with a strength of T, and the eventual decision is to give the entry a truth value of ~ or false? In this case, because the rule is monotonic, if the preconditions of the rule are true, the conclusions must also be true. Because the contention process has decided that the conclusion is not true, the preconditions must not be true. So, when this happens, CycL does the following:

1. Generates the set of assertions (s u v1) that made the antecedent of the monotonic rule true.

2. Makes some number of these assertions false.

Well, how does CycL select which ones to make false? First of all, it immediately rules out any of them that are monotonically true (have CF = 100). So at this point CycL has a set of facts $F = \{f1, f2 \ldots\}$, where each f_i is an assertion of the form (s u v1) and has CF T. One of these f_i must be selected, and its CF must be reduced to Unknown. We keep doing that until the antecedent is no longer true; that is, until the monotonic rule ceases to be satisfied.

Okay, so how is the "best" f_i chosen at each cycle of that procedure? The way in which this is picked is as follows:

1. If there is a fact f_i that is known to be less likely than all the members of F, that fact is picked to have its CF reduced to Unknown. In CycL, such "less likely than" information is expressed by creating slot entry details for each member of F and listing some of those members in each other's #%lessLikelyThan slots. So if (the unit representing) one of the f_i lists all the others in its #%lessLikelyThan slot, that's the less likely fact that will be picked.

2. If there is no such f_i, pick any of the facts whose #%moreLikelyThan slot is empty (*note*: #%moreLikelyThan.#%inverse.#%lessLikelyThan).

3. If no such f_i exists, there's a contradictory "cycle" of lessLikelyThan assertions! Don't lose sleep over it, just pick one of the f_i with the smallest number of entries in its #%moreLikelyThan slot.

Does the above scheme usually work? Yes, in two ways. First, when there isn't too much semantic knowledge, it's about as good a syntactic scheme as we can have. Second, when it fails, it points out some missing #%moreLikelyThan link, which can then be added to the KB to prevent that (class of) mistakes in the future. And speaking of failing, yes, it does indeed sometimes lead to the wrong answers:
Say we have two incommensurable rules

- Rule J: $A \rightarrow B \wedge C$

- Rule K: $\neg B \rightarrow \neg A \wedge \neg C$

And suppose that, at the moment, A is believed with strength T, and B with strength - (that is, $\neg B$ is believed with strength T). We'll also assume, for simplicity, that each of A and $\neg B$ has exactly one source (one justification); that is, we didn't have to consult our 5×5 table to come up with their present certainty values.

So, given that situation, either rule J or K could "fire" at this moment. But the two rules block each other. (Two rules of the form $a \rightarrow b$ and $c \rightarrow \neg b$ *don't* block each other, because there is no mention of the conclusion on the left-hand side, as in standard default logics.) If J is run first, the strength of B rises to $\sim$ (because the newly asserted value, T, combines with the current value, -, to produce the net CF, namely $\sim$), C is asserted with strength T, and rule K no longer will try to run. If rule K is run first, the strength of A is lowered from T to $\sim$, and C is asserted with strength -. So the states of A, B, and C will all be different depending on the order of evaluation of the rules! If J is run first, then those three facts wind up with CFs of T, $\sim$, and T. If K is run first, they wind up with CFs of $\sim$, -, and -.

Ideally, both rules should be used "in parallel" and the conclusion should be that the CF of C winds up as $\sim$. Also — probably — the CFs of A and B should remain unchanged, namely as T and -, respectively. Notice that this is the same result we get by running the two rules in each of the two possible orders and then combining (using our 5×5 matrix) the different results.

A similar sort of problem occurs when CycL has two rules that are commensurable, but the overridden rule is forward and the other, stronger rule, is backward.

6.6. Structures (Including Scripts)

The notion of structure is ubiquitous: we speak of the structure of a person, of a manufacturing process, of an argument. It is one of the most common clichés and — consequently — difficult to define precisely. After a great deal of thought, experiment, trial and error, more thought, more error, etc., we have arrived at what we now believe to be an adequate representation of structure in Cyc. It's not marvelous, but frankly we're relieved we found *some* adequate way to represent it!

In an earlier section, while differentiating between an IndividualObject and a Collection, we mentioned that *the relationships that hold between the different parts of the IndividualObject* are central in defining the IndividualObject. This set of relationships, conceived of as an object in its own right, is referred to as the *structure* of the object.

Let us suppose we were describing a telephone. The constraints that describe a phone fall into two basic categories:

- Constraints that describe a part by itself (for example, specifying the color of the metallic underplate, or specifying the size of the digit buttons)

- Constraints that relate the different parts of the object to one another (for example, the telephone cord plugs into the lower left side of the telephone body; the underplate is connected to the bottom of the body). This second class of constraints is what really defines the structure of the object as more than just "a set of its parts."

For example, the StructureOfFred is represented by its own unit in Cyc, and pointed to in the "structure" slot of Fred. StructureOfFred contains (1) a list of intrapart constraints that the parts of Fred must satisfy singly (for example, the fact that his head must be an instance of HumanHead), and (2) a list of interpart constraints (including spatial arrangement, functional linkage, relative size, etc.).

The crucial thing about the structure of Fred is not the list of his parts (that list sits on the Fred unit) but rather the lists of constraints on those parts (those lists sit over on the StructureOfFred unit). It is those interrelationships that define, that *are*, the *structure* of Fred.

Often, one of the defining features of a category is the structure of the instances of the category. Various attributes of things — not just their instanceOf — often are determined by their structure. It is therefore important to have a representation scheme that allows Cyc to do, inexpensively, things like compare structures and define simple similarity norms.

At a fundamental level, the structure of an object can be expressed *(in principle)* by means of a sentence in the constraint language (see section 2.3.1). However, that would be too cumbersome in many cases — that is, the scheme we just explained would be unacceptable. So, for the special case of representing structures, we shall deviate from the pure constraint language in the interest of computational efficiency.

Writing sentences of the form "There exists exactly n . . ." could get cumbersome. So structures could also be viewed as a more concise way of stating the type of constraints mentioned above.

The full extent of this deviation will be clear from the examples later on; in essence, what we'll allow is the giving of temporary variable names to parts of an object, "inheriting" them from its partOf if necessary, and a special syntax for stating the type (allInstanceOf) of each part and the multiplicity (number of such parts) in the object.

Because we could possibly have many orthogonal divisions of the components of an object (such as the physiological division of the human body versus the anatomical division versus the evolutionary division), a clear distinction is made between these by allowing a *set* of structures for any object, as opposed to a single one.

Our fundamental hypothesis in the efficient definition of structures is that there are many broad but useful structure clichés. That is, there are a relatively small number of commonly occurring sets of relations with sets of objects that largely define the overall approximate structure of the object.

One such common structural cliché — one such set of relations — is the following: "two objects, one of which is some kind of processing device, and the other of which is a peripheral, and they are connected by an information channel such as a wire."

Another common structural cliché is: "a number of very similar events occurring in parallel, and that parellel process is repeated serially for a while."

Hopefully by now you get the idea of what a structural cliché is. [By the way, we should acknowledge that the cliché work was originally sparked by discussions with David Chapman and Phil Agre, from MIT.]

The next step — which we are currently working on — is to collect the corpus of the few hundred most widely used structural clichés, and then compare them to one another, thereby using them to generate a set of relations with which to compare two structures. From that exercise we hope to derive an especially good set of interstructure relations. Why? Because these structural clichés are assumed to define the basic structure of a great many objects, rough comparison of structure must (we hope) often boil down to a comparison of the structural predicates used in clichés.

In addition to making the *comparison* of structures computationally tractable, having these primitives should make it easier to *represent* structures.

At a symbol level, these structural clichés are really nothing more than n-ary predicates and are hence represented in the constraint language as structural predicates. The structural predicates are usually predicates of a high arity when expressed in the constraint language (they are like scripts that take a large number of actors).

Every structure may have substructures, and there is yet a different set of relations for how the substructures interrelate and fit together to produce the structure.

Because one of the defining characteristics of most categories is the common structure of its elements, the structure is often one of the default inherited properties of objects. So even though we might have StructureOfFred, we rarely create structures just for Fred. Instead we create a structure that is the default structure for all humans.

For instance, the unit Telephone represents the set of all telephones. It inherits the default physical structure of a (stereotypical) telephone down to its allInstances: to wit, that it consists of a handpiece, a body, a handpiece-cord connecting the two, and a wall-cord connecting the body to a phone-outlet. Notice how we represent the five parts of a phone, plus the relationships and constraints among them:

```
Telephone
  instanceOf: Collection
  genls: CommunicationDevice HomeAppliance
  canHaveSlots: teleHandset teleBody teleHandsetWire
                teleOutletCord teleOutlet
  allinstances: Telephone15, Telephone99,...
    weightInLBs: 1
    hasStructure: TelephoneStructure-Physical
                  TelephoneStructure-Functional
    heightInCM: 11
    lengthInCM: 20
    depthInCM: 11
    .
    . ← other default properties of a typical telephone
    .
```

```
TelephoneStructure-Physical
  instanceOf: PhysicalStructure
  structureOf: Telephone99,...
  partsList: ((x TelephoneHandset 1)
              (y TelephoneBody 1)
              (z TelephoneHandsetWire 1)
              (w TelephoneOutletWire 1)
              (v TelephoneOutlet 1))
  partsSlot: physicalParts    ← w,x,y,z repr. physical parts of a phone
                                This gets inherited from PhysicalStructure.
  structureConstraints: ((2ObjsConnectedByAWire x y z)
                         (2ObjsConnectedByAWire y v w))
```

```
relnsToFunctionalStruc:
                ((embeddedIn TSF:teleMike x)
                 (embeddedIn TSF:teleSpeaker x) (embeddedIn
                 TSF:teleNumberAccepter y)
                 (embeddedIn TSF:teleInUseDetector y)
                 (appendageOf (x storageStandFor ) y)   ?
                 (appendageOf (y storageStandFor ) y))   ?
    specStructures: PrincessTelephoneStructure-Physical
              1940sBlackTelephoneStructure-Physical
```

```
2ObjsConnectedByAWire
  instanceOf: StructurePredicate
  genlPreds: 2ObjsConnectedByACord    ← e.g., a Bolo, a tincan telephone, mountain
                                        climbers roped together,…

  expressionArity: 3
  arg1type: ElectricalComponent    ← v1 will be locally bound to 1st argument
  arg2type: ElectricalComponent    ← v2 to the 2nd argument
  arg3type: Wire    ← v3 to the 3rd argument
  expansion: ((Connected v1 (end1 v3))    ← arg1 ctd to one end of wire
    (Connected v2 (end2 v3)))) ← arg2 ctd to the other end
```

Note: We prefer this special syntax (that is, with partsList, etc.) simply because it is easier to say this than to state something like (ThereExists x (u parts) (IsA x TelephoneHandset)) . . . for every part of the object. In practice these expressions on structures get converted to regular constraint language expressions and are then translated into appropriate inference template instances for 'implementation'. From that perspective, most of this is just a tool at the epistemological level to allow us to state things with less effort.

If we had specific "partsSlots" on the object, like *telebody*, which would point from the telephone to its body part, we could use that slot as a skolem function and not use a "local variable" y, on the partsList slot, above, where we said (y TelephoneBody 1). This is shown below.

```
TelephoneStructure-Physical
  instanceOf: PhysicalStructure
  structureOf: Telephone99,...
  partsList: ((teleHandset TelephoneHandset 1)
             (teleBody TelephoneBody 1)
             (teleHandsetWire TelephoneHandsetWire 1)
             (teleOutletCord TelephoneOutletWire 1)
             (teleOutlet TelephoneOutlet 1))
```

```
partsSlot: physicalParts
structureConstraints: ((2ObjsConnectedByAWire teleHandset
                         teleBody teleHandsetWire)
                        (2ObjsConnectedByAWire teleBody
                         teleOutlet teleOutletCord))
relnsToFunctionalStruc:
             ((embeddedIn TSF:teleMike teleHandset)
              (embeddedIn TSF:teleSpeaker teleHandset)
              (embeddedIn TSF:teleNumberAccepter teleBody)
             (embeddedIn TSF:teleInUseDetector teleBody)
             (appendageOf ((u teleHandset)
             storageStandFor) teleBody)
             (appendageOf ((u teleBody) storageStandFor)
             teleBody))
```

Note: In the relnsToFunctionalStruc slot of TelephoneStructure-Physical, the variable TSF:teleMike refers to one of the parts specified on the parts list of the unit TelephoneStructure-Functional (we just abbreviated it TSF).

Similarly, TSF would have a slot called relnsToPhysicalStruc, whose entries would be constraints referring freely to teleMike, and referring to TSP:teleHandset by prefacing it with the name of the unit it comes from (in this case, TelephoneStructure-Physical, which we abbreviated TSP). Just as the relnsToFunctionalStruc slot of TSP held the various structural relationships, so the relnsToPhysicalStruc slot of TSF holds the various functional relationships among the TSF: and TSP: parts.

The *specStructures* of a structure are similar, "whole" structures that are a little more specialized: they generally have some additional parts, and may override some of the information as well. For example, PrincessTelephoneStructure-Physical indicates a species of phones that have dial-lights, and 1940sBlackTelephoneStructure-Physical have straight wires (phones in general might have straight or coiled wires) and must have colorOfObject: BlackColor for all of their major physical parts.

The *subStructures* represent just some of the parts and (hence) just some of the structureConstraints. In a way, the unit we've shown represents a telephone plugged into an outlet. It could point to a subStructure that didn't mention the wall cord or the outlet, that just represented the more basic notion of a telephone handset and body connected by a wire — that is, TelephoneHandset&BodyStructure-Physical.

Another important use of subStructures is to break down the relations that hold between the parts into different categories. For example, if we were to take the structure of a type of process such as "driving a car over a snake," this structure could be broken down into a temporal structure (which talked about the speed we would need and the temporal relations between the different acts, such as the Aiming endsBeforeTheStartOf the Crushing) and the spatial relations between the different actors involved in the event (such as the snake being under the tires of the car at some moment).

It is important to separate *spec-* and *sub-structures* from each other and from structures that represent individual parts of the object. For example, there is a unit called TelephoneHandsetStructure-Physical, but it is neither a specStructure nor a subStructure of TelephoneStructure-Physical (nor should it be!). You and Cyc can "get to it" from TelephoneStructure-Physical via the partsList slot, which points to TelephoneHandset, whose hasStructures slot points to (among other things) TelephoneHandsetStructure-Physical.

Actually, what we represented above is pretty static. We haven't captured the dynamic, temporal nature of the telephone at all. We could have named that unit SpatialTelephoneStructure-Physical, created another one called TemporalTelephoneStructure-Physical, and made both of them subStructures of a third unit that would really deserve the name TelephoneStructure-Physical. TemporalTelephoneStructure-Physical would, in turn, talk about electric currents, ringing noises, sound wave transducings going on, the dial turning, etc. (It wouldn't talk about speaking words, or hearing them on the other end, or what it really *meant* when someone turns the dial or puts down the receiver; those would be part of TelephoneStructure-*Functional*.)

Although it is not true for *sub*-structures, it *is* generally the case that *the specStructures of U are precisely the structures of specs of U*. For example, take one of the specStructures of QuadrupedStructure-Physical, say DogStructure-Physical; now observe that Dog is indeed a spec of Quadruped. And, conversely, if you take any spec X of Quadruped, look at any of X's hasStructures, they can and should be specStructures of QuadrupedStructure.

Some structures are a *mob* of parts of one type, repeated over and over again: the segments of a caterpillar, the coils in a coiled telephone cord, the pitches in a cricket match, etc. Often, the nth part is related to the $n+1$-st part (or to some number of neighboring parts). Examples of this are Fibonacci numbers (each one is the sum of the preceding two); the gradually diminishing bones in a dinosaur's spine; etc. For instance:

```
OccursInSerial
   instanceOf: RepeatedStructurePredicate
   interpretedStrRelns: ((StartsAfterEndOf v2 v1))
   argType: Event
   howManyPredecessorsNeeded: 1
   minNumberOfRepetitions: 1    ← inherited from RepeatedStructurePredicate
   maxNumberOfRepetitions: Infinity    ← also inherited from there
```

This defines a repeated structure predicate, OccursInSerial, similar to the nonrepeated structure predicate 2ObjsConnectedByAWire we saw above. OccursInSerial takes a list of (any number of) events, and for the $n+1$-st event, requires that it begin after the ending of the nth event. Because we need only one predecessor, only two variables, v1 and v2, are required. In the case of Fibonacci, howManyPredecessorsNeeded would be 2, and v1, v2, v3 would be meaningful to refer to in the various constraints listed on the interpretedStructureRelns slot.

Note: Although we've primarily used physical objects (such as Telephone and Fred) in the above examples, keep in mind that this notion of structure applies to each IndividualObject, including each event, each argument, etc. We've mentioned *scripts* in Cyc before; in a way, they define the structure of (a class of) events. The next section examines that in detail.

6.6.1.   Structure of Dynamic Systems.   Each dynamic system (process) is represented in Cyc by a script. The slots that appear on a script unit — for example, Walking — are more or less the same as the ones that appear on a unit describing a static structure, for example, the unit Telephone.

However, dynamic systems have the following three additional elements that are worth representing:

- The preconditions that must be satisfied by the set of actors in order for the script to occur

- The "parts" from which a script is built are of two very different types: the various "actors" and the various "subevents" in which they participate

- The changes that (would) occur if/when the script is carried out

Because dynamic systems have these three additional aspects to capture and represent in Cyc, each Cyc script has several additional slots — slots not found on static structures:

- To represent the preconditions, we use a slot called *preconditions*. Its entries are just constraints expressed in the CycL constraint language. It is not recommended that users directly enter information on a script's preconditions slot; rather, we recommend using one or both of the following two important specSlots of preconditions: necessaryPreconditions and sufficientPreconditions.

- Because the parts fall into two categories — the subEvents and the actors — two specSlots of the partsList slot are used in its stead: actorList and subEventsList. (partsList is still heavily used when representing static structures, such as Telephone.)

- The changes that result because of the script are represented using the slots changeConstraints, finalStateConstraints, and others.

What sorts of entries are found on changeConstraints and finalStateConstraints? They're expressions in the constraint language, of course, and their main "predicate" is usually an instance of ChangePredicate. ChangePredicates are similar to the StructurePredicates. Here are some of the existing instances of ChangePredicate (this is a very small sample set):

```
IncreaseInNumberOfParts
ComingIntoExistence
CeasingToExist
ChangeInState
IncreaseChange
DecreaseChange
QuantitativeIncreaseChange
QuantitativeDecreaseChange
```

Some of the important types (that is, specs) of ChangePredicate include:

```
QualitativeChangePredicate
IntangibleChangePredicate
PhysicalChangePredicate
DifferenceChangePredicate
ReplacementChangePredicate
PrimitiveChangePredicate
```

```
QuantitativeChangePredicate
ContinuousChangePredicate
DiscreteChangePredicate
```

Let us look at a typical expression involving one of these ChangePredicates. Let Fred001 be a temporal subAbstraction of Fred, representing him on the day he robs a bank. Let's consider how we'd represent the change that says that Fred001 goes from being a RespectedPerson to a WantedCriminal. This would be stated as:

```
(ChangeInState Fred001 RespectedPerson
    WantedCriminal)
```

What are the temporal semantics of this statement? It means that there exists a subAbstraction of Fred001 — let's call it Fred001before — that was an instance of RespectedPerson and that was contiguousBefore Fred001; and there exists another subAbstraction of Fred001 — let's call it Fred001after — that is an instance of WantedCriminal and that is contiguousAfter Fred001. We — and Cyc — generally won't bother creating those subAbstractions, we — and Cyc — just know that, in principle, they could be created, and that that's the meaning of the constraint

```
(ChangeInState Fred001 RespectedPerson
    WantedCriminal)
```

So the semantics of each of these change predicates has built into it some information regarding the temporal subAbstractions, and thereby lets us express things at a higher level of abstraction.

As another example, here is how we could use a different ChangePredicate to represent the change in Fred001's wealthiness slot:

```
(IncreaseChange Fred001 wealthiness)
```

If we knew how much loot he'd absconded with, say a million dollars, we could have used the *Quantitative*IncreaseChange predicate, which takes an extra argument, namely the absolute amount of the change.

(*Note to purists:* We might, at first blush, think of a script as being simply an *n*-ary predicate with the *n* different actors as the arguments. This is not really adequate, however, because we are interested in talking about other, "deeper" parts of the script, such as the subEvents. On the other hand, the list of changes *is* a high-level "summary" of the script that intentionally ignores those details. From this perspective, it is reasonable to think of the ChangePredicates as nothing more than predicates in the constraint language.)

6.6.2. Defining Slots with Schemata.   There are a number of slots, such as #%structureConstraints, #%activityConstraints, #%purposeConstraints, and #%goalStatement, that take as their entries constraint expressions with variations in the syntax, special variables, and so forth. For most of these slots the range of allowed constraint expressions is quite large. In the past, each time one of these was created, we would write a special piece of code to draw all the inferences based on the intended semantics of the slot. This is bad for several reasons:

a. It should be easy for anyone to define one of these slots, use them, and have the system draw the intended conclusions.

b. Since these slots take arbitrary constraint expressions it is virtually impossible to get an efficient implementation of them as they are.

c. Since each of these has a slightly different semantics, it is quite hard for these things to share the code that implements them.

6.6.2.1.

INTRODUCTION TO SCHEMATA

What follows is a description of the scheme that allows us to do the following:

a. We define the intended semantics of our new slot in the KB.

b. Whenever we enter an entry E on this slot this definition will be used to get a (context independent) constraint expression that expresses the semantics of E.

c. Cyc can translate this constraint expression into an appropriate inference feature (e.g., inheritance) for efficient implementation.

This basically attempts to draw a distinction between "inference features" such as inheritance, horn clause rules, etc., and "representation features" such as activity details, structures, etc., whose main purpose seems to be to help us to organize the information in a more easily understandable (for humans) form.

The details of schemata will be illustrated through the example of #%structureConstraints:

```
#%Str1
  #%structureConstraints ((#%connectedTo
                     (u #%legPart) (u #%torso)))
```

Let us suppose we have a proposition P sitting on the #%structureConstraints slot of a structure #%Str1. For the moment assume that the only free variable in P is the symbol u. What does this really mean? We could say that it "means" the following:

$$((li∀u)hasStructure(u\ Str1) → P(u)$$

Since P ranges over (possibly complex) predicates rather than units, this is a second-order schema rather than a first-order schema. The feature code generator can only deal with the latter.

Let us take the case where P is (#%connectedTo (u #%legPart) (u #%torso)). So we can now substitute for P(u) in our original expression to get $(∀u)hasStructure(u\ Str1) ⇒ (\#\%connectedTo\ (u\ \#\%legPart)$ (u #%torso))

Translating this into the constraint language, we get

(#%LogImplication (#%hasStructure u #%Str1)
(#%connectedTo (u #%legPart) (u #%torso)))

We can now give this to Tell (that is, the epistemological level to heuristic level translator) which converts it into an appropriate inference scheme for actual implementation. Although the symbol u has a special meaning in entries on #%structureConstraints, once the definition is in place, the context dependence is apparent. The sentence given to Tell has no special symbols (except for '*rule*, which is discussed later).

Let us look at one more example before we start looking at the actual slots. The slot #%goalStatement takes as its entries pairs of constraint expressions where the first element in each pair is any constraint expression and the second one is of the form (<predicate> arg1 . . .) where the args are either variables or constants (they can't be expressions like (u s)). If (P1 P2) is a #%goalStatement for a GoalSet #%GS1, the semantics is:

$$\#\%goalSetOf(a\ GS1) ∧ \#\%believes\ (a\ P1) → \#\%hasGoals\ (a\ P2)$$

Not separating the #%believes and #%hasGoals parts of #%goalStatements can lead to problems. Consider saying that a patient wishes that his wound will heal soon — his goals surely don't include having the wound, but his beliefs include it and he does hope that it heals soon. Of course, the first part could simply be #%True and we expect eventually to loosen the restriction on the syntax of the second part.

```
#%GS1
  #%goalStatement ((#%hasWound a #%Wound1)
          (#%QualitativeChange #%Wound1 #%size
            #%DecreasingQualitativeChange
                  #%TheNearFuture))
```

Entries on #%goalStatement have more structure than entries on #%hasStructure, where we denoted the entry by just P. So in order to define the meaning of schema slots in general, we need to be able to "declare" the structure of the entry. We show how to do this by using the single entry slot #%entryStructure:

```
#%structureConstraints
  #%definingSchema ((#%LogImplication (#%hasStructure u rule)
  proposition))
  #%entryStructure (proposition)

#%goalStatement
  #%definingSchema ((#%LogImplication (#%LogAnd (#%hasGoals
            u rule)(#%believes u P1)) (#%hasGoals u
            p2)))
  #%entryStructure ((p1 p2))
```

Some points are in order here —

a. The symbol 'rule is a special one that will be used to denote the unit on which the slots #%structureConstraints or #%goalStatement will occur.

b. The special symbols that will be used in the constraint expressions should be used in the schema in the same sense; for example, the u used in the schema is used in the same sense in which it is used in the constraint expression. (These are the ones that, when combined with the schema definition, lose their special interpretation.)

c. The #%instanceOf of #%structureConstraints and #%goalStatement is #%SchematizingSlot.

6.6.2.3. FREE
VARIABLES IN
SCHEMATA

Let us now consider the case where there are other free variables in the constraint expression. For example in the case of the slot structureConstraints, one is allowed to "declare free variables" using the slot partsList.

The first thing we need to do is to specify which slot holds the "free variable declarations." This is stated using the slot #%quantificationSlot. So #%quantificationSlot(#%structure Constraints #%partsList). The entries on the slot #%partsList quantify the variables (other than u) that are free in the expressions on the slot #%structureConstraints and in addition specify an instanceOf constraint on the binding for the variable. So if we had the entry (x #%Col1 1) on #%Str1.#%partsList and the structure constraints included the constraint (#%s1 x u), Cyc obtains the quantification for x by converting (#%s1 x u) to (#%ThereExists x (u #%physicalParts)(#%LogAnd (#%allInstanceOf x #%Col1) (#%s1 x u)))

After this, Cyc can convert it to what we actually meant, that is,

(#%LogImplication (#%hasStructure u #%Str1)
    (#%ThereExists x (u #%physicalParts)
        (#%LogAnd (#%allInstanceOf x #%Col1) (#%s1 x u)))).

Though this seems to be the right one, let us take a look at another structure. The debatable point about the intended semantics concerns the quantification. It looks as though the intended quantification is a universal quantifier and not an existential one. Consider the by now familiar example of telephone structure.

```
TelephoneStructure
partsList ((x #%TelephoneBody 1)(y #%TelephoneReciever 1)
  (z #%Buttons 9))
structureConstraints ((#%connectedTo x y))
```

This is ambiguous since this does not say that a phone has exactly one telephone body and receiver. If we knew that, we could give you that information plus an existential translation to get a universal translation. So the debatable point concerns whether slots such as partsList specify that "exactly n parts of type Foo are there" or say that "at least n parts of type Foo are there." This ambiguity is resolved by doing the following — we use the slot #%atLeastQuantifiedVars which will contain the entries that are quantified in an "at least n" fashion. The default is *exactly* (this choice was made by looking at the KB). So the slot #%atLeastQuantifiedVars sits on TelephoneStructure, and for the variable z (buttons) we would say #%atLeastQuantifiedVars

(TelephoneStructure z), since in most phones there could be many more buttons.

So for the telephone body, etc., we can convert this to

```
(ForAll x (u physicalParts)
  (ForAll y (u physicalParts)
    (LogImplication (LogAnd (allInstanceOf x #%TelephoneBody)
                            (allInstanceOf y #%TelephoneReceiver))
              (#%connectedTo x y))))
```

and this translates into a horn clause that is quite simple to handle.

The slots such as partsList, activityList, etc., are instances of #%ExistentialQuantificationSlot and are assumed to have the syntax (*<symbol or role-chain> <collection> <number or composition detail>*)

There is one more issue to be resolved. In our translation, we came up with the slot #%physicalParts out of the blue. This was because #%physicalParts was presumably the entry for the slot #%structurePartsSlot on the unit #%Str1. Associated with each instance of #%ExistentialQuantificationSlot we have a slot called #%quantPartSlot. So we have #%quantPartSlot(#%partsList #%structurePartSlot).

If the cardinality of the entries is more than one and the variable is quantified in an "at least fashion," this expands out into a larger expression.

6.7. Space

How should we represent "pieces of space," such as are occupied by physical objects? And how should we represent spatial relations between such pieces of space (relations such as "inside", "knottedWith", "abutting", "parallelTo" . . .)? And what are the most useful spatial relations?

Given the analogy between space and time, and the symmetry between these two substances in the overall ontology of Cyc, maybe we can closely follow what we did for "pieces of time" and for "temporal relations," and thereby come up with a notion of an ECSR (easily conceptualized spatial region) and a small set of powerful spatial relations (such as inside, piercing, and so on).

6.7.1. Abandoned Attempts.   *Try 1:* We attempted to take our 49 temporal relations, view them as relations on one-dimensional space, and Cartesian-product them three times. Not only did that lead to an awful lot of relations

(117,649 to be exact), but most of the ones we looked at were bad. Even worse, we believe that the set still omitted most of the known useful ones! Oh well, it was a reasonable thing to try.

Try 2: We carried over *something* from the Time case to the Space case. Instead of trying to carry over the list of final relations, we just transferred the methodology of *looking at a small number of interesting points*. We then generalized that to include looking at a very small number of interesting edges and surfaces as well.

Before going deeper into the problem, let us consider the essential differences between spatial and temporal representation. There are two main reasons for these differences:

- Time is just one dimension, whereas space is three dimensions.

- Somehow there does seem to be some difference between space and time in the way we perceive these things. For example, you can go backward in space to "undo" motion a lot more easily than you can go backward in time to "undo" your mistakes. Time has a preferred direction, and a notion of entropy, whereas space does not.

Related to the second reason above is the following point. Although the question of the variation of spatial relations over time is of great importance, even the meaning of the notion of "the variation of temporal relations over space" seems fuzzy, if not downright meaningless.

Because Cyc is, after all, an account of the consensus reality of humans, we must take this apparent asymmetry seriously and expect it to be strongly reflected in the representation.

6.7.2. Try 3: An Ontology of Models of Space (Our Current Hope!). Now we can describe the approach that is currently being pursued, a scheme for representing spatial relations between objects.

6.7.2.1. A BRIEF REVIEW OF WHAT'S INVOLVED IN "REPRESENTING"

Before we actually get into the details of the representation, let us briefly review some of the basics of representing that hold good for any domain; let's also look at some of the implications of our conclusions for our attempts to represent space.

An *ontology* to describe a particular domain could be said to contain two basic kinds of elements — a set of categories and a set of relations that hold between instances of these categories. In any domain, the categories that must exist (for something such as Cyc) include all the different kinds of primitive entities that can be recognized in that domain (that is, those that are not merely composites formed by the agglomeration of other entities). Given such a set, we can look for the relations that hold between the elements of these categories. Once we have those, we can generate further relationships and entities that are composite in nature. The fundamental set of entities we use defines our basic abstraction of the domain; and different kinds of compositions of these elements form different kinds of new abstractions. A number of questions come up at this point. The first one is whether these different abstractions are needed. This is an important question, because the presence of new abstractions could cause many problems — like having to decide when to use which abstraction!

Soon, we will show how this all applies to spatial reasoning. We will pick one primitive representation — a spatial object as a set of points — and then construct various abstractions built from that primitive one. For example, we will develop a model of spatial objects built around surfaces; around solid objects; around equations; around devices; and so on.

6.7.2.2.
ABSTRACTIONS FOR SPATIAL REASONING

Before we try to justify the need for spatial abstractions built from the primitive one (the set of points), let us consider what are some of the desirable properties of an ontology.

There seem to be two main properties that ontologies must satisfy: *epistemological adequacy* and *pragmatic adequacy*. For an ontology to be epistemologically adequate, we should be able to state whatever we want to state in that domain using the ontology. For an ontology to be pragmatically adequate, we should be able to state commonly-stated things in a relatively easy fashion, and we should be able to infer commonly-inferred conclusions in a relatively easy fashion.

There is no *a priori* reason why a single ontology should be able to serve both purposes. In fact, except for some very simple domains, no one ontology does suffice. Why? We need one ontology that attempts to capture the most primitive notions of the domain, or the ontology won't be epistemologically adequate. But such a low-level ontology is likely to be inefficient in dealing with the common cases.

Building new abstractions from this basic abstraction has the potential of making it easier to handle some of the tasks of translating from one abstraction to another. So, given the inherent complexity of spatial representation, we have decided to develop a number of abstractions, each of which is suitable (optimized) for some category of spatial representation and reasoning tasks. Because this work is still in progress, what follows is a brief description of each of the levels of abstraction and how they relate to the other levels.

6.7.2.3.
ABSTRACTING A SPATIAL OBJECT AS A SET OF POINTS

The abstraction we shall choose as our epistemologically adequate abstraction is the point-based abstraction of space. The basic entities that exist at this level include points, sets of points, forces, masses, velocities, etc.

(Forces can be applied only to infinite sets of points. We may not talk about the force on a point, or its mass; we can talk only about its acceleration.)

Every point may have a position with respect to some coordinate frame of reference indicated by a triplet. A point in space may be part of an object. So, in this scheme, we would define the shape of a cylinder by specifying a set of constraints (including some equality constraints) on the different coordinates of a point, constraints that tell whether or not it is a part of that cylinder.

Two kinds of relations may hold between pairs of points (or between sets of points). These are the spatial and spatio-temporal relations. The basic *spatial* relations are the analogues of the relations in the temporal domain, namely, *above, below,* etc. However, there is an imminent explosion in the number of relations that can arise as compositions of these primitive relations holding between the extreme points of objects in each dimension. That's why the simple spatial analogue of our 49 (by now 51) temporal relations (above) didn't work.

That is, it is easy to conjure hundreds of useful slots from the basic spatial primitives, largely because of the existence of three dimensions as opposed to time's one. There are two basic approaches to solving this problem, and presumably a combination of these should finally provide the answer.

Approach 1: Restrict the number of combinations of the primitive relations. Though at first sight this seems absurd, at least a preliminary examination seems to indicate that only a small spectrum of the possible combinations of the primitives are needed. Some of those needed include containment (along one dimension), overlap (and its inverse), abutting, completely above (and completely below).

Approach 2: Have primitive relations only for one of the dimensions, and, instead of having these primitives (and the composite relations) be binary predicates, make them *ternary* predicates with the third argument being the dimension. This can be done because the compositions of the relations are always compositions of the primitives along just one direction. That is, composite relations such as the following are not worth remembering and representing explicitly, as they are no more than the sum of their constituent one-dimensional relations: *"the topmost point of one object being above the others and the leftmost point being to the right of the others."*

The second class of relations are the *spatio-temporal* relations. Some of the basic spatio-temporal relations include stronglyConnectedTo and looselyConnectedTo. These indicate the constraints on the changes in the spatial relationship with time. As can be seen, these relations define the basic notions of solid, liquid, etc.

The basic computations using this abstraction are closely related to the basics of continuum mechanics. As expected, doing these computations for the average real-world situation is far too difficult. So why bother having the set-of-points abstraction? Two reasons: it is the only one that is epistemologically adequate, and it helps to "root" and organize the other abstractions.

Okay, then, let's look at some of the abstractions that are useful for pragmatic reasons.

But before we can talk about abstractions for pragmatic purposes, we need to have some idea of some of the tasks we are interested in performing. They include the following:

- Predicting the behavior of some given device

- Diagnosis — determining which one of a disjunct of possible structures can account for an observed behavior

- Manufacturing — synthesizing a sequence of processes that will produce a particular shape

- Design — synthesizing a shape to account for a particular behavior.

Unfortunately, the descriptions of these four tasks themselves refer to spatial concepts, such as "the behavior of a device." As we go through some of the proposed abstractions, we shall see how we can talk about notions such as behavior more easily using these abstractions.

6.7.2.4.
PRAGMATIC
ABSTRACTION 1:
MECHANICS
(EQUATIONS AND
DIAGRAMS)

The first abstraction we shall talk about is the mechanics abstraction. This is actually a class of abstractions, all of which are related to the solution of problems such as those given in freshman mechanics books. Actually, a rather large class of problems can be formulated into the framework used in these books.

At one end of the spectrum formed by these models are the equation-level descriptions of systems. The kinematic and dynamic equations used to describe systems could be thought of as representations of the systems (usually combined with the laws of dynamics, etc.).

At the other end of the spectrum are representations corresponding to the diagrams that usually accompany these problems. The basic entities that exist in the abstraction for representing these diagrams include the following: objects (usually only one- and two-dimensional), forces, moments, velocities, etc.

The relationship between objects is in terms of geometric constraints between specific points on the objects.

Two classes of forces are recognized here: surface forces (for example, contact forces) and body forces (for example, gravity). Corresponding to these are two classes of points on objects of interest to us. The first class includes the points of contact between objects (note that the location of these points changes as the point of contact changes). The second class of points are the center points, such as the center of mass.

The locations of all these points are described using a triplet of coordinates. The forces are described by specifying the object they act on, their magnitude, and either their direction or the distance of two of their orthogonal components from the contact points of the object on which they act.

The shape of objects is described purely by the geometric constraints that apply between the different relevant points considered on the object.

An argument can be made that this is the level that determines/specifies the behavior of the system. Also, having gotten a system into this representation, we know a reasonable amount about how to solve the equations that result from this representation. Hence, a considerable amount of the problem of determining the behavior will be that of transforming the representation into this abstraction.

6.7.2.5.
PRAGMATIC
ABSTRACTION 2:
SOLIDS

The next pragmatic abstraction we shall consider is the solids abstraction. Here the basic elements are primitives such as cubes, cylinders, etc. Whereas the mechanics abstraction emphasizes the behavioral aspects of a system, this one is more about the geometric properties.

The relations between instances of these primitives are again divided into two categories, spatial and spatio-temporal. Although the spatio-temporal properties are approximately the same as in the point abstraction, one of the spatial relations — namely, "touching" or "inContactWith" — gets a little more complicated.

When two objects (such as cylinders or cubes) are in contact, it is important to specify the locations *on* the objects that are in contact. Such locations are called *patches*.

Patches are sets of points; they are usually on the surface of the object. Each type of object has some number of types of patches, and the location of instances of each of these can be specified by some number of parameters (specific to that kind of patch).

For example, the patches on a cylinder fall into two categories, namely, those on the cylindrical surface and those on one of its ends. Different parameters are used to specify the locations and sizes of each of these types.

There are two main purposes for using this notion of "patches." The first purpose is to allow special-purpose routines to be used easily to compute distances, etc., between different patches (and thereby the distance between different points of interest). The second purpose is to keep us from having to create a large number of units corresponding to these points of contact. Using these parameterized patch categories allows us to refer to these points using functions that map from these parameters to the patches.

The next issue that comes up in this abstraction (and marginally in others) is that of representing *orientation*. The orientation of an object is described as a minimal set of parameters that must be specified such that, given the location of a point on the object and these parameters, we can determine the location of the rest of the points.

So specifying the relative orientation of objects is equivalent to specifying a set of constraints on these parameters. Because there may be more than one such minimal set, a decision has to be made as to whether more than one set or a single set should be used.

A question that crops up as soon as we try to break down an object into cylinders, etc., is: What does it mean to be considered an instance of a cylinder? We could either define these as precise cylindrical objects, and so on, or admit more fuzzy definitions of cylinders (for example, by using some measure of the cylindricity and so on). Because most real-world objects that we have to describe are not perfectly cylindrical, we chose the later definition. (In a sense, this moves some of the responsibility of choosing a good approximation on to the user.)

In addition to the positive versions of these different primitives, we also admit negative versions (in order to be able to produce holes, tunnels, etc.).

Related to this is a distinction we make between two kinds of spatial properties — the spatially monotonic and spatially non-monotonic predicates. The spatially monotonic ones are relations, such as *contains,* that are such that if the partial description of a system has this property, the addition of more positive solids to the system will not cause the system to lose this property. On the other hand, properties such as "the ability of the object to roll" don't have this property; for example, if we drive a nail a little ways into a rolling-pin's outer surface, it no longer rolls.

6.7.2.6.
PRAGMATIC
ABSTRACTION 3:
THE DEVICE LEVEL

There are a number of other abstractions that abstract objects as being, for example, simple polygons (for path planning) or surfaces (for determining aesthetic considerations, certain manufacturing operations, etc.). Let us take a closer look at one just more abstraction, though — namely, the device level abstraction.

Consider the problem of representing the spatial concept inherent in the common-sense notion of a table. The immediate problem that faces us is the fact that tables come in a wide variety of possible shapes; for example, some have four legs, some have a pedestal base, and so on. However, all these different shapes have a lot in common, which is not too surprising since they all satisfy a similar functionality.

This suggests that the representation of things like table, which are really defined more functionally than structurally anyhow, should be at the functional (or mechanical) level of abstraction.

This is not 100-percent satisfactory, however, because many possible shapes other than those in which tables commonly come would have the same representation (and functionality) as a table in the mechanical level. Thus, we need some additional constraints.

So what is needed is a slightly more constrained level, such that the representation of *table* in that new level would have a single representation in the mechanical level abstraction and a much smaller set of extensions in the solids abstraction than that possessed by the mechanics abstractions instances. This level is called the device level.

The device level has many entities that correspond to the notion of functional primitives; for example, wheel, lever, etc. Because the representations in this level have unique equivalents in the mechanics domain, in order to talk about the relationships that may hold between objects in this level, we can simply use the same relations we used in the mechanics abstraction.

There are some problems, however, in that the geometric realizations of a particular relation in the mechanics abstraction could be a rather large set. Given that the device abstraction should have a smaller mapping into the geometric level, we need to reify each of the relations in the mechanics abstraction into a more specific one. So some of the relations that exist at this level include notions such as "connectedByBall&SocketJoint", "hingedTo", etc.

We earlier relaxed our definition of the term *cylinder* to mean a fuzzy sort-of-cylindrically-shaped thing. Now we have another abstraction that again tries to provide fuzzy geometric definitions of objects. How are these two abstractions really different? The answer is that the variations of the shape in the device level are irrelevant to the functionality of the object, and this is not true of the variations in the solids level.

As we mentioned earlier, given an object at this level, more than one geometry for the system could correspond to this device description. In a sense, we could view these geometries as forming an extension of the device description. Viewed this way, it seems to be reasonable to specify a preference criterion on the different extensions. So, given only that a something was a table, we could assume that it was a standard table (with four legs, etc.); and getting some contradictory information later on could cause us to revise this default inference.

A similar view can be taken of the transformation between other levels of abstraction. In this case (in going from the device level to the solids level) the preference partial order is guided largely by the empirical observation that most tables are four-legged. In other cases (for example in going to the mechanics abstraction), other kinds of preference criteria (for example, a preference for abstractions that make the computation simpler) could be used. This is the basic approach being pursued to solving the problem of going from one abstraction to another.

6.7.2.7. GENERATING NEW SPATIAL ABSTRACTIONS

Let us conclude this section by taking a look at some of the issues related to the general problem of deriving new abstractions.

Suppose we had a single (epistemologically adequate) ontology to start off with. And suppose we are doing some problem solving using this abstraction. Now when we look at the proof trace, it might be possible to replace complicated terms with more simple ones, with the idea being that the proof gets vastly simplified and still yields the same answers. Then the class of problems for which the abstraction defined by these new terms will be useful corresponds to the class of problems to which the specific problem that was being solved belongs.

This approach views the problem of generating new abstractions as equivalent to term substitution in traces of instances of problem-solving. Some standard types of substitutions seem to account for the generation of a number of abstractions.

However, some major problems turn up on closer examination. The space of possible terms to substitute seems extremely large, and often it is not possible to prune this space purely on syntactic grounds. The other major problem is that we need not just one but a large number of the possible proofs, because it is possible that some term that appears in a longer proof (a term that can be substituted to yield a very short proof) will not appear in a slightly shorter proof. Another problem is that it seems hard to predict the non-monotonic transformations from one abstraction to another by this term substitution approach. So, for now, at least for the problem of developing abstractions of space, the approach has been to *manually* identify some of the useful abstractions.

7. Mistakes Commonly Made When Knowledge Is Entered

Representation of knowledge is an art, not a science, let alone a well-understood technical craft. In finger painting, it's hard to be "wrong," to truly make "a mistake." In some other art forms, mistakes are instantly apparent (for example, the art of juggling chain saws and flaming daggers). Unfortunately, someone "entering knowledge" can be wrong and yet not feel the ramifications of the error for a long time.

So what representation mistakes are commonly made by new users of Cyc? This section will enumerate some of them. Along with each mistake is a brief discussion of why we consider it to be a mistake and what harm would accrue in the long run from its commission.

Most of these stories are true; only the names have been changed to protect the innocent (that is, to protect the writers from the wrath of the guilty parties).

7.1. Confusing an IndividualObject with a Collection

The process of entering something in the Cyc KB often involves taking some English sentence and translating it into CycL. Unfortunately, in English, there is much ambiguity, especially about individuals versus collections. The sections that follow discuss some sample English sentences.

7.1.1. "An Engineer Is a Person"; "Casey Jones Is an Engineer".

In this situation, it is tempting to go to the unit #%Engineer and say that it is an instance of #%Person. However, this would be wrong; it would mean that #%Engineer represents a *particular* person, for example, a person born on a certain date, in a particular hospital, etc. However, this is not what we want to say. What we are trying to say is that if we take any engineer, that engineer will be an instance of Person.

In other words, we are trying to say that there are certain things that fall into the *class* represented by the unit #%Engineer, and all these things are elements of the *class* represented by #%Person. This means that the class #%Engineer is a spec (that is, a subclass or subset) of the class #%Person. Therefore, #%Engineer should be an instance of #%Collection (which means that it is a class), and it should have a genls of #%Person.

WRONG	RIGHT

`Engineer`
`    instanceOf: Person`
	`Engineer`
	`    instanceOf: Collection`
	`    genls: Person`
	`    specs: TrainEngineer,`
	`        ElectricalEngineer...`
	`    instances: CaseyJones...`

Notice that if #%Engineer were an instance of #%Person, it couldn't legally have genls or specs or instances — just as #%Fred can't have those slots, for example. Only instances of #%Collection can have genls, specs, and instances.

Each Collection C has a definition, a characteristic function. You can view C as consisting of the set of all things satisfying that definition. For instance, PrimeNumber is a collection, and its definition is "a number divisible only by 1 and itself." Anything that satisfies that definition is an instance of PrimeNumber. In other words:

> X is an instance *of Y if and only if X itself satisfies the definition of Y.*
> X is a spec *of Y if and only if X defines a collection, and* all its instances *satisfy the definition of Y.*

So TheNumberThirtySeven is an instance of PrimeNumber, but OddPrimeNumber and ThePrimesFromThirtyToForty are specs of PrimeNumber. And that's also why Engineer is a spec of Person, not an instance of Person; and why CaseyJones is an instance of Engineer, not a spec of Engineer.

7.1.2. "Hackers Like Lisp". Because the unit #%Hacker represents the collection of all hackers, it seems reasonable to go to this unit and place the slot #%likes on it with the entries #%Lisp and #%Noodles. However this would mean that the *class* Hacker — an abstract set! — likes Lisp and Noodles, when really what we mean is that *each member* of that set likes those things. What we really want to say is that we want each and every instance of Hacker to inherit "likes: (Lisp Noodles)" as one of its default slot/value pairs.

`WRONG`	`RIGHT`
`Hacker`	`Hacker`
`instanceOf: Collection`	`instanceOf: Collection`
`genls: Person`	`genls: Person`
`allInstances: Guha, Lenat`	`allInstances: Guha, Lenat`
`likes: Lisp, Noodles`	`likes: Lisp Noodles`
`specs: SymbolicsHacker...`	`specs: SymbolicsHacker...`

That little indentation makes a lot of difference! What it means is that when we say Guha is an instance of Hacker, then Guha is assumed to like Lisp and Noodles.

Actually, it's illegal for the unit Hacker to have a likes slot at all, because the makesSenseFor of likes is (say) Person, and Hacker is a Collection, not a Person. So Guha can have a likes slot, but Hacker can't.

This is arguably a confusing situation — but just keep in mind that what is true about every element of a class is not necessarily true for the class itself. Some examples:

FiniteSet: The set of all finite sets in the universe. Every single instance of this must have "finite?: T", but FiniteSet itself has "finite?: NIL", because there is an infinite number of different finite sets.

HumanCyclist: The default interestingness for each instance of this class is High, but this set itself is of only moderate interestingness.

Texan: Each instance of this class has "allInstanceOf: American", but Texan itself lists American on its allGenls, not its allInstanceOf, slot.

We could represent the middle example as:

```
HumanCyclist
   instanceOf: Collection
   allInstances: Lenat, Guha...
      interestingness: High
   genls: Person, Cyclist
   interestingness: Moderate
```

In most cases, the confusion arises because of — not in spite of — the fact that the slot makes sense only for instances of the collection. The examples above just happen to be slots that are legal for certain collections and their instances (that is, the slots interestingness and allInstanceOf).

When we say "GermanPeople are interesting," there's genuine ambiguity about whether we mean (a) the set of all German people is an interesting set — for example, it has a prime number of members — or (b) each German person is by default pretty interesting. But when we say "GermanPeople have blue eyes" it's clear that we can only mean that each German person by default has blue eyes — a *collection* can't have eyes at all.

English lets us get away with this sort of sloppiness, because humans have common sense and can figure out, from context, what the speaker must have intended. But we want things represented unambiguously in Cyc. Eventually, Cyc will be able to help more and more with this chore. Some rudimentary examples of this are occurring already; for example, Cyc disambiguates " . . . red conductor . . . " by examining each possible meaning and using general knowledge to estimate each one's plausibility.

Even in its present embryonic state, Cyc would object to a user trying to place "eyeColor: Blue" on GermanPerson and could suggest that it should be placed as an indented slot/value pair beneath allInstances of GermanPerson.

Actually, it's a little hairier than that — namely, Blue is the default eyeColor of the *physical body* of any instance of GermanPerson. That is,

```
GermanPerson
   instanceOf: Collection
   genls: Person, GermanAnimal
   allInstances:
     physicalBody:
       eyeColor: Blue
```

So how does Cyc handle this? First it recognizes that the assertion GermanPerson.eyeColor.Blue is illegal, because a collection can't have eyeColor. Next, it notes that the "allInstances" slot has very high metaphorSensibility, so inheriting to GermanPerson.allInstances is likely to be what's meant. But that isn't quite legal either, because each GermanPerson is a CompositeTangible&IntangibleObject. But that's okay, because each GermanPerson can have a physicalExtent which (in turn) can indeed legally have "eyeColor: Blue". Whew! In other words, it looks for an overall high-valued metaphorSensibility path from GermanPerson to some units that could have "eyeColor: Blue". If there is one, it's a good bet that that's what the user intended. If there's a small set of nearly-equally-good possibilities, then the user should be given a menu of them. If there's a large set or an empty set of such possibilities, Cyc should just signal an error and have the user be more precise.

For now, though, the knowledge enterer must keep in mind that Cyc's abilities to help disambiguate sloppy entries is very small. They must take some care in disambiguating English sentences themselves. And being very precise about sets versus instances is an important, frequent part of that disambiguation process.

(*A note to purists:* If we were to dispense with all collections in Cyc, this problem would go away. But in earlier chapters we argued for the very high utility of allowing explicit collections to exist and be represented in Cyc.)

7.1.3. "Human Cyclists Drive Toyota Trucks".

The intent here is that each human Cyclist has his/her own Toyota truck and drives it. Let's assume that the collections HumanCyclist and ToyotaTruck are already present in the system. How, then, should the sentence be represented? We present three wrong ways to do it, and three right ways to do it.

DOUBLY WRONG	WRONG	WRONG
HumanCyclist	HumanCyclist	HumanCyclist
instanceOf: Collection	instanceOf: Collection	instanceOf: Collection
genls: Person,Cyclist	genls: Person,Cyclist	genls: Person,Cyclist
allInstances: Guha...	allInstances: Guha...	allInstances: Guha...
vehicle: ToyotaTruck	vehicle: ToyotaTruck	vehicleIsA: ToyotaTruck

The first way is wrong because a collection can't drive a vehicle; only individual objects like people can!

The second way is wrong because each individual person drives a particular Toyota truck, not the set of all Toyota trucks; that is, you can drive a truck but you can't drive a collection.

The third way is wrong because a collection (HumanCyclist) can't drive a vehicle that is an instance of ToyotaTruck; only individual people (like Guha) can. But we can combine the second and third wrong ways into one right way, namely by saying that each instance of HumanCyclist inherits "vehicleIsA: ToyotaTruck". That's the first of the several right ways below:

RIGHT	RIGHT
HumanCyclist	HumanCyclist
instanceOf: Collection	instanceOf: Collection
genls: Person,Cyclist	genls: Person,Cyclist
allInstances: Guha...	allInstances: Guha...
vehicleIsA: ToyotaTruck	inheritedSlotConstraints:
	DrivesAToyotaTruck

```
vehicleIsA                      DrivesAToyotaTruck
   instanceOf: Slot                instanceOf: ConstraintOnASlot
   hasAnInstanceOn: vehicle        slotsConstrained: vehicle
   entryIsA: Collection            slotConstraints:
   entryIsASpecOf: Vehicle            ((#%ThereExists v1 v
                                   (allInstanceOf v1 ToyotaTruck))
```

The "tie" between vehicleIsA and vehicle is given in full-blown form on the semanticExpansion slot of the vehicleIsA unit and in concise form on the hasAnInstanceOn slot of the vehicleIsA unit. What it means is that if Fred has vehicleIsA: ToyotaTruck, then (at least) one of Fred's vehicles is an instance of the class ToyotaTruck.

The second acceptable way of representing the fact that each HumanCyclist drives a ToyotaTruck is to inherit an inheritedSlotConstraints entry to all instances of HumanCyclist — that is, to inherit to them the DrivesAToyotaTruck constraint. If we do things this way, the Guha unit (because it's an instance of HumanCyclist) will automatically get an inheritedSlotConstraints slot with the entry DrivesAToyotaTruck. That constraint, in turn, says that (one or more of) Guha's vehicles must be a Toyota truck.

There is yet a third acceptable way to encode this same knowledge. If we had a separate unit representing the *structure description* of HumanCyclist, we could include a *part* of that structure that was a ToyotaTruck and was the vehicle of the (other part that was a) human cyclist. This is a pretty awkward way to do it, and we recommend using one of the first two. However, if we wanted to say that every human cyclist owns exactly three Toyota trucks, and one is blue, and the other two are the same color as each other, then it would be better (easier, more concise) to use the *structure description* scheme.

A fourth acceptable way to encode this knowledge is depicted below. The idea is to define a new slot, vehicleType, that sits right on HumanCyclist. Its semantics is "each instance of HumanCyclist has a vehicle that is an instance of ToyotaTruck." That definition of vehicleType is stated to Cyc by giving vehicleType a slot called hasInstancesOn, filled with the entry vehicle.

```
HumanCyclist
   instanceOf: Collection
   genls: Person,Cyclist
   allInstances: Guha,...
   vehicleType: ToyotaTruck
```

7.1.4. Process versus ProcessType; Person versus PersonType.   Another common source of confusion between Collections and IndividualObjects is due to the presence of units such as ProcessType, EventType, SubstanceType, PersonType, SlotType . . . This was discussed in earlier chapters. Consider the difference between ProcessType and Process:

```
Process    (the most general element of ProcessType)
    instanceOf: ProcessType
    allInstanceOf: ProcessType, Collection,
        Thing
    genls: Thing
    allGenls: Process, Thing
    specs: SomethingExisting, Event,
        InstantaneousProcess...
    allSpecs: Process, SomethingExisting, Event,
        InstantaneousProcess, Walking...
    instances: NIL
    allInstances:
        FredWalkingHomeOn30July1988At5pm...

ProcessType
    instanceOf: CollectionOfCollections   (we may
        just have Collection here)
    allInstanceOf: CollectionOfCollections,
        Collection, Thing
    genls: Collection
    allGenls: ProcessType, Collection, Thing
    instances: Process
    allInstances: Walking, SomethingExisting,...
      allGenls: Process   (every ProcessType must be a spec of Process)
```

As we said earlier, Process is a collection whose specs include Walking and SomethingExisting and whose instances include all the various particular *events* in the world. ProcessType is a collection whose instances are Process and its specs. Process is the most general member of ProcessType; any instance of ProcessType must be a spec of Process. But not vice versa (e.g., Event is not a ProcessType).

Why should both of these units exist? In some sense, onlyProcess is dispensable. Any slot/value pair we used to say on Process we could now place indented under the allInstances slot of ProcessType.

But each of them is worth keeping around, for two reasons at least:

- Certain very important slots start making sense for these collections

- They provide an intermediate layer of taxonomy between the top-most concepts (Thing, Collection) and the lower-level ones (Walking, FredWalkingHomeOn30July1988At5pm)

What do we mean "intermediate layer"? If Process and Event didn't exist, then all the direct specs of Process (SomethingExisting, InstantaneousProcess . . .) would become direct specs of IndividualObject. If ProcessType didn't exist, SomethingExisting, Eating, Walking . . . would all be direct instances of Collection. Neither of those alternatives is pleasant to contemplate — Collection having thousands of entries on its instances slot, or IndividualObject having thousands of entries on its specs slot (note that we don't mind, and can't avoid, their *all*Instances and *all*Specs slots being large).

Having such intermediate levels is a good idea for three reasons:

- Some statements are true "at that level" and inherit down to more specialized cases

- It speeds up doing searches and classification and recognition

- It reduces the cognitive load on human users of the system. (A similar economic argument might explain why people seem to have "natural kinds")

Because there are going to be different kinds of classes, maybe we can group similar kinds of classes again into classes, and say something about these "sets of sets of units." Yes, we can. That's how we get the various . . . Type units, such as ProcessType, EventType, PersonType, etc.

We said above that one of the three reasons for having such units is that we sometimes have things to say about them. What's something "special" that we might want to say about one of these units, say the unit ProcessType? A trivial thing is that all its instances are processes. But there's something less trivial we can say. Any slot that originates on (that is, appears on the canHaveSlots of) an instance of ProcessType will probably have "temporallyIntrinsic?: T". This was explained in section 6.2.4.1.

7.2. Defining a New Collection versus Defining a New Attribute

Suppose we want to say that each FireEngine is (typically) red. We have three possible ways of doing that. One is to create a unit for the color red, and create a slot called colorOfObject that maps any tangible object to its color:

```
FireEngine
  allInstances
    colorOfObject: RedColor
```

In order for this to make sense, we'd have to worry about defining RedColor, too. An apparently simpler — but less general — solution would be to define a special attribute called red? — that is, a slot whose only legal entries are T and NIL:

```
FireEngine
  allInstances
    red?: T
```

A third way to handle this would be to define a new collection, called RedObject — the set of all red objects — and make this a genl of FireEngine:

```
FireEngine
  genls: RedObject
```

Or, if you really just mean "Fire engines are *usually* colored red," you could write this as

```
FireEngine
  allInstances
    allInstanceOf: RedObject
```

That is, anytime you find out that something is a fire engine, a good default guess is that it is also a red object.

Which of these three alternative solutions should we choose: Defining a new slot and qualitative-value (colorOfObject and RedColor), defining a new T/NIL-valued slot (red?), or defining a new collection (RedObject)?

There is no "right" or "wrong" answer. Each can be done, and Cyc can and should relate different colors to one another even if we choose more than one way to represent them: for example, RedColor, blue?, and WhiteObject. Nevertheless, we have evolved a policy based on aesthetic and economic grounds:

If there's a specific reason to define the collection, then do it. Otherwise, don't! If you don't define a collection, you have to choose between the general slot and attribute-value on the one hand and the T/NIL-valued

slot on the other. If the qualitative value would have more than one or two siblings (in this case, other colors), then prefer the general slot and attribute-value; otherwise, just define the predicate (the T/NIL-valued attribute).

Let's try to apply this policy to the FireEngine color problem.

What are the different justifications for defining explicit named collections? We discussed this much earlier, back in sections 4.1–4.3. Here are four reasons for defining a new collection C:

- When C would get a canHaveSlots. That is, all — and only — instances of C should legally be able to have a certain slot. For example, only instances of Number can have a squareRoot, so squareRoot would appear in the canHaveSlots of Number, and that's a good justification for having the collection Number hang around explicitly in the knowledge base.

- When we have only an intensional definition for the collection, and we can't just list all the instances. Three examples are Number (which has an infinite number of instances) and OddPerfectNumber (we just aren't sure which, if any, numbers fall into this category) and LispAtom (we can write a Lisp function that acts as a "characteristic function" for this collection, but it's probably not a good idea to try to create a list of all the atoms in the system).

- When we have something to say about the set itself (as opposed to saying something that holds for every element of the set). An example of this is the cardinality of the collection GreekDeity, or the birthRate of IndianPerson.

- When a large number of default properties get inherited to the instances of this collection. In Cyc, we can inherit along any slot, so this is merely an aesthetic criterion, not a hard-and-fast rule. It's simply empirically true that in almost all such cases it seems "intuitive" to people to have such a collection, and it enables various sorts of speed-ups and cachings to take place in Cyc.

So: Should we bother defining RedObject? We think it's a close decision, but we have settled on the answer No. Okay then, should we define the T/NIL valued slot red? The policy stated above says not to, because there would be a large collection of such slots — many hundreds of them — one for each color; for example, there would be beige?, chartreuse?, magenta? . . . So we're left with the first choice, which is indeed what's in Cyc today: that is, we defined just one new slot (colorOfObject) and several qualitative-values (RedColor, BeigeColor, etc.), which are all instances of a new collection, Color.

7.3. Attaching Meaning to a Unit's Name or Its #%english Slot

7.3.1. Names Considered Harmful.   As you must have realized by now, Cyc is *not a knowledge base oriented toward the different words in a particular language; rather, it's aimed at capturing the most frequently used concepts encountered in day-to-day living. Because the existence of these concepts is sometimes independent of the existence of words to describe them, a possible question is: why bother having names for the concepts?

Part of the answer is that *the names are scaffolding that helps us now, in the early stages, as we build up the Cyc KB.* Eventually, the names can all go away (for example, they could be replaced by randomly generated symbols).

Some of the units in Cyc will relate to language use — for example, #%TheEnglishWord"Red", which has slots pointing to various other Cyc units, such as #%RedColor, #%CommunistIdeology, etc. They wouldn't have their readable names anymore, but that wouldn't matter. Cyc would "accept" and "generate" English sentences as part of its task, just as it would handle any other problem. Of course, the unit #%TheEnglishWord"Red" (whatever it was called — say #%G00083) *would* have a slot containing the string "red," and this would be the bridge between the nameless version of Cyc and the user (or natural language interface).

Although we see this as being possible (circa the end of this century), we likewise see little reason for going out of our way to give the units meaningless names, especially during the initial stages of the project. It makes life easier if we can recognize the printed forms of these units — for example, #%RedColor.

However, this decision is fraught with hidden danger: new knowledge enterers tend to recognize and understand "too much" from these expressive English names — more than is there in the rest of the unit!

Closely related to this are problems like:

- The name of one unit was "DanishFurniture". The person who entered it forgot to tie it to #%Denmark, and accidentally tied it to #%Danish (a type of sweet roll) instead. For a year, people used this unit without noticing the error, because they accessed it by name and the name seemed right.

- The names of two units were "Pencil" and "WhiteBoardMarker". Unfortunately, nobody bothered saying much more than that their genls include #%WritingImplement. As far as Cyc was concerned, the two units were indistinguishable. (We developed tools to prevent this sort of error in the future, by automatically classifying new units and asking about undistinguished (*sic*) new units. But the knowledge enterers were then unhappy about being dragged off-track so much. We have some ideas for how to fix this problem and will be trying them out in the coming months.)

• The name of one unit was "ThinPencil". Can you guess what it means? Right. Unfortunately, the person who created it meant "a thin beam of light," but later people used it as if it were a writing implement. Someone was even "kind" enough to add that as another instanceOf of the unit. So two very different concepts, which should have been represented by two separate units, got wrongly "merged" and intertwined thanks to the name.

• The name of the unit was #%FredEatingOn4July1988. Is that a *spec* of Process — that is, a collection with three instances (each of which is an event) — or is it an *instance* of Process — that is, itself a single event? In the case of #%FredEating we can *guess* that it's a spec of Process, and in the case of #%FredEatingLunchOn4July1988 we can *guess* that it's an instance of Process. But this relies on heuristics like "humans rarely define and name singleton collections."

Some clearer naming conventions would help, but those are no substitute for clear thinking — for clear disambiguation by the knowledge enterer.

7.3.2. #%english and Other Non-machine-understandable "Documentation". Another danger arises from the use of slots like #%english, which contains a documentation string about the unit. Although this helps another user later figure out what the original creator of the unit intended, sometimes users just read that documentation string and do not pay attention to what the unit itself really says (in the slots that really define the unit).

You can think of the #%english slot as just being a very long "name" for the unit, and then almost all of the advice in section 7.3.1 applies to it.

One solution here is to generate the value of this slot automatically for each unit. Then, as you enter a new unit, you can scan its evolving #%english summary. If there's something wrong there, or something missing, the way to correct it is to add or remove entries from other slots of the unit.

7.4. Overspecific/Overgeneral Information

This error is not so much an error as "poor representation taste." Let us suppose we want to say that the age of any person is neccessarily less than that of his/her parents. This seems to be a perfectly appropriate thing to say, and we say it to Cyc. Later, we realize the profound truth that the fact is actually true for all living things, not just people. It's almost lunchtime, so we decide just to leave the overspecific information in for a while, and then we forget to reposition it in its proper, more general place. A year later, someone mistypes a horse's age, realizes that a constraint is missing, and puts in a nearly-identical constraint that applies just to horses. And so on.

In fact, we should go one more step and say that the age of anything is less than the age of those agencies causing it to come into existence. For example, the age of a toy is less than that of the machine that made it, and less than the age of the human operator who ran that machine. The age of the earth is less than the age of the sun. This very general principle, when applied to the specific case of animals being produced by their parents, yields the specialization we started out to say. (Aside: we should go even further, if possible, to explain *why* the creator is always older than the creation.)

It is certainly not *untrue* to say "people are younger than their parents," but it is *overly specific*. It is a waste not to say something that is just as easy to state and encode in Cyc and that is vastly more general.

So much for over over*specializing*. Alas, we must also be careful not to over*generalize*. Even if a fact that was absolutely true for a class C is still "sort of true" for a larger class C', it might lose some of its certainty; it might be only metaphorically true; or it might be true only today.

Many truisms in sociology have this tendency toward overgeneralization — if we are not careful, we state modern-day customs as if they were universal codes of behavior.

Another form of underspecialization arises from the fact that the same English word can take on various meanings depending on the surrounding context — the sentence in which it's embedded. The term "genls" means the same thing no matter where it's used. It's tempting just to state that Child is a spec of Person, for example. That's a true fact, but there's something else, something special, in the relationship between Child and Person — something that's different from, say, the relationship between Battleship and Ship. Namely, each person was once a child, and in fact started out as a child. So we defined a new specialized version of the slot genls, called superAbstractionType, which points from Child to Person. (By the way, the relationship "new specialized version of the slot" is itself a relation represented in Cyc: the specSlots slot of genls pointed to superAbstractionType.)

So it is important that the right slot be used. Otherwise, there is the danger that what is really represented is not the same as the interpretation given by those creating/browsing through the units.

Another manifestation of this malaise creeps in through the makesSenseFor and entryIsA of the various slots. Often, users can find, while browsing through slot space, that a slot has an incredibly general makesSenseFor or entryIsA. For example, for a while, each person could have the slot #%excrementIn; every unit in the system could have the slot #%likesToEat; and so on. The creators of those slots didn't bother to worry about what their makesSenseFor should be — they just stuck #%Thing there, and went on their merry way.

This is actually a special case of the extensional representation not keeping track with the intensional representation. Maybe only instances of animals, represented in the Cyc KB, have a #%likesToEat slot. So *extensionally*, Cyc does "know" that the makesSenseFor of likesToEat is Animal. But *intensionally*, on the makesSenseFor slot of the unit likesToEat, it might still have an *overly general* value like Thing.

Because most new knowledge is entered via copy&edit, the extensional knowledge we just mentioned is far from worthless. The danger is that it might diverge from a weaker set of intensional knowledge, and that must be guarded against.

(If the *intensional* representation were too *specific*, we'd have found out in short order. For instance, if we'd put #%Person as the makesSenseFor of likesToEat, then the first time we tried to say Fido.likesToEat.DogBiscuits the system would complain about the violation, and we'd fix it.)

It is important that both these practices — over- and under-generalization — be avoided, especially in these early days when Cyc is unable to be adequately skeptical. In later years, it should have enough existing knowledge to match against that it should have a decent chance of detecting cases of under- and over-generalization.

7.5. Accidental Duplication of Effort

Before creating any unit (be it a slot or a non-slot), users should ensure that a unit to represent that concept does not already exist in the KB.

Theoretically, the system can find such duplications — but it can only know which other units subsume this new one *at the current moment*.

We have built a tool that lets users constantly monitor which other subsuming units there are, as they enter a new unit. The idea is that users shouldn't stop telling the system more facts about the new unit until (a) the new unit is distinguished from all existing units, or (b) they realize it should be merged with one of the existing units.

There are more insidious types of duplication — for example, a set of units that carves up X in a slightly different fashion than some other set of units does. It's okay to treat these as separate units, but at the very least they should appropriately point to each other (that is, list each other in the proper slots).

For now, the policy is that users should (1) become acquainted with the relevant corner of the knowledge space before they enter new knowledge, and (2) try to find a unit corresponding to the one they have in mind before they try to create it.

The second of these is actually a pretty big win, because the way users find a unit is to begin telling the system things about it. If the unit already exists, they'll find it; if not, they've already specified most of what Cyc needs to know to create the unit! Moreover, the last few units that subsumed this new one, before it became truly unique, are likely to be good ones to have up on the screen anyway, because they should be related to this new unit, the units they point to will likely be related to it as well, and there may be some knowledge on them that should be pushed to a higher, more general unit.

8. Conclusions

8.1. Conclusions about the Cyc Philosophy/Motivation

With the exception of a few specific topics (notably, liquids and time), AI has more or less ignored the zillions of important special-case things that any intelligent agent ought to know a lot about. Other fields (for example, philosophy, cognitive psychology, and anthropology) have paid some attention to these, but their paradigms make their inquiries and their results hard to "operationalize" by those of us trying to build an AI. Even the relevant AI work we have cited in this book has been done pretty much in isolation and remains largely unrelated to the rest of AI.

We could also consider much of the knowledge in expert systems as relevant, but the problem of systems being done in isolation goes double for such systems! Expert system building to date has capitalized on this isolation — on the fact that the builder can tailor the program to the task: making just the necessary distinctions, treating time only as required by the task, using just one simple type of inference mechanism, and so on.

Integrating all these special cases is a big problem — a really big problem — and hence is generally not even mentioned much in polite AI society. Unfortunately, it is not merely a big problem, it is on the critical path to achieving an artificial intelligence.

Instead of tackling that problem head on, AI seems to have divided into two camps, each of which has found its own way to go around it:

- *Camp 1*: One camp is the "knowledge engineers," who are doing a brand of scientific applications programming. They use AI tools and representation languages, but basically they've got a specific job to do and they do it, often very successfully — and that's it. "What's that, a global ontology? How interesting. Now, if you'll excuse me, I have to finish this expert system by next Friday."

- *Camp 2*: The other camp is the "neats," those who are doing a brand of mathematics or physics. They are trying to understand the way that intelligence works, to crystallize the equivalent of the Maxwell's equations of thought.

It might even be possible, in principle, to derive the zillions of specific facts and heuristics required by camp 1 from the much smaller set of general ones sought after by camp 2; but that's like trying to solve automotive engineering problems using just Newton's laws. We're trying not just to understand our world but to solve tough problems in it efficiently; hence, we need the special cases.

But we don't want to go into camp 1 either, for two reasons. First, the magnitude of all the world's knowledge — that is, all the specific knowledge that might ever wend its way into any expert system — is staggeringly large, probably beyond the manpower capabilities of the human race to encode (at present). Second, the specific knowledge changes from year to year and from day to day and would soon become out of date even if we could represent all of it today.

As for why we care about the broad coverage, see the early chapters of this book. In essence, we believe that the current brittleness problems with expert systems are the result of their inability to fall back on ever more general knowledge, and on their inability to analogize to superficially far-flung specific knowledge.

In the course of the last few years, our work has evolved slowly, inexorably, from the center of camp 1 toward camp 2, so that by now we don't quite fit the paradigm of either. We've come to see the need to have both camp 1 and camp 2 kinds of knowledge and approach to research, and — perhaps even more importantly — all the stuff in between, the middle-level knowledge that both camps currently pass by: knowledge like "once something dies it stays dead," "members of the same species can breed," "the cost of a manufactured item is usually the cost of its parts, plus the labor and overhead in assembling the thing, plus a moderate percentage for profit," and "cars today go around 55 m.p.h. between American cities."

8.2. Conclusions about the Global Ontology

After all, we are trying to build an agent that's intelligent only in this world, not in all worlds that might have been. If it can handle the small number of general rules from camp 2, the zillions of specific pieces of knowledge from camp 1, and the millions of items that fall "in between," then we'll be happy.

It doesn't matter if it's awkward to state, using our ontology, some of the facts and rules that might have been worth knowing, in some other universe (for example, one in which the speed at which you move is a function of the direction you want to head in; or one in which each object can be in exactly two places at once; or one in which substances are infinitely divisible and have no granularity; or one in which a person can have more than one age at a time; etc.).

The implication of all that is as follows:

> *As we work out the ontology, and we come upon a decision about how to represent something, or whether to represent some distinction, it's okay for us to take a look at the real world and make a decision.*

A large number of key decisions, some apparently counter-intuitive ones, have indeed been made in working out the Cyc ontology:

- Pieces of time need to embrace both point-sets and solid intervals

- We usually reason only about time-pieces that are a small number of compositions of these operators:
  $\cap, \cup, \circ -$, repeat, and name.

- We usually reason about time-pieces using only about 50 particular relations: contiguousAfter, startsAfterStartOf, coTerminalWith . . .

- Stuff (the set of all pieces of all substances) is a spec of individual

- No harm accrues from combining (the unit representing) an event with (the unit representing) its time interval

- People and other agents are composite tangible/intangible objects

- Tangible objects (and composites) are events (and have durations, etc.)

Some of these decisions may be wrong, but most are probably "correct enough." *Not* to commit to making such decisions is a less fruitful path than making them and occasionally being wrong. We'll find out which ones are wrong, and how serious that wrongness is, as we develop our system: as we try and fail to represent some thing in Cyc, as Cyc tries and fails to solve some problem that it ought to be able to solve given what we believe it "already knows," etc. In those cases, we expect to be able to extend our ontology.

Perhaps we will have to back up in some sense — perhaps all the way back to the start. But we're willing to take that gamble; we believe that such catastrophes are, like coincidences in Gelernter's geometry diagrams, "possible but astronomically unlikely."

8.3. Conclusions about Common Mistakes in Using the System

Ever since Ed Feigenbaum's and Josh Lederberg's success with Dendral, more than twenty years ago, one of the AI dreams has been that "all that is needed to build an expert system for task X is expertise in task X."

The dream has been elusive; building successful expert systems has demanded expertise in representing knowledge as well as in the task domain. Unfortunately, that expertise could not be learned mechanically, just by reading some AI textbook, but rather had to be assimilated slowly, by apprenticeship to a "master." Knowledge engineering is — currently — a talent-based artistic skill, one that is slowly progressing toward becoming a well-understood technical procedure. When Cyc exists, it should be a useful component in that procedure.

The flurry of early successes with Dendral, Mycin, and their fellows led to the premature heavy use of the technology by industry, notably American industry. But there was a tremendous shortage of qualified (that is, apprenticed) knowledge engineers. American industry, however, was not to be daunted (unfortunately). It responded to this shortage by simply *relabeling* some of its programmers as knowledge engineers. We believe it made this mistake partly because of the *mislabeling* of this job as "knowledge *engineer*" instead of "knowledge *artist*," which would have been a more accurate title and which might have given the corporations pause before they reslotted employees into that category.

These people did — and are doing — the best they can. Namely, they continued the same sort of scientific-and business-applications programming they'd been doing perfectly well before. That is, they closed their eyes, they imagined the algorithm they would have used if they were allowed to write in C or Fortran, or whatever, and then they encoded that algorithm in the awkward (from that point of view) syntax permitted by their AI tool.

This has led to lots of expert systems with a small number of very big rules; it has led to expert systems that simulate assembly language (for example, having rules like "If state = 805 and x>43, then set state to 806").

At a higher level, it has led AI to get an awful lot of credit it doesn't deserve and an awful lot of blame it doesn't deserve.

The trouble is that the builders of these systems haven't "bought in" to the true knowledge engineer's frame of mind: telling the program what to *know*, not what to *do* step by step. That is, the idea that one can get a program to gradually achieve competence by incrementally dumping more and more knowledge into it, even without having a full understanding of how that knowledge will be used in the future.

The most serious danger we foresee with failing to use Cyc, or misusing it, is the analogue of this expert system misuse problem. That is, the danger that Cyc's users might do one of the following:

- Misuse the various inference schemes, say by overworking one poor scheme (such as toCompute, or slotConstraints, or inheritance) while ignoring the rest. This is like people who learn a few words in a foreign language and never bother to learn the remaining ones because they can sort of "get by" with that limited vocabulary.

- Use all the various inference schemes in CycL but not bother to tie in the application's KB with the existing Cyc KB. Like learning a foreign language, learning to use Cyc properly requires a large investment up front. Cyc is not well suited to a naive user walking up, writing a small Expert System, and walking away forever. Maybe one day, once Cyc knows enough and has the right sorts of interfaces, it will be. But for now, it requires that users study and understand the global ontology, buy in to that ontology, and hook their represented concepts into the appropriate places in that existing KB.

So to build an expert system, more than expertise is needed, and to build a common-sense KB, more than common sense is needed.

8.4.   The Current State of Cyc

8.4.1.   The Current State of the Cyc Knowledge Base.   Although it's the wrong measure to make a big deal about, most people are curious about the "raw size" of the Cyc KB. As of mid-1989, there were about a million primitive "pieces of data" in the Cyc KB, mostly individual entries in the values of slots. These are dispersed across roughly 50,000 units. About 6,000 of these units are Collections, 148 of which are actually specs of Collection (that is, sets of sets) and 103 of which are specs of Slot (that is, sets of slots). About 4,000 different kinds of slots exist in the KB. There are about 4,100 different kinds of processes and scripts (Process.allSpecs), and they have a total of 9,400 instances (that is, Process.allInstances). There are 1,700 specs of TangibleObject, having a total of 2,321 explicitly represented instances. About 2,000 units explicitly represent constraints on slot values. There are 900 types of IntangibleStuff (IntangibleStuff.allSpecs), and they have a total of 9,900 instances (IntangibleStuff.allInstances).

The strengths of the KB are, of course, its breadth, covering (or at least touching upon) the topics in the Encyclopaedia Britannica *Propaedia*. Only a very small fraction (less than 1 percent) of the topics in a desk encyclopedia are covered. And the KB contains an even *smaller* fraction of the knowledge required to understand, for example, a typical *National Enquirer* article.

Two points are worth making about these numbers.

First, the fraction of the KB that's built is too small to expect much "power" from yet. We have always predicted that the knee of the curve would be somewhere in the 10–50-percent range of consensus reality knowledge, and we're still down around the 0.1-percent level. It should still be possible to see isolated flashes of useful common sense reasoning (that's linear with the KB size), but fruitful analogies will be rare indeed (they're quadratic with the KB size, so a size of .001 means only one millionth of the analogies we'll eventually hope to generate could be generated now).

Second, we're right on schedule. Our plan has been to stay small until about now, entering just enough knowledge to come up against the tough representation and reasoning problems we have to "crack" and spending most of our effort on finding adequate solutions for them. And that is precisely what we've done.

8.4.2. The Current State of CycL. There isn't much to add about the current state of CycL, either. It is up and running, in CommonLisp, on Symbolics Machines of all sorts, Sun3s, TI ExplorerII + s, MacIIs (with Ivory boards), and (with some conversion) VAX machines. The user interface and full knowledge server environment is debugged now only on the first of those types of machines, Symbolics, but we expect the class of machines it runs on to expand by mid-1990 to include most or all on that list.

If it helps you gauge the speed of the system (it's not clear why it should!), CycL can process about 2,500 primitive (Level 0) operations per second. A complicated inheritance operation that causes a reasonable amount of rippling will take several seconds to finish "percolating." That's one big reason that the current UE (unit editor interface) has a background process that does such propagating things and a foreground process that keeps paying attention to the user.

The reason we say not to take these timing numbers too seriously is the following. Most of our functions were put together "in the obvious way." If the system (or that part of it) runs quickly enough, we never improve it. When some part of it runs too slowly, we run metering tools, see where the time is going, and optimize the function a little (or, rarely, we nontrivially revise/alter its algorithm or, even more rarely, alter both the algorithm and the underlying data structures) and repeat that until it all runs "fast enough" again. So inheritance propagating to a thousand units now takes "a few seconds" because that's the minimally acceptable (to humans) time period.

One day we *will* hit some real complexity-bound time-limits; probably that's the day we'll look into C, or a parallel Lisp machine, or a Cyc distributed across N Lisp machines, or even some sort of "Cyc Machine."

8.4.3.   The Current State of the Knowledge Editing Environment.   In chapter 2, we described the UE, MUE, and Knowledge Server utilities. Together, these form the Cyc "knowledge editing environment."

Figures 8–1 and 8–2 (which were also shown in chapter 2) show the textual pane-based unit editor (UE) screen and the rectangle-based museum floor plan editor (MUE) screen. Both of these are quite striking in color, and much additional information is provided as well; unfortunately, all that is lost in the figures because of their being black and white.

A thin horizontal bar near the bottom of the UE screen shows the Knowledge Server (KS) status: Is this machine talking with the server?; is the server up or down?; how long are the background process queues there and here?; etc.

The MUE works very quickly; users can jump from room to room in a fraction of a second and can traverse the KB from "one end to the other" (for example, ten "jumps") in about ten seconds.

For more information on these editors, please see section 2.2; also see [Shepherd, 1988]. Here, we'll just make a few timely observations.

One interface idea that seems to be working out well is not separating the interface from the debugging tools; in other words, browsing, editing, debugging, solving a problem, etc., all are done through the interface. (Of course, it would be nice if Cyc noticed the user's "mode" and reacted accordingly.)

Another interface idea that's working out well is the notion that we can try things out best by talking to Cyc and seeing the ramifications. What does that mean, concretely? It means that we can do some operations, entering a mode (a "state") in which constraint violations and such are merely displayed dynamically — that is, don't cause error breaks. Then, as we do more and more to the KB, hopefully that list of current constraint violations gets smaller, finally becoming empty, at which point we can "record our state," because we're once again consistent. (Of course, we're generating transcript files all along, in case of machine failure, but that's something quite independent of this last point.)

What's the alternative to this? One would be to have users enter some sort of complete no-error-checking mode — that is, as if they were just using a text editor.

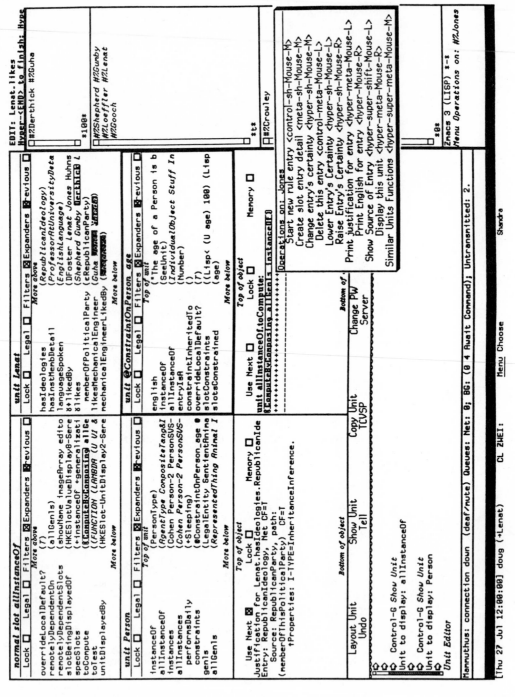

Figure 8-1: The Default (UE) Configuration

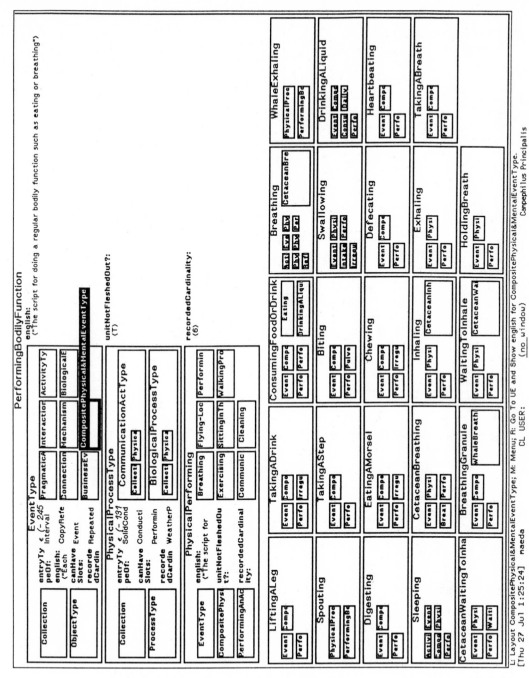

Figure 8-2: The Default Museum Editor Configuration

One interface idea we tried was a dismal failure. Our original KB browser was a node&link (graph) editor. This worked like a dream at first. As the number of nodes in the system crossed the 5,000 mark, though, the dream became a nightmare. Either (a) the arcs got longer and more cluttered, to the point of unreadability, or (b) we had to give up the fixed positioning of nodes in "knowledge space," which was an idea we liked because users could build up expertise and familiarity with where each node was. We finally opted for another choice: (c) re-think the interface and start over, which is what led to MUE.

There have been a few *interface-specific* "errors that new group members commit when first learning to use Cyc." For instance, people often don't pay attention to whether they're transmitting or not — until it's too late. Here's a less obvious error: if our background process is wedged (for example, reporting an error), more and more operations can "pile up" in the background. That, in turn, increases the chances that some of the operations we're now doing locally might not be legal by the time they're done over on the server. Or, because the after-effects of our local operations aren't propagated in this state, it might increase the chances that some subsequent locally-performed (that is, by us on our machine) illegal operation wouldn't be noticed as being illegal for quite a while *(until the background process starts up again and catches up to that point).*

8.5. The Future

8.5.1. Cyc's Final Exam — Where We Hope To Be in Late 1994.
In brief, the goal of our project is to break the brittleness bottleneck once and for all. Less briefly, we could state some "final exam" questions for Cyc in late 1994. No, we don't expect Cyc to be all-wise then, but we do hope to have moved by then from the manual "brain surgery" mode of knowledge entry, to a more "Socratic dialogue" knowledge acquisition metaphor. These "final exam" questions would be:

1a. Build an expert system in Cyc and show that it is *better* than building it from scratch (that is, in a conventional expert system building shell). *Grading:*
   How much better is it, and in what ways? For example, does it rely less on experts, having some of its knowledge acquired by reading texts or via discovery?; is it less prone to attempt to answer questions out of its area of expertise?; does it provide more comprehensible explanations of its behavior?; is it better able to cope with unanticipated problems?

1b. Build two expert systems in Cyc, on related topics, neither project knowing much about the other. Show that they can *share* each other's knowledge productively. "Sharing" means that the whole is more than the sum of its parts — that the combined system does *better* than just the union of what the two individual systems could do. "Better" includes such dimensions as: a wider range of problems can be handled, more correct answers are generated, fewer mistakes are made, the system is more easily understood by the user, and/or it is faster. *Grading:*

> How consistent and repeatable is this phenomenon?
> How synergistic, potent, or at least time-saving, is it?

2a. Communicate with Cyc in English, by dint of a natural language understanding program built largely by ACA's Human Interface project, which is deeply, recursively intertwined with Cyc. The understanding process includes disambiguation, resolving anaphora and ellipsis, as well as more sophisticated tasks such as recognizing and handling hyperbole, metaphor, and humor. After being understood, the new communication will then be added to Cyc's KB. If it was a question, then Cyc's answer will help gauge its understanding of both that query and of its existing KB. *Grading*:

> How well does Cyc do at the Turing test?
> How well does it answer tough (for example, metaphor-laden) questions?

2b. Demonstrate that, based on 2a, the Cyc project is no longer needed. The massive hand-coding knowledge representation effort can be wound down and eliminated by the end of 1994. In its stead, Cyc will grow by assimilating textbooks, literature, newspapers, etc. It will also have access to, and models of, numerous large data bases to call on as needed. In place of the knowledge enterers will be a cadre of teachers, to elucidate confusing passages, to discuss and educate rather than to continue to practice brain surgery upon Cyc's KB. *Grading*:

> Is language understanding now the dominant mode of entering new knowledge into Cyc?

3. Demonstrate that Cyc can learn by discovery. This goes beyond the sort of "learning by being programmed" of 1a and 1b, and beyond the sort of "learning by reading" of 2a and 2b. It includes deciding what data to gather, noticing patterns and regularities in the data, and drawing from those patterns useful new analogies, dependencies, and generalizations. This sort of learning may go on either *proactively* ("at night" or on idle machines) or *dynamically* as needed in the course of solving some tough problem. *Grading*:

What discoveries are made? How significant are they? How frequent? "Discoveries" might range from new technical hypotheses, to metaphors of unusual pedagogical power, to simplifying reorganizations of bodies of known facts.

4. Have Cyc be the major "consensus reality KB" for the world. Dozens of projects, throughout academia and industry, make use of Cyc, build new knowledge into it, and send and receive constant updates to keep the KBs consistent. Cyc becomes thought of as *the knowledge utility,* much like an electric or telephone utility today: something everyone plugs into and is happy to pay for. Just as, today, no one would even *think* of buying a computer that didn't have an operating system and that couldn't run a spreadsheet and a word processing program, we hope that by 1999 no one would even *think* about having a computer that doesn't have Cyc running on it.

8.5.2. Progress Toward that Final Exam.   Much of the current effort on Cyc is designed with the final objectives in mind; or to serve as an early warning of likely failure.

We're working with several collaborative projects to evaluate the adequacy of Cyc's representation language, and to show at least a few instances of knowledge sharing, falling back on general knowledge, and analogy. We're also encouraging academic AI researchers to use Cyc as a substrate, even today, on which to do their research.

Even at this early stage, we're coupling Cyc to a natural language understanding system (being developed by Elaine Rich and Jim Barnett at MCC). Cyc can input some English sentences, assimilate them, and, when appropriate, respond to them. The system can currently handle only the most general knowledge ("Can a person eat Kansas?"), plus a few slivers of competence (for example, those dealing with computer sizing, which is one of the collaborative applications mentioned in the previous paragraph).

Again, at this stage, at least anecdotally, we're pushing Cyc to discover some novel analogies, functional dependencies, subtle inconsistencies in its KB, and useful new generalizations. We have two machines constantly running and dedicated to this sort of introspective "dreaming" activity.

Finally, we would also like to thank the 1990–1994 AI community for their terrific cooperation and collaboration in growing and testing Cyc. So please get busy!

References

Adams, James L., *Conceptual Blockbusting*, Addison-Wesley Reading, MA 1986.

Davidson, *Essays on Actions and Events*, Oxford University Press, New York, 1980.

Green, C. C., R Waldinger, D. Barstow, R. Elschlager, D. Lenat, B. McCune, D. Shaw, L. Steinberg, Progress report on program understanding systems, Memo A1M-240, CS Report STAN-CS-74-444, Artificial Intelligence Lab, Stanford University, August 1974.

Greiner, R., and D. Lenat, "RLL: A Representation Language Language," *Proceedings of the 1st AAAI Conference*, Stanford, CA, 1980, pp. 165–169.

Hayes, Patrick, "The naive physics manifesto," in (D. Michie, ed.) *Expert systems in the microelectronic age*, Edinburgh: Edinburgh U. Press, 1978.

Lakoff, G., and M. Johnson, *Metaphors We Live By*, University of Chicago Press, Chicago, 1980.

Lenat, Douglas, "Computer Software for Intelligent Systems," *Scientific American* 251, Sept. 1984, pp. 204–213.

Lenat, Douglas, A. Borning, D. McDonald, C. Taylor, and S. Weyer, "Knoesphere: Expert Systems with EnCyclopedic Knowledge," *Proceedings of the IJCAI–83*, Karlsruhe, 1984, pp.167–169.

Lenat, Douglas, and J. S. Brown, "Why AM and Eurisko Appear to Work," *Artificial Intelligence* 23, 1984, pp. 269–294.

Lenat, Douglas, and E. A. Feigenbaum, "On the Thresholds of Knowledge," *Proceedings of the IJCAI–87*, Milan, 1987. Also available as MCC Technical Report Number AI–126–87, May, 1987.

Lenat, Douglas, M. Prakash, and M. Shepherd, "Cyc: Using Common Sense Knowledge to Overcome Brittleness and Knowledge Acquisition Bottlenecks," *The AI Magazine*, vol. 6, no. 4 (1986), pp. 65–85.

McCarthy, John, "First Order Theories of Individual Concepts and Propositions," in (J. Hayes, D. Michie, and L. Mikulich, eds.) *Machine Intelligence 9*, Chichester, England: Ellis Horwood, Ltd., 1979, pp. 129–147.

Minsky, Marvin, *Society of Mind*, Simon & Schuster, New York, 1985.

Norman, Don, *Psychology of Everyday Things*, Basic Books, New York,1988.

Rosch, E., "Natural Categories," *Cognitive Psychology*, vol. 4 (1973), pp. 328–350.

Russell, Bertrand, *An Enquiry into Meaning and Truth,* Unwin, 1950; Paper-backs, 1950.

Russell, Bertrand, *Human Knowledge, Its Scope and Limitations,* Unwin, 1948.

Russell, Stuart, "Analogy by Similarity," in *Analogical Reasoning,* David Helman, ed., Reidel, Boston, 1988.

Shepherd, Mary, "Tools for Adding Knowledge to the Cyc LSKB," *Proceedings of the IEEE International Workshop on AI for Industrial Applications,* Tokyo, 1988, pp. 365–369. Also available as MCC Technical Report ACA–AI–068–88, February, 1988.

Touretsky, David, "Implicit ordering of defaults," *Proc. 5th AAAI,* Austin: Morgan-Kaufmann, 1984.

Uemov, A.I., *Problems of the Logic of Scientific Knowledge,* Dordrecht, 1970.

Vinge, Verner, *True Names,* Blue Jay, New York, 1984.

INDEX